STRUGGLE AND SUBMISSION:

R. C. ZAEHNER ON MYSTICISMS

By William Lloyd Newell

Foreword by Gregory Baum

Library of Congress Catalog Card Number: 80-6295

For my mother
    Mary Agnes Newell
    December 12, 1908 - December 13, 1980

To do the godly things and laugh
as if it were a task

i

PREFACE

This is a book about the work of Robert
Charles Zaehner who held the Spalding Chair of
Eastern Religions and Ethics at Oxford University
as well as being a Fellow at All Souls College.
He professed history of religions there from
November of 1953 until his death in November of
1974. Behind him he left a corpus of books which
ranged from a Pahlavi dictionary to a commentary
on the Bhagavad-Gītā after running through Sufi
texts, works on mysticism in general and several
theologies of religions. He spoke frequently on
the BBC and wrote just as frequently-at the rate
of almost a book per year. He spoke of Marxism
and Drugs, turgid theologians and his beloved Pope
John, of Zoroastrianism and Heraclitus, of Aldous
Huxley and Hugh of St. Victor. His works were
frequently weighted with authority--as when he did
his Zurvan, A Zoroastrian Dilemma,[1] and his commentary on the Gita which Geoffrey Parrinder said
was "probably the most important commentary on
any non-Biblical text to appear in this century..."[2]--and at other times the work of the
gifted amateur, which is an honored tradition in
England. He was so exciting and infuriating that
the distinguished Canadian scholar, Wilfred Cantwell Smith said of his Concordant Discord:

> There is a fair deal of repetition in the
> work, especially of quotations; and the
> reader at times is not sure whether he is
> on a merry-go-round, or is actually going
> somewhere. A merry-go-round of such engag-
> ing colour, boisterous sound effects, and
> bouncing intellectual activity, however, is
> itself perhaps no mean achievement.[3]

---

[1]Oxford, 1955.

[2]A review in "Rel. Studies," 7, p. 169.

[3]A review in "Journ. of Rel.," 53, 1973,
p. 381.

Smith howled with outrage in the same review when Zaehner asserted that Buddhist sorrow/wretchedness (Skt.=Dukka, the starting place of Indian religions) was the virtue of hope in Buddhism. Smith found this assertion incredible.[4]

But Zaehner could inspire fear as well in his readers. Paul Younger, reviewing Zaehner's Hinduism (Oxford, 1962), The Convergent Spirit: Towards a Dialectics of Religion (London, Routledge and Paul, published in the United States as Matter and Spirit: Their Convergence in Eastern Religions, Marx, and Teilhard de Chardin, New York, Harper, 1963) found Zaehner's baptism of the hopes of the age--Catholicism and Marxism--frightening because it would mean the end of religion as he knew it: which meant that history was dealing the death blow to Protestantism and leaving a convergent Marxism and Roman Catholicism in its place.[5]

The small, birdlike, Zaehner, whose rheumy, color-faded eyes darted about in a clay colored face, misted blue from the smoke of Gauloise cigarettes, could be fearsome indeed. He was a volatile figure worthy of the best steel of his age. He fought and flailed cant and hypocrisy as only the critic can. He was famous, but never popular; loyal, but never blindly so; brilliant, but not above egregious self-contradiction; shy before pain, but not above spilling scholarly blood.

From this skein of works came two sets of theses which we set out to follow from source to end. In doing so, I poured through all his written materials and the critical reviews which attended them. My findings took up four hundred and seventy-two pages. It seemed that Zaehner

---

[4]W. Cantwell Smith, art cit., p. 380.

[5]Paul Younger, in "Theology Today," 23, 1966-67, p. 438.

propounded five theses in his scholarly career.
In pulling these out of his works and fashioning
them into something orderly, for Zaehner was a
probing systematizer, but not--above all--orderly,
I found that Zaehner proved his most important
theses--which I shall call numbers one and two,
and merely indicated the direction the other
three would take.[6] These "indicators" took him
seventeen years, and most of his corpus, to
write. What the first two theses proved was corroborated by the rest of his works, but it did
not seem essential that I do anything in this
book but set out his proven theses, and merely
indicate in brief compass what he encompassed in
extenso in his indicator theses. Hence I wish
to set out fully his first two theses as the meat
of this essay. They contain the seminal ideas
which became a systematics of religious experiences when Zaehner's empirical approach got off
the boards.

Spy for His Majesty in Teheran, Marxist-
humanist, historian of religions, theologian, con-
vert to Catholicism; Zaehner was all this and
more. He tried to fashion a total system of
theology from his work as historian, and from his
experience as a dedicated Christian. To do this
he began with a systematics of religious experience. His work was always in reference to something, when it was not straight textual exegesis
of Pahlavi, Sanskrit or Arabic religious texts.
So he wrote his first systematics of religious
experience to clear up the elegant muddle Aldous
Huxley had made of things by running all religious experiences and drug mysticism into one

---

[6]Just before he died he burnt himself out of
some of the most beautiful rooms in All Souls, and
said to us students that it should not have happened as the chair which had started the conflag-
ration which all but cost him his life had been
doused by decanted water--implying that no blaze
should have started where a gentleman had taken
the care to douse it with something, seemingly,
wetter than ordinary water.

unified experience, albeit on the transcendental level. Zaehner could not abide this type of dabbling, especially since it was done by one so sophisticated--whose work always commanded respect on the part of serious readers.

So he began to analyze Huxley's statements and also those of Hindus, Buddhists and Muslim Sufis and to place them alongside the writings of Christian mystics, and he found fundamental differences. The more he worked, the more radical the differences became until three essentially different experiences described themselves: the first was Nature Mysticism--this was the experience of Huxley and so many others; the second was Isolation Mysticism, the 'mother experience' of Indian Religion--based as it is on the self-induced states of yoga; and the last is the Mysticism of Love to be found in Christianity, but also in theistic Hinduism and Islam. These three separate experiences evolved upwards from the first to the third. Obviously, this was not so clear historically, but it seemed so to Zaehner on the level of ideas. He held to his systematics of mysticisms until his death in 1974. His Marxism and his love for Teilhard de Chardin caused him to incorporate their insights into his thoughts and so he became a theologian and set up the beginnings of a theological systematics as well. He died before he could finish them off. But what we have of his thought on mysticisms can serve by itself as the basis for both a theology of religions and a firm-based theology of religious experience. The three types of experiences can be used as a foil against which the spiritual director can listen to his/her directee and judge true from false mysticism, healthy from unhealthy movements, and move beyond religious mysticism into the mysticisms of matter and their angelic as well as their diabolic manifestations.

This book is a hard, dry academic treatment of a wildly exciting man. It is so because so much cant and downright foolishness has been

fobbed off in the name of both spirituality
(mysticism) and ecumenism. I would like to
make this a modest beginning in both fields towards an honest appreciation of both mysticisms
and our sister religions. If I succeed, if only
on the crudest and most fundamental level, to
set a base for further discussion, tne work will
be worthwhile.

My thoughts go out to Professor Gregory
Baum of the University of St. Michael's College,
Toronto, Canada, who first planted the idea for
this book when I was his student a few years
back. I had also been one of Zaehner's students
for two years at Oxford. Professor Baum felt
such an exciting man should not go unstudied.
By the time I had gotten to St. Michael's, I had
become more interested than ever in theological
methodology. How does one go out to others--be
they other religions or just others whom one is
studying in order to bring succour for their
pain? I had become convinced that one's own
interiority had to be involved in judging the
other. Leo Baeck, the great Jewish scholar, said
that science measured the world and religion
judged it. I accepted that more and more. How
could my Catholic interiority go out, become
vulnerable to the objects of my study, change
me and then return to me to be judged theologically? All such study had to involve me sub-
jectively and consciously--i.e., I had to both
raise my biases to the conscious level to use
them and to see their limits in the work at hand.
In doing this book on Robert Charles Zaehner I
put to paper the fruit of both watching him
work and having him savage my own limping efforts
at getting beyond phenomenology to involve myself
in a more intimate way in my work--more intimate
because more of my interiority (in Rahnerian
jargon, 'subjectivity') was engaged in the work.
As I got deeper into the work I became ever more
convinced that I was on the right track. I was
changing, but my work was coming out accurately.
I had begun this with my Master's thesis at

vii

Harvard's Center for the Study of World Religions. There, my essay on Nagarjuna's idea of Nothingness involved my Catholicity unabashedly, yet the delightful Professor Nagatomi was kind enough to say, "Yes, you see us correctly all right." My work was crude, but in going out and being changed, in involving my own subjectivity with that of the Buddhists, I had returned intact--like Zaehner, who also used his Roman Catholicism as a methodological base--having seen the Buddhists in a fair and accurate way.

I offer this book, not so much as a work in the History of Religions as a work in Roman Catholic Spiritual Theology. I don't mean this to 'cop out' of rigorous scholarship on the historical level--I have used those techniques to the best of my abilities and training at two great universities--but I am more interested in stepping back from the texts and the phenomeno-logical 'bits and pieces' patterning levels of method to work in my own religion in order to serve my people and their spiritual needs. Having been a priest for twenty years, I am more than ever convinced that we Christians are all called to a mystical knowledge of Christ. Just where does this fit with our everyday experi-ences? Just where does it fit with the religious experiences of our sister religions--which are real and noble experiences? This is what this book is about.

I cannot thank Gregory Baum enough for his patience and many kindnesses. I owe him much, not only as mentor, but as a shrewd discerner of where my own strengths lay. Footnotes are for my hunches--as proofs for my intuitions. He knew this and listened, as did Professor Nagatomi. I owe them both much. To the men of the Jesuit houses in Toronto who lived with me as this was written, I owe a deep debt of gratitude. All writers are a bit 'cracked,' and no more so than when they are in the creative process.

The Jesuits of the Maryland Province have my
deepest gratitude for giving me the time and
financing, along with their encouragement, to 'go
to it' and get my thoughts down on paper. In
particular, Jack Haughey has my thanks for insist-
ing that "You'll be published." The Jesuits of the
Woodstock Center also have my deepest gratitude as
well for providing me with the facilities and com-
radeship necessary to maintain the 'will to publish.'

Since lastness is not leastness, I wish to
thank Liz Holmes especially for her patience,
humor and peacefulness in putting this manuscript
to paper.

If this is a dull book, it's my fault. If
it's a useful one, dear reader, thank an old
English spy, a Japanese Buddhist and a Canadian
Catholic for their time and encouragement.

Woodstock Theological Center
Georgetown University
Washington, D. C.

February 17, 1981

ix

There are several historical reasons why
Christian thinkers have come to recognize the
universal significance of religious experience
and adopt a more open attitude toward the world
religions. The intellectual climate created by
German Idealism and the search for the meaning of
universal history impelled some 19th century
Protestant thinkers to acknowledge God's presence
in the great non-Christian religions. Later,
it was the advance of secularization and the growing indifference toward things spiritual that
made Christians look to members of other religions
as possible allies in a common cause. Pope
Paul VI, on his trip to the East, joined repre-
sentatives of the Asian religions in common
prayer. It was, moreover, the bad conscience
produced in Christianity by its prolonged identification with colonialism and oppression, that
urged many Christian theologians to repent of
their past contempt for non-Western cultures, to
recognize the validity of the world religions,
and to acknowledge God's redemptive presence in
them. Many theologians followed the hunch, for
the most part without trying to demonstrate it by
empirical research, that the world religions, in
varying degrees of clarity, expressed the same
gracious divine mystery that was revealed in the
scriptures and proclaimed by the church. These
intellectual trends made some theologians argue
that the world religions communicate in an obscure
and implicit manner what Christianity reveals
explicitly, while others went even further by
suggesting that the same mystery of salvation
offers itself in all religions, and that no one,
not even the Christian tradition, can make a
claim to universality. These 'ecumenical'
approaches are today found among Catholic and
Protestant theologians.

Let it be said that this is not the only
new approach to religion found in contemporary

theology. There are Christian thinkers who argue that all religions, including historical Christianity, suffer from all sorts of ideological distortions and hence become instruments of divine redemption only to the extent that they actually serve peace, brotherhood (sisterhood), and social justice in the world. This is a minority view. The 'ecumenical' approach actually predominates in today's theology.

William Newell's book examines the extensive work of a brilliant scholar, the late Robert Charles Zaehner, professor of Eastern religions and ethics at Oxford, whose studies constitute a powerful argument against the 'ecumenical' approach to religion. Historical research can demonstrate that the world religions are really different. They raise religious questions from entirely different starting points. While their literature contains similar phrases and their practise similar gestures, the similarities disappear once the phrases and gestures are understood in their historical context. Zaehner turns his anger especially against contemporary secular authors who have become fascinated by religion, especially by mystical experience, and who try to show that the world religions, however different, actually aim at the same thing. Religions are separated by different teachings and institutions, but once you reach a higher plane, the level of spiritual experience--so they argue--the walls separating the religions disappear and truly spiritual people meet in the same search for union with God. Typical for this position is Aldous Huxley who in his famous Perennial Philosophy tried to set out the essential unity of the mystical way in all the religious traditions, and who in a later book, The Doors of Perception, went so far as to claim that the ecstasy produced by mescalin was identical with mystical experience pertaining to the world religions. Against Huxley and his allies, Robert Zaehner instituted his great scholarly polemics.

Zaehner's arguments for the unbridgeable differences between religions also raise questions in regard to the 'ecumenical' approach to the world religions adopted by many Christian theologians today.

Newell offers a detailed, critical account of Zaehner's argumentation. By a careful analysis of the religious literature Zaehner is able to demonstrate the differences of the spiritual perceptions of the religions, and through a typology of religious experience, he provides the student of religion with useful paradigms to engage in a more faithful reading of the classical religious texts. Even the language of the mystics with its accent on unity and inutterability is capable of analysis. Zaehner provides a systematics of mysticism that enables him to do justice to the unitive experiences mediated through the world religions and yet distinguish very clearly between cosmic unity experienced in nature mysticism, the unity of the soul and its ground in what he calls isolation mysticism, and the unity of God and man in theistic mysticism. Newell's presentation of these paradigms and concepts provides theologians with sensitive tools for studying Christian spirituality and the contemporary turn to religious experience. But what should theologians think of spiritual experiences outside of the Christian tradition?

Newell outlines what a theology of the world religions should look like if Zaehner's viewpoint is taken seriously. Newell argues that Zaehner's method represents a more concrete, historical approach to the study of religion, one which recognizes the cultural mediation of human consciousness and the impact of historical conditions on man's perception of reality. By comparison, the 'ecumenical' approach implies a Platonic view of human history where every people has direct access to the divine in independence of their concrete struggle to build and sustain their society. Newell argues that a more

historical understanding of people's self-
constitution favours Zaehner's view that not
only their self-understanding but even their
ecstasies are culturally mediated. The hermit
on his deserted island experiences the unutter-
able through symbols and language handed on by
his religious tradition.

Newell's approach shows how deeply religions
and their mystical traditions are linked to the
societies in which they flourish. His argument
also seems to imply that through social struggle
and cultural change the followers of the religions are able to experience a transformation of
consciousness, which in turn may lead to new
religious experiences, a significant re-reading
of the ancient texts and a new interpretation of
the traditional symbols. The world religions,
including Christianity, remain alive.

Newell's critical examination of Zaehner's
systematization of the world religions is a
challenge to contemporary Christian theology.

Gregory Baum

TABLE OF CONTENTS

PREFACE   iii

FOREWORD   x

TABLE OF SYMBOLS

CHAPTER I: ZAEHNER'S WORK AND METHOD   1

    (A)   Zaehner's Five Theses: His
        Work   1

        (1)   Thesis Three: Religions
            Diverge   5
        (2)   Religions Seem to Converge   24

    (B)   Zaehner's Method   40

CHAPTER II: THE PHILOSOPHIA PERENNIS   53

    (A)   Huxley Et Al.   55

        (1)   Et Al.   55
        (2)   Huxley   63
        (3)   Frithjof Schuon   64
        (4)   Hegel and Schuon   73

CHAPTER III: ZAEHNER'S FIRST CATEGORY:
NATURE MYSTICISM   79

    (A)   Huxley's Experience   80

        (1)   The Meaning of Huxley's
            Experience   88

    (B)   The Rest of the Argument Con-
        cerning Nature Mysticism   112

    (C)   Summary on Nature Mysticism   133

CHAPTER IV: RELIGIOUS MYSTICISMS   145

CHAPTER IV - continued

   (A)   The Religious Use of Nature
        Mysticism   145

       (1)   The First Step in
             Religious Mysticism
             in India is Nature
             Mysticism   146

CHAPTER V: ISOLATION MYSTICISM   159

   (A)   Samkhya   159

   (B)   Religious Monism   177

   (C)   Summary of Hindu and
        Muslim Isolation and
        Monism   209

CHAPTER VI: THEISTIC MYSTICISM   215

   (A)   Ruysbroeck's argument
        against Beghard Quietism
        and Zaehner's use of it
        for his argument   222

   (B)   Zaehner's thesis:
        Vedānta's goal (emptiness)
        is Theism's beginning.
        Hence they are different.   236

CHAPTER VII: SUMMARY AND CONCLUSIONS   251

   (A)   Summary   251

       (1)   Nature Mysticism   251
       (2)   Religious Nature
             Mysticism   263
       (3)   Mysticism of Spirit:
             Isolation Mysticism   268
       (4)   Christian Mysticism   279

APPENDICES   295

    Appendix I: An Appraisal of Zaehner
    on Abū Yazid   295

    Appendix II: Al-Junayd   309

    Appendix III: Al-Ghazālī   315

BIBLIOGRAPHY   321

INDEX   345

TABLE OF SYMBOLS

S/P	=	Mysticism Sacred and Profane
H/M	=	Hindu and Muslim Mysticism
S/T	=	At Sundry Times
C/Sp	=	The Convergent Spirit
Xt/O	=	Christianity and Other Religions
D/Xt	=	Dialectical Christianity and Christian Materialism
E/R	=	Evolution in Religion, A Study of Sri Aurobindo and Teilhard de Chardin
Drugs	=	Drugs, Mysticism and Make-Believe
S/G	=	Our Savage God
Xt/W	=	"Christianity and the World Religions"
C/D	=	Concordant Discord

CHAPTER I

ZAEHNER'S WORK AND METHOD

(A) Zaehner's Five Theses: His Work

Zaehner's first two theses, with which I shall occupy myself in this book, have to do with refuting what is called the philosophia perennis of Aldous Huxley and many of his followers and those who think like him. This is not the same thing as that philosophia perennis spoken of by neo-Scholastics like Etienne Gilson. What Huxley meant was that there was one divine Reality which was "substantial to the manifold world of things and lives and minds. But the nature of this one Reality is such that it cannot be directly and immediately apprehended except by those who have chosen to fulfill certain conditions, making themselves loving, pure in heart, and poor in spirit."[1] Further, Huxley adds that it is not only philosophy which is rooted in this unity since, "All Science...is the reduction of multiplicities to identities."[2] Huxley had an experience under drugs which he termed the same as that had in both Christianity's Beatific Vision and that in Hinduism termed the experience of Sat, Chit, and Ananda,[3] which is the ultimate experience for Hindus. Thus all experiences are the same behind their phenomenal packaging. Zaehner disproves this by showing that Huxley and the many who think like him assume that all are the same,

---

[1]Huxley, Aldous, The Perennial Philosophy, Harper and Brothers, New York and London, 1945, p. viii.

[2]Ibid., p. 5.

[3]Huxley, Aldous, The Doors of Perception, Penguin ed., 1954, pp. 18-19, Middlesex, England.

1

but never prove it.[4] Specifically, Zaehner agreed
with Huxley that his experience was mystical, but
it was not theistic but something Zaehner called
pan-en-henism, which is a term in which the sub-
ject/object relation melts away into a euphoric
experience of almost limitless expansion of the
ego. So it was mystical, but a mysticism of
another sort from the Christian and Hindu experiences referred to above.

So this is thesis number one, which refuted
Huxley, and his assertion that he had found a
surrogate for religion, on Huxley's own grounds.
The second thesis takes off from there, at the
same time as it is refuting Huxley, to attend to
the host of scholars who hold that mystical
experiences are the same, on the upper--
transcendental--level; that if one goes beyond
the phenomenon, or the given expression in a
religion, it is the same as that found in other
religions whether theistic or monistic. Zaehner
says that this is not so, because the mysticisms
are radically different, even when they look or
talk alike. In refuting this, text by text and
religion by religion, Zaehner set up his systematics of religious experience, which consisted of
carving out categories which allowed one to see
the interrelatedness, yet difference, of religious
experiences. I shall deal with these two theses
in detail, since they are the meat of this book.
But what Zaehner did after he solved the difficulty in thesis two was to shift over into a
manifestly theological mode and erect a theology
of religions built on the insights of his first
two theses. This showed in detail that Nature
Mysticism (pan-en-henism) is different from Monism
and Sāṁkhya-Yoga (both manifestations of basic
Indian religion, which he termed Isolation Mysticism), and that they were both different from

---

[4]Zaehner, R.C., <u>Mysticism Sacred and Profane</u>:
<u>An Enquiry into Some Varieties of Preternatural
Experience</u>, Oxford, 1957, p. 2.

theism and *vice versa*. These first two theses meant, basically, that the religions may look alike at times, but that they say radically different things and begin from radically different points; and that if there is similarity, it is "between Christian orthodoxy and non-Christian heterodoxy."[5] So orthodoxies do not pan out to be the same at all, when compared. It is the heresy which looks like the other religion--e.g., some forms of Ṣūfism which are manifestly like Hindu monism.

Zaehner set out, therefore, to take the rest of his life's work from the base he laid down in his Mysticism Sacred and Profane, and its companion volume, Hindu and Muslim Mysticism.[6] His systematics of mysticisms is a rather simple affair once boiled down: There are different mysticisms, different in form and content; as different as one Aristotelian form is from another. The rest of his thought builds on this simple framework laid out in his inaugural lecture: i) religions are talking about different things, and ii) there is a "development of theism from an originally atheist creed (and along with it) the growth of the idea of a Divine incarnation and a Divine Mediator in all the great religions; and I have indicated that this idea arises not in accordance with, but in opposition to, the whole sense and tenor of all the non-Christian sacred books. Similarity, then, there is: but the similarity is between Christian orthodoxy and non-Christian heterodoxy."[7] The paramount themes of

---

[5]Zaehner, "Foolishness to the Greeks," An Inaugural Lecture delivered before the University of Oxford on 2 November, 1953, apud Zaehner's Concordant Discord, Oxford, 1970, p. 429.

[6]Zaehner, Hindu and Muslim Mysticism, N.Y., Schocken Books, 1960.

[7]Zaehner, Concordant Discord (hereafter C/D), p. 443.

Zaehner's first lecture, and indeed of the rest of his intelletcual life, are: divergence and growth in religions. What makes his thought so interesting is how he places these themes in juxtaposition with one another and with the secular world, with which his faith was in competition.

Competition is a watchword for Zaehner. If it was the philosophia perennis which placed his feet to the fire, thus triggering a knee-jerk reaction of literary works by him, then it should be remembered that the philosophia perennis saw no need for competition since, at the highest level, all religions are the same thing anyway. There can be no competition in such a system. There can be only peaceful acceptance of what one is. Truth is found only at the top; on the local level religions are merely relatively true and valid; relatively true, and locally valid. Competition is alien to this cast of thought. Zaehner's leitmotif is that there is a radical difference among religions. When one sets up a pattern, then, what begins to appear among the religions is divergence. The first application of Zaehner's thought, logically, would be to show such. This he did with the publication of his At Sundry Times, an Essay in the Comparison of Religions (published in the United States as The Comparison of Religions, Religion East and West, Boston, 1962).8 Where Huxley et al would see a continuum among religions, Zaehner saw gaps, yawning gaps; not only doctrinal chasms, but such a difference as exists between soul and soul. The principle of individuation makes it that the substance of an individual is so intimate to his nature, so umbilically linked with it, that it cannot be communicated without destroying that substance and making a mockery out of that which would unite it in such a way with another.

8At Sundry Times (hereafter S/T), London, Faber and Faber, 1958.

4

What stance would this place one in in a religion which is, by nature, a missionary religion? It would put him in competition with other revelations. Ninian Smart asserts that this is precisely what happened in Zaehner's At Sundry Times. Smart said that in an age in which Natural Theology was lacking among the competing revelations, a defence of Christianity must include the Christian faith as fulfiller of other systems.[9] So both Zaehner's Catholic faith and his scholarship in history of religions met in producing theses three through five.

(1)   Thesis Three: Religions Diverge

It will be argued that Zaehner saw his religion as a mysticism; and that that is too narrow a base on which to propose a systematics of religions is rather obvious. But this contention does not accurately reflect the whole of Zaehner's position, nor the problems he worked out of to produce his system. It is not that Christianity is a mysticism, it is that mysticism is the ground for dialogue between East and West. This will be especially true when Christianity faces Indian religion; and Indian religion comprises Hinduism, Buddhism and Jainism, and abuts Taoism and Zen in Zaehner's view of things. Zaehner says that if Christianity is to fulfill Gentile hopes it is in terms of mysticism. Further, since both Hinduism and Christianity are mystical, then the ground for dialogue will be their respective mysticisms.[10] Obviously, the religions themselves are something else essentially--if anyone can deal well with essences in religions; but what Zaehner and I are dealing with now is the ground for a debate, a dialogue, a meeting.

---

[9]Smart, Ninian, review in "Jour. Theol. Stud.," on S/T, NS 11, p. 239.

[10]Zaehner, S/T, p. 173.

Zaehner said that the religions of the world describe a pattern of growth. First he sought to find a typology. He found that religions fell into two groups: opposing the religions of the East to those of the West he came up with Indian religion as one type and the religions of Israel as another. Each develops along similar lines. Each began as a national religion; and another religion developed from each: Buddhism from Hinduism, and Christianity from Judaism. Approximately six hundred years after the daughter religions were founded two new religions, or at least major religious groupings, were founded: namely, Mahāyāna Buddhism and Islam.[11] In each case the old religion rejected the new. Growing in tandem to Jewish religion was the religion of Iran, Zoroastrianism; running parallel to Indian religion was Taoism. Both were somehow connected inwardly to the religions of Israel and India respectively. Zaehner stresses, however, that the parallelism is in form, not content.[12]

In comparing one religion to the other Zaehner begins to develop ideal types. Semitic-Christian religion is a prophetic religion; a religion in which one hears God and must obey his wishes. But Indian religion does not begin with obedience to God. In fact, salvation among the Indians is not from sin, but from the human condition. Man is born once in the West, but severally in the East. In India life is the evil, but man is good. Hence Indian religion is for Zaehner mystical. So he proposes two types of religions: prophetic and mystical. The former is an obedience to a Presence, the latter a technique

---

[11]Zaehner, Christianity and Other Religions, Twentieth Century Encyclopedia of Catholicism (1964), published in England as the Catholic Church and World Religion (hereafter referred to as Xt/O), pp. 14f.

[12]Zaehner, Xt/O, p. 15.

which prescribes the method whereby one can experience, not believe in, immortality here and now.[13] Two other types aid in understanding Zaehner's system. When considered as a mystical religion, or a series of them, Indian religion and Taoism in China, and Zen in Japan, are religions which Zaehner calls Solidary; i.e., they are not community based as are the Semitic religions which demand that one be seen as part of a corporate religious entity. These religions of the East are, on the contrary, isolationisms in which one narrows the base of one's life so that what is left after the Fall, and its shattering of the imago dei, can be dealt with in a way which leaves man capable of some taste of immortality-at least here and now. This "taste" is to be had alone, and not in concert with one's fellows. Hence Zaehner's denomination "Solidary." Semitic religions, which include Judaism, Christianity and Islam, and which are allied to Zoroastrianism by Zaehner, are, on the contrary, communal religions. These he calls religions of Solidarity. To these he adds Confucianism in China. Thus his religions are Prophetic or Mystical, Solidary or Solidarity affairs.[14] Zaehner determined the Prophetic/Mystical terminology when dealing with religions as divergent. The Solidary/Solidarity typology revealed itself when he considered the possibilities of religious convergence.

There is, further, a mysticism of love. This is based on the universal acknowledgement of two selves in man; one an empirical self, known as what we ordinarily conceive of as man; the other the deeper, transcendental, immortal self. This

---

[13]Ibid., pp. 15-17 Passim.

[14]Zaehner, The Convergent Spirit, Towards a Dialectics of Religion, London, Routledge and Kegan Paul, 1963, pp. 21-44 passim (hereafter C/Sp).

latter is known as the image of God in man in the West, and it is not too far off from this in the East, mutatis mutandis. Buddhism and Hinduism set off after the deeper, transcendent self. This is done by scotching out the empirical self. Theirs is a mysticism of self, an experience of absolute oneness without any conscious reference to God as distinct from oneself.[15] This is Zaehner's view of Indian religion. One interested in what he calls isolation falls into the Sāṃkhya system of Hinduism. One interested in the same experience, but discerning no metaphysical difference between the Self and the Absolute, falls into advaitan Vedānta in Hinduism. Lastly, Nature Mysticism is a form of experience in which one feels the barriers have fallen completely between object and subject. Here there is no question of good or evil, religious or non-religious. This form of mysticism can be had by anyone, in any religion.[16] In the religion of love, one deals with the union of God with the second, transcendent, self. There is no union with God in Isolation Mysticism, since there is no union with anything in it. It is the lopping off of everything save the transcendent self. There is no union in monistic Vedānta either, since there is only identity there. Union is possible only in a theistic, love, mysticism, in Zaehner's view of things.

Next, Zaehner discerns two categories of religions: i) the this-worldly, which stress the need for right conduct. Into this class fall Judaism, Islam, Protestantism and Confucianism. And ii) other-worldly religion, in which one can reach the timeless-transcendent within oneself. Among these are Theravada Buddhism, Hinduism and Taoism. In between the two extremes stand Mahāyāna Buddhism, Neo-Confucianism, reformed (Gītā) Hinduism, that of Tagore and Gandhi, and

---

[15]Zaehner, Xt/O, pp. 19-20.

[16]Ibid., p. 20.

the Catholic Church. Zaehner isolates Islam to
the category of a special case.[17]

The Fall, and man's way of reacting to the
human condition attendant on it, determines the
shape and direction of religions for Zaehner. The
religions of the East are psychologies and empiricisms, for him, since they do not go in for
speculation about reunification. They batten on
what is salvageable in the mess in which man is.
What is possible is to experience immortality in
bliss without involving the body. The body is a
trammel for this spirituality. The religions of
the West (Judaism, Zoroastrianism, and Islam) see
man as a unity--more the first two than the third.
Christianity fits into the Judaic-Zoroastrian
mould for Zaehner.

In the Fall the lower soul disobeyed the
higher, and thereby God. Seen through the eyes of
Eastern religion, Eve is the lower soul since she
has the power of reflection and decision. The
lower soul wanted to go it alone. She tempted her
master, who was the higher (transcendent) self,
who ate with her and fell. The resultant fall
caused man's center to recede to the unconscious.
The ego was now at war with itself since the other
self (conscience) reproved it constantly.[18] Man's
state, in this construct, was one in which the
higher soul was in exile in the unconscious. It
was a state in which the ego could not follow the
body without getting into trouble. There just
wasn't any harmony or unity between body and soul,
and between soul and soul, within man.[19] So the

---

[17]Zaehner, Xt/O, p. 22.

[18]Ibid., p. 138.

[19]Ibid.

9

Fall relegated the transcendent to the unconscious, where Zaehner says it is the pearl of great price. It awaits discovery there. Early Indian religion discovered it, but thought its journey had ended there. But Zaehner says that it had just happily rediscovered the Self, not God.[20]

In Buddhism's Lotus Sutra Zaehner sees the Buddha being transformed "into the God-man Christ." But this Sutra and the Gītā both agree that realizing one's own soul is just the beginning. Love brings one into God's presence, and love only. There is none in Nature Mysticism. The Lotus Sutra said that men should not only go into their own timeless essence, but should partake of the Buddha nature, which is the ground of man's nature, being itself as creature, not as Creator.[21] For Zaehner, as far as the Tao is concerned, the nameless Tao has been named: it is Jesus.[22] The bhakti (devotion) cults of Krishna in India are just too sugary for Zaehner. There is no terror in them, and there must be terror in religion, since it is in life. But the Gītā's Krishna is more real because there is tragedy and pathos there in the fact that the warrior must kill his brothers in order to fill out his caste-duty. So there is tragedy and love in the Gītā.[23] It is a fuller religious expression than the cult of Krishna dallying with the cattle girls (gopis), which is all sweetness and lacks the balancing effect of pain and tragedy.

---

[20]Ibid., p. 140.

[21]Ibid., p. 142.

[22]Ibid., p. 143.

[23]Ibid., p. 144.

For Zaehner religions diverge according to how men react to the Fall. First, he begins with Hinduism. In Hinduism the oldest Scriptures, the Vedas, are not concerned with God's dealings with man in history, but with the gradual revelation of God's and man's natures. They are a quest for the Absolute, in Zaehner's estimation.[24] Later, the Upanisads ended by stating that man's inmost essence is identical with the Godhead (Chāndogya Upan. 3.14). Zaehner says that except for his doctrine of love and union this teaching is almost exactly like that of Thomas Merton's two-self hypothesis. The Upanisad sees only absolute oneness; there is one being, not two, in man and things.[25]

In India, long before the Upanisads, yoga was a practice in which one punched through the empirical self and went on to the transcendent Self. The immortal Self is the eternal substratum of man's being. This immortality, Zaehner hastens to add, does not mean living forever--as it would in Christian circles. It means that one has conquered death by attaining to a form of existence impervious to the depredations of death.[26] The yogin sees all in space and time subject to death. His goal is to attain to a state beyond the space/time continuum; for there is no death where there is no time.[27] This is a thoroughly empirical approach to religion, which, however, since it is the nub of Indian religion, makes the religion thoroughly unworldly. Liberation from mortality is the aim of Indian religion: mokṣa (Skt.= liberation) means something beyond what man considers the world. It is a

---

[24]Zaehner, Xt/O, p. 23.

[25]Ibid., p. 26.

[26]Zaehner, "Christianity and the World Religions," an art. in Blackfriars 41, 1960, pp. 256-71, p. 260 (hereafter Xt/W).

[27]Ibid., p. 260.

11

freedom from all that is world. This makes Indian religion quite mystical for Zaehner.[28] The prophet makes one historical, bound to find God in time and place. The seer would have none of this. Empirical religion makes one unworldly. A personal God leading his people through history to a final meeting and happiness in the eschaton is utterly meaningless to this brand of religiousness.[29] Yoga, being based on the Sāmkhya system of thought, sees two eternities comprising things: time (Skt.=prkrti), or matter if you will, and the timeless and spaceless substance we call the soul, and which the Sāmkhya names purusa (Skt.=man). The goal of all this is the "dis-union from all that is not man's own eternal self."[30]

Secondly, Buddhism, as found in its earlier variety, Theravada, and following the example of the Buddha himself, is not theoretical like the Upanisads. On the contrary, it cuts away what it considers irrelevant and "mumbo jumbo" in the Brāhmanas, the texts dealing with the earliest Hindu ritual, and contents itself with dealing with an empirical method of finding liberation.[31] Both love and hate are scotched out as passions, attachments to be scorned. The house is on fire; don't ask who made the house, or who rooms in it; get out. So the God-question and the man-question (theology and anthropology) are irrelevant to the Buddha and to most Buddhologists. Zaehner says that the Buddha himself never did solve the problem of why the heap of parts people call man is worth saving. But try to save him the Buddha did. Zaehner goes out on a limb, therefore, in affirming the courageous view that the Buddha taught a

---

[28]Zaehner, Xt/W., art. cit. p. 260.

[29]Ibid.

[30]Ibid., p. 261.

doctrine of the transcendent Self like Sāmkhya's
doctrine of the puruṣa. The Pali canon of
Buddhistic scriptures says we are to make the Self
one's refuge.[32] But, in the final analysis, all
the Buddha himself claimed was but a way to
liberate the individual, nothing more. The rest
was added by the Buddhists. Buddha was a psycho-
logist more than the founder of a religion, and
certainly no savior--nor did he claim or intend to
be. The way was to the inside, to the within of
the individual. So Buddhism is a representative
par excellence of the type of religion Zaehner
calls Indian Religion. It is the type which "seeks
the kingdom of God within you."[33] It is a moral
religion, containing half the Decalogue, but not
the part concerning God.[34] It battens on the part
of man which is deathless; this is beyond the
empirical self; what one calls it is irrelevant.
It is an experience of deathlessness within death
(the essence of Buddhism is "Nirvāṇa is Saṁsara";
i.e. bliss is within suffering and death; seek the
within).

Thirdly, if Buddhism represents one type of
religion, Zaehner says that Judaism and Islam
represent one which is radically other: prophetic
religion. He says, "The contrast between the two
types of religion was great enough to make the
partition of the subcontinent of India almost
inevitable--for Islam is everything that Hinduism
is not, and conversely Hinduism is everything that
Islam is not. The two seem mutually incompat-
ible."[35] To the Jew God is the Presence who
guides them through history, who speaks and
expects obedience. Man's attitude towards God

---

[32]Zaehner, Xt/O, p. 28.

[33]Ibid., pp. 29-31.

[34]Zaehner, Xt/W, p. 263.

[35]Ibid.

13

is one of listening and obedience. Zaehner says
that this climate is "wholly foreign to" mysticism;
that the OT is foreign to mysticism in general.
Not only this, but the only mysticism Zaehner says
Judaism permits, that of the medieval era, is
"reluctant to speak of union." So Indian mysticism is so far from being a possibility to Judaism that it is a blasphemy even to countenance
anything like Nirvāṇa in it--since Nirvāṇa is the
experience of the immortal in man. In Judaism
only God is immortal, however.[36] Jewish mystics
will admit that communion with God is possible, but
never union. Zaehner said that, on the whole, the
Jews thought of the persistence of the nation,
but "they never gave any thought to the immortality of their own souls"; i.e., not until they
met Zoroastrianism during the Babylonian captivi-
ty and derived such a notion from them.[37] It
was the prophet Zoroaster who first proclaimed the
responsibility of the individual, and its immortality as an individual.[38]

Samkhya deems it a singular disaster that
man's nature, his purest essence--his soul--was
ever mixed up in matter. Zaehner says that this
view is re-echoed by Plato and the Gnostics. But
for both Jews and Zoroastrians man is what
Zaehner calls "a single unfractionable being, and
the union of body and soul was essential to his
very nature."[39] Hence, personal survival entered

---

[36] Ibid.

[37] Ibid.

[38] Ibid.

[39] Ibid.

14

late into Judaism, and then it came from the outside: Zoroastrianism. Both religions saw an end time, a judgment, and either bliss or punishment ensuing (and, for Zoroastrianism, bliss after punishment).

So Zaehner concludes that the two types of religion could not differ more on what is good for man: for the Jews/Zoroastrians the good means deliverance from evil; for the Indians liberation means from "matter and time..." which are evil for Indian religions.[40] There is between the great religions, therefore, what Zaehner terms an "absolute gulf" because they rarely speak of the same things. For Jews what is vital to religion is God and man's "true rela- tion" with him. For Indians the only good worth vying for is the realization here and now of deathlessness, of the bliss within; "...whether there is one god or many or none at all is not felt to be important, and what happens to the body and the mind which is dependent on it cannot be of the slightest consequence to the soul."[41] Zaehner sees no basis of agreement between the Jewish/Zoroastrian/Muhammadan religious tradi- tion and the Indian one. But this does not put the situation beyond redemption. Zaehner says it is stark, not hopeless, "For Indian religions did not stand still."[42] This is the watchword for Zaehner's thought: development. Religions develop. The Sāṁkhya-Yoga and Buddhist aspects of Indian religion thought that because they had experienced the eternal, they were the Eternal. But there was another strand of thought develop- ing alongside the situation, to the extent that:

---

[40]Ibid., p. 265.

[41]Zaehner, Xt/W, p. 265.

[42]Ibid.

15

"They thus identified what is a purely
psychological condition with a metaphysical
construction; or, to put it another way,
they identified a state of mind in themselves in which time had been transcended
with the Great Being that transcends all
things including time. And from this again
they concluded that all things in essence
are one, and that thus God is All, and since
the soul is also identical with God, the
soul is also All. So did the pantheistical
trend which is so strong in Hinduism
begin."[43]

Zaehner says that this Hindu pantheism is known as
Vedānta. This form of Hinduism drives the two
religions, Hinduism and Judaism, farther apart,
since, where Buddha left the question of God on the
shelf, Vedānta reintroduces him as an impersonal
ground of the universe, with which the soul is
identical.[44]

Fourthly, Vedānta is only one strand of
Hinduism. There is another: Bhakti, i.e., the
religion of devotion. The religion of the monks
and the philosophers was Vedānta, but the
people's religion brought the gods back to the
fore; and from the gods the people chose Viṣnu
and Śiva as the paramount deities. Both these
deities related to their devotees in terms of
intimacy and offered them succor. But it was the
former god who interested Zaehner since his
incarnation, depicted in the Gītā, was made for
men when times were hard and demanded help
from on high.[45] Even before the Gītā, however,

---

[43]Ibid., pp. 265f.

[44]Ibid., p. 266.

[45]Zaehner, Xt/W, pp. 266f.

Hinduism changed gradually from the impersonal notion of the Brahman to a personal god. In the Śvetāśvatara Upaniṣad one finds three stages of liberation: i) the first is the integration of the whole self around the transcendental self, ii) then the higher self illumines the eternal within man, and iii) lastly, when the self sees time/eternity, it intuits God. God has entered the picture, but not to love or be loved. Mysticism thus far, in Hinduism, is knowledge (Skt.=jñāna). In Christianity, on the other hand, mysticism is love and knowledge.[46] The first five chapters of the Gītā acknowledge classical Indian spirituality in which one can realize the Brahman through the use of yoga (i.e. one can become a Brahma-bhuta), without god's help. But as the god Krishna, who is an incarnation of Visnu, unfolds his revelation to the warrior Arjuna, it appears that moksa (liberation) is not the end of the journey, bhakti (devotion) is. Zaehner maintains that bhakti slowly became Hinduism's living religion.[47]

Fifthly, in Chinese religion Zaehner sees something which could not be more different from Indian thought. In China both spirit and matter are equally real and valuable. Further, rather than an endless concatenation of lives, as in India, Chinese man lives but once. While he lives, matter and spirit are inseparable; but they do not speculate about them in the afterlife. For both Confucianism and Taoism salvation means integration into the Tao-into the cosmic order.[48] Taoism looks back longingly to a unity which man

---

[46]Zaehner, Xt/O, p. 33.

[47]Ibid., pp. 34-7.

[48]Zaehner, Xt/O, p. 74.

enjoyed before the Fall, which Fall imposed a
false personality on man's natural self. This
false person makes man makes man multiply himself
and his powers, careening him further and further
away from his pristine simplicity.[49]   Taoism seeks
to integrate man's parts into what the Buddhists
(Mahāyāna) call emptiness (Skt.=śūnyatā). This
emptiness is the stillness of the world beyond
time. Zaehner finds this theme in all religions.[50]
Taoism is a religion which seeks only to let things
alone; leave them alone and they will be all right.
It is a religion firmly rooted in a boundless
optimism in man's natural goodness. The world has
a built-in harmony. Let things alone, and, like
water, the harmony will seek its level. Zaehner
finds Taoism very much in the mould of Rousseau's
naturalism.[51] This optimism is half like Ur
Buddhism and its early Mahāyāna reform, that of
Nagarjuna, which closely approximated the teaching of the Buddha himself in that it saw man as
irretrievably good. Buddhism says that man is
good, but the world is evil, full of sadness and
pain: wretched. When Buddhism came into China,
therefore, it had a basis on which to build. With
its principle of upaya (Skt.=skill in means),
which allowed it to become a world religion
flourishing beyond the confines of India--in endow-
ing it with the power to change to suit the time
and clime in which it found itself--it battened
on the Taoist optimism and began to build itself
into Chinese life.

Taoism, therefore, is a natural religion, and
its mysticism is natural, too, in Zaehner's sense
of that word; i.e., in touch with matter in a way

---

        [49]Zaehner, Concordant Discord (hereafter,
C/D), p. 229.

        [50]Ibid., pp. 233-6.

        [51]Ibid., p. 237.

18

which is euphoric--happy to experience--which is, in turn, an experience of deathlessness as it removes the limits of the ego, which are space and time. There, all is One and One is all.[52]

Confucianism, in Zaehner's estimation, is a humanism. He calls it a "Way of Man." It began as a person, Confucius, and ended as a principle. Hinduism begins with gods and ends with a saviour. Confucianism is the most realistic of religions in worshipping both god and mammon.[53] It deals with both the good and the evil in the human situation in opting for a synthesis. Confucianism is the religion of the Mean; it takes its stance in the middle, between polar opposites. Like Taoism, it asserts that the harmony of the cosmos comes without effort, but that man's harmony demands sweat and effort. Confucianism aims at a restoration of the series of interconnections and interdependencies among men, and with its head the Son of Heaven, and with all nature. Among the competing views of human nature Mencius' triumphed: man is good, so whatever is human is good and accords with the Way (Tao).[54] The Way lies in the Mean, the median between polar opposites. In Confucianism, therefore, life consisted of a delicate filagree of relationships. This is why Confucians hated Buddhism (Mahāyāna) so much; it broke up the chain of relationships it so earnestly sought to re-forge. Mahāyāna is a religion of no love: compassion, always; love, not at all. The optimum state for Mahāyāna consisted in Emptiness (Skt.=śūnyata); and there is no love in an emptiness-of-self-for-the-sake-of-bliss (Nirvāna). Compassion is not love; there is a radical difference. It is on the way to love of the other because he is other, but in Mahāyāna there is not any other; and one has difficulty establishing that there is even a self. So how

---

[52]Ibid., p. 237.

[53]Zaehner, C/D, p. 257.

[54]Ibid., p. 263.

can there be love? This is a fundamental point
with Zaehner. If the religions are the same,
ultimately, how is it that their differences are
irreconcilable, especially when referring to
Buddhism? Christianity centers around and builds
up from a fulcrum of love; not so Buddhism.

This is the nub of Zaehner's thought. The
religions are talking of different things. Compassion and Emptiness and Nirvāna are not love in
themselves.[55] Zaehner seems to be basing his
thought on the reality of language; i.e., its
ability to express something metaphysically and
epistemologically real. If what the religions
are saying, after an examination of the best and
most orthodox of theist thoughts, is radically
different, then the religions must be radically
different. Otherwise language is nonsense. What
you will see in my analysis of the philosophia
perennis is that it tries to get out of its
philosophical cul-de-sac--in which language is meaningless if all religions are saying different
things but meaning the same thing--by asserting
that it has certain and unattainable knowledge
that what it says is true. It denies ultimacy
to all faiths, but like every gnostic system, it
demands faith in its own unverifiable doctrines. The
philosophia perennis is, therefore, no more than
another religion--and a sect at that--in setting its
ultimacy over against the ultimate claims of
other religious exclusiveness. Its inclusiveness
will be shown to be really special pleading for
its own Vedānta doctrine. Hence, it is an
exclusiveness using inclusivist language.

What Zaehner calls Natural Religion is one
built up on the reasonableness of things.[56]
Here one need not have faith in a god; not a

_____

[55]Cf. Zaehner's C/D, pp. 267-69 for a fuller
treatment of this.

[56]Zaehner, C/D, p. 35.

personal god anyway. It is the religion of western
intellectuals, in Zaehner's eyes. It is Rousseau's
religion, the religion of the French Revolution.
He calls it quintessential Enlightenment thought.[57]
He deprecates it because it is the undemanding
religion of western burghers which allows men to
see the same philosophy in all religious forms:
this is the philosophia perennis.[58] No wonder
Zaehner went to such lengths to tie it down and
identify it in both its eastern and western forms.
Natural Religion has its goal in the meeting of
Buddhism with Taoism in China, where Nirvāna is
Saṁsara; i.e., the world itself is peace, so let
it be![59]

Neo-Confucianism is a synthesis of Buddhism,
Confucianism and Taoism; the latter stands midway
between Confucianism and Buddhism. In Neo-
Confucianism there is a concept called ch'i,
which is matter in motion. The Great Vacuity,
in the Marxist sense, is matter in its most
subtle form.[60] (Śūnyatā is a Mahāyāna term;
it is the ultimate state of bliss attained
in the knowledge (Skt.=jñāna) that everything is void, which knowledge is a blissful experience, not the end-product of man's
lucubrations, but the term of meditative
practices and asceticisms.) Matter (ch'i) is a
substance composed ambivalently of yang and yin,
which correspond to the Samkhya notions of
purusa and prakrti, albeit in a superficial way,
according to Zaehner.[61] In this system the subject becomes the object when one sees that the

---

[57]Ibid., PP. 36ff.

[58]Ibid., p. 38.

[59]Ibid., p. 269.

[60]Ibid., p. 271.

[61]Ibid., p. 272.

principle of all (which the Neo-Confucians call Li) is the same in all for all. This is the tathatā (suchness, the Buddhahood, which is to know by experience that one is the Buddha) of Buddhism and the Tao of Taoism. Zaehner says that the principle Li becomes the Logos, the philosopher's God. So mysticism becomes a politics in Neo-Confucianism.[62] Natural Religion has pulled it all together in Neo-Confucianism: a blend of the old mysticism, Taoism, and the old humanism, Confucianism, given the old forms so as not to confound and scandalize the people.[63]

But it is the tie-in with mysticism and philosophy which seems to intrigue Zaehner. It all smacks, in the West, of the philosophia perennis. The same mentality as manifested in Mahāyāna and Taoism crops up in Neo-Confucianism and in the West in Huxley's and Frithjof Schoun's works, and now even in the work of the eminent American scholar Huston Smith.[64] In this mindset, everything is tied together in a knowledge-experience which only the few have. What the rest have, though the forms be several, is the same if only they knew it. Zaehner has turned the tables on Huxley et al. in seeing the connection between so many of the religions of the East, which religions have become the piety of those in the West who cannot stand the absoluteness of form found in the great religions of the West: Judaism, Christianity and Islam.

---

[62]Ibid., p. 281

[63]Huston Smith's The Religions of Man, Harper Colophon, 1958, pp. 156,7 Passim.

[64]Huston Smith has published a new book in which he claims to be an adherent of the philosophia perennis, viz., Forgotten Truth, the primoridal tradition, N.Y., 1976. cf. p.x.

So he pulls all this together by his use of
the myth of the Fall. Fallen man has intuited
that there is something seriously wrong with him;
he is out of joint with others, God and even with
himself. Religions differ according to how man
deals with his half-angel, half-beast nature;
which is, consequently, half mortal and half
immortal. Zaehner says that all mysticisms have
tried to slay the beast, the mortal in man. He
states that this is the secret of the Buddha's
Enlightenment: he has slain the beast and
tasted immortality while alive. He has, thus,
split man apart, body from soul, mortal from
immortal. The Buddha affirmed by experience
what Christianity knows by faith, and Zoroaster
by revelation: that the soul is immortal. By
dying, God showed his love for man, which was
foreshadowed in the Gītā. These three, therefore,
state that these religions are different from
Christianity, but that all the major religions
are the repositories of true revelations, and,
therefore, true mysticisms, which seem to be
working out of the revelations. This is what
he means by entitling his first book after his
Sacred and Profane (1957) and its companion
volume, Hindu and Muslim Mysticism (1960), At
Sundry Times (1958). He meant to say that God
had revealed himself in diverse ways at "sundry
times" to the various religions; this, quoting
Hebrews 1:1.[65] So Zaehner asserts, it is not
the religions, but God who has posed the conun-
drum of History of Religions:[66] they claim to
be exclusive, but no explanation seems satisfy-
ing either to the adherents of any religion or
to those looking from the outside. So, since it
is God who has revealed these truths, this from
our own New Testament, then only that which the

---

[65]Zaehner, S/T, p. 28.

[66]Ibid., p. 29.

23

religions themselves accept as orthodox is worthy
of consideration, in Zaehner's estimation. The
religions themselves should look after their own
revelations and say what corresponds to them and
what does not. Each revelation is unique, therefore, separate and to be tended by those who share
the revelation/experience-of-it in the religious
community which we call religion. It appears that
this is what Zaehner is trying to say in setting
up his third thesis. Hence, what do these
religions mean? He makes them point to Christ by
seeing both Indian religion and Iranian (Zoroastrianism) as a better praeparatio evangelica than
Greek religion. But this preparation theme forms
his fourth and fifth theses.

(2) Religions Seem to Converge

Zaehner's fourth thesis is that religions
converge on Christ who fulfills their best hopes.
He says that the Taoist-Sāṁkhya experience (i.e.,
the yoga experience of stripping all away to one's
immortal core in order to experience it) in Japanese garb is Zen. Zen is the experience of the
eternal in oneself. But this is not all there is
to Buddhism. With the admission of outside help
in Buddhism, the religion radically changed.
Originally, it was held that only one's own powers
are needed to experience one's Buddha Nature, and
this is still the thought and teaching of the
older Theravada branch of Buddhism. Now grace
could allow one to experience one's Buddhahood.
Further, the Lotus Sutra makes a god of the
Buddha; it allows one to go beyond Nirvāna to a
state beyond all opposites--a state which it calls
parinirvāna (Pali).[67]

Zaehner assays Zen as a Nature Mysticism, a
rubric which he hammered out when dealing with

---

[67]Zaehner, C/D, pp. 279-84.

Huxley, and which I shall pay due attention to shortly.[68] Zaehner thinks that the bridge between Zen and Christian love is to be found in the Hindu notion of bhakti (devotion), where the yogin must leave his integration to become attached to God.[69] The Taoist, Neo-Confucian and Zen experience seem to be the discovery of the transcendent Self beyond time and eternity.[70] Here, love means that one must leave the god of the self and seek the Self of God.

As Buddhism developed, a triune Buddha evolved in popular devotion and philosophy. This comprised the Dharma Buddha, the Buddha-kaya (which was the Buddha's glorybody), and the Cosmic Buddha. Using its device of upaya (Skt.=skill in means, which allowed the religion to become worldwide and adaptive, unlike Hinduism which is tied to land and unbending traditions) Buddhism changed and evolved as it went from country to country. Zaehner feels that it is better to compare this Buddhist Trinity to the three aspects of Jesus, than to the Christian Trinity--as do many Western scholars. The three aspects he chooses are: i) the logos, which corresponds to the Dharma Body of the Buddha, ii) Christ as risen, which corresponds to the Body of Bliss, the Buddha-kaya, and iii) the body of the child Jesus and that of the Crucified Jesus, which Zaehner calls the construct body.[71] This is not a very cogent theology on Zaehner's part, but it showed that his mind was changing as he got down to the brass tacks of applying his basic intuitions--written up in his first two books

---

[68]Ibid., pp. 294-7, passim.

[69]Ibid., pp. 297-301, passim.

[70]Zaehner, Xt/O, p. 87.

[71]Ibid., p. 89.

25

on mysticism, Sacred and Profane and Hindu and
Muslim Mysticism. Zaehner began to see the
possibility of a religious convergence as being
more than merely "verbal" and "fictitious."[72]
When he began, this was the trap he discerned
in so many who plotted the lines of putative
religious convergence. But as he continued his
empirical study of the religious texts he found
that there was, indeed, a possibility of convergence.

He concludes, not unnaturally, that all the
religions, as they develop, "seem to draw ever
nearer to Christianity."[73] This is the key to
Zaehner's mind, as it grew and changed. He made
his thoughts out to be an apologetics, based on
empirical studies of texts, done rigorously on
the linguistic level, and moving over into the
interpretative level. Theologians see these and
recognize that they are a theology; historians
seeing them, claim them as pieces of interpretation.[74] I shall take up these thoughts in the
next unit of this chapter, on Zaehner's method
and method in general, in which Bernard Lonergan
mentions that theology gives the literal meaning
of symbols, and that history of religions tells

---

[72]Zaehner's inaugural lecture, art.cit., in
C/D, p. 429.

[73]Zaehner, Xt/O, p. 99.

[74]The historian of religions, T. Gelblum, reviewing Zaehner's H/M in "Bull. of the School of
Oriental and African Studies," 25, 1962, said that
what Zaehner was doing was "reinterpretation," and
seems to imply that this is a legitimate function,
whether or not the interpretation is correct--which
he implies is probably closer to the latter since
Zaehner's methodology is "subjective." But
interpretation is not a moot point for Gelblum at
all (p. 173).

which are equivalent, and no more.[75] There seems
to be a battle brewing between historians of
religions and theologians. Both claim rights of
interpretation.

But, to continue Zaehner's line of thought,
he says: Why should the religions not converge
since it is God who guides them all? He cites
Nirvāna as an example that God left his impress
on all the world's religions. It is better
equipped as a religious symbol than is the Old
Testament, to tell us about the eternal in man;
the OT, in Zaehner's estimation, tells us only
about God the eternal, not man the eternal.[76]

Zaehner asserts that each religious tradition
has the same types of mysticism in it but with an
emphasis on different aspects. Indian religion
emphasizes moksa (liberation from time and matter),
while Christianity emphasizes union with God.[77]
The religions of the East emphasize contemplation
and the eternal within, a motif which has withered
in Christianity since the Reformation. Zaehner
thinks that orthodox Protestantism has killed the
mystical tradition in its lands, and made it suspect within Catholicism.[78] The Buddha had such
mystical experiences, the lack of which Zaehner
decries in the West. The Buddha had achieved
peace, then having attained it, opted for compassion on men who had not gained it; this,
since peace is not the end of the journey.
Zaehner's interpretation of this appears in his
Concordant Discord where he says that having
attained real peace (Nirvāna or Satori in Zen)

---

[75]B. Lonergan, "The Ongoing Genesis of Methods," apud Studies in Rel. 6,4, 1976-77, p. 354.

[76]Zaehner, Xt/O, p. 99.

[77]Zaehner, C/D, p. 302.

[78]Zaehner, Xt/O, p. 130

means that one is beyond first peace. The latter
is that which one has when one possesses the Self
in joy, and has become one with Nature; in a
theistic system we would call it a unity with
God, the two being by no means the same, as we
shall see in the chapter on Nature Mysticism.
Zaehner sees as the link between Zen's Satori and
theism in that doctrine in the Gītā which takes
pleasure in the good of all.[79]   That which, in
Christianity, is the same as the Buddha's peace
is the emptiness talked of by the Christian
mystics of St. Victor, Hugh and Richard, in which
there is an emptiness (which we can call first
peace), then, and then only, is there love (or,
in theism, what can be called second peace).
Richard calls the first peace self-contemplation
and the second the contemplation of God.[80]

Startlingly enough to Christians, but not to
Indians, Taoists or Zen adepts, the Self alone
can restore man's original state, which was one
of bliss and peace.   This places one at the apex
of the soul, where Zaehner spies the possibility
of any convergence in religions happening.   It is
here that they will meet, if meet they shall.
Zaehner becomes more sanguine about this possibility as he gets older, and broadens his thoughts
through his having to write on all the major
religious traditions, not just his original
fields, which included Zoroastrianism, Hinduism
and Islam.   The state of first peace is of
enstasy, in which a being is at peace in the Self.
The second stage, note Zaehner does not say
"state" here, but uses a term which demands a
religious evolution, is one of ecstasy which

---

[79]Zaehner, C/D, p. 304.

[80]Ibid., pp. 305-12, passim.

28

going out to the Other in peace and love. This
latter is theism for Zaehner.[81]

On what level does Zaehner see religious convergence? He says it seems to be possible on the
level Hindus call natural, dreamless sleep
(samādhi in Sanskrit); he hastens to add that this
trance state is not one which contains any love.
It is, therefore, a convergence in what Zaehner
has learned to call Nature Mysticism, a level in
which the nature mystics become one with their
ground, which is matter. But, as the Muslim
mystical writer Abū Yazīd has discovered, this
stage is just a start, not the end.[82] This stage
is one characterized by the inflation of the ego
until subject and object have become one, and
the resultant unity can truly be called the All.
In theistic mysticism the unity of soul found in
the first stage is shattered in many by God. God
shatters his own image in man in order to prepare
him for the nuptials he has prepared for his beloved.
This is what John of the Cross called the Dark
Night of the soul. Anything which reptures
the concord between body and soul is an abomina-
tion. There must be concord between the two,
ultimately. Zaehner is emphatic in stressing
this point. Body and soul demand unity in a
theistic system, but this is not so in "emptiness mysticism," which is the mysticism of
India, Taoism, and Zen. The unity, or concord,
shows up in how one acts, in theistic mysticism;
if there are evil fruits then the mysticism is
evil, no matter how blissful or peaceful.[83]
Again, the trap one may lay for oneself in using
potent tools like yoga, or the techniques of
Ṣūfism, is that they are so efficacious that the
subject may mistake the resultant expansion of

---

[81]Zaehner, C/D, p. 313.

[82]Ibid., p. 317.

[83]Ibid., pp. 320-33.

the ego for God.[84]

So Zaehner says there is Nature Mysticism,
then there is the experience of the self as the
image of God (sāmkhya in Hinduism and Ṣūfism in
Islam), and then there is love/union mysticism,
the mysticism of the love of God. Mysticism
moves in an evolutionary pattern for Zaehner. It
is the same pattern he discerns in religions
themselves. Mysticism moves up from Nature
Mysticism to love mysticism; both mysticisms and
religions act in the same way for Zaehner. This
is his paramount thesis in his theology of religions. He thinks that Nature Mysticism is God's
creation before sin, and man, spoilt it by growing up.

He says that both in the Lotus Sutra of
Buddhism and the Gītā of Hinduism man must leave
the fragment of enjoyment he possesses in his
experience of the eternity in the Self, since it
is not enough. Man must leave this rest behind
as defective in order to be free to be one with
the Lord. He asserts that convergence seems to
happen in the incarnation theme of Christianity
and Hinduism. In both, God becomes man to reveal
himself--the unknown God opens up to man. Further,
convergence appears in the duality of selves in
both Buddha and Christ: they both have an
empirical self (body) and a transcendent body
(self).[85]

He says that Adam lives on in us as our
Transcendent Self. This Self is crucified with
Christ; it dies to pride--the pride of the
Buddhist arhants (Skt.=adepts) and other mystics
whose experience allows them to possess themselves
to the exclusion of all others, and love--and rises

---

[84]Zaehner, Xt/O, p. 132.

[85]Zaehner, Xt/O, p. 145.

with Christ in charity, which is love of the Other. Eve is the empirical soul, which is to be integrated with the higher soul--the inner soul--which is her consort. She goes through Adam into Christ, and thus to God. Here the original doctrine of the Buddha is turned upside down, even more than it was with the Lotus Sutra. The Buddha came to free man from matter, the cause of pain. Christ came to free man in matter.[86]

Zaehner employs the old axiom o testimonium animae naturaliter Christianae as his instrument of convergence among religions. Man's highest aspirations in Judaism and the Far East point to the Incarnation. The other religions have not accepted Christ because, though Christianity is easy to accept de jure as the true faith, in praxi Christians do not act in a very holy way. But the best aspirations of Hinduism, and both Theravada and Mahāyāna Buddhism, point to a somewhat natural appetite for deification.[87] This is so because the highpoints of Hindu and Buddhist aspirations are these: incarnation (Viṣnu) in Hinduism, and compassion in the Buddha, and the long-suffering compassion of the Bodhisattva. Christ fills out what these shadows indicate. He is the true Messiah of the Jews, the true Krishna and true Bodhisattva of the Hindus and Buddhists, respectively. Zaehner, therefore asserts in Thesis Four that the Catholic Church is the Middle Way between the absolute transcendence of Islam and Judaism and the absolute immanence of Hinduism and Buddhism; it is midway between the quest for individual salvation in Indian religion and corporate spiritual maintenance in China. Transcendent and immanent, individual and collectivity

---

[86]Ibid., p. 146.

[87]Zaehner, Xt/O, p. 146.

31

meet in Christ. He affirms that the Catholic
Church brings an earnest of mystical union to
ordinary men in the Blessed Sacrament. The
sacrament fills the gap between matter and spirit,
God and man.[88] And, finally, Jesus fulfilled
Zoroaster's revelation that, in the final days,
the whole man--body and soul--will live in harmony
with God as an individual and as part of a
corporate entity; together at least with all his
brothers and sisters.[89]

Zaehner's fifth thesis deals with the convergence of Christianity and Marxism in matter.
He views the Church as standing for Marxism's
ideal of solidarity, which Engels thought was
reflected by religion and philosophy anyway. So
Zaehner places both on a convergent path; Christ
and Marx are not necessarily and always inimical.
He says that individualism, such as the existen-
tialist preoccupation with it is, in Lenins'
words, an "infantile disease." There is, therefore, for Zaehner, a convergence in things:
Marxism with Christianity, especially with Catholic Christianity, and Christianity with the best
in Indian, Jewish, Zoroastrian, Muslim and
Chinese religions.

Zaehner's thought pulls itself together
under the rubric of matter and its mysticism. The
mystics of matter are Teilhard and Engels. Its
prophets are Christ and Marx. So Zaehner pulls
the two types of religions--mystical and prophetic--
together through the unifying power and evolutionary thrust of matter. He does all this by
confronting Christ with Marx, just as he did in
confronting Judaism with Buddhism, to see if any
common denominator exists between them which can
throw a unifying umbrella over the brawling

---

[88]Ibid.

[89]Zaehner, Xt/W, pp. 270f.

themes and divergent religions he has thus far
treated. The unifying factor is matter. It
allows Christ and Marx to come together without
destroying either, and to do so in a way which is
ongoing and in process. It would seem that
Zaehner's is an Hegelian system which deals with
opposing forces and ideas--the religions and their
expressions in cult, mysticism . . . It allows
them to converge on a higher level, which level
is not a static synthetic thing, but a dynamic
process which must constantly clash and renew itself in order to keep both the religion (Christianity) and the flow of history, which is matter,
on the move to its consummation in a solidarity.
This is precisely Zaehner's concept of Marxism,
separate as individuals, and together as the convergent realities.

So God clashes with matter in his two incarnations: that of the Holy Spirit losing itself in
matter in its first Incarnation, which was creation, and that of Christ's forgetting of self in
his Incarnation. The latter is an _amnesia_, in
Zaehner's view of it, in which the _Logos_ empties
himself in a way which is self-forgetting, a kind
of amnesia. This amnesia is overccme as Jesus
comes to his majority in full self-awareness and
self-fulfillment. His growth is an _anamnesis_,
a remembering of God back into the world through
matter, the Incarnation.[90]

But if God clashes with matter in his two
incarnations, Zaehner has matter clash with God
in Marxist criticism. The result is what Hegel
called an "overreach," which Emil Fackenheim

---

[90]Cf. Zaehner's C/Sp. pp. 189,192; also C/D,
ch.XX; and especially his Dialectical-Christianity
and Christian Materialism, Oxford, 1971,
pp.80ff.

terms "perhaps Hegel's most important term...(which is)...the decisive condition of the possibility of the complete philosophic thought."[91] This overreach is the dynamic element in the process allowing the clash of God and matter to converge and resolve on the level of history and religion--all of which becomes either religious history or history of religions, in my appreciation of what Zaehner says: it depends on where one comes from, religion or history, whether the endproduct's emphasis is religion or history.

Zaehner can reverse the process nicely, using the dialectical device of chiasmus, making Word become Flesh and Flesh become Word.[92] In so doing he allows what is happening in Nature Mysticism to be redirected back into world history by God so

---

[91]Fackenheim, Emil L., The Religious Dimension in Hegel's Thought, Beacon Press, Boston, 1970, p.98. Cf. p.256, note no. 35 where Fackenheim says that overreach--a translation of Aufgehoben--is a term overlooked by Hegel scholars. He says it is universally neglected. He cites its occurrence in several key passages in Hegel, but cannot even find the term indexed in the Hegel-Lexikon (ed. Hermann Glockner-2nd ed.: Stuttgart, 1957) or in any lexicon which he consulted. Overreach allows not only the possibility of philosophic thought for Zaehner, but it allows him to deal with the convergence of religions with Christ, and with secularity--Marxism--as well.

[92]Zaehner, C/D, chapters 17 and 20 deal with this in detail.

that man's intimacy with matter does not have to
be non-historical, as it is in his rendering of
this mystical type.

Zaehner finds that evolution is the point of
convergence between Christianity and Marxism. Both
depict the world on the move, upwards, towards
something higher. Solidarity has described the
movement of religions thus far for Zaehner, and it
does not desert him now.

Teilhard based his thought on matter on a
personal experience of matter, what Zaehner calls
Nature Mysticism. Zaehner says that it is also
what is called cosmic consciousness. Teilhard
concluded that God's revelation was to be the
matter of Nature Mysticism, which was a matter
undifferentiated. Zaehner corrects this for his
own uses by saying that the revelation from God
would be through matter, but matter personified
in Christ, and this a Christ crucified. Teilhard's revelation leaves us open to the godless-
ness of Nature Mysticism and also its amorality.
But Teilhard corrected himself by making a distinction between a pantheism of identity and
one of unity--the one is a mysticism of matter
and the second a mysticism of the love of God,
in which there was "unity at the top, by ultra-
differentiation."[93] But Teilhard's unamended
thought makes matter look very much like Jung's
God, in Zaehner's estimation. So, Zaehner concludes that Teilhard's theology is flawed due
to its lack of any appreciation of Jesus on the
Cross. Teilhard's view of suffering was too
harsh for Zaehner; so harsh as to seem unchris-
tian. So Zaehner says that the union Teilhard
calls for is through a differentiated matter,
which is Christ crucified; and that the change
which Teilhard made in his thought, in setting
up a distinction between pantheisms--one Natural

---

[93]Zaehner, Drugs, Mysticism and Make-
Believe, London, 1972, p. 179.

35

and one Christian—came as he neared his death, and Zaehner's came as he neared his own.

So he found he had to reject Teilhard's unchanged works because there was not any Christian way of interpreting suffering and evil in them. In the end, Zaehner comes back to his original categories of mysticisms in order to understand and use Teilhard's thought. Zaehner, using his own categories of mysticisms, found that Teilhard was a nature mystic in his unreconstructed thought; and this would put Teilhard where he protested he did not want to be: viz., beyond good and evil in the embrace of a seductive matter. Hence Zaehner had to correct the faults in Teilhard's thoughts on original sin and sin in general, as well as readjust Teilhard's notions on God. At bottom, what he found faulty with Nature Mysticism is that its concept of convergence took the place of goodness in time; Zaehner said that in eternity there seemed to be no need for good nor evil because the opposites coalesce there; but there is a crying need for good and evil in time, otherwise it would be the <u>reductio ad absurdum</u> of mysticisms.[94] Men sorely need the distinction between good and evil in order to live their lives. If men do not need them when in the throes of an experience of Nature Mysticism, then they need them when it wears off.

When Teilhard said in his Parable of Matter that "all is but one" in heaven and that "nothing is precious save what is yourself in others and others in yourself,"[95] Zaehner interpreted this as what he calls "dialectical thinking in the tradition of Heraclitus, of Nicolas of Cusa, of Hegel, Marx, and Engels." "The whole universe

---

[94]Zaehner, D/Xt, p. 73.

[95]<u>Ibid</u>., p. 5.

operates through the clash of opposites, but these opposites are never mutually exclusive but interpenetrate each other so as to form a final harmonious synthesis."[96] Thus Zaehner sees Teilhard as having made a "radical departure from classical Christian theology." This is so because Teilhard is basing his thoughts on evolution rather than on the inner workings of theology. So, Zaehner feels that Teilhard is far closer to Marx and Engels than to Thomas or Augustine, and that the last named has been a disaster in Christian theology because of his stand on matter and the flesh.[97] Zaehner lionizes Teilhard for the latter's view that the separation of matter from spirit represents a heresy. For Zaehner, seeing his own theology in Teilhard and Balzac--the latter for his remark that the Church is to turn around the phrase et verbum caro factum est to read "flesh became Word"--matter is instinct with spirit. The temptation of matter is that it tends to make man want to return to a lower state of consciousness in which all is diffused, and in which one is united once again with all living things; in which one is innocent, penetrates all things, and knows no good or evil.[98]

So Zaehner ends his thought by seeing Marxism and Christ meeting in, for want of a better word, a "spirituality," or a theology of man's evolution through God's devolution (i.e., two incarnations). Zaehner, therefore, accepts Engels' and Marx's concept of the rise of matter towards thought and up to a level which will allow men to become free and just. He fuses it with Teilhard's mysticism of matter being spiritualized through Christ--who

---

[96]Zaehner, C/Xt, p. 5.

[97]Ibid., p. 6.

[98]Ibid., p. 7.

was materialized through the Holy Spirit--and ends
with an apologetics which is at once a spiritual
theology and a theology of history. For Zaehner,
religion reflects nature.[99] This is quite Marxist.
He sees God's imprint on nature where the Holy
Spirit became one with matter in creation and the
Son of God became man in the Incarnation.[100]
Zaehner must tackle the question, here, "Is there
a Natural Religion, as there is a Nature Mysticism?" He uses the terms Natural Religion in the
pejorative sense to show the use the bourgeois
West made of the Nature Mysticisms and Monism of
the Orient. But he certainly seems to be moving
in the direction of saying that religion is
connatural to man since God is imprinted in nature.

Nature, or in Marxist terms, man's real conditions, is the basis of Zaehner's thought and method
all along. Zaehner's thought, Marxist thought and
Indian religious mysticism are all empiricisms.[101]
So Zaehner mines Teilhard for his apologetic
value. For Zaehner, Teilhard did not stand by himself, but only in relation to Marxism and his own
Catholic faith. Teilhard's ultimate value, for
Zaehner, lay in showing all that the Church is the
logical fruit of evolution. So Teilhard reverses the
Marxist criticism that the world is heartless, and
"fulfills and perfects and baptizes the insights
of Marx and Engels, and brings the heart of Christ
into a heartless world."[102]

Thus Thesis Five should read: God has buried
himself in the world's stuff on two occasions:
Creation and the Incranation. So God has

---

[99]Zaehner, C/Sp, p. 168.

[100]Ibid., pp. 189-91.

[101]Ibid., p. 164.

[102]Ibid., p. 186.

directed the movement of matter, thought and man
from the beginning. Marxist analysis treats of
these real conditions, as far as empirical
analysis can go. Teilhard's value for Zaehner's
empirical study and theological interpretation
of the same situation is that he has related
spirit to matter; has put a heart into it, over-
coming the heartlessness of Nature Mysticism--
which is a peak state, depicting a long-term drive
of matter on the move upwards. In formulating
Marxism in Christian terms Zaehner found Teilhard
of great value. Hence, things seem to be con-
verging in nature. Marxist and Christian convergence are the two hopes for the world, and
they are not necessarily inimical hopes.

In sum, Zaehner's thought comes down to this:
i) Huxley's experience was true mysticism, but of
a type which is called Nature Mysticism. Hence
it is not the same as Theism, since there is no
God in it, necessarily. ii) There is, in Indian
thought, a common strand of "spirituality" which
Zaehner calls Isolation Mysticism. It is yoga,
plain and simple. It is dualistic in its
Sāmkhya form and monistic in its Advaita form.
Hence, it is not Nature Mysticism, since neither
are expansions, as in Nature Mysticism, but the
exact opposite: man contracts to exclude all
but eternity and its immediate experience. Theism
is an experience of God as other, not of Self as
God-as we have it in monism. God is the All-
powerful. This is not the same as Isolation
Mysticism, in which one can see the Self as the
Absolute, nor is it Nature Mysticism in which the
ego becomes the All. Hence each of the three
types of mysticism is different from the other.
Therefore, Huxley's philosophia perennis is
false in asserting that all are, ultimately, the
same. iii) Since the mysticisms are not only
different but divergent, so are the religions.
They diverge because of the way they face up to
the human situation after the Fall. Semitic
religions go one way, India another and China
another. iv) But India and Iran describe, in
their religions, a praeparatio evangelica, which

Zaehner sees as even better than the Greek one. So
convergence is possible in that there seems an in-
nate tendency to theism and love mysticism. Fur-
thur, Jesus fulfills the best hopes of India, Iran,
Judaism and China by being Incarnate God, Resurrected man, Compassionate One, Messiah and Recon-
ciler of human situations and the one to Tao the
Tao. v) Marxism and Christianity are not necessarily inimical, and are the only hopes for the
age. Both describe a world on the move to convergence, but it is a convergence in love as well
as justice.

I have chosen to treat the first two of these
theses, since they are the basis for all the rest
and seem to be the only ones which Zaehner had
time to demonstrate fully. A knowledge of them,
furthermore, is sufficient to know in extenso
what Zaehner's thought is all about. But before
one sees his thought laid out point by point, it
is well to note his method, which was somewhat
different for an historian of religions, and which
shaped his thought. The way he asked questions
shaped his answers ahead of time.

(B)   Zaehner's Method

Zaehner's methodology is forthright, simple
and controversial; but it is not always stated
explicitly. He believed in doing history of
religions and not dwelling too long on preparatory
details such as method. His method, however, is
pivotal for any understanding of what Zaehner does.
In the first term of his incumbency in the
Spalding Chair in Eastern Religions and Ethics,
which was the Fall term of 1953, Zaehner hurled
the challenge of his scholarly life. In his
inaugural address, "Foolishness to the Greeks,"
he said that Mr. Spalding's wishes for the incum-
bent were: that he i) "...interpret, compare, and
contrast these (religious) systems; ii) (and) to
bring them together in closer understanding,

harmony and friendship."[103] Zaehner feels that
the first request is well within the competence of
a university professor to accomplish. But the
second is likely to produce a harmony which is
"...apparent, verbal, and therefore fictitious."[104]
He says that this is so because the religions talk
about something radically different from one
another. The distinctions between them and among
them are essential ones; for when a religion
asserts that the individual and the absolute are
one it is meaningless to speak of a unio mystica
which means that two are united in one, because
only an unitas mystica is indicated by the experience, and the latter denotes that there is only
one entity involved.[105] He is, therefore, less
sanguine about the possibility of bringing about
harmony than he is about his ability to "interpret,
compare and contrast" religious systems. Hence
he states that he can perceive (see) the other
religions and understand them more easily than he
can perceive any harmony, let alone bring it
about. His latter three theses concern themselves with the possibilities of harmony. His
first two deal with perceiving the other religious
systems and describing any order or patterns that
they may indicate.

Zaehner's method clarified itself for him as
he went along in his first work: that of refuting
the philosophia perennis. So his starting point
is in his hunch that Huxley and his colleagues are
seriously in error. In this his faith, his
interiority, played a major role for him. The
most obvious thing about religions for him was
that they were different. This sure knowledge
came about through his faith as much as his

---

[103]Zaehner, C/D, art.cit., p. 429.

[104]Ibid.

[105]Ibid., p. 443.

professional life as historian of religions.
Zaehner's method counts his own religious faith
and his personal experience of what he will call
Nature Mysticism as being important to his work.
He knows what the religions are talking about,
and he will not accept that either Huxley or
those he calls "agnostics" know religions because
the first will not go out to others and allow them
to change him, but projects a pre-conceived notion
of them; and the second cannot see the interiority
of religion because it is not scientific to do so--
i.e., it ruins one's objective basis to use data
from either the interiority of the religious
experience or one's own interiority.

Firstly, then, Zaehner's approach is empirical. He takes what the religions say is orthodox
as the object of his study. The religions themselves are the best judges of what expresses
their experiences, rites and beliefs.
Zaehner took what they said was good and worked
from there. The similarities so many discern
between the religions, which similarities indicate
the essential sameness of religions for the protagonists of the philosophia perennis, are really
between "Christian orthodoxy and non-Christian
heterodoxy."[106] So what Zaehner uses as an object
of perception, the object to be studied, is what
the religions in question deem worthy of consideration, and nothing else. He perceives them as
different:

> It is then only too true that the basic
> principles of Eastern and Western, which
> in practice means Indian and Semitic,
> thought are, I will not say irrecon-
> cilably opposed; they are simply not
> starting from the same premises. The
> only common ground is that the function

---

[106]Zaehner, C/D, art. cit., p. 443.

of religion is to provide release: there
is no agreement at all as to what it is
that man must be released from. The great
religions are talking at cross purposes.[107]

So, if religions are to be compared they have to
be seen. If they are to be seen, only orthodoxy
is worthy of consideration.

In all this, however, we must not forget that
Zaehner's perception performs two functions for
him: firstly, it sees the other religions, primarily through their texts; secondly, it is a
flail seeking to thrash his enemies. He "sees:
that Huxley's and positivist "objectivity" are
not all that they claim. The former refuses
to go out to the other and allow it to speak to
him (change him); the latter refuses to accept
any subjectivity even when it studies religiousness, the most subjective of things. So Zaehner
says that Huxley's style must be put in its
place as flawed methodologically; this, since it
is a methodology so exclusive as to reject any
position but its own--at the same time that it
claims to accept all as equal. It is quite
exclusivist and not eirenic at all. Zaehner
senses this and, though he never explicates it,
his work goes about savaging Huxley's flawed
position. He feels as deeply that the so-called
"objective scholars" of religions, so much in
fashion in these days in the arts and humani-
ties faculties of modern universities, are not
so objective at all. He feels that, at best,
he and they could give no more than an honest
attempt at accuracy and objectivity. And if
this is so in the arts and sciences, he could go
on to say, "In religion I very much doubt
whether it is possible to be either (accurate
or objective); for if it is true that it is the
Infinite which is the subject of these studies,
what can this have to do with the various

---

[107]Ibid.

objects of scientific inquiry which, of their very
nature, are concerned with the finite and defin-
able?"[108] He goes on to say that the theory is all
well and good, but in practice what emerges is
dullness and, more to the point, the fact that
"complete objectivity is never attainable in
practice except in minute points of scholarship."[109] Geoffrey Parrinder heaped kudos on
Zaehner's commentary on the Gītā, an attempt to
cut through the nonsense attending that holy book,
by showing it to be a combination of all Indian
spiritualities, culminating in theistic devotion
religion (Skt.=bhakti). The fact that Zaehner's
is a more honest method than are Radhakrishnan's,
which sought to impose a monist philosophia
perennis outlook on the book, or even Rudolf
Otto's, which sought to impose a preconception that
there was an Ur Gītā lurking in some darksome corner, is attested by Parrinder's statement that
they "...have sought to impose their own views on
the text...Zaehner (however) takes the Gītā as a
whole and his conviction that it is far more
unitary than most scholars have been willing to
concede was a dominating factor in deciding to
write his own edition...(Zaehner's is a) book of
monumental importance and constant fascina-
tion."[110] So, Zaehner's work was quite successful,

---

[108]Zaehner, C/D, p. 9.

[109]Ibid.

[110]Parrinder's article, cit.supra. pp.169f.
Zaehner's Zurvan, A Zoroastrian Dilemma,
Oxford, 1955, written before he took the Spalding
Chair, was the most compelling reason for his
being chosen for it. It was his masterpiece of
"objective scholarship" until the study on the
Gītā appeared. Further, Zaehner's Hinduism,
Oxford, 1962, is a minor classic of putting down
in brief compass such a congeries of ideas and
deities as is Hinduism.

though based on his interiority as well as the other's religiousness and the texts which emanated therefrom.

This first step in Zaehner's method demanded that he take the bits and pieces offered by the other's religions in order to see what they mean. This is to say that one takes the bits from another and compares them with one's own religiousness to see if they are equivalent. If not, why not? If so, why so? This Zaehner did in his first two works against the philosophia perennis (Sacred and Profane and Hindu and Muslim Mysticism). It is the task of first sight that occupied him there. Just what did text by text mean? And he proceeded just in that fashion: text by text. He tested every assumption, including his own. The fact that his is a modern methodology is shown by his changed attitude as he allowed the other religions to modify him. One can easily see this in his Concordant Discord and his Convergent Spirit. But this is to get ahead of myself. First sight "sees" the other in terms of himself and in terms of one's own position. Comparison demands just that: comparison. In doing so Zaehner validated not only his own scholarly conclusions, but he did it also because the process allowed him to authenticate/validate his own basis and that of the other under consideration.

So not only do Zaehner's professional qualifications equip him to "see" others, but his faith and experience of it and of mysticism equip him to see and judge the others as well. These are organs of perception for him. Not only did he have a religious basis from which to work, but he also had an experience of what he would later call Nature Mysticism while a schoolboy at Tonbridge School. He had to struggle with this experience to find a rubric under which it could live in his experience. He details this in his

<u>Our Savage God</u>.[111] His conclusion was that this experience had nothing at all to do with God. He went in the other direction at first, but at last came to the conclusion that he had a non-religious experience which had been mystical. So his faith and his experience of it and his experience with Rimbaud's poetry, which had triggered off his own mystical experience, were the ambiance in which he worked.

This first level of the methodology, the search to see equivalencies in the bits and pieces, is a search for unity. The falsification of this step is a preconception that there is not just a unity to be found, but an identity behind all religious phenomena. This is the fallacy Zaehner perceived in the <u>philosophia perennis</u>: it assumed what it should have been setting out to prove: unity or identity. Ninian Smart recognized Zaehner's value when he perceived that the latter's <u>At Sundry Times</u>, a work written unabashedly with a Roman Catholic bias, had accurately assessed the realities of things: that religions were in competition with one another. Smart said that revelations meant competition, for they all seem to be somewhat missionary.[112]

Further, the falsification of this first level, that of first sight of the object, is to make personal faith an organ of distortion. Zaehner knew this. He said that because of it he could never guarantee his work. He goes further, though, and says that neither can the so-called objectivists.[113] He foresaw Frits Staal's

---

[111]Cf. Zaehner's S/G, London, Collins, 1974, pp. 210-215.

[112]Smart's review article, on Zaehner's S/T, in <u>Jour.Theol.Stud.</u>, NS 11, p. 239, April 1960.

[113]Zaehner, C/D, p. 9.

mordant criticism of his methodology, written in 1975 in the latter's <u>Exploring Mysticism</u>,[114] when he wrote in <u>Concordant Discord</u>, in 1970, "Any man with any convictions at all is liable to be influenced by them even when he tries to adopt an entirely objective approach; but let him recognize this from the outset and guard against it. If he does this, he will be less liable to deceive himself and others."[115] Staal says that this is impossible, and that only an intellectual/ rationalist approach, cleansed of all bias, can perceive the religiousness of another. Zaehner foresaw this objection and said in his <u>At Sundry Times</u> that no one who has been without religious experience, or admits to it, or admits it into his working moments, can do the job.[116] This is doing religion from the inside in which one proceeds from one's interiority to that of another. This is precisely what W.C. Smith meant by method in his "Essay on Method."[117] It is also what Gadamer seems to be driving at in reviving prejudice as a virtue in the medieval sense.[118] Prejudice for him is an organ of perception which authenticates one's own and another's interiority by seeing the other in the sense we have used "seeing" here: perceiving the reality conveyed by religious symbol, be it rite, text or spoken word. This, obviously, moves our understanding of the methodological process away from method into the hermeneutical circle and

---

[114]Staal, Pelican ed., pp. 73-75.

[115]Zaehner, C/D, p. 9.

[116]Zaehner, S/T, pp. 12-13.

[117]Cf. W.C. Smith essay, p. 154 <u>apud</u> <u>Religious Diversity, Essays</u>, ed. by W. Oxtoby, Harper and Row, N.Y., 1976.

[118]<u>Apud</u>, H.G. Gadamer's <u>Truth and Method</u>, Seabury, 1975, pp. 238f.

into an ontology of understanding.[119] What I
have portrayed thus far is a description of how
one goes out to another's being with one's own.
Underneath all method, and underneath the
philosophia perennis, is a philosophical question:
what does all this say of the reality of symbols
and of the Real itself? It is my judgment, after
reading Zaehner and the Huxleyites, that he perceived that the latter did not accord any reality
to religions at all, but only to their own
disciplina arcana. They have destroyed not only
religious language in making it so relative, but
they have reduced religions to absurdity. This
is an ontological-epistemological question, ultimately.

So the bits-and-pieces level of history of
religions was based, for Zaehner, on a bias that
they were parts of Wholes which had meaning. This
level means to find not only equivalencies among
one's own and others' bits and pieces--over against
the Gestalt of a religious Whole--but one seeks to
obtain an Einfühlung as well. This means for the
coiner of the phrase, Hendrik Kraemer, as well as
for his mentor, Brede Kristensen, that one develops a feeling into the disjecta membra of
another's religion. Kristensen said that this
afforded one religious growth in the process,
as well.[120] In "getting into" another's religious symbols one must say what they mean literally.
This goes beyond equivalency and means that one
interprets it, even on this primary level. It is
the first judgment one makes about the religiousness of the other. As such it brings one's

_____

[119]Ibid., p. 261

[120]Cf. Brede Kristensen's The Meaning of
Religion, trans. by J.B. Carman, Martinus Nijhoff,
the Hague, 1960, taken from the introduction by
K. Kraemer, p.xxxi.

interiority, one's religious faith or lack of it,
into play. For both Zaehner and Kristensen/
Kraemer "seeing" meant having a religion of one's
own.

This first level admits, therefore, that there
is an outer and an inner level to the bits and
pieces. The scholar must deal with the text, for
instance, as text--with all the literary/historical
devices at his disposal--in order to interpret it.
But the inner dimension means that he must "listen"
to it from the inside, and this demands that one
be religious in order to get to the inner level.
This is why Zaehner rejects the agnostic/objective
approach in history of religions. It disallows
entry into the inner meaning of the phenomenon.
All one can do, otherwise, is skirt around its
outside dimension. So the text is the outer dimension and the Eifühlung the inner dimension. In
stretching out to the other one changes, or grows,
as it were. Also in doing this Zaehner and others
like him authenticated himself in a way which
constantly changed. He had to stretch and change
constantly. This seems to be what Bernard
Lonergan meant when he said that modern method
does not deal with laws and principles, but
changes to meet the facts.[121] This seems to be
what Gadamer means by using one's prejudice in
order to understand. It means that the bits and
pieces, being understood, begin to coalesce in
the perceiver as a theme: it is the task of the
historian to thematize what the other has lived.[122]
This is precisely what Zaehner did with what he
saw: to look for themes and patterns. And this
is the second level of the task. It is a level
which tests both the subject and object for
authenticity in a more clear way. But the test
began on the bits-and-pieces level. Both
Zaehner and Lonergan agree that in this age, an

---

[121]Lonergan, art., cit.supra, pp. 342-4,
passim.

[122]Ibid., p. 349.

49

age of a methodological loss of innocence, authenticity is never taken for granted.[123] Zaehner's corpus in his more apologetic period, beginning with At Sundry Times, published in 1962, was a constant challenge to himself as well as those with whom he felt he was in competition.

What this second stage looked for was the Whole which the symbol or text bespoke. No symbol is disconnected from its Whole or Gestalt. Meaning is found on the first level. But it is a meaning concerned with what the part means over against an analogous part in one's own religious system. The second stage of the method, that of pattern-seeking is a descriptive method, a kind of phenomenology. Zaehner did not like the word phenomenology. I used it in his presence and he stiffened appreciably since it smacked of Husserl's thought, which was too systematic for him. He accepted phenomenology only as describing both bits and pieces and getting at the "big picture" suggested by the emerging pattern.[124] This is a method which demands of its practitioners that one really know what religions are all about. It demands a feel for the religions not given to everyone, and certainly not, in Zaehner's estimation, to those without religion or a deep sympathy for it, at the very least.

In step one, many similar bits and pieces turn up. But Zaehner felt strongly that similarities or look-alikes did not mean that things were essentially the same in religions as in other enterprises. One has to be constantly on the lookout for making the mistake of seeing unity where there is none on this level, or else the upper levels will demand a fictitious unity or identity where there is none in reality among the religions. Things which are similar in the

---

[123]Ibid., p. 349.

[124]Zaehner, C/D, p. 10.

50

different religions are frequently quite dissimilar
in reality. When the Buddhists, for instance,
speak of "nothingness" (Skt.=śūnyatā) or emptiness
as being the optimal state they are in no way maintaining, as do some in the West, that this is the
same as Meister Eckhart's nothingness or that of
the apophatic tradition of Christian mysticism from
the time of the Pseudo-Denys on down to our time.
The one is a psychological state of unity with the
Self. The latter is a state of unity with
another: God. There is a radical and critical
difference here. So comparison begins with step
one, the bits and pieces. But it really begins
to take on meaning when one steps back to say
Quid significat? Patterns and directions among
religions reveal not only their inner meaning
but also their meaning vis-à-vis others. Meaning
is a function of relationship here. When the
philosophia perennis denied any meaning other than
a relative one to religiousness it neutered relations among them, and any meaning at all.

Thus, the second level or step in the methodology begins to stretch out to the religion itself as a complex of patterns and realities larger
than discrete bits and pieces. It begins to
touch the Whole. Zaehner does not think he can
touch the Whole of religion without seeing a pattern, and he cannot see the pattern without
authenticiating both his own perception of himself
and that the religions have of themselves. He
rejects Huxley and the positivist objectivists
since they refuse to deal with Wholes: the
former, since they reject that there are any
other Wholes; the latter since they cannot deal
with an interiority and validate it.

Zaehner used the first and second level of
his methodology in refuting the philosophia
perennis in his Mysticism Sacred and Profane and
Hindu and Muslim Mysticism. The third level, that
of judging the overall meaning of religions themselves, he saves for the rest of his works. He
needs only the bottom levels to refute, text by

51

text, mystical type by mystical type, those
who say all religious experiences are the same.
This third level is the level of theology. It
tells the literal meaning of the systems and
patterns. It deals with Wholes as Wholes. The
first level deals with the Whole as in its tiniest
part. The second level sees the Whole as it patterns itself. The third level takes religion as
a whole and compares it with other religions. At
bottom, it assumes that the religions are different. Zaehner tackled that assumption and proved
it to be true. This means that those who assume
that religions are not different, ultimately--and
all religions are ultimate systems--accord no
value to theology at all. Schuon proved that
when he said that religions did not take their
truths seriously at all.[125] But this third level
of discussion cannot take up our time here,
interesting though it is, since I content myself
in this book only with the first two.

---

[125]Frithjof Schuon, The Transcendent Unity of
Religions, Faber and Faber, London, p. 32.

CHAPTER II

THE PHILOSOPHIA PERENNIS

What bothered Zaehner about Aldous Huxley was not only what he said, but that he was so eminent; so that both he and those he held under his umbrella, at least in the West, could not be taken lightly. In his The Perennial Philosophy Huxley laid down the outlines of that hypothesis which so exercised Zaehner: viz., there is one divine Reality which is "substantial to the manifold world of things and lives and minds. But the nature of this one Reality is such that it cannot be directly and immediately apprehended except by those who have chosen to fulfill certain conditions, making themselves loving, pure in heart, and poor in spirit."[1] Those in every time and religion who have chosen to seek the Real have left us their accounts, and Huxley rehearses many of these in this book. Thus the apprehenders of the one Real range from Lao Tzu to Eckhart, from Śankara to Ruysbroeck, from William Law to Kabir, from Philo to Jalāl-uddīn Rūmī. All had perceived the oneness beneath the multiplicity through the agency of intuition.[2] But it is not only philosophy, but also natural science, which is rooted in this unity for Huxley; this, since "All science...is the reduction of multiplicities to identities." No intermediary is capable of affording one the intuition of the One.[3] Only one alone can scale these heights. It is like Plotinus' flight of the alone to the Alone. Ultimately, religions

---

[1]Huxley, Aldous, The Perennial Philosophy, Harper and Brothers, N.Y. and London, 1945, p. viii.

[2]Ibid., p. 5.

[3]Ibid.

and religious community mean nothing to the Huxley camp.

Zaehner gagged on this as reductionist. He protested that religions and religious experience were protean and not so transcendentally simple. But if Huxley and his pusilla grex (sic),[4] as Zaehner called them in his inaugural at Oxford, exercised him, it was one book in particular which sent him sallying forth into print. Huxley's little The Doors of Perception was published in 1954.[5] Its importance outweighed its lack of heft in Zaehner's estimation. It purported to offer a surrogate for religion and religious experience: mescalin produced in Huxley an experience of true mysticism, and he hastened to offer it to all and sundry. Mescalin is a derivative of the North American peyote plant--itself a derivative of the cactus plant. Huxley had flogged his philosophia perennis for a good while, in which he lauded the mystical intuitions of the great mystics, but he had not had any such experiences until his con- trolled experiment with mescalin. His convic- tions, previous to this, were that there was no difference, at bottom, between his experience and any other form of mysticism. Secondly, those in the Hindu and Muslim fold who defended their religious experiences wrote of them to the effect

---

[4]Zaehner calls Huxley et al this in his inaugural (C/D, p. 443). The faulty grammar (it should read: pusillus grex) is strange since Zaehner had done a good bit of Latin at Tonbridge School before going up to Oxford, yet both he and his editors let the error persist as late as C/D, published some seventeen years after it was delivered in 1953.

[5]The Doors of Perception and Heaven and Hell, Penguin ed., 1974, originally published by Chatto and Windus, London, 1954.

that the monist and theist experiences were identical. These two factors, Huxley and his stripe, and the monists, gave rise to Zaehner's first book as the Spalding Professor: namely, Mysticism Sacred and Profane, to be followed by its companion volume, Hindu and Muslim Mysticism.

Zaehner characterized Huxley's philosophia perennis as an outlook which held that ultimate truths were inexpressible, but that these same truths were the same everywhere and in all times. Hence "revealed religions" are only relatively true since truth is absolutely one and they differ so markedly in their various dogmas.[6] Zaehner gets down to naming Huxley's colleagues in the philosophia perennis almost at once in Sacred and Profane. But before I take this up further, it would be wise to go deeper into the mechanics of the philosophia perennis than does Zaehner. He spends most of his time refuting it, but does not go into it sufficiently to do justice to this essay, which concerns itself precisely with the philosophia and its refutation by Zaehner. I am most interested in Zaehner's systematics of mysticism, but he arrived at it through his devastation of the philosophia perennis.

(A)   Huxley Et Al.

(1)   Et Al.

I shall introduce the reader to Huxley's thinking slowly, by backing into it with a review of those who think like him in matters of mysticism. It is a way of thinking which interests us here. Zaehner begins by citing the eminent Islamicist, Professor A. J. Arberry, who said, "It has become a platitude to observe that mysticism is essentially one and the same, whatever

---

[6]Zaehner, S/P, p. 27.

may be the religion professed by the individual
mystic: a constant unvarying phenomenon of the
universal yearning of the human spirit for
personal communion with God."[7] Next he names
Dr. Enid Starkie, in whose work on Arthur Rimbaud
he says that the poet reached the state without
orthodoxy which religious mystics seek: namely,
union with God.[8] But it is Arberry's eminent
predecessor in the Chair of Arabic at the University of Cambridge, E. G. Browne, who is
spokesman for what Arberry terms a platitude:

> There is hardly any soil, be it ever so
> barren, where it (mysticism) will not
> strike root; hardly any creed, however
> stern, however formal, round which it
> will not twine itself. It is, indeed,
> the eternal cry of the human soul for
> rest; the insatiable longing of a being
> wherein infinite ideals are fettered and
> cramped by a miserable actuality; and so
> long as man is less than an angel and
> more than a beast, this cry will not for
> a moment fail to make itself heard.
> Wonderfully uniform, too, is its tenor:
> in all ages, in all countries, in all
> creeds, whether it comes from the Brahmin
> sage, the Greek philosopher, the Persian
> poet, or the Chinese quietist, it is in
> essence an enunciation more or less
> clear, more or less eloquent, of the

---

[7]Sūfism, An Account of the Mystics of Islam,
London, Geo. Allen and Unwin, 1950, p. 11, apud
Zaehner's S/P, p.ix of the Introduction.

[8]Starkie, E., Arthur Rimbaud rev. ed., London,
Hamish Hamilton, 1947, p. 422, apud Zaehner's
S/P, p.ix.

aspiration of the soul to cease altogether from self, and to be at one with God.[9]

There is nothing intrinsically wrong with this assertion, but placed in conjunction with Huxley's contention that, since the expressions of the experiences of the various religions bear such similarities, then they are merely expressions of an ultimate truth, and partial expressions at that. This truth is the philosophia perennis itself.[10] It is based, moreover, on the experience of all religions.[11] Zaehner is saying that Huxley's fundamental error consists in making look-alikes essentially the same.

Next Zaehner applies the cudgel to Ānanda Coomaraswami, whom he terms "an unusually well-equipped Oriental scholar," and the self-styled commentator on Vedānta, Rene Guenon, who loses little love for orientalists due to their opposition to any unbiased treatment of mysticism as a religious phenomenon.[12] Zaehner goes on to say that it is not so much the members of the religions themselves, but these purveyors of the philosophia perennis, who form the bulk of the opposition to his type of inquiry. The most modern exponents Zaehner names are Frithjof Schuon,

---

[9]Browne, E. G., A Year Amongst the Persians, London, Adam and Charles Black, 2nd ed., 1950, p. 136, quoted in Margaret Smith's An Introduction to the History of Mysticism, London, Macmillan, 1930, p. 2, apud Zaehner's S/P, p.x.

[10]Zaehner, S/P, p. 2.

[11]Ibid., p. 14.

[12]Ibid., p. 30.

whose The Transcendent Unity of Religions[13] displays his esoteric metaphysics, and W. T. Stace, whose Mysticism and Philosophy offers a systematics of mysticism. Zaehner never went too deeply into Schuon's thought in his books, though he was to mention him incisively in his At Sundry Times[14] and his Concordant Discord.[15]

Stace seems to have gored Zaehner's ox in his Mysticism and Philosophy, for the latter quips that Stace is "very keen on unmasking doctrinal bias in others, even going so far as to attribute Martin Buber's interpretation of his own experience after mature reflection to the 'environmental pressure of the culture to which he belongs': in other words, he is accusing him of intellectual dishonesty...Yet Stace is far more guilty of bias than Buber ever was, for at least Buber had had an experience and, so far as is known, Stace had not."[16] Stace drives in the wedge by footnoting Zaehner's pet peeve and using one of Zaehner's favorite authors to do his work for him; for Stace brings in the Flemish mystic Ruysbroeck to prove that Christians have emptiness experiences just like Orientals; so he says, "Professor Zaehner thus disagrees with the view which I am maintaining, that the experience described in the Mandukya Upanisad is in all essentials the same experience as that of the Christian mystics."[17]

---

[13]Translated by P. Townsend, Faber and Faber, London, 1953.

[14]Zaehner later calls this type of thinking the "Indian tendency" in his At Sundry Times, p. 36.

[15]C/D, pp. 38, 44, 438.

[16]Ibid., p. 200, apud Stace, p. 157.

[17]Stace, op. cit., p. 97, note no. 44.

This is it in a nutshell for Zaehner. He cannot abide that hypothesis. He is so exercised by
Stace since he sets great store by Buber's rehearsal of his own experience and appraisal of it.
Buber, in the passage which Zaehner quotes in
Sacred and Profane, and which he recalls over and
over in the rest of his corpus,[18] is trying to
affirm the reality of dualism--of an I and Thou
dyadic relationship--before the counter-affirma-
tion that deep down there is only "...the one
primal being unconfronted by another."[19] Zaehner
thinks so much of what can be construed as Buber's
reply to Stace's philosophia perennis that he
quotes it as the very first words in his Sacred
and Profane; and it becomes, as it were, Zaehner's
colophon:

Now from my own unforgettable experience
I know well that there is a state in
which the bonds of the personal nature
of life seem to have fallen away from us
and we experienced an undivided unity.
But I do not know-what the soul willingly
imagines and indeed is bound to imagine
(mine too once did it)--that in this I
had attained to a union with the primal
being or the godhead. That is an
exaggeration no longer permitted to the
responsible understanding. Responsibly-
that is, as a man holding his ground
before reality--I can elicit from those
experiences only that in them I reached
an undifferentiable unity of myself
without form or content. I may call
this an original pre-biographical unity

---

[18]In his C/D Zaehner uses it on pp. 97-8,
203; in H/M on pp. 17-18; in S/T, on pp. 91-92;
in Drugs... on pp. 90, 91, 101.

[19]Buber, M., Between Man and Man, London,
1947, p. 34.

and suppose that it is hidden unchanged
beneath all biological change, all development and complication of the soul. Nevertheless, in the honest and sober account
of the responsible understanding this
unity is nothing but the unity of this
soul of mine, whose "ground" I have
reached, so much so, beneath all forma-
tions and contents, that my spirit has
no choice but to understand it as ground-
less. But the basic unity of my own soul
is certainly beyond the reach of all
multiplicity of all the souls in the
world of which it is one-existing but
once, single, unique, irreducible, this
creaturely one: one of the human souls
and not the "soul of the All;" a defined
and particular being and not "Being;"
the creaturely basic unity of a creature,
bound to God as in the instant before
release the creature is to the creator
spiritus, not bound to God as the creature
to the creator spiritus in the moment of
release.[20]

Thus does Zaehner, by his first utterance, set a
coda to his inaugural, and inaugurate his lively
career as historian/theologian. Buber's experience and explanation are paradigmatic for Zaehner,
as we shall see. In this brief compass can be
found the type Zaehner called Nature Mysticism,
Love Mysticism and the possibility of Isolation
Mysticism of the monist type.

His mentioning of Ānanda Coomeraswami as one
of Huxley's fellow travellers was not itself
followed up by Zaehner. In an article which
appeared in a work under the editorship of
Christopher Isherwood, entitled Vedānta for the

---

[20]Zaehner, S/P,v, and Buber, op.cit., pp.
24-25.

Western World, Coomeraswami says, "the essentials
of Christianity, of Buddhism in its two forms,
and of Hinduism are one. Here it is the
philosophia perennis, here the Eternal Gospel."
He goes on to say, "(There is a) common thought
manifesting its power under different forms."[21]
This seems to be right on the mark. The religions
and their contents are, ultimately, one; and that
oneness is Vedānta. The monist never quite understands theism and seems, persistently and annoy-
ingly, to undercut any discussion with theists by
saying that he accepts us all. But he accepts us
theists as monists, which is his "doctrine," not
that of theism. This is what Zaehner fought
throughout his life. The philosophia perennis,
no matter which form it took, according to Zaehner,
had Indian Vedāntin roots. Coomeraswami strength-
ens Zaehner's contention here when he says that the
religions do not borrow from one another, but
draw from a common source, which is a way of life
we have all forgotten.[22] This seems to be drop-
ing its monism in favor of a higher truth, but it
is exactly this higher truth that monism teaches:
get rid of proximities, even relatively ultimate
ones, and ascend to the universal level where
the Self (read ātman) is the Ultimate (read
Brahman) by a direct knowledge of the Truth (read
identical with the Absolute, or in Sanskrit
a-dvaita, which means non-two).[23]

---

[21]Article entitled "Hinduism and Buddhism,"
p. 295, Viking, N.Y., 1945, 69th printing.

[22]Ibid., p. 296.

[23]Coomeraswami adds that our great fault is
ignorance (Skt.=avidya). Since all roads lead to
God, take the most suitable one; which means any
road which suits one. (art.cit., p. 297). This
is Hinduism plain and simple. He means that we
can choose the Marga (way) which is our caste duty,
and the God of our choice (Iṣṭadevatā=chosen
deity).

Isherwood himself says in his article in the
Vedanta volume that these are the elements of
Vedantin philosophy: i) Man is divine by nature,
ii) life's aim is the realization of one's
divinity, and iii) lastly, "all religions are
essentially in agreement."[24] What this means,
explains Isherwood, in practical terms, is this:
although the saints of different religions are so
dissimilar their experience is the same. This
means that one realizes that his nature is the
ātman, the Hindu Self-ultimate, which is identical
to the Real. What it boils down to is this: I
am the Real. He says that what the Christians
call mystical union is the same as the Hindu
ultimate state samādhi.[25] That this is a gross
misstatement, one that anyone versed in Christian
Mysticism would not make, eludes Mr. Isherwood.
Samādhi is a trance state which has nothing to do
with God nor does it care to. It is the complete
loss of the empirical self in the transcendent
Self (ātman) in an euphoric state of sleep, which
Hindus call samādhi. This is, obviously, not what
the Christian means when he says that he is one with
God the Father, Son and Holy Spirit in love and
through grace; for both are distinct metaphysically. This fundamental error persists all throughout the writings of the philosophia perennis.
Isherwood says that each religion is a different
form of yoga, and that Vedānta seeks to synthesize all religions into something monist; that
exclusivist religions cannot do so because they
are exclusivist, and that his is an inclusivist
religion. This is an important point to remember.
Hans Küng, in his On Being a Christian, says
that Hinduism is just as exclusivist as is
Christianity. Further, Küng notes that phenomenology of religion, which Isherwood and his colleagues are using here in comparing like with

---

[24]Isherwood, introduction art. to his book,
p. 1.

[25]Ibid.

like, is faulty in comparing and elaborating the
likes in religions but not doing much with the
dissimilarities among them.[26] He blasts Zaehner's
predecessor, Radhakrishnan, for his Nineteenth
Century liberalism in affirming that all religions
are one. Underneath all this, in Hinduism, Küng
perceives an exclusivism in that it absorbs other
religions into itself. At bottom, Küng asserts,
Hinduism is exclusivist in its claims. Quoting
Karl Jaspers, Küng says that it is true that
there are common features among religions, but
that one cannot integrate these "archtypal men"
into a totality. He says that men are disparate,
and that is the most obvious thing about them,
again quoting Jaspers. One cannot combine all
men into a single man. And Küng adds that one
would have to be naively ignorant to miss the
fact of religious divergence.[27] So we come to
Isherwood's most brazen monist declaration:
there is only one real, and nothing else. For
him the One may be personified in an "infinite
number of aspects."[28] This is monism with a
vengeance, and it seems to be behind and under
the eirenic unity statements of the _philosophia
perennis_. If one were to abide this statement,
one would no longer exist. That is not the concept which prevails in the religions of the West,
and Zaehner would have none of it for himself.

(2) Huxley

Huxley himself said that there were two
types of religious experience: i) one type is

---

[26]Küng, Hans, On Being a Christian, Collins,
London, 1977, pp. 101f.

[27]Küng, op.cit., p. 103, quoting K. Jasper's
Die massgebenden Menschen, München, 1971, p. 206.

[28]Isherwood article, p. 10.

that had in the philosophia perennis: it is a
direct intuition of the godhead, which was made
possible because the heart is pure; this type
is non-mediated and non-induced; ii) the other
type is self-induced; it is the type had in
religion, which is an emotive experience brought
on by either the "passion" or "beauty" of religion.
At bottom, Huxley says, such experiences in religion are self-induced.[29] So, for Huxley, an
experience which is about God is not the experience of the philosophia perennis. The latter
experience is a direct awareness of the deity in
a heart mortified of even its noblest emotions.
Huxley, rightly, fears the identity of an emotion
about God with God himself.[30] This makes religious
emotion an end in itself.

For Huxley, the philosophia perennis concerns
itself primarily with "the nature of the eternal,
spiritual Reality."[31] Huxley's point in all this
is that, since the self is supernatural anyway,
then all that is left to it is to polish the
mirror by asceticism in order for one's divinity
to shine out spontaneously and without mediation-
by way of religion or anything which gets in the
way of Ultimacy. Asceticism on the part of the
chosen is Huxley's point. It is an elitism which
he espouses.

(3) Frithjof Schuon

If Huxley's philosophy seems slanted towards
asceticism, one should not be fooled: it is a
philosophy he advocates, not a religion. Better,
it is a religion of method, beginning with man.

---

[29]Huxley's Perennial Philosophy, op.cit.,
p. 255.

[30]Ibid., p. 257.

[31]Ibid., p. 125.

This is what Zaehner will call the Isolation
Mysticism of Sāṁkhya-yoga. At bottom, Huxley
is advocating Yoga with a thin and beautiful
patina of mystical texts of every hue covering
it. It is as exclusive as one can get: namely,
complete isolation of a person in the Self, which
is the One. His yoga is monism, not the dualism
of the Sāṁkhya, even though it uses God as does
Sāṁkhya: i.e., as a tool for self-discovery.
Huxley's religion is a "method," not an obedience
to an eternal Law such as the Decalogue, or to a
God. If Huxley's thought is beautiful but ascetical, Schuon is equally as lofty but more out in
the open as a philosopher of method religion.[32]
I shall dwell for a few pages on his thoughts
since Zaehner knew them, rejected them, and fought
them empirically by going at Huxley and the
monists text by text. A more thorough explanation is due the reader, however, as Zaehner
gives it only through his devastation of Huxley's
hypotheses.

Briefly what Schuon says is this: firstly,
there is an uncreated part of man which he calls
Metaphysic. It is not philosophy, which is
created and discursive, and must deal with things
not quite certain. But metaphysic is of the
Intellect, which is the name he gives to that uncreated part in man. The knowledge which Intellect affords man is beyond reason and faith; it is
absolute in its certitude because, in it, knower
and known are identical.[33] This is, obviously, a
form of monism: an identity of knower and known
on an absolute level means that, in the language

---

[32]As opposed to a religion of grace, which is
"outside help" in achieving one's goals, method
religion is one in which one achieves the goal if
one knows a technique or method for its procure-
ment.

[33]Schuon, The Transcendent Unity of Religions,
cit. supra, p. 11.

of Hinduism, Ātman is Brahman, or the Self is the Absolute. Dogmatic language, the coinage of religion, translates the truths of Intellect into relative truths. On the level of Intellect truth is absolute.[34]

Religion, furthermore, depends on revelations in order to "see," and therefore cannot distinguish between the symbol and the truth it contains. But Metaphysic does not depend on relative revelations and can distinguish between symbol and the truth it mediates.[35] Philosophy is never more than what it expresses. Further, it cannot reach the level of Metaphysic, which is the level of the transcendent, by itself. Metaphysic, however, is always more than what it expresses, and that more is always a certainty. Philosophy can express the truths of Metaphysic, but it cannot reach them unaided or contain them fully. If philosophy endeavors to prove God's existence, and religion believes it without proof, Metaphysic knows that God exists through direct evidence which is absolutely certain.[36] Schuon says, "...in the present state of humanity such evidence is only accessible to a spiritual elite which becomes ever more restricted in number."[37] Beneath the symbols of religions are the truths of Intellect, which these very religions might be unaware of because they have absolutized the relativity of dogmatic statements and symbols within the religion itself.[38] The theme of elitism seems to be a constant in each of these systems.

---

[34]Ibid.

[35]Schuon, op.cit., p. 11.

[36]Ibid., p. 11f.

[37]Ibid., p. 12.

[38]Ibid.

Secondly, all integral traditional civilizations know this Truth. That this seems to contradict the elitism in point number one does not bother Schuon, who now taps into the works of Rene Guenon for some of his thoughts. Zaehner put Guenon into the same basket as Schuon, i.e., as being protagonists of the philosophia perennis.[39] So, it is not just elite individuals who share this thought, but also civilizations which have stayed on the primordial level have retained the Truth in question.[40] He begins to clear up our mystification when he says that such civilizations are to be found in all traditional religions; but that the religions as presently constituted deal only with the Truth on the external level. Union among religions, however, cannot be had on this exoteric, external level, but only on the inner, esoteric level. Besides, Schuon adds, it would deprive religion of its raison d'etre if one were to unite now on the esoteric level. So religion as we know it, with all its rites, dogmas and paraphernalia, is merely an ephemeral phenomenon with no lasting connection to Truth. Schuon does not accord to religion(s) any ability to symbol Truth at all, but only truths. The Whole is never to be found among religions, but only among the coterie, or civilization, which is on the primordial level. That there is a yawning gap in logic does not seem to bother Schuon: namely, that if the traditional civilizations are within the religions then the religions must have an umbilical link with the primordial tradition. So, Schuon says that the union of men of religion is on a transcendent level "without prejudice to any particular form."[41]

---

[39]Zaehner, S/P, p. 30.

[40]Schuon, p. 13.

[41]Schuon, op. cit., p. 16.

Further, a religious dogma is a dogma because it has confused the idea with its form. Dogma can see things only from one point of view. Apparently, no dogma can hold the Truth in a full way. Schuon seems to deny to all forms of communication any ability to translate Truth or evoke it, even if the Divinity should will it to be so, as it did in Hinduism with the mantra, yantra and tantra which are words, geometric designs and rites instinct with the power to evoke the divine, respectively, and in Christianity with its belief that God demanded that some rites be done to evoke his presence; e.g., the Sacraments and the Mass.

Thirdly, Schuon begins to get to the nub of his ideas about religion here: dogma, though a limited idea exoterically, is an unlimited symbol esoterically. So the religion chooses the man, not vice versa.[42] The esoteric is in control of religion. God does not seem to enter the picture in any central way here. Truth seems distinct from the deity. So, each exoteric tradition claims to be the truth because "the exoteric point of view, being concerned only with the individual interest, namely salvation, has no advantage to gain from knowledge of the truth of any other traditional religious forms."[43] Schuon adds what he seems to think an exculpatory clause, which really slanders each traditional religion, when he says that, at base, religion is not interested in other truths, because it is not interested in its own truth.[44]

So, there is only one truth which the divinity distributes under various forms; but no form is

---

[42]Ibid., pp. 29 f.

[43]Schuon, op. cit., p. 31.

[44]Ibid., p. 32.

unique and exclusive since, by definition, other forms can express the same.[45]

The exoteric is related to the esoteric as an external form is to its spirit. He adds, "...only spiritual authority places itself at the level of naked and integral Truth,"[46] which Truth is the preserve of Schuon's elite scattered about the religions. Which religions he means seems to come out when Schuon makes a plea for his own brand of modern Ṣūfism, scorned by many of the orthodox in Islam, when he delivers Judaism and Christianity from fault in so particularizing their truths that Islam had to reject them. The universalism preached by esotericists like Schuon seems to be monism as philosophy and an exclusivism as theology. He makes all symbols, except those of Islam, particular and corrupt.

Fourthly, essentially esotericism is the preserve of an elite which is "restricted in numbers." Here is the central point of Schuon's thought: inferior levels of thought are absorbed or integrated by the superior levels so that the inferior levels cannot really be said to exist, ontologically speaking.[47] So, on this level, the world does not exist. Secondly, God is surpassed by a Supra-Personal Divinity, of which the personal God is merely what he calls "the first determination" from which flow what we call phenomena. Obviously those on the exoteric level cannot admit that their world is not real because they cannot "see" the Truth, which is above world, God and all truths. Schuon admits that, at bottom, this looks like pantheism, which he thinks is merely a

---

[45]Ibid., pp. 33 f.

[46]Ibid., p. 48.

[47]Schuon, op. cit., p. 53.

continuity between the finite and infinite; but for him both the finite and infinite are identical.[48] So we have a Muslim saying that there is a God above God, and that all are identical with the Ultimate, and yet he claims to be Muslim. Zaehner will take care of these claims in due time, but for now, it is well for us to see what is at the bottom of the eirenic claims of the philosophia perennis.

Running across the protagonists from Huxley, through Coomeraswami, to Radhakrishnan, to Guenon, and Isherwood, and now Schuon, we see that it is monism, at bottom, and that it accords no other religious form any room in which to maneuver since it has maneuvered theism into the corner of particularism and relativity from which it cannot emerge unless it comes out monist. Schuon says, openly, that theism is an exoteric and, therefore, limited and false argument. Further, he says that theism proves its weakness by seeing them as pantheists, but he will not be called such by theists.[49] He says that it merely means that all is One, and that finite and infinite exist in continuum, which continuum indicates that both are identical. So he says that what he means is that Being and phenomena are identical. He chides theisms for calling it pantheism, and he is correct, it is not pantheism, it is monism, pure and simple. Zaehner saw this in the philosophia perennis and made the proper distinction between pantheism and monism, and between pantheism and that form of Nature Mysticism which he termed pan-en-henism, as we shall see in the next chapter. So theism is false for Schuon because it is limited; and monism is true because it is unlimited. It does not seem that Schuon's vaunted universalism is so inclusive at all; he seems to be making a special

---

[48]Ibid., p. 55.

[49]Ibid.

plea for monism in Islamic Ṣūfism and Vedānta,
from which Zaehner thinks the former derives. At
bottom all these writers seem to be quite at home
with Indian Vedanta of the Advaitan, non-two-or
monist, if you will, variety.

In praxi, Zaehner saw that this would lead to
a fuzziness between good and evil which would allow
much that we call evil to go unchallenged. What
we would call evil Schuon calls a negative cosmic
principle drawing us away from our Principle. We
have personified this negative tendency in religion in calling it the Devil.[50] Schuon calls it
by the Hindu term tamas--which we shall see in our
treatment of Sāṁkhya-yoga. It is a downward force
filled with laziness and darkness. But the esoteric level cannot call that which Schuon calls
tamas, or the Demiurge, an evil since it is so
natural; and since it is the principle of creation.
Tamas, in drawing us away from our principle,
simply allows us to exist. So even the holy needs
tamas in order to exist. He concludes that tamas
is neutral, neither good nor evil. It is independent of good and evil. A thing is good,
therefore, if it leads to the goal of esotericism,
which is unity. It is good even if religions
think it evil. The good in esotericism is whatever leads one to concentration. At bottom, esotericism seems to be a contemplative method which
aims at putting one back at one's source in order
to enjoy it. This is yoga pure and simple. The
Self is the imago dei, which is the ātman in
Hindu parlance. Whatever leads one to one's
source, one's supernatural nature, to quote Isherwood again,[51] is good. Schuon adds that whatever
serves for contemplation is good, and goes on to
say that religious morality "is never made for
the benefit of contemplatives only but for that

---

[50]Schuon, op. cit., p. 63.

[51]Isherwood, art. cit., p. 1.

of all men."[52]

Fifthly, hence the esoteric is the same
Metaphysic for Schuon. Both are universal. The
metaphysical way is a universal way and the religious way is particular. Esotericism, which he
calls the initiatory way, makes use of asceticism
as method, not as religion. It is a method used,
"to pass beyond individuality and consequently
beyond every interested viewpoint."[53] This last
remark is interesting because Schuon defines
religion as an interested point of view, which
interest is self-interest homing in on salvation.[54] So esotericism is a religion of method,
which method is yoga; the latter induces the
intellection which is a form of gnosis for Schuon.
Like Huxley, Schuon admits that asceticism activates one's divine nature. Grace is not needed.
One is supernatural by nature, by right. Contemplation activates this divine nature and allows
one to know (Greek=gnosis, Skt.=jñāna) that the
contemplator and contemplated are identical.
Zaehner would call this level Nature Mysticism,
since all it is is the coalescence of subject
and object. What Schuon seems to be driving at,
though, is that this is a form of intellection
in which the subject is the One, which is monism.
So asceticism merely removes the obstacles to a
grace which is due one by dint of one's divine
nature. Asceticism is never penitential in esotericism, but it is always so for theisms.[55]
This is an extremely important point since, as we
shall see, the tipoff for Rimbaud that his Nature

---

[52]Schuon, op. cit., p. 65.

[53]Ibid., p. 73.

[54]Ibid., p. 23.

[55]Schuon, op. cit., p. 73.

72

Mysticism was not truly Theistic Mysticism, a mysticism of love, was that it did not turn him to God nor did it make him penitent.[56] This seems to be one of the shibboleths between theistic mysticism and non-theistic mysticism: penitence always comes into play where there is a God of love and forgiveness, and is not necessary--and gets in the way--where there are other legitimate, and different, forms of mysticism such as that induced by yoga.

Ultimately Schuon's problem with religions is that no religious symbol can be anything but relatively absolute. He wants more and cannot find it on the exoteric level. Only the esoteric level places him on the level of the Absolute.[57]

(4) Hegel and Schuon

There is a peculiar resemblance in Schuon's desire to get man on the level of the Absolute to Hegel's thoughts about the same thing. Obviously, Hegel never placed himself above God, never denied the possibility to philosophy to reach Truth, as does Schuon. But Hegel and Schuon share a few things in common, which it would be well to keep in mind as we go into Zaehner's work in the next, and succeeding chapters.

One of the things Schuon, and his colleagues in philosophia perennis, shares with Hegel is that intellect is given an infinite power. Schuon gives man's nature as supernatural, by which he means that he can activate the self in man and raise it to the level of infinity. So, with Hegel, who radicalizes Kant, reason is made infinitely self-active. In making reason infinite

---

[56]Zaehner, S/P, pp. 82 f.

[57]Schuon, Gnosis, translated by G. E. H. Palmer, John Murray, publisher, London, 1959, p. 35.

Hegel radicalized all German idealism.[58] And, in this line, it should be remembered that Hindu monism is an idealism in which method (read yoga) can raise mind (ātman, or self) to the level of the infinite. German idealism shares much in common with mainline Indian thought. And quintessential Indian thought is yoga, whether it is monistic advita or dualistic sāṁkhya or bhakti, as in the Gītā. Hegel's philosophy desired to overcome all dualisms in life, and so does the Hindu religion of method in reducing man to his simples: matter and mind, and casting off the former for the latter. Hegel confronted historical Christianity by making the reason infinite: if reason is infinite, what of Christ?[59] The philosophia perennis poses just such a challenge to historical Christianity when it makes all religious phenomena relative, so that Jesus' history does not seem to have any more ultimacy than that of a Hindu avatar, and no ultimacy is claimed for such by Hindus.

But where Hegel and Schuon et al. have the greatest similarity is in the way they look at other religions. In Hegel's The Phenomenology of Mind the whole process of the appearance of the Absolute to us looks very much like the philosophia perennis, except that the latter maintains that all was supernatural to begin with, whereas one must be raised to that level in Hegel's system. However, the idealism looks the same in both systems as does the limitedness of religion.[60] The modes of religions differ because they are

---

[58]Fackenheim, Emil, op. cit., p. 226.

[59]Ibid., p. 228.

[60]Hegel, trans. with an introduction by J. B. Baillie, introduction to Torchback edited by G. Lichtheim, Harper, N.Y., 1967, p. 683, Chapter VII, Religion. Notes on Hegel by Lichtheim.

different modalities of the Absolute. Each modality of the Absolute is different; so each religion is different. Therefore many religions are necessary; but the Absolute is one. This is very much like the cast of mind found in the philosophia perennis. Hegel's thought pushes to establish "the truth that Spirit is the only reality for the more finite spirit approximates to the state of claiming to be self-contained the more is it dependent on universal self-consciousness."[61] So, for Hegel, reality is essentially spiritual. Hinduism would not cavil at this at all. It wished to escape from the space/time trammel in order to realize its nature, which is spiritual. It certainly is not material. So, "if the truth is the whole," and only so is "truth self-complete and self-explaining, and if reality is essentially spiritual--then experience only finds its complete meaning realized in the principle of Absolute Spirit."[62] The final chapter, or phase, of Hegel's thought is the appearance of the Absolute among men. It will always be limited, finite. "When (the Absolute) appears in and through these modes of finitude we have the attitude of Religion. Since these modes, as we saw, differ, the religious attitude differs; and accordingly, we have various types or forms of religion. Each of these forms, in and through which the Absolute appears, is circumscribed in its nature and process; each is per se inadequate to the revelation of complete absolute self-consciousness: hence the variety of religions is necessitated by and is indirectly due to the failure of any one type and the inadequacy of every single type to reveal the Absolute completely.[63]

---

[61]Hegel, op. cit., p. 683. Lichtheim's notes.

[62]Ibid., pp. 683 f.

[63]Ibid., p. 695, notes preceding Hegel's "Natural Religion."

When Hegel talks of what he calls Natural
Religion he states that the religions are illus-
trations of principles, and are true in doing
that. As mediators of truth the religions do not
seem true to Lichtheim, Hegel's commentator.[64]
This is farther than Schuon would go. Religions,
for the latter, are true in a most limited sense,
not the Real, but true.

But Hegel shows the greatest similarity between his thought and what was to be the philosophia perennis, when he said, "The series of
different religions, which will come before us,
just as much sets forth again merely the different aspects of a single religion, and indeed of
every single religion, and the imagery, the conscious ideas, which seem to mark off one concrete
religion from another, make their appearance in
each."[65] Underneath it all there is only one
religion for Hegel: Christianity. All others were
merely phases of it. Schuon and Huxley have simply
turned the tables on him and made the one religion
their own monistic Ṣūfism or Vedānta--for they are
both Indian monisms, the one in Indian garb and
the other in Muslim.

Huxley and Schuon may have been influenced
by Hegel, or they may not have. I have given
this section on Hegel, not to impress one with an
eruidition I do not possess, and not to defend
the similarity so as to state that it is the
missing link, but to show how pervasive this mentality was and is which states that there is
basically only one religion, and then go on proving it by relativizing everyone else's in terms
of one's own. Hegel did it to the Orientals and
Greeks. Huxley, Radhakrishnan, Schuon, etc., do

---

[64]Ibid., 695, notes.

[65]Hegel, op. cit., p. 696.

it to Christianity. Each does it in terms of
one's own system. Christians make all theisms
and monists make it all monism.

Finally, the philosophia perennis I have laid
out for the reader is here so that you may see
that, underneath all, it is both a pervasive system and quite contemporary. Huston Smith's latest book, cited above, which caps a distinguished
career, is professedly a philosophia perennis.
And it is a system radically different from any
theism. This little disquisition on this persistent system of thought, goes into its mechanics
in a more speculative way so one may see it all
together in one place. Now I shall switch to
Zaehner's method, in which he goes through text
after text to establish that Huxley is wrong by
setting out three types of Mysticisms: Nature
Mysticism, Isolation Mysticism and the Mysticism
of Love (Theism).

So, in a word or two, since Zaehner does this
nowhere in short compass, the philosophia perennis
states:

i)   man: a) he is divine by nature; b) the
     aim of life is to realize one's own
     divinity; and c) all religious asceticism
     is good only for activating what is there
     anyway: being the Absolute.

ii) religion: a) all religions are essenti-
     ally the same; b) only the elite can
     realize their divinity; c) dogmas can-
     not contain the Whole in a way which
     really communicates it; d) religions
     merely represent, in a tentative, tem-
     porary way, the Primordial Tradition,
     back towards which man tends; e) and
     no penitence is necessary for the true
     contemplative in the exoteric tradition;
     and f) hence religion is not necessary
     for the elite except as a tool of con-
     templation which brings about, dis-
     positively, not efficiently, the removal

77

of the obstacles of man's being himself: which is an identity of the self with the Absolute.

iii) God is not necessary to this system, except as a temporary and ephemeral entity. God is useful, but not ultimate. The Self beyond the Self is the Ultimate. And that each man is (Ātman is Brahman). Though only the elite will realize this through the philosophia perennis. Hence, the philosophia perennis is a religion of method, a yoga, which is not religion as known in the Judeo-Christian mould. It is a technique, not an obedience to God and love of him.

iv) Good and Evil: whatever activates one's nature is good, whatever keeps one from realizing that one is the Absolute is evil. What is called religious morality is useful, but not necessarily the truth.

At bottom, the philosophia perennis is an exclusivism, despite disclaimers to the contrary, which is, philosophically, a monism: the Real Self is the Self, and the world is not that real. It is a form of Indian religion (advaitan Vedānta) in western dress.

CHAPTER III

ZAEHNER'S FIRST CATEGORY: NATURE MYSTICISM

Zaehner defines mysticism in Christianity as a "...direct apprehension of the deity."[1] The average Christian is rarely aware that God is present in him by grace in any way which would bring him more than a modicum of certitude, but in a mystical state he knows it in a way which is immediate. Faith is not needed in such an experience in the way it was before the experience; while it is happening his faith becomes the forum in which God appears to the exterior or interior senses or to the mind. In India, on the contrary, faith is not needed at all; one need only know the technique to induce the state of awareness called samādhi (Skt.=trance sleep) in which one has the direct awareness of the Self (ātman) which the Hindus call jñāna (Skt.). The Christian's mystical experience has nothing to do with telepathy, visions, auditions, or the other paraphenomena of mysticism--which both saint and sinner can experience, as well as the hysterical personality.[2]

Christians see mysticism, therefore, as a union with God, and non-theists see it as union with a principle. The Christian believes that he is brought to union with God; and the advaitan Hindu, for instance, thinks that a pre-existent union is merely brought to light. Both are union experiences, but Zaehner is quick to distinguish between them.[3] The Christian experience is a dualism where God and man are separate; but the Hindu experience is one in which there is really

---

[1]Zaehner, S/P, p. 31.

[2]Ibid., pp. 31 f.

[3]Ibid., p. 32.

no separation or distinction between the Self and
the Absolute. So Hindus see the two as one; the
removal of the illusion which forced man into a
position of thinking he was two is the method of
"Method Religion" whereby one is brought to a
knowledge of what one is and has been all along.
The Christian mystic is in process of becoming
something he has not been: united with God
fully.   The Hindu is in process of removing the
obstacles to seeing what he has been and is: the
Absolute.   Zaehner adds the distinctive feature
between the two mysticisms when he says that the
Christian will never go so far as to say he is God,
while that is really what the Hindu means when he
says Atman is Brahman, and tat tvam asi (Thou art
that), which is the touchstone saying of Indian
mysticism.

So Muslims and Jews can rest easily with
Zaehner's definition since the reality of God is
not impugned. He is still God and man is still
separate and creature, even in union; the distinction between creature and Creator perdures
in theistic mysticism. The distinction never was
in non-theistic mysticisms.

In a non-religious mysticism union is still
the essence of the experience. It is a union
with nature in which the ego is enlarged to become
the All. This is what Zaehner thinks Huxley's
experience was: real mysticism, but Nature
Mysticism; true mysticism, but not religious
mysticism. This is the thrust of this chapter:
to define Huxley's experience, and that of a host
of others--from whom I have chosen a few mentioned
in Zaehner's works-and to declare it true mysticism in which man is in touch with his material
nature; and in which there is neither any religious function nor experience, nor any God present.

(A) Huxley's Experience

When Aldous Huxley published The Doors of

80

Perception[4] he hurled a challenge which Zaehner
could not let pass: that drugs are a "religious
surrogate."[5] Zaehner accepts Huxley's assertion
that he had experienced something preternatural.
But, Huxley adds, this preternatural experience
is religious, holy. This Zaehner will dispute.
One of Zaehner's sorrows was that Protestantism
had changed Christianity radically. It did so by
doing away with the mystical side of religion, in
doing away with monasteries and convents in order
to found a secular spirituality which the layman
could follow--a laudable aim. But it did it in a
way in which it is manifest that mysticism is not
only not an aim in the great Protestant divinity
schools, it is hardly taught; and it is not included in the spirituality of the youngster aiming
at ordination either. Schleirmacher tried to over-
turn this shift in goals when he turned away from
Kant's ethics to the irrational side of religion,
but neither theologian made up the religion, and
neither changed it. It had been made during the
Reformation as a Christian spirituality for the
world, and made well. Zaehner never disputed that;
but it had not included enough of the mystical side
of Christianity, that side which dwells on the King
within. Weber recognized this when he said that
Protestants wish to subdue the world, while the
Chinese wish to adapt to it. It is a difference
of mentalities which Zaehner decries: the one
wishes to deal with the King in his Kingdom, the
other with the King of the Kingdom within the very
person himself. Zaehner could be a bigot about
Protestantism, which had "done him in" at Tonbridge school. He loathed Evangelical Anglicanism, and extended his experience of it to all
Protestantism, the lack of which is proved by the
presence of Protestant mystics: they stand out as

---

[4]Cit. supra.

[5]Zaehner, S/P, p. 1.

81

different in Protestantism, different from the mainstream; while in Catholicism they are part of the mainstream and are not much to get worked up over.

In his field, history of religions, Zaehner felt that this slant in Protestantism made it somewhat lopsided when facing religions based on experience (mysticism) like Hinduism and Buddhism. There, religion is not a matter of faith; the Eastern religions experience immortality in the yogic-type of trance which Zaehner sees as quintessential Indian religion. They experience immortality now. Religion for the Indian is something to be experienced, not just professed. Zaehner feels that the reverse is true in the West where we have lost contact with the religious issues India dealt with.[6]

In his reading of the religious books of the East, Aldous Huxley became convinced that there was such a thing as a philosophia perennis, the chief hypothesis of which is that beneath all religions there is an "ultimate truth of which all religions were only partial expressions."[7] Huxley had had no religious experience which could be called mystical before he took part in the mescalin experiment which was to launch him into publishing The Doors of Perception. Zaehner contends that, steeped as he was in the books of the East, it was no coincidence that Huxley's experience was replete with expressions deriving from the religions of the Orient. Zaehner seems to doubt whether such would have been so if Huxley had not been so conversant

---

[6]Ibid., p. 2. He spent much of the rest of his life proving this very contention.

[7]Ibid.

with Eastern religions. Mysticism, for Zaehner,
seems to color itself in hues well known to each
mystic; which is to say, each mysticism, and
a fortiori, each religion experiences mysticism
in a way which is connected to its roots--ethnic,
cultural, social-economic...

At eleven o'clock in the morning Aldous Huxley
took a mescalin pill. It took half an hour to take
effect; an effect which lasted for eight hours. He
was sitting in his study and looking at an arrangement of flowers in a vase, an arrangement which
displeased him esthetically. As the drug took its
effect, esthetics became irrelevant, for he no
longer looked at an odd flower arrangement but saw
what "...Adam had seen on the morning of his
creation--the miracle, moment by moment, of naked
existence."[8] Asked whether the flowers pleased
him, he replied that it was neither agreeable nor
disagreeable. It just "is."

"Istigheit," he said, "wasn't that the word
the Meister Eckhart liked to use?" "Isness."
The Being of Platonic philosophy--except that
Plato seems to have made the enormous, the
grotesque mistake of separating Being from
Becoming, and identifying it with the mathe-
matical abstraction of the Idea. He could
never...have seen a bunch of flowers shining
with their own inner light and all but quiver-
ing under the pressure of the significance
with which they were charged; could never
have perceived that what the rose and iris
and carnation so intensely signified was
nothing more, and nothing less, than what
they were, a transience that was yet eternal
light, a perpetual perishing that was at
the same time pure Being, a bundle of
minute, unique particulars in which, by
some unspeakable and yet self-evident

---

[8]Zaehner, S/P, p. 4.

paradox, was to be seen the divine source of all existence."

He goes on:

> I continued to look at the flowers, and in their living light I seemed to detect the qualitative equivalent of breathing--but of a breathing without returns to a starting-point, with no recurrent ebbs but only a repeated flow from beauty to heightened beauty, from deeper to ever deeper meaning. Words like Grace and Transfiguration came to my mind, and this of course was what, among other things they stood for... The Beatific Vision, Sat Chit Ānanda, Being-Awareness-Bliss-for the first time I understood, not on the verbal level, not by inchoate hints or at a distance, but precisely and completely what those prodigious syllables referred to. And then I remember a passage I had read in one of Suzuki's essays. "What is the Dharma-Body of the Buddha (the Godhead, Suchness, the Void)?..."[9]

Zaehner might have mentioned that Huxley's Perennial Philosophy,[10] in its treatment of Eckhart, had used the word "istigkeit."[11] It does not decay Zaehner's argument that he does not mention this as an old thought of Huxley's, but he might have strengthened it had he done so.

The answer to Huxley's question was "the hedge at the bottom of the garden." This was put to a Zen master. His reply was geared to stop

---

[9]Zaehner, S/P, pp. 4-5, apud Huxley, op.cit., pp. 12-13.

[10]Harper Brothers, London, 1945.

[11]Huxley, op.cit., p. 30.

questions, to lock up the mind in irrelevance so as to make it transcend discursive reasoning. But Huxley understood it, saw it, "...as clear as day, as evident as Euclid."[12] Now the colors in his room were glowing, brighter, with a "profounder significance...so intrinsically meaningful, that they seemed to be on the point of leaving the shelves to thrust themselves more insistently on my attention."[13] So Huxley concludes that these correspond to Zen experiences, and both he and his investigative helpers conclude that these are common to "mystical experience in general."[14]

Zaehner notes that practically a commonplace in mystical experience is the transcendence of space and time. Huxley's experience is no exception. Space ceased to matter very much to Huxley. The mind's function had shifted to perceiving things, not spatially, but in terms of intensity and profundity of meaning, of seeing a pattern of relationships. Space still existed, but Huxley was concerned with its predominance. As to time, Huxley maintained, "My actual experience had been, was still, of an indefinite duration or alternatively of a perpetual present made up of one continually changing apocalypse."[15] He seems to mean, by this, that time flowed back and forth between eternity and a series of revelations; that is, that time had ceased, but activity had not, that one was still vigorous, in fact more so than during normalcy since the revelations were

---

[12]Zaehner, S/P, p. 5.

[13]Ibid.

[14]Zaehner, S/P, p. 5.

[15]Ibid., p. 6.

such heightened experiences.

The investigation proceeded to external objects. Huxley's attention was turned to the furniture. First he perceived it as would a cubist: a pattern of lines, horizontals, diagonals...etc. But then the objects took on what Huxley described as "...the sacramental vision of reality." Everything seemed imbued with an inner light, with infinite meaning. Gazing at a bamboo chair he was taken out of time and not only saw, but became the chair: "...not merely gazing at those bamboo legs, but actually being them--or rather being myself in them; or, to be still more accurate (for "I" was not involved in the case, nor in a certain sense were "they") being my Not-self in the Not-self which was the chair."[16] Zaehner adds that this language is borrowed from the Vedānta of Hinduism and from Mahāyāna Buddhism, and that it sounds like sheer lunacy, except that its extraordinary nature leaves it quite vulnerable to such interpretations since there is no language with which to describe such an intense and radical experience.[17]

Later on in the telling, Huxley mentions that things had achieved a great importance, but not

---

[16]Ibid., p. 7, apud Huxley's The Doors of Perception, op. cit., p. 15.

[17]Vedānta is a branch of Hindu philosophy feeding off the later scriptures called the Upanisads. Mahāyāna is a late reform of Buddhism which began to stress the use of philosophy to induce the experience of the usefulness of life, and thus to throw one open to the Emptiness of all, which emptiness (śūnyatā=Pali) is the locus of nirvāna. So, amid life, if one seeks it, there is Bliss.

people or the relationships which attend them. He had become a Not-self, and persons are selves. So his grey flannel trouser legs took on a place of supreme importance, while he avoided even eye contact with his wife and a very close friend, both of whom were in the room with him.[18] Listening to music, he went into what he described as "pure contemplation." This state continued when he was led into the garden. There he gazed at a trellised pergola on which was a climbing rose. The beauty of this ordinary sight was "...inexpressibly wonderful, wonderful to the point, almost, of being terrifying. And suddenly I had an inkling of what it must feel like to be mad."[19] Zaehner battens on this to say that something had gone haywire; that Huxley should have remembered that the clinical use for mescalin was to produce a state "akin to schizophrenia." So Zaehner concluded that Huxley's pure contemplation had a link with madness. This is an important note in the definition of what Zaehner came to call Nature Mysticism. Faced with a chair which looked "like the Last Judgment," Huxley began to panic. Zaehner quotes him as saying, "This...was going too far...even though going was into intenser beauty, deeper significance."[20]

Huxley summarizes the experience thusly: i) thinking is not impaired much, if at all; ii) sight is so intensified that it regains some of "the innocence of childhood," when concept did not dominate sense so; iii) space is diminished as something interesting, and time diminishes almost to nothingness; iv) will is impaired quite

---

[18]Zaehner, S/P, p. 8.

[19]Ibid., p. 10.

[20]Ibid., p. 11.

a bit, and Huxley found himself in a state of apathy, almost complete, since the things which normally compel action have lost their force before things more interesting; v) the things which were more interesting, "better" in Huxley's own words, were interior and exterior as well.[21]

Zaehner sees the importance of Huxley's book in the fact that the latter, whose eminence was not disputed, had posed the problem: viz., that a drug experience is close to a genuine mystical experience.[22]

(1) The Meaning of Huxley's Experience

What Zaehner took from Huxley was the first outline of what he was to call Nature Mysticism. He preferred another term to Nature Mysticism, namely, pan-en-henism, but Nature Mysticism is better for our purposes, and might have served Zaehner more had he used it originally because the pan-en-henism term is not as inclusive as the other term. However, pan-en-henism, a Zaehner neologism, came out of his empirical studies of Huxley, and is quite useful as far as it goes, as we shall see now.

(a) Zaehner conceded that Huxley had under-gone a preternatural experience; his first. Pre-vious to this he had known contemplation only in its discursive forms: viz., in poetry, painting or music.[23] But Zaehner says that what Huxley had called contemplation of a discursive type is not contemplation at all, since contemplation of its nature is never discursive: it is intuitive. The mind stops. Hence, when Huxley wrote of the philosophia perennis, Zaehner contends that he was

---

[21]Ibid., pp. 11-12.

[22]Ibid., p. 12.

[23]Zaehner, S/P, p. 14.

merely intellectualizing--he looked in from the outside and never entered the sacred precincts until his mescalin experience, which was the genuine thing for both Huxley and Zaehner. This experience came long after Huxley had written about his *philosophia perennis*. Huxley had had a predilection for mystics and mystical experience. Before his mescalin experiment he had felt that such an experience is based on the experience of the religious mystics of every faith and religion.[24] He felt that there was one soaring idea behind a multiplicity of religious expressions. His conviction, Zaehner reiterates, was merely intellectual, not experiential. Huxley's conclusion, which looks for a unity concept under which all can fit, is based on the similarities among the experiences, not on their essences.[25] Thus, Zaehner makes his first point: Huxley had a truly preternatural experience; but he began to conclude to a universal from one experience--which is an untruth, as well as a logical fallacy.

(b) Zaehner's first attack on the *philosophia perennis*, *ex professo*, came when he made his second point: that mysticisms differ both as to substance and approach, and that Huxley seems to have overlooked this fact, having been taken by similarities between and among mysticisms. Zaehner begins his argument by making an innocent remark about Huxley's love for mysticism. He was interested in it because he saw in mystics a claim to have broken away from the empirical self and into a new mode of perception. The element in all mysticisms which compelled Huxley was that mystics had gotten away from the humdrum; had obtained release from the ego. Huxley earnestly wanted release from ordinary relationships, and for his ego, room to expand. Huxley said:

---

[24]*Ibid.*

[25]*Ibid.*, p. 15.

89

That humanity at large will ever be able to
dispense with Artificial Paradises seems
unlikely. Most men and women lead lives at
the worst so painful, at the best so monoto-
nous, poor and limited that the urge to
escape, the longing to transcend themselves
if only for a few moments, is and has always
been one of the principal appetites of the
soul.[26]

(c) Hence Zaehner concludes that "This is
rather a bold generalization; but it is a generalization that is typical of the intellectual and particularly of the intellectual who has been born
and bred in an industrial civilization. The "urge
to escape, is, of course, the mainspring of
Gnosticism, and particularly of Manichaeanism
which described the body as a "carrion and a
prison," a satanic substance in which the heavenly
soul was unnaturally confined."[27] This is an
important, and not offhand, remark on Zaehner's
part. Gnosticism is an elitisim for Schuon. In
another book treating the philosophia perennis
Schuon calls it Gnosis.[28] Zaehner goes on to say
that the religion of Mani was one of escape and
release, and that he and most heretics were "egg-
heads" and appealed to the intellectual. Further,
Zaehner scores Huxley's urge to escape as being
neurotic; that Huxley's stuff was not what William
James called "healthy-minded." The clincher to
Zaehner's argument is that most men fall into the

---

[26]Zaehner, S/P, p. 15.

[27]Ibid., apud H. C. Peuch, Le Manicheisme,
son Fondateur, sa Doctrine. Publications du
Musée Guimet, Paris, 1949, pp. 82-83; Zaehner
refers us to his Zurvan, A Zoroastrian Dilemma,
Oxford, 1955, p. 169, for remarks on Gnosticism.

[28]Cit. supra.

"healthy-minded" class.[29] Zaehner leaves us hanging in mid-air with that remark about James, something he would do frequently in his writings, only to come back pages later, to switch the metaphor, and draw the strings around the package he has been meticulously wrapping all along, but not always without misplacing some of the wrappers. He ties up this package twenty-six pages later when he clears up just what James thought a "healthy-minded" mysticism was. For him it was one not indulged in by those trying to escape life. Sick mysticism was the escape of the frightened and ill for James, and Zaehner accepted this rubric as his own.[30] I shall take up James in conjunction with Huxley to show how the type Nature Mysticism evolved for Zaehner, but first let me finish Zaehner's remarks about Huxley's "sickness" of soul.

Zaehner launched into an analysis of Huxley's life and motives in order to explain just where his experience fitted into a larger scheme of things in both Huxley's life and his own budding systematics of mysticism. Zaehner opines that Huxley's mind is a product of his intellectualism. He began his adult life as a rebel, rejecting the conventional forms of society. He found that this led him to a rejection of sexual mores, which resulted in what Zaehner terms "new and deeper bondages."[31] The ensuing slavery to his passions brought what Zaehner terms "as harsh a slavery as that imposed by any political system."[32] His

---

[29]Zaehner, S/P, p. 16.

[30]Ibid., p. 42, apud James, The Varieties of Religious Experience, London, Longmans, Green and Co., rev. ed., 1902, pp. 388-9.

[31]Zaehner, op. cit., p. 17.

[32]Ibid.

revolt ended in the desire to escape from the
self.[33] He realized what the great religions had
taught about such slavery, Zaehner says, and
sought a religion which would supply escape from
his predicament. He was fully conscious that his
unhappy predicament was intimately connected with
the self. He was both unhappy and introspective
by nature, and he knew that he was unhappy.
Zaehner says that the realization of one's predicament of unhappiness and of one's self as the
beginning of that sad state is "the beginning of
religion."[34] The preoccupation with self is the
font of malaise in two major religions: Hinduism
and Buddhism. It is precisely to them that Huxley
turned. And why not? says Zaehner, "...for though
the Gospels teach that one must die to oneself in
order to live, this is only one of many Christian
teachings, whereas both Hinduism and Buddhism
regard the elimination of the ego as the sine
qua non of "liberation" or "enlightenment," and
never tire of saying so...that Christianity was
far less clear in teaching that unhappiness and
the ego are one and the same thing than was either
Buddhism and Hinduism...etc."[35] This is the background out of which Huxley's thought and religious
experience came; and it was a life from which he
earnestly sought escape.

He takes Huxley to task precisely for this
desire to escape; not that he sought private
escape--that was his own business--but that he
sought to provide everyone with a highway of
escape. This seems to bother Zaehner no end.

---

[33]Ibid., p. 16.

[34]Zaehner, S/P, p. 17.

[35]Ibid.

He chides Huxley for not recognizing the many
good, generous souls,

> ...whom everyone likes and who do good to
> others, not by any conscious effort, but
> simply being what they are...These do not
> feel any need for escape, nor can they
> be attracted by any religion which
> offers them only this (though I do not
> suggest for a moment that Hinduism and
> Buddhism have nothing further to offer,
> for obviously they have): for they have
> been made whole, and it is only what is
> partial or maimed that can feel the
> need for completion. Thus, for them,
> the word "escape" has very little
> meaning.[36]

I leave Zaehner's pointed, yet somewhat meandering treatment of Nature Mysticism, as it reveals
itself in Huxley's experience and writings, for
a short treatment of William James. The latter
also had an experience of what Zaehner saw to be
Nature Mysticism, but he had as well some distinctions which are quite useful for our argument.

James' experience of Nature Mysticism is
mined by Zaehner to fill out his type called by
that name and to further his argument against
Huxley and the philosophia perennis. James
experiences pretty much the same as Huxley did,
though through the agency of nitrous oxide, not
mescalin. James had no axe, such as the
philsophia perennis, to grind, so his evidence is
all the better for its freedom from bias. James
found that normal waking consciousness is just one
form of consciousness, and that if properly
stimulated, various kinds of consciousness will
bob to the surface which are "...discontinuous

---

[36]Ibid., p. 18.

with ordinary consciousness. Yet they may deter-
mine attitudes though they cannot furnish formulas,
and open a region though they fail to give a map.
At any rate, they forbid a premature closing of
our accounts with reality...my own experiences...
all converge towards a kind of insight to which I
cannot help ascribing some metaphysical significance. The keynote of it is invariably a reconciliation...as if the opposites of the world...
were melted into unity..."[37] All things became,
not one genus for James, but one species.[38] So
the experience was unitive and the unity reconciled opposites. These are two notes in Zaehner's
definition of Nature Mysticism: unitive, which
is to be found in all kinds of mysticism, and the
reconciliation of opposites. He will perceive,
here, the danger of being beyond good and evil,
as we shall see.

Zaehner finds James' words particularly startling since he is so healthy-minded when seen alongside Huxley. Where the latter was neurotic and
wished to escape from the self, James' experience
was not anything of the sort, and did not come out
of any desire to be escapist either. James, on
the contrary, inclines away from these states of
deliverance which are strictly for the morbid of
mind. He advocates instead, a religion for the
healthy-minded who need no ecstasies to rid them of
the fetters of the ego.[39] For James, the healthy
do not need deliverance. Not only is James
weighty for making a distinction between healthy-
minded and unhealthy mysticisms, but he is
especially cogent for Zaehner in affirming that

---

[37]Zaehner, S/P, p. 42, _apud_ James, _op. cit._,
pp. 388-9.

[38]_Ibid._, p. 42.

[39]Zaehner, S/P, pp. 42 f.

there is such a thing as Nature Mysticism at all.
This is all Zaehner really wanted of him.

The notes of the experiences come out, further,
when James speaks of the like experience of others.
Zaehner accepts what James quotes of Tennyson as
being preternatural when the latter said:

> I have never had any revelations through
> anaesthetics, but a kind of waking trance--this
> for lack of a better word--I have frequently
> had, quite up from boyhood, when I have been
> all alone. This has come upon me through
> repeating my own name to myself silently,
> till all at once, as it were out of the
> intensity of the consciousness of individu-
> ality, individuality itself seemed to dis-
> solve and fade away into boundless being,
> and this not a confused state but the
> clearest, the surest of the surest, utterly
> beyond words--where death was an almost
> laughable impossibility--the loss of person-
> ality (if so it were) seeming no extinction,
> but the only true life. I am ashamed of
> my feeble description. Have I not said
> the state is utterly beyond words?[40]

But, though it is preternatural, though it con-
firms the note of immortality experienced and the
loss of ego, Zaehner homes in on what is most
important for him in discerning the difference
between this healthy experience which he will call
Nature Mysticism and the experience of union with
God in love: there is nothing of God in Tennyson's
experience at all. Hence it can be hardly
described as theistic mysticism. In fact, Zaehner
adds, it is significant that the poet never
thought to connect these experiences with God.[41]

---

[40]Ibid., p. 37, apud James, op. cit., p. 384.

[41]Zaehner, S/P, p. 37.

Next Zaehner chooses from James' litany of examples of such experiences that of Amiel's _Journal Intime_ and one from Malwida von Meysenburg, a German idealist. In both the same symbols recur: earth, heaven and sea. There is a recurrent theme of the unity of all such things; there is the same certainty of immortality as was found in Tennyson. In Amiel's work the world seems to breathe. In fact, he mentions the Holy Ghost, and Zaehner launches into his theological theme of God inspiring matter with his breath so that it can come alive and move upwards to thought, and thence to God.

Zaehner goes to Jung for an explanation of these phenomena.[42] But Jung is found wanting. In fact, none of the explanations fully convinces Zaehner of their cogency. But the salient feature of all is that Zaehner is now calling it the "natural mystical experience," and what is ever more important, that the evidence for its existence and universality is "...overwhelming."[43] So the experience shows that the without and the within of things are one and that the space/time continuum has been transcended. This unity of the interiority of man with extra-mental reality is no mere unity with local pixies and elves for Zaehner; nor is it for James. The latter puzzles over the list of experiences he has presented in order to bring order to them. Zaehner is doing precisely that, slowly and surely. James leaves us with the thought that he would not brush aside the experience he and others had as "mere illusion."[44]

---

[42]_Ibid._, p. 40, Zaehner refers to Jung's _Psychology of the Unconscious_ as being his source, but he leaves us with no particulars.

[43]_Ibid._, p. 41.

[44]Zaehner, S/P, p. 41.

Zaehner is always on the lookout for that
element in the philosophia perennis which makes
whatever aids contemplation and its attainment as
the good and the opposite an evil. Over and over
again he discerns in Nature Mysticism the danger
which the reconciliatio oppositorum poses for
mysticism and those engaged in it. When James said
that his own experience under nitrous oxide
"...soaks up and absorbs its opposites into
itself"[45] Zaehner reminds him of his own rubric
called "diabolic mysticism" in Varieties of
Religious Experience, and that he seems to have
forgotten it in not recognizing in his own experience that the reconciling of opposites is one
thing, but their absorption of the one into the
other is highly dangerous; and James, he notes,
seems unaware of the danger. Zaehner says that
both the Ṣūfīs and Catholic mystics, like St.
Teresa of Avila, maintain that there may be
mystical experiences which are really only visita-
tions by the Devil. Saint Teresa claims to have
had such. James saw the possibility in cases of
insanity where, under what he calls "delusional
insanity," there may be instances of:

> diabolical mysticism, a sort of mysticism
> turned upside down. The same sense of
> ineffable importance in the smallest events,
> the same texts and words coming with new
> meanings, the same voices and visions and
> leadings and missions, the same controlling
> by extraneous powers; only this time the
> emotion is pessimistic: instead of con-
> solations we have desolations; the meanings
> are dreadful; and the powers are enemies to
> life. It is evidence that from the point
> of view of their psychological mechanism,
> the classic mysticism and these lower

---

[45]Ibid., p. 42, apud James, op. cit.,
pp. 388-9.

mysticisms spring from the mental level,
from that great subliminal or transmarginal region of which science is beginning to admit the existence, but of which
so little is really known.[46]

Zaehner moves very carefully here since he has
touched on to an area which is quite difficult to
handle. It is the rendezvous point for psychology,
history of religions, mystical theology and psy-
chiatry, and no one has yet given a sufficiently
cogent explanation of the phenomena outlined or
yet named them properly. So Zaehner says that this
"transmarginal region "...seems to be an adumbra-
tion of what Jung now calls the "collective unconscious" or what the Canadian physician Bucke
calls "cosmic consciousness." It seems to Zaehner
that this is the vast area of archetypal race
experiences which Jung deals with in his collective
unconscious. Huxley too touched on the phenomenon
and called it Mind at Large. The problem in
Zaehner's eyes is phrased in Jungian terms; it is
not Jungian psychology _per se_. The integration of
the collective unconscious, the personal unconscious and the conscious is integration and salvation, for Zaehner. The unconscious level is the
irrational and bestial level of man since it
"recognizes neither good nor evil." Both Avicenna
and Ghazālī, the latter a philosopher and Ṣūfi
master, demand that the job is to take charge of
this area and control it. No explanation would
satisfy Zaehner that such wildness and horrors
derive from union with God. This holds true for
Huxley's mescalin experience as well. So Zaehner
says that there is something irrational here,
something which Lonergan and scientists call in-
authentic,[47] which his methodology cannot handle.

---

[46]Zaehner, S/P, p. 43, _apud_ James, _op. cit._,
p. 426.

[47]_Art. cit._

98

So Zaehner, like the empirical scientists, creates
a rubric--as the scientists create a surd number--to
handle the imponderable area just uncovered. He
says that he will assume that there is an area
which he will call the collective unconscious or
cosmic consciousness, since it is obvious that
there is something in man and men larger than
personal consciousness. Buddhists call it the
vijñānālaya (Pali=reservoir of consciousness),
which Zaehner says could be Jung's anima and the
prāna of the Hindus; the latter term means the
breath or spirit which animates the universe. It
is neither good nor evil. When it unites with
good it looks good, and when it is one with evil
it seems to be evil. Huxley said that there is
both original virtue and original sin in it.[48]

What helps our argument here? Nothing seems
to be terribly certain. We are dealing with a
grand assumption, and a certainty of confusion.
The only certain thing is that neither monism nor
theism explains the state of affairs: one is
not realizing that the Self is the Absolute,
nor is one in union with a loving God. Another
state is depicted here. This, Zaehner and those
who argue, with James, for a natural mystical
state, call by the name Natural Mysticism.
The state depicted is ambivalent, both divine
and diabolic, both manic and depressive, depending on whether one speaks theologically or psychologically. So Zaehner says that there seems
to be a deity in the one state and a devil in the
other. But it is ambivalent, nothing is stable,
and the states of both theism and monism are quite
stable. Hence Zaehner says that Nature Mysticism
has another note to add to its definition: moral

---

[48]Huxley, The Devils of Loudun, Chatto and
Windus, London, 1952, p. 104.

ambivalence. He uses, but does not assert proof
for, the rubric of psychology called collective
unconscious as a term of convenience to speak of
the mixed bag which pours forth from a subject under
the sway of the experience. History of religions
can go no farther. It has carved out another line
in the picture of Nature Mysticism: moral ambivalence. So Zaehner says theology may have to take
over later. And later he will use mythology to
pull his chestnuts out of the fire. The Fall and
original sin seem a proper explanation for him in
his At Sundry Times, Convergent Spirit, Concordant
Discord, and especially his Drugs, Mysticism and
Make-Believe and his Our Savage God. The latter
two deal with the savagery of Nature Mysticism,
especially that had in drug experiences.

So James has led us further than we were in
establishing the argument. The experience is to be
taken seriously; it is fairly universal; it deals
with one's experience of immortality; with the loss
of the ego; with the reconciliation of opposites
(moral ambivalence) which Zaehner says is to be
rooted in what psychology calls the collective
unconscious; and does not deal with God as theism
knows it or with monism as Indian religion and
Islam know it; it is, in a word, a complete unity
with Nature which may be happy or terrifying.

Zaehner hurled his most barbed comment at
Huxley in saying that he never fully satisfies
the differences or relationships between his
mescalin experience and the ecstasies of those
living lives of heroic virtue. Huxley's point is
that Christianity should baptize mescalin since it
satisfies the fundamental urge of religion, which
is to escape from the self. He never explains
his experiences, therefore, over against that of
the saints: he does not answer the question,
is it good? Is one better, more loving?
Kinder...? So Zaehner faults him on this

score.[49] The ecstasy of the saint always makes
him better; Huxley's did not.

Again, Zaehner states that Huxley's ideas
suffer from confusion because he swings from
identifying his experience with the Beatific
Vision to offering it as a surrogate for alcohol.[50] In his Doors of Perception Huxley states
that his experience is like the Beatific Vision and
the Sat Chit Ananda experience of the Hindus:
that he understood them beyond the verbal level
"...precisely and completely..."[51] Zaehner will
not accept Huxley's explanation that what he had
was the same as the vision of God as generally
understood by Christian theology. Further, he cannot accept that a vision of nature is a substitute
for a vision of God, even though it is a nature
transfigured.

If one is to know the difference between a
Christian vision and one which is not, the best
way to find out is by comparing it with the real
thing. So Zaehner brings in a vision of Blessed
Henry Suso as a basis of comparison. He says it
is a typical Christian mystical experience.

It happens, no doubt, that when the
good and faithful servant enters into

---

[49]Zaehner, S/P, p. 20. Zaehner cites Huxley
for lumping the sick and well together and making
for all a religion of the sick. The neurotic
lives by introspection and is bound sooner or
later to seek escape. The healthy, even the bored
proletariat of Ananda Coomeraswami, another advo-
cate of the philosophia perennis, do not seek
escape from the self, only from a dull environment.

[50]Ibid., p. 20.

[51]Ibid., p. 20, Huxley, Doors of Perception,
pp. 12-13.

the joy of his Lord, he becomes intoxicated with the immeasurable abundance of the Divine house. For in an ineffable manner, it happens to him as to a drunk man, who forgets himself, is no longer himself. He is quite dead to himself, and is entirely lost in God, has passed into Him, and has become one spirit with Him in all respects, just as a little drop of water that is poured into a large quantity of wine. For as this is lost to itself, and draws to itself and into itself the taste and colour of the wine, similarly it happens to those who are in the full possession of the blessedness. In an inexpressible manner all human desires fall away from them, they melt away into themselves, and sink away completely into the will of God. If anything remained in man, and was not entirely poured out of him, then the Scripture could not be true that says: God is to become all things to all things. Nevertheless, his being remains, though in a different form, in a different glory, and in a different power. And all this comes to a man through his utter abandonment of self.[52]

This is true not only in Christianity. Zaehner says that hundreds of passages from Muslim mystics say the same thing: that one is lost, but in God; that the loss is not total, but is a union; that all one's being remains, though in another form. He goes on to say that Huxley's experience takes him in the opposite direction from that of theistic mystics. The former is atomized into the objective world, whereas theistic mystics experience a total absorption in God, who is seen to be totally

---

[52]Ibid., p. 21, Suso, <u>Little Book of Eternal Wisdom and the Little Book of Truth</u>, tr. J. M. Clark, London, Faber and Faber, 1953, p. 185.

distinct from them and from the objective world.

Christian mysticism gives us the deification of the soul in God, and the loss of consciousness of all things except God. Huxley gives us as a Christian experience, "...the identification of the self via the "Not-self" with the eternal world to the exclusion, it would appear, of God; for... Huxley...fails to identify his Not-self with God though he does not feel this to be incongruous in the case of the "Dharma-Body of the Buddha."[53] Huxley says that he has experienced Christian mysticism without benefit of God as agent or object. Zaehner says that this is a radical falsehood.[54]

Why Zaehner did not hoist Huxley on his own petard is a mystery to me. In Huxley's The Perennial Philosophy Huxley has a chapter entitled "Tantum religio potuit suadere malorum" (Chapter XX) in which he leads with his chin in saying, with William Law:

"Now religion in the hands of self, or corrupt nature, serves only to discover vices of a worse kind than in nature left to itself." "Turning to God without turning from self"--the formula is absurdly simple...as it...explains all the follies and iniquities committed in the name of religion. Those who turn to God without turning from themselves are tempted to evil in several characteristic and easily recognizable ways. They are tempted, first of all, to practice magical rites, by means of which they hope to

[53]Zaehner, S/P, p. 22.

[54]Ibid., p. 24.

compel God to answer their petitions...
For, let there be no mistake, sacrifice,
incantation and "vain repetition"
actually do produce fruits, especially
when practised in conjunction with physical
austerities. Men who turn towards God
without turning away from themselves do
not, of course, reach God; but if they
devote themselves energetically enough to
their pseudo-religion, they will get
results...some of (which) are doutbless
the product of autosuggestion...[55]

Further, in his The Doors of Perception
Huxley becomes, in his mescalin experience, a Not-
self, which means that he has expanded to include
all, to become the All. It does not mean that he
has left himself in the sense of the Christian
and Muslim, or the Hindu or Buddhist, for that
matter, mystical traditions. Zaehner could have
done Huxley in with the merest mention of this passage from the Ur work, Perennial Philosophy, but he
did not. Either he did not know that passage, or
he did not need it. D. M. Lang's review of
Zaehner's Mysticism Sacred and Profane says of the
effect of Zaehner's argument, "After pulverizing
poor Mr. Huxley, Professor Zaehner discusses
'Nature Mysticism'..."[56]

Huxley raised the question of whether drugs
could be used as an aid in procuring for one union
with God, but after raising it he drops it.

---

[55]Huxley, The Perennial Philosophy, op. cit.,
pp. 243-44.

[56]Lang art. in Bulletin of the School of
Oriental and African Studies, University of London,
XXI, 1958, pp. 185-187, p. 186.

Zaehner faulted him for that.[57] Further, Huxley
feels that Christianity should have sacramen-
talized alcohol since it alters consciousness much like mescalin. But Zaehner cites St.
Paul's stern rebuke of drunken Agapes in I Cor.
11:20-22 to refute Huxley, to prove that, in all
these assertions Huxley is "...admittedly both
incoherent and self-contradictory."[58] What
Zaehner does to Huxley's argument in all this is
his reductio ad absurdum of the latter's position.
For Huxley, religion is primarily an escape from
the ego; and all the great mystics have escaped
their egos, have become Gods, Not-selves, too.
Mescalin and alcohol do the same thing. They give
one the ability to shake off the ego and afford
one a glorious feeling of release. Hence, they
are essentially religious. Then they must be
good. But Zaehner mines St. Paul to the effect
that Christ came to make us whole, not ecstatic.
One may have ecstasies, but they mean nothing,
since alcohol can do the same. Christian mysticism is more than ecstasy. It is union with God.
There is none of this in Huxley's argumentation
for ecstasy. Zaehner hastens to add that one
should not mistake ecstasy for grace since it
can come to both saint and sinner alike: witness
diabolic ecstasy. Further, ecstasy can be produced by drugs and alcohol, but that means only
that there is an ecstasy, not a Christian one.
Hence, Huxley is both confused in making graced
union identical with an alcoholic fog, and a drug
high; and he is wrong since such states mean
nothing at all about whether or not one has genuine Christian or Muslim mysticism; counterfeits
abound in mystical states.[59]

---

[57]Zaehner, op. cit., p. 24.

[58]Zaehner, S/P, p. 25.

[59]Ibid., pp. 25 f.

Zaehner gives us an outline of what the
philosophia perennis looks like on the basis of
the evidence thus far presented. For Huxley, religion and mysticism are this: i) one cannot
express the ultimate truths of religion with words;
ii) these truths are necessarily the same everywhere; iii) hence, revealed religions can be only
relatively true since they differ on so many major
points; each religion is tailored to the clime and
to its clients; iv) the only heresy is in thinking
one has the exclusive possession of truth; v) all
religions are facets of one truth presented in
different ways according to time, and to the
development of the people; vi) the truth lies in
the experience of the mystics; it is one in
thought and language; this should speak for
itself.[60]

Zaehner outlines his objections to Huxley's
thought thus. First off, few of the authors holding these thoughts in general, and Huxley in particular, define what they mean by a mystical experience, and when they do it is too vague to be useful. Secondly, to say that all mystics speak with
one language throughout the world will not hold up
within one religion, let alone in many. Thirdly,
if one includes Huxley's experience as mystical,
then one must also have to include manic-depressive
states as well since they are much like that induced by Huxley and the enthusiasms of conventional
mystics.[61]

To balance off his objections to what he considers a false concept of mysticism, Zaehner poses
his schema of mysticisms for the first time; and
this is his prime thesis, that there are mysticisms, not a mysticism: firstly, there is what
he calls the pan-en-henic experience (from the

---

[60]Zaehner, S/P, p. 27.

[61]Ibid.

106

Greek all-in-one) in which one feels one with the
All, and that all is one. This sort of experience
is usually termed pantheistic, but Zaehner measures
the words used in such experiences very carefully,
and they come up without any God at all, let alone
seeing God everywhere. Such experiences as "When
I am inseparably this and that, and this and that
are I; when I experience the other person as myself and the other, as myself, experiences me" are
what he would call pan-en-henic experiences.
The Kausītakī Upaniṣad sums it up as "Thou art
this all" (Skt.=idam sarvam asi=Kaus. Up. 1.6).
This is not pantheism, it is Nature Mysticism, or
what Zaehner terms pen-en-henism. It is to be
found in later Ṣūfi writers in Islam and in Huxley's experiences when he said that he was a Not-
self in their Not-self, or that he was a Not-self
in the Not-self which was the chair.

A more useful term than Zaehner's neologism,
over the long run, is Nature Mysticism. As he
went on he sharpened his definition of this type
appreciably. His method floated, as a good method
will, with the situation, and allowed him to face
religious fact with an explanation, not force his
explanation on the religious facts.

Zaehner's second classification is monism, for
now. It accords no reality to phenomena whatsoever, none on the absolute level, anyway. This
seems, at first blush, to be the same as the pan-
en-henic experience, especially when one is
plunged into, for instance, Indian monism in the
Upaniṣads--which mixes pan-en-henism, monism and an
incipient theism with an abandon and relaxedness

which leaves Westerners limp.[62] Monism's heart is
the statement that the individual soul is identical
in an unqualified sense with the Absolute, essentially and substantially.[63]

There is already a pattern appearing for
Zaehner: two forms of mysticism are apparent. To
these Zaehner will add a third: the mysticism of
love, which is the normal Christian variety in
which one is united with God in love. The theological basis for this type is the Christian truth
that man is created in God's image and likeness;
and that this image can be united with God. Thus
the mysticism of love and Vedānta monism are distinct from the pan-en-henism of nature mysticism.
They are also distinct from each other: Christian
love mysticism is not monism, and Vedānta monism
is not Christian love. The soul retains its
identity in Christianity; it does not melt in God.
Non-dual Vedānta (the adherents of which do not
accept "monism" as an accurate term but prefer
advaita, which means non-twoism or non-dualism) is
180 degrees in the other direction: there, the
soul is God, and God is the soul. The two are completely identical. As time wore on Zaehner worked
out a good rule of thumb for discerning the difference between pantheism and monism: when god

---

[62]Hindu Vedanta is replete with monism,
especially such statements as: i) Thou art that
(Skt.=tat tvam asi from the Chāndogya Upaniṣad
6.9ff. It means "you are the Real," "that which
is All is one's soul." ii) This Ātman is Brahman
(This individual soul is the Absolute), taken from
the Māndūkya Up. 2; in Skt. this is ayam atma
brahma; iii) I am Brahman (taken from the
Bṛhadāranyaka Up. 1.4.10) which is aham brahmasmi
in Skt.; and iv) Consciousness is Brahman
(prajñānam brahma in Skt.), taken from Aitareya
Up. 5.3.

[63]Zaehner, S/P, p. 28.

becomes world, that is pantheism; when he is one's soul, that is monism.[64] I should add to this that what he seems to be saying about Nature Mysticism is that when the ego expands to become the All, that is pan-en-henism. It is different from pantheism because there is no god in the All, only ego; and because it is the reverse of pantheism in direction. Nature Mysticism is All-in-one-ism whereas pantheism is One-in-all-ism. The first begins and ends with the ego; the second begins with God and ends with creatures. Nature Mysticism, for Zaehner, begins and ends with the ego; it means that the ego is atomized into creatures considered as material in an intimacy which can be both euphoric and identical: that is to say, the ego becomes identical with creatures for a while psychologically. Nature Mysticism is never a philosophy, it is always a psychological experience. One does not philosophize over it. It is, therefore, neither philosophical nor religious per se. Later it will be seen that it can be religious (in Hinduism, with the early Upaniṣads) but it is only so per accidens. It can also be induced, as we have seen with Huxley's drug experience. But forms of asceticism can induce it as well. It can also happen spontaneously, as we shall see with Proust's experience.

So Zaehner has begun to carve out his first category and introduce the other two mystical categories. He turns his scorn on Huxley and Schuon for their arrogance in feeling that only they can get to the truth since their methodology is free of any religious bias. Both Huxley and Schuon think their level superior to that of any religious or philosophical vantage point. Hence only they can discern truth, in the final analysis. Zaehner would have none of this since it made religious truth a lower truth, which was to make it not truth at all in the philosophical sense, since, for them,

---

symbol is never really connected with what it
points towards: the Truth of Metaphysic.

My argument has begun to form the notes of
Nature Mysticism into something cohesive. In
doing so I have shown a pattern of mysticisms ris-
ing out of Zaehner's typologies of Nature Mysticism, Monism and Mysticism of Love. In applying
his definition of mysticism to Huxley's experience,
Zaehner found that it was mystical, but preternatural, not theistic mysticism. Huxley said that
his experience was of the Beatific Vision and the
Hindu Sat Chit Ananda (Being, Thought-Mind, and
Bliss); and Zaehner says that this is "...to state
or imply an obvious untruth."[65] Zaehner's reasons
are simple: the extreme Vedantin position-which
realizes the self as the One which has no second-
is the opposite of Huxley's being Not-self in the
Not-self in the chair. The experiences are not
the same and demand different explanations. Simply
put: Huxley's experience was an expansion of the
personality in which he became the all--the chair
represented the loss of the subject-object relation
in an expansion of the personality. The Vedanta
experience is not an expansion at all. It is a
realization of complete unity-through-isolation of
the self from all that is not itself. The end
result is the realization that one is Being, self
is Brahman, or that the self is God. Huxley's
and Vedanta's experiences are, therefore, radically
different. But Huxley forces a conclusion that his
is the ultimate Hindu experience of Sat Chit
Ananda, and that it is the Christian Beatific
Vision. Zaehner will not and cannot let this
falsehood pass. He plainly calls it an untruth.[66]

---

[65]Zaehner, S/P, p. 33.

[66]Ibid.

110

Therefore Huxley's experience is true mysticism. His explanation of it is nonsense. He has neither experienced the Vedānta experience nor the Christian experience of union.

Further, in his remarks on the unconscious and diabolic mysticism Zaehner hits on a fact: the level touched in Nature Mysticism is ambivalent morally, containing elements of both good and evil. For Zaehner the unconscious is the home of both good and evil; the irrational and diabolical recognize no good and evil. So unconscious for Zaehner means irrationality; this implies both good and evil existing in a dialectical relationship, conflicting with one another but not judging. Good and Evil exist in a rather flat world where there are no peaks to point out the depressions. Zaehner recognizes a gap between the experience of natural mysticism and that of diabolic mysticism. In the latter one is not in union with God or with nature, but with something he calls the collective unconscious. Zaehner explains that his "collective unconscious" is the same as the cosmic consciousness spoken of by Bucke. But the flaw in Zaehner's argumentation here is that he slips into the language of the healer, and mixes up his methods too much. He is an historian of religions who moves over into theology when necessary. To move further into the healing arts is to confuse and weaken his argument. I do not take as seriously what he says about the collective unconscious being the best explanation of what is going on in Nature Mysticism, but offer it as the direction in which part of Zaehner's thought is moving. What is important in this part of Zaehner's argument is that it is a description of what is happening-and he has said that his method is to describe, at its best[67] -and not an explanation. What he described is an uprush of the contents of man's inner life.

---

[67]Zaehner, C/D, p. 10.

He calls it collective unconscious. That may be unfortunate since it is a technical term for Jungian psychology. But his description is of value since what appears is the ambivalence of one's nature-good and evil, male and female, commingling and converting into one another. In saying that it is a revelation of one's pre-biological unity--which is Buber's explanation of his own experience[68]--Zaehner is giving an explanation of it which seems useful for an historian of religion. In its expansive, non-terror phase, which is to say in its healthy manifestation, Nature Mysticism is a happy intuition of one's closeness to matter. To go further would be to impose explanations which the argument, thus far, does not warrant.

(B) The Rest of the Argument Concerning
      Nature Mysticism

Thus far Zaehner seems to have demolished Huxley's claim to have had either a Christian or Hindu mystical experience. It is one called Nature Mysticism. More data, however, is needed to fill out the rest of what I see in Zaehner's concept of Nature Mysticism.

Perhaps, among all the nature mystics he treated, Zaehner had the deepest affection for the Englishman, Richard Jefferies. Jefferies had broken with all religious institutions and with any notion of a personal God. He could brook no God handing out rewards and punishments. His experiences, ecstatic though they were, did not blind him to the savagery of human existence, something which would haunt Zaehner so much that he would publish his last book, a brilliant, meandering, repetitive and depressingly sad book

---

[68]Between Man and Man, op. cit., pp. 24 f.

called <u>Our Savage God</u>, about just such savagery in man's condition. For Jefferies, Providence was an insult to man's intelligence; he was an atheist, and his ecstasies have no room in them for any God. But the very Nature which produced such euphoria in him in his contemplation of earth, sun, sea and trees is quite different to him. Moreover, Nature is not only indifferent to man, it is hostile to him; this, even though his experiences almost identified him with sun, sea,...etc. Yet, even though this be so, Nature could produce in him a state of timelessness in which subject and object became one, and in which Nature was experienced as being animated by a subtle force. Finally, he is not only timeless, but he contains within him all space and its contents.[69]

What Jefferies adds to my argument is that: i) his experiences happened spontaneously; ii) they were not experiences of any God at all; iii) instead they were experiences of Nature; iv) and both subject and object are one; v) he became timeless; vi) and experienced nature (matter) as being alive; vii) lastly, his experience was an expansion of the ego to include all things.

Zaehner's explanation of the life—force animating Nature was to call it by the Hindu name <u>prāna</u> (Skt.=breath, life force, vital force).[70] This seems a useless exercise since it is looking for union in religions before one has put the pieces of his pattern together. He is getting ahead of himself in this, and his argument suffered thereby.

---

[69]Zaehner, S/P, <u>apud</u> Jefferies' <u>The Story of My Heart</u>, London, 1912, pp. 43-45, 81-82.

[70]Zaehner, <u>op. cit.</u>, p. 49.

Next, Zaehner turns to Proust to develop his argument. Marcel Proust (1871-1922) was a French man of letters whose analytical and psychological novels of French manners are filled with strange and impressive characters. His health failing, he retired to write, with striking memory for details, about his times in the salons of France, whose darling he was, in search of a means of evoking those good old times in the face of a protracted and vicious neurosis which forced him to his bed. He wishes to overcome the ravages of time by writing these novels (hence the title of one of them, À la récherche du temps perdu (in fifteen parts or volumes). His life became a quest to overcome time, to see beyond the transitory and frivolous to the permanent.

In the face of mortality Proust details one of his experiences of Nature Mysticism in his Du Coté de chez Swann. Zaehner sees the description of Proust's mental state and subsequent mystical experience as Proust's life in miniature. The author had returned to his house after taking a walk. He was tired and dejected. His mother offered him some cakes upon his return. In a state of boredom and depression he began to take tea and eat the Petites Madeleines. He says, outlining the mystical experience which ensued:

> But at the very moment when the mouthful
> mixed with the crumbs of the cake touched
> my palate, I shuddered, as I took note
> of the strange things that were going on
> inside me. An exquisite pleasure had
> invaded me, -isolated, with no idea of
> what its cause might be. Immediately
> it had made the vicissitudes of life in-
> different, its disasters inoffensive,
> its brevity illusory, -in much the same
> way as love operates, filling me with
> a precious essence: or rather this
> essence was not in me (author's emphasis).
> I had ceased to feel mediocre, contingent,
> or mortal. Whence should this strong joy

114

have come to me? I felt that it was connected with the taste of the tea and the
cake, but that it transcended it infinitely
and could not be of the same nature.
Whence did it come? What did it mean?
How to lay hold of it?[71]

It is interesting to note that Zaehner assess-
es this experience, and the rest of like experiences which Proust had, as akin to what is called
satori in Zen. Satori is a complete integration
of the personality and total unification of the
faculties of soul and mind. It comes to one whose
mind is emptied and readied for the experience by
a course of asceticism sedulously followed for a
long period of time. Then, even little things can
set off the experience; which experience is, when
healthy, always joyful, a direct intuition of one's
immortality--the exact opposite of the transitory.[72]
Proust's experiences freed and liberated him of
his longstanding neurosis. Time had melted, and
death became meaningless.[73]

The integration of his personality is a rather
interesting variant of Nature Mysticism, which
usually takes a direction of expansion of the ego
to become the All. Here, however, we do not see
any expansion but a gathering of his powers
causing in them, and in him, a wholeness, a healing. This is a fact retailed to us at length and
with tremendous attention to detail in Proust's
very long novel series. He was healthy again
and had found something of eternity. The health
was permanent, but the intuitions and enjoyments
of eternity transitory, but sufficient to go on
for a long time. These experiences are not

_____

[71]Ibid., p. 53, apud Proust's work, Vol. i,
pp. 872-3.

[72]Ibid., pp. 54 f.

[73]Ibid., p. 57.

extraordinary, or restricted to the gifted, but when they happen they are of extraordinary power.[74] So, if the other nature mystics found the experience euphoric, Proust found it curative as well. They expanded, but he pulled into a tight bundle, which smallness meant health for him. In becoming compressed, Proust's experience is very much like the Isolation Mysticism I shall treat in the next chapter. There, one pulls into a small bundle, as well, in order to be able to enjoy immortality for long periods of time. But Proust's and this state are only look-alikes. Proust's state was integrative of all his powers, but Isolation is divisive--it pulls matter from spirit and time from space in order to be only spirit enjoying the Self. Proust's experience encompassed both body and spirit. This is its difference from what Zaehner calls Isolation Mysticism. It is a pity he does not inform us of this, since it is quite important and, lacking this information, very confusing.

It is noteworthy that Proust did not fall into the trap so many nature mystics fall prey to in interpreting their experience in a pantheistic way. Proust was a very analytical person who knew Catholic theology and practice quite well, yet not only did he not explain his experience pantheistically, as did so many others, but he did not even explain it in terms of God. There was no God in any of Proust's healing experiences which we call Nature Mysticism.

---

[74]I had such an intuition of immortality while studying Islam at Oxford. One afternoon, while studying Muslim theology, I looked up from my desk to be subject to an overwhelming feeling and intuition of not only my immortality, but, in fact, of being an immortality. My ego was replaced by another, deeper, person, who was me, but was not patient of my everyday knowledge and experience.

116

Proust's statement that another self emerged from the experience is of the utmost importance here, since it is one of the key distinctions to be made in Nature Mysticism, and in mysticism generally. In Proust Zaehner saw that there were two selves: one is the workaday one, the one men normally see as the only self. It may be called the empirical, transitory self. But the second self is the real one, seemingly dead, but brought to life in such ecstasy situations. Proust found this second self within him, and saw him as a stranger to him, though at the same time, himself. The second self partook of an environment beyond space and time, though still in it; which partook of eternity though it was not identical with it. This, Zaehner says, is the status of angels, according to St. Thomas. It is what Thomas called aevum, or aevaeternity.

So Proust did not experience an enlargement of the personality which caused him to merge into Nature; he felt a contraction which was healing. His was not an experience of God or of gods in any form. He went beyond time to experience, beyond the empirical self, the true Self.

Zaehner, next, turns to Rimbaud for assistance. Arthur Rimbaud (1845-1891) was a teenage prodigy of French poetry. He began to write when he was ten, and some of his best writing was done when he was fifteen. His experiences of ecstasy were the enthusiasms of Nature Mysticism. They advance our argument since they indicate that: i) one can induce such states; ii) that there is nothing of God in them even when God language is used; iii) another person, the Self, emerges united with Nature, and which is both one's personal soul and seems to be universal, or collective as well; iv) it seems to be the mysticism of the early Upaniṣads (the Nature Mysticism of the Vedānta); v) it is capable of being corrupted into what can be called Devil's mysticism, and vi) true Christian mysticism is attended by prayer and a desire for penance.

117

Rimbaud's Nature Mysticism, therefore, seems
to be more complicated than anything we have yet
encountered. As a very young man he thought to
storm heaven by descending through hell. This, he
thought, would produce a psychosis and open him,
ultimately, to the joys of heaven. So, he induced
a psychosis as a kind of ascetical-mystical technique, much like Shamans do, and very like the
techniques of Ṣūfism as well. His temporary madness could and did induce what we can call a preternatural experience and state; but, unhappily,
the view of God which he so earnestly sought, without benefit of God's grace, never came.

His desire was to dissolve into what he called
the universal mind, which appeared to be a level of
mind which is both personal, since it is connected
with him, but trans-personal, or universal as well.
It is like what Huxley called Mind at Large, and
something like Jung's collective unconscious.
When Rimbaud achieved this universal mind, or the
experience of it, he was no longer himself but
someone else: he appeared to be the Self, spoken
of by Proust. His mysticism is a function of his
esthetics, his poetics. For him the function of
the poet and the seer are identical. He said,
"I say that we must be seers, we must make ourselves seers;" and what he seems to have been
driving at is that the true function of the seer
was to find the true Self beyond the empirical
self, what he calls "...the real self dormant
below the busy ego."[75] Zaehner's statement that
this is the function of all Indian spirituality
seems appropriate since they too are in search of
the timeless ātman at the base of the ephemeral
ego, the Self beyond the ego; and they too see
the function of life to be in induction of those
states which produce not only the experience of
the Self, but its perduring presence on the

---

[75]Zaehner, S/P, p. 57, apud Rimbaud's
Oeuvres Completes, p. 270.

118

conscious level.[76]

When Rimbaud attains the level of universal mind the ideas of that mind flow forth naturally. He means by this that these ideas are identical with Nature, but that even though man functions by these ideas, none has collected them fully. He says,

> People acted by it, wrote books from it: that is how things went on, man not working upon himself, not having yet woken up, or not being yet in the fullness of the great dream. Civil servants, writers! Author, creator, poet, -such a man has never existed.[77]

Zaehner states that this level put Rimbaud on the level of what Hindus call the ātman, which is the level of the Brahman, once ātman (Self) has been experienced directly. The Brahman is the universal principle which Rimbaud seems to be talking about, and Rimbaud's "great dream" is the Hindu concept of māyā (=illusion, Skt.), and that the "other self" is ātman in Hinduism.[78] So there seems to be a connection between what Zaehner calls Nature Mysticism and a religious state in Vedānta, produced (induced) by the classic Indian ascetical technique Yoga.

Rimbaud's technique for inducing his mystical states was based on his idea of Nature: that all things and everybody develop naturally back to Nature. In this he looks to Zaehner like

---

[76]Zaehner, S/P, pp. 63 f.

[77]Ibid., apud Enid Starkie's Arthur Rimbaud, rev. ed., London, 1974, p. 253.

[78]Zaehner, op. cit., p. 65.

Rousseau,[79] and to me like Indian Nature Mysticism which seems an end to time and a return to a state of unity we had before we were born. This is a state in which each person participates in a communal form of life in which his personal ego is united with that of the group, and whose ideas share those of the group. It is a level in which life is more important than the individual and the tribe more valuable than any of its members. It is what Lévy-Bruhl called participation mystique,[80] a rubric which Zaehner would use to great advantage when explaining just how Nature Mysticism works out among the religions. For my purposes here this concept of universal mind is important since it is the level of consciousness to which those in Hinduism, Buddhism, Taoism, Zen and those in the West who experienced it have arrived via a variety of routes. It seems that the experience of it means that one has experienced matter thinking. I shall elaborate on this in my conclusion, at the end of this chapter.

Rimbaud jettisons any theory of asceticism, such as the slow discipline of the Christian monk, or the Hindu yogi. He abandons discipline for maximum disorder of the senses; this, to find the other self. Once it is found, one must obey it; it is below (beyond) good and evil. The universal mind, in Zaehner's estimation, is the materialist's mind, not the God of the Christians, as some claim, and as Rimbaud himself claimed initially. It is the absolute material base like the early Hindu Brahman, which the Hindus saw as food to be eaten, and breath to be breathed. Union came through the dissolution of the conscious personality and flight to the unconscious.[81]

---

[79]Ibid.

[80]Zaehner, S/T, p. 76.

[81]Zaehner, S/P, p. 65.

120

Rimbaud thought of himself as Nature, and his energies were to get back, through poetry and madness, to Nature. He says, "O Nature! O ma mère," in one of his letters. Having reached nature, which it was in his power to do--through poetry and by inducing madness--he thought that he reached a state of omnipotence like a god.[82]

This is a trap into which many nature mystics fall. They believe themselves to be God or a god. Zaehner points this out by saying, "Theistic (and dualistic) mystics have always abhorred this doctrine..."[83] He quotes the mystical doctor of Islam, Ghazālī, to the effect that love of the world and love of God are always mutually exclusive.[84] So, it seems that the way cut is to make a distinction between two types of mysticism here: the one is a mysticism of God, which produces good fruit in one's life; and the other is a mysticism of the devil, which produces an evil life. Zaehner does just this, and goes on to quote the author of the Cloud of Unknowing to the effect that, "...for I tell thee truly, that the devil hath his contemplatives as God hath his."[85]

Is Rimbaud's a mysticism of God or of the devil? Zaehner answers that it is of the latter. Rimbaud's technique for getting beyond the self to the Self was by the "derangement of all the senses. Every possible form of love, suffering, and madness; he searches for himself, exhausts all

---

[82]Zaehner, S/P, p. 66.

[83]Ibid.

[84]Ibid., apud Ghazālī's Kīmiyā-yi Sa'ādat, Tehran, 1319 A. H. (solar), vol. ii, p. 617.

[85]Ibid., p. 67, apud Cloud..., London, 1952, p. 63.

the poisons within himself, keeping only their quintessences. Indescribable torture in which he needs all faith, all superhuman strength, in which he becomes, above all others, the great invalid, the great criminal, the greatest among the damned--and the highest Sage! For he reached the unknown! and even though, in his madness, he should lose the understanding of his visions, he will have seen them."[86] Zaehner sees this as devil's contemplation, and, again quoting the Cloud of Unknowing, he says, "the true mystic, 'desireth not to un-be' for that were devil's madness and despite unto God."[87] I should add a further distinction to all this. Seeking God is, obviously, a theistic (sometimes polytheistic) enterprise. Seeking the self, however, can some-times be good, when one does not say that one is seeking God, but knowingly and willingly sets out to court the Self. Such is quintessential Indian spirituality--which produces good fruits in its following. Yoga seeks the Self and its enjoyment in Bliss (nirvāṇa). So this is not diabolic. When, however, one sets out to seek God, and really only wants the Self--the transcendent, im-mortal aspect of man--it can frequently result in what Ghazālī, Christian and Indian mystics see as diabolic.

This leads me to my next point about Rimbaud. He sought not only mysticism; he sought it to get to God himself, whether God wanted this or not. He sought not the God of Nature, but the God of his first communion.[88] He tried the shortcut to God through the putrefaction of every type of

---

[86]Ibid., p. 64, apud Rimbaud, op. cit., p. 270.

[87]Zaehner, S/P, p. 67, apud the Cloud..., op. cit., p. 61.

[88]Ibid., p. 68

perversion and the use of alchemy.[89] What he
achieved was true ecstasy; but he never did
achieve union with God, nor did he claim to have
achieved such. His ecstasy "oned" his personality with Nature, dissolved the ego in it,
expanded his personality and, thus, plunged the
ego beyond the good and evil into the "other."
He called this experience, later, a lie.[90] His
"other" was the second person, the Self, we have
spoken of. He never, however, achieved peace
through the attainment of this ecstasy. What
Zaehner calls perversion in Rimbaud's life was a
way to ecstasy paved with absinthe, drugs and
homosexuality.[91]

But what did Rimbaud contact in his experiences of lunacy and ecstasy--which lunacy seems to
be the manic phase of the manic-depressive psychosis? Zaehner called it "...an overwhelming unconscious content and a psychological reality.
Rimbaud had been seeking the 'God of Abraham,
Isaac, and Jacob,' what he found was a wildly
irrational joy that dissolved his ego in a flash
of lunatic exultation in which God had no part."[92]
What I can take from Zaehner, therefore, are two
points: i) there is no God there; ii) and it was
a level of the soul which is unconscious, a level
which is overwhelmingly powerful and full of joy
and wildness. Zaehner merely points this out.
It might be desirable to define these experiences
and their relations to the religions further, but
that is precisely what the religions themselves

---

[89]Ibid., apud Starkie, op. cit., pp. 124-37.

[90]Ibid., p. 68.

[91]Ibid., p. 68.

[92]Zaehner, S/P, p. 68.

123

cannot do. Zaehner's Nature Mysticism seems to be at the intersection point of the theisms of the West and the theisms and other spiritualities of the East. The question of their definition and interrelatedness is the question, and not the question I face in this essay. What I am doing here is pointing out that Huxley et al. are wrong; theirs is not a theistic experience but one of Nature Mysticism. Further there are two other mysticisms called Isolation and the Mysticism of Love, and these are different the one from the other, too. The point-by-point development of this argument is my job in this book. As a counterpoint I shall indicate a few of the problems which this systematics of mysticisms raises, such as the fact, here stated, that lunacy, Nature Mysticism and the Yogas of the East meet in their ecstasies, and to merely indicate for the reader possible explanations in aiding one to see which are wholesome (orthodox) and which are unwholesome experiences.

When Rimbaud rejected his experience as being one of God, and called it a lie, Zaehner says that he is being too hard on himself, for there is a real experience there. Zaehner points out the fact that Rimbaud was wildly happy in his episodes of lunacy-mysticism. Rimbaud said, "I wait on God like a glutton," but he never found him.[93]

There are two last points about Rimbaud which further our argument. First, though he was gluttonously awaiting God, he had a conversion of sorts. He calls it a conversion of "sorts" because it was not a free one, but was forced. In the novel in which he details all his ecstasies, Saison en Enfer, he calls this conversion "Fausse Conversion." He began with feelings of

---

[93]Zaehner, S/P, p. 68, apud Rimbaud, Oeuvres Completes, cit. supra, p. 236.

revolt against God, and then flipped over feeling that all his sins had been forgiven. Zaehner's point here is interesting to note since it throws into relief the relation of the manic-depressive psychosis and Nature Mysticism. He says that this feeling of freedom from sins is "so characteristic of the manic-depressive psychosis that it would be rash to assume that anything of the sort has happened unless, of course, we are prepared to admit that acute mania and mescalin experiences are also direct divine interventions."[94] So, from feelings of deep self-hatred in which he said, "I succeeded in extinguishing all human hope in my spirit. Like a wild beast I pounced blindly upon every joy that I might throttle it.'[95] The poet says that this flip, or conversion, was false, that there was nothing of God in it. I conclude that it was manic; and indicate that there seems to be a link between mania and Nature Mysticism--a link which Custance's experience will reinforce when I take him up next.

What is ever more important in seeing the difference between Nature Mysticism--for that is what Rimbaud experienced--the lunacy should not detract from the nature of the experience, which shares all the notes of Nature Mysticism: namely, expansion of the ego, timelessness, being one with the All, a lack of God in the experience and a feeling of intense joy--and the other mysticisms I will outline in the rest of this essay is Rimbaud's rule of thumb for discerning the difference between Christian and Nature Mysticism--wholesome or diabolic. He says that Christian mysticism leads one to prayer and peace, but that he had neither of these in his experiences. Hence, he

---

[94]Ibid., p. 73.

[95]Ibid., p. 70, apud Rimbaud, op. cit., pp. 220 f.

125

concluded that his were other than Christian experiences. I add to these two the concept of Schuon, which I alluded to above, that there is no penance there either. What I am saying, is what Zaehner affirmed, that Nature Mysticism is the experience of the <u>philosophia perennis</u>. The <u>philosophia</u> places a metaphysical construct on it, but the experience is the same.

Even though God is mentioned <u>nominatim</u> by Rimbaud, Zaehner says that "What...is entirely lacking is any direct apperception of the divine presence; and from the theistic point of view... this is what marks off that form of mysticism which results or is alleged to result in union of the human soul with God, from all others. For Rimbaud 'divine love' is still an abstraction, something suggested by '<u>le chant raisonnable des anges</u>' it is not an intense personal relationship."[96] There was nothing personal between God and Rimbaud in the experience. All he spoke of were abstractions and notions, not devotion and love. When Rimbaud used Christian symbols and quotes the usages of the Church as his by faith we should not let that keep our eyes off precisely what he is saying. Rimbaud had a Catholic youth, and died a Catholic--after a life spent in what is euphemistically termed "European mercantile ventures"--which meant that he engaged in the Arab slave trade in Africa and the Near East, his poetry being finished before he was hardly out of his teens--we can say that what his experiences denote is not Christian mysticism but that which Zaehner calls Nature Mysticism.

So Rimbaud adds to the argument: i) that lunacy is akin to Nature Mysticism, i.e., the manic phase of lunacy; ii) that there is nothing of God there, even though He be referred to, because there is no desire to pray and no peace

---

[96]Zaehner, S/P, p. 74.

present; iii) that there is a divine contemplation and a diabolic one--the latter being a form
of self-hatred in which one wishes to get rid of
the self; iv) that the Vedanta mysticisms contain
one which is Nature Mysticism, i.e., I shall later
maintain that this mysticism is not religious per
se, but can be used by religion; v) that Nature
Mysticism is in touch with the Self beyond the
empirical ego, which is the nature of Yoga, the
technique of Vedanta and of all Indian spiritualities.

Zaehner's interpretation of this experience of
Rimbaud's is extremely interesting and important
for my argument. Rimbaud's euphoria was one of a
returned innocence in which one was at one with
his Self. Secondly, one can induce it by oneself.
Thirdly, Zaehner says that it is the Limbo spoken
of by Catholic theology. It is a post-lapsarian
Eden. I agree with Zaehner, but only up to a
point. I agree with him that Rimbaud found the
ecstasy of Limbo.[97] But Zaehner did not say that
he found the peace expected there, albeit a peace
without God. Zaehner is guilty of a flagrant con-
tradiction in this, but it is not enough to
destroy his point: one can induce a state of
ecstatic mysticism. This is in line with his
point about Indian spirituality, to which I shall
return in the next chapter on Isolation Mysticism,
echoed by Ruysbroeck in his work against the
Beghards, that, if one knows the technique, one
can by oneself attain the emptiness of peace.[98]
If one accepts what Zaehner says--that Limbo was
the hell Christ went to after his Crucifixion--then
one may save Zaehner's point. But it does not
seem necessary. He has made a valid point in the
fact that one can induce the state. His interpretation is self-contradictory, but that does not

---

[97]Zaehner, S/P, p. 81.

[98]Ibid., pp. 170-72.

derogate from his main point that one can induce
it and that it is not of God.

The manic experiences of John Custance add
some useful notes to our concept of Nature Mysticism. While in his manic states, which lasted not
for days but for months at a time, Custance
believed himself endowed with the attributes of
God. He believed that one carried a deity in oneself and that he got in touch with this deity during his ecstasies. So he became the Sun, the
energy-life-force of the world, its elan vital,...
etc. All that God endows the world with, Custance
became.[99] When Custance is soaring with ecstasy
he feels that he is a god, but when the mania
passes, and sanity once more prevails, he no longer
feels endowed with immortality, bi-sexuality and
all things past, present and to come.[100] Custance
is aware of the dilemma: that mania and mystic
states share a kinship. What seems to happen here,
and Zaehner keeps reminding us of this--one would
think to restore order in the lushness of detail to
be found in his books--is that one keeps mistaking
one's soul, and the direct experience of it, either
in mania (the sick form of Nature Mysticism) or in
healthy Nature Mysticism, as in Jefferies' case,
for God.

Custance's experience bears a striking resemblance to that of the Rāja-yoga school of Hinduism.
Like the yogins, Custance felt a tingle in his
lower spine. Zaehner points out that this is precisely where the experience begins in Kundalini
yoga. Custance had a distinctive warmth in the
solar-plexus before the experience began. This is

---

[99]Zaehner, S/P, p. 91, apud Custance's Wisdom,
Madness and Folly: The Philosophy of a Lunatic,
London, 1951, p. 37.

[100]Zaehner, S/P, p. 92, apud Custance,
op. cit., p. 37.

to be found in yoga, too. The rāja-yogins believe
that there is a power coiled at the base of the
spine which the yoga technique awakens. As it
awakens it rises up the spine; as it does it
alters consciousness and endows the yogin with
the powers latent in him and affords him visions
and bliss. When this power reaches the brain it
detaches the yogin from mind and body; the soul is
freed.[101] The conclusion here is that kundalini-
yoga is a method for inducing trance states which
I would call acute mania. It is the same experience which Custance had, though the latter's
happened spontaneously and through morbidity.[102]
I shall outline just what the purpose of Yoga is
in the next chapter, which is on Isolation Mysticism. But, for now, suffice it to say that Yoga
is more than a method for inducing states which
include manic phases. It may be used to induce a
selfish mania here in the West, but yogins have no
such self-centered motives on Hinduism's highest
level. What it looks like to Zaehner is that the
yogins practices yoga to release their pent-up
libido, or psychic energy, and that this resulted
in expansion. So, Custance's mania locked divine,
but it is a state of morbidity in which the elements of Nature Mysticism are present. It is
Nature Mysticism gone haywire. Custance's god and
Nature are identical, and Zaehner is quick to see
pantheism here. I agree. While in this state
Custance's ego dissolved and he became many
beings; e.g., ancestors, gods, devils, his friends
become himself...etc. This goes beyond good and
evil; beyond time and death, heavan and hell uniting in the springs of the soul. The pattern of

---

[101]Ibid., p. 97, taken from Vivekanands's
Rāja-yoga or Conquering the Internal Nature,
Advaita Ashrama, Almore, 1951, p. 57.

[102]Zaehner, op. cit., p. 97.

Nature Mysticism is firm; so firm that even a morbid state corroborates the elements found in its healthier manifestations.[103]

Here it is time to introduce one of the central distinctions to be made in Nature Mysticism. Islam will help us out here. Zaehner goes to the mystical writer Qushayrī for our information. In Islam there are two key virtues: hope (Arab.=raja) and fear (Arab.=khawf). These are the paramount virtues in Ṣūfism. To these states correspond the two chief states of Nature Mysticism: namely, expansion (Arab.=basṭ) and contraction (Arab.=qabḍ). It looks like basṭ accurately describes the expansion phase of Nature Mysticism. What qabḍ describes is depression. Qabḍ (contraction) is the utter abandonment "to oneself in oneself." The contraction side looks very much like what Custance described when in the "down" phase of his illness and what William James describes in his chapter on the sick soul. In it the constricted soul is overwhelmed by a sense of sin; in fact, the soul is utterly alone during the state of constriction. His only companion is his sin. Custance said that he felt only disgust for his body and for himself. He was in pain and suffered from fear. Expansion, on the contrary, takes delight in the body. It is filled with a magic, man-like power. Constriction, for Qushayrī, Custance and James leaves one completely alone, depressed in his sin, in a feeling of self-loathing. St. Teresa of Avila, when writing about her own sense of sin, however, said that her very sinfulness called out to her of the mercy of God. She was not depressed in her sin, instead she was aware of love and salvation in it.

Zaehner draws the conclusion that contraction is the depressed side of schizophrenia-of the

---

[103]Ibid., p. 92.

manic-depressive psychosis.[104] He went beyond
his brief in doing this. What contraction is is
the down side of Nature Mysticism, and it looks
like the down side of the psychosis.

If fear and hope are concerned with future
things in Islam, and in the rest of the Western
religions, expansion and contraction concern themselves with the present. Qushayrī says that contraction corresponds to the fear found in beginners in the mystical life; and expansion is the
state of the hopeful at the same stage. Contraction comes to those obsessed by damnation.
Expansion follows upon learning something favor-
able or welcome.

Qushayrī even lays down rules of conduct for
those experiencing these polar feelings. When one
experiences contraction he should not struggle
since exertion only increases the morbidity. One
should do nothing when in that state; i.e., nothing
to overcome it. Submission to the state allows it
to pass. When in a state of expansion one should
keep quiet and observe the rules of good manners.
The movements will dictate that one should give
vent to wild enthusiasms but the canons of good
breeding should hold one down and quieten them.[105]
Qushayrī seems to call these phenomena by our
terms for them: namely, mania and depression.
What Zaehner concludes is that expansion is mania
and depression is contraction. What seems to be
more proper from the evidence is that expansion
is, as Zaehner rightly concludes Nature Mysticism;
but contraction is the diabolic mysticism he
spoke of before, which looks like depression. He
seems to have proved his case for diabolic mysticism, but he is walking on thin ice when he
speaks of modern psychology.

---

[104]Zaehner, S/P, p. 94.

[105]Zaehner, S/P, p. 86.

131

Qushayrī and Zaehner both say something important and useful for my argument. It is that both
Christian and Muslim mystics see expansion as a
trap, since the devil can counterfeit such states.
The Muslim says that God sets the trap, since he
wished to test the wayfarer. The danger is
greater in the beginner since expansion, which is
purely a natural (and I might add, ungraced, or,
more barbarically, an "ungodded" state) phenomenon can easily be mistaken in the beginner for
progress. Contraction possesses no such charms for
anyone, beginner or adept.[106]

What all this means to my argument is that
expansion is a Nature Mysticism, or a manifestation of it. Contraction is a recognized phenomenon, which can be a natural morbid state, or the
diabolic side of Nature Mysticism--the terrors and
spirit-crushing nature of this side of Nature
Mysticism is easy to discern, but the diabolic
nature of some expansions is very difficult to
discern. They are good if they lead to good, and
evil if they lead to evil. The expansion side
always leads one towards being above law, but this
is not evil in se. What is the tipoff is whether
one begins to lead an evil life over the long haul
of things. Huxley gives us a key to the "exalted"
nature of diabolic mysticism when he says that the
expansion side which leads to evil is a "downward
transcendence."[107]

So it seems that Nature Mysticism is a
phenomenon recognized, in its mechanics, by others
than Zaehner. The name is not the same, but the
thoughts add up to what Zaehner has been talking
about. Now, I must pull my argument together and
summarize Nature Mysticism and draw my conclusions

---

[106]Ibid., p. 87, apud Qushayrī's Risāla,
pp. 32-33.

[107]Ibid., p. 140.

about it and plot the course for the next
chapter dealing with Isolation Mysticism.

(C)   Summary on Nature Mysticism

What I have done thus far is introduce the
problem which exercised Zaehner, namely Huxley's
assertion that his was the same experience as
that had in Hinduism and Christian mysticism.
What I have shown is that it was a true preternatural experience because it threw him out of
the bounds which we call normal existence-expansion
of ego, dissolution of space/time continuum, feeling of immortality...etc.-and that it appears to
be an experience of pan-en-henism. Hence it is
not a Christian experience at all, for there is
no God involved at all, let alone union with him
through His grace. Huxley's argument was that
one could induce the Christian experience through
drugs. This has been shown not to be so. Something can be, and was, induced by drugs, but it
is not a loving union with the Christian Trinity.
Hence, thus far Huxley is wrong. His experience
is not Christian.

In the next chapter, in which I outline Isolation Mysticism, composed of Sāṁkhya-Yoga,
Advaita and Theravada and Mahāyāna Buddhism, as
well as Taoism and Zen, I shall demonstrate that
Huxley's experience was not any of these either.
It was an experience of Nature Mysticism. I
have demonstrated this. The fourth chapter shall
also cap the argument by nailing down just what
the differences between Huxley's and a Christian
experience are, and how a Christian experience is
different from Isolation. So, in doing-in
Huxley I refute his philosophia perennis by proving that the mysticisms are radically, philosophically and psychologically different.

Just what, then, is Nature Mysticism? It
appears to be: i) a preternatural experience in
which, ii) the ego is expanded to identify with
all things, iii) and thus to unite itself with
its objects, iv) in a way which carries it beyond

133

space and time, v) beyond good and evil, vi) where personal immortality is assured, vii) and where no God is necessarily involved, viii) thus making it a mystical experience, but not necessarily a religious one at all, ix) in which one is aware of his intimacy with his environment, or, put another way, in which one's material side becomes aware of itself.

(i) The most obvious thing about Nature Mysticism is that it is an experience, but what kind? It seems, without doubt, to be one beyond the ordinary, beyond the normal, natural happenings of our workaday existence. It is for this reason that we must look for a descriptive word which means beyond the ordinary or natural. Since it is not an experience of divine origin, which is to say that it is ungraced by nature (not that it cannot be graced per accidens, as it seems to be in the Vedānta of the early Upaniṣads, which are a Nature Mysticism), I have settled on the word preternatural.

It is an experience which may be momentary, as in the case of Proust and Zaehner's youthful experiences, or of quite long duration, as in the case of Custance. Further, it is not an illusion of the poetic or arty since it appears to be a universal phenomenon which is irrefutably powerful to those who have had it. It is just too powerful, therefore, to deny its existence.

(ii) Secondly, it is an experience in which the ego is expanded to include all things, or put another way, in which the ego becomes the All. This phase of the phenomenon is euphoric, joyful. One comes to know not only all things in terms of immediacy and intimacy, but one becomes All things. Such expansion is called bast by Muslims who affirm the existence of this movement to become All. The danger here is that a beginner will not only mistake this movement for spiritual progress, but he tends to mistake himself for God. Becoming the All is an overpowering experience in which, as

Buber said, one must be careful to know the difference between the self and God.

The other movement, which vectors off in a countervailing and frightening direction, tends towards complete self-loathing and isolation from all things in one's sin. Muslims call this phase qabd which means contraction, a word which aptly describes what psychologists mean by depression.

Thus, it appears that not only are we dealing with a form of mystical experience, but it is one which looks very much like the two phases of that psychosis called manic-depressive. Custance's enthusiasms are only a small indication of the wealth of material which can be adduced to further substantiate this. I only mean, here, to indicate that there is a relationship here between psychosis and Nature Mysticism, a relationship which may only be a similarity, but which appears stronger than that. What may be worth further investigation is the fact that this expansion seems to free the contents of a very deep level of man's psyche, which contents manifest a commonality with those of other men. They seem, in fact, to be transpersonal, or beyond personality, and more like a race consciousness, if one permits such a barbarism. What seems factual here is that we are in contact with something both deep and communal. That part, at least, is verifiable and useful to both historian of religions and theologian as they sift through the data here presented to give its equivalency (history of religions) and its literal meaning (theology). Equivalently, the contents of these enthusiasms seem to be like those to be seen in the manic phase of psychosis. Literally they seem to be the seminal things in man's psyche spoken of by such theologians as St. Augustine. What is useful to our argument about Nature Mysticism is that they reveal a subliminal unity of men and things, a unity which transcends personality. More than that is too conjectural.

135

(iii) Since mysticism is, by definition, a unitive experience, what we have here has fulfilled that condition admirably. It is a unity of man with all things, not just with himself. In fact the unity we detected was with things beyond man. Only per accidens, in the case of Proust, do we see what can be called a psychological healing, or integration of man's powers with himself, or of ego with the transcendental Self. Zaehner made too much of the healing side of this phenomenon, so promising was it. There may be some connection between mystical technique and psychotherapy, as David C. McLelland and David Bakan have pointed out elsewhere.[108] What has been demonstrated is that this experience can heal as well. But what is important for my argument is that Nature Mysticism exists and that its essentials are well attested. Proust's integrative experience was healing, for sure, but what is more, it was an experience of what we call Nature Mysticism. Such mysticism is different from religious mysticism.

Identity with the All can either be pantheistic or pan-en-henic. A rule of thumb which allows one to discern which is which is this: if I am the All, one is dealing with Nature Mysticism; if there is only the All and I am That All (Skt.= tat tvam asi-That thou art), then one is dealing with monism. This is a critical difference, as we shall see in the next chapter on Isolation Mysticism, which mysticism includes a monist side. So "I am the All" means that I am one with Nature. The ego is united with the object in Nature Mysticism, but not identified with it.

---

[108]McLelland, in his The Roots of Consciousness, Princeton, N.J., 1964, the chapter entitled "Psychoanalysis and Religious Mysticism," p. 121, in which he mentions the extensive work done on this matter by David Bakan in his Sigmund Freud and the Jewish Mystical Tradition, Princeton, Van Nostrand, 1958.

Monism means that the transcendental Self--which
is the immortal aspect of man, far beyond the
empirical ego--is identified with the object so
that what one sees is an illusion. What one sees
is the Self. Monism is a philosophical intrusion
into the Nature Mystical experience which pushes
it further than a simple union of subject and object. Nature Mysticism is a psychological experience. The question here is, does Nature Mysticism
seem very close to Isolation Mysticism/Monism? My
answer is: Very close. The distinction will come
out in the next chapter. For now, I have established that Nature Mysticism is a unitive experience, which describes what happens, and does not
give it any philosophical standing or make any
metaphysical system to explain it. It is a very
primitive level of experience, albeit powerful, in
which one is "oned" with all things, and per
accidens, sometimes gathered with one's powers in
an inner healing. Such inner healing gives the
ego over to the higher Self, so there is less an
unio here than an integritas. It is less mystical
than curative. Mysticism, then, is, by definition,
union.

Such union can be quite restful because it
pulls one beyond the self in an emptiness spoken
of by Zen, Taoism, Hinduism and Buddhism. Ruysbroeck, the Flemish mystic, also spoke of such
rest as being on the way to Christian mysticism,
but only a beginning in which there is more self
and no God per se.

In pulling one away from the self to go out
and be united with the All there is union of subject and object. This is affirmed in experience
after experience. It can happen spontaneously
or be induced by a method such as yoga or by
drugs. But the effect is invariably the same.
One falls away to be replaced by a larger ego-
note I do not say Self, since that level comes
with Isolation Mysticism and religious mysticism.
Suffice it to say that Nature Mysticism deals
only with a unity on the ego level, which level

137

can, for all intents and purposes, be considered
as a material thing. Such material includes all
that we call mind, as well as body. It does not
include, however, the deepest level of man, which
is his immortal Self. So Nature Mysticism's
union is a material (in the atomized, undifferentiated, or larger sense of the word) union in
which man is intimate with his roots and environment.

(iv) and (v) Since this experience pulls
one beyond space and time it seems to thrust one
away from the necessity of good and evil. There
seems to be an inner dialectic working here in
which the ties to the space/time continuum having
been removed, one feels no need to think about the
consequences of one's acts. In Taoism, where there
is a dialectical process working with its yang/yin
principles of being, ultimately, the good becomes
evil and vice versa. This seems to be the root of
the diabolic possibilities of Nature Mysticism,
its corrupt manifestation. Rimbaud certainly had
what I would call Nature Mysticism; the fact that
he induced it by going to brief periods of madness
should not deter us from seeing that his unity
with earth, sun and stars, his feelings of being
one with the All, etc., were genuine Nature Mysticism. The medievals in the West recognized this
side of what we call diabolic Nature Mysticism in
the phenomenon. They called it diabolic possession. It was an expansion usually followed by a
crashing depression. They noticed, further, that
after the feelings of euphoria, there would be a
coalescence of the without and within of things-
what we are calling being united (subject with
object) with the All. And, lastly, close on the
heels of this experience is a blunting of one's
moral sense, or, what is worse, a distortion of
it. This they named possession, according to
Zaehner.[109] Hence what I am speaking of is

---

[109]Zaehner, S/P, p. 101.

nothing new. I am just giving it a new name and systematizing it for my uses against the philosophia perennis.

(vi) Death seems to be an impossibility to those who have intuited their immortality. Being beyond space and time thrusts one intc the area of immortality. It is merely one of the logical sequelae of being thrust out of the space/time continuum. One's normal links with this world are broken and what is left is existence without needing space--which gives one a feeling of omnipotence, since only God is everywhere--and being beyond time gives one the immediate perception of a reality we only knew by dint of discursive reascning or through the offices of our faith: namely, that we are immortal. This feeling is only momentary, ordinarily, but quite enough to last one indefinitely.

(vii) and (viii) There is no God involved necessarily in this experience. This is to say that it is not a theistic experience. The God of Abraham, Isaac and Jacob, the God of the Christians, the Allah of Islam and the high Gods of Hinduism, Viṣnu and Śiva, are simply not involved. There is no interrelation with anyone here at all, and this is the essence of theism. Even Islam comes to have God dealing with his creatures with love, in orthodox Ṣūfism. The other theisms, Christian, Jewish and Hindu, are replete with what Buber called the I-Thou relation in which God and man are commercing in mutual love and affection. Huxley said quite frankly that his wife, present at his mescalin session, meant nothing to him during this experience; in fact, none of our subjects presented in this chapter speaks of anything but the self. It is an experience of the self uniting with others, but not as equals. The ego is the starting point of the experience and its terminus. No other means anything to the ego in this experience, and a fortiori, no Other-God-either means anything to him or appears. When a god is mentioned it either proved ersatz, as in

139

the case of Rimbaud's false conversion, or it
seemed pantheistic, as with Custance. Pantheism is not a relationship of God with man or vice
versa. It bespeaks an identity, not a relation.
Hence, there is no God present in this experience
in the theist sense. If a god (pantheism) appears,
as it does in the early Upaniṣads, which are
experiences of Nature Mysticism, it is not God who
appears but man united with his environment calling
that a god, not the God. This is the inter-face
between Nature Mysticism and something religious.
Nature Mysticism per se is not religious because it
does not do anything religious.

Religion begins when man intentionally and
willingly attends to his fallen, alienated,
state. It is better to speak of an alienated
state here, rather than with a fallen state, since
the Fall is a Western myth. Religion seems to
begin when either God or man does something about
man's alienation. Semitic religion, as I have
said, has God making the first move towards man.
This is a theistic process pure and simple.
Indian religion, and I have included Hinduism,
Buddhism and, since they manifest a parallel pattern, Taoism and Zen, puts the emphasis on man
doing something about his sad estate in setting
out to do away with sadness by using its Yoga
technique which strips man of all relations,
which are the roots of sadness and woe. Such
religion ends with an immediate experience of
bliss (Skt.=ānanda) which can be called, likewise
nirvāṇa (Buddhism), śūnyatā (Buddhist "emptiness,"
Mahāyāna variety), and satori (Zen); the Taoist
emptiness is much like Buddhist, and may be
later influenced by it-since Buddhism came into
China with great effect.

Nature Mysticism involves none of this. It
is far too primitive to boast of any God or technique so eloquent in its results as is Yoga. It
is an end in itself, as thus far stated. It can
have a religious use, however. Then it is the
first step before the proper religious doings,

which begin when either God or man begins to
empty the ego bulging with selfishness (seen
pejoratively) or with the fullness of Nature
Mysticism. Nature Mysticism is, therefore, a
fullness of the ego; it is the best man can hope
for without religion. This seems to be the
reason why Zaehner called it Limbo, a place of
supernal happiness for man, but devoid of God.
This may not, on balance, be a bad way of putting it since Limbo is a place for the good but
religionless. At its best Nature Mysticism is
good, but religionless. It does not go further
than the ego euphorically in union with itself
and with all things in a happy conjunction which
carries it away from all human concerns such as
time (death) and place (responsibilities). At
its worst, it is a diabolic flagellation of the
ego by itself, and other side of the ego, self-
contraction (hatred) coming to the fore to take
command. This is not religious either. It is
the opposite of religion since no religion
preaches the destruction of either ego or Self.
Hence diabolical Nature Mysticism is not religious. And expansive Nature Mysticism is not
either, since it tends to self-worship, and no
religion, whether Semitic or Indian, allows such
a breach of religious polity such as "Egolatry."
In itself, therefore, Nature Mysticism is either
good or evil. Zaehner said it is neutral in
making it ambivalent, but good is not neutral, nor
is evil. Value is not neutral, and Nature Mysticism is a value experience since it is mystical.
It is the first step towards the sorting of
values, which is a chief facet of religion. Since
Nature Mysticism has difficulty with its values,
in recognizing none, it cannot be said that it is
religious at all.

(ix) This next point is not an established
one, but it is an extrapolation made from the
preceding. If Nature Mysticism can be said to be
the bubbling up of one's collective side from

141

within the psyche, which side is considered un-
touched yet by religion, and which can be, therefore, considered material in the broad sense, then
Nature Mysticism is matter becoming aware of
itself. When the euphoria wears off, which it does
all too soon, then one becomes, normally, painfully
aware of his isolation from others and even from
this inner content of his own makeup. Matter has,
thus, become aware of itself, when man is aware of
a collective side of his makeup; that he is not
just himself, but is somehow one with his environment (it is not personalism yet, by a long shot).
Matter has been experienced as something alive in
Nature Mysticism. In saying this I have moved from
saying what the experience indicates to saying what
its equivalent is. Matter experienced alive is
Nature Mysticism. I am still in the realm of
history of religions, which deals with equivalencies among the phenomena it compares. Nature
Mysticism is an experience of things alive in us
and us in them, not only spiritual things like
people, but sun and sea as well. Man, considered
as a personal environment--which is to say part of
the environment we see who is person--is environment
(matter in a diffused sense) aware of itself. We
have just edged ourselves toward theology in stating the literal meaning of Nature Mysticism. Up
to now we have just put it together piece by piece,
and in doing so have demonstrated that Huxley's
assertions are false concerning his claims to have
experienced the Hindu and Christian mystical experiences. Huxley is wrong, but his experience is
true, i.e., true Nature Mysticism. I have defined
what I see as Nature Mysticism by taking my
material from Zaehner and making systematic sense
of it. Now I am moving into the inter-face
between history of religions and theology and making a statement, taken from Zaehner,[110] into one

---

[110]Zaehner's first chapter, in his Dialectical
Christianity and Christian Materialism, entitled
"The Throes of Matter" (pp. 1-29), takes up the
question of matter coming together in thought and
self-awareness, and sees it in an evolutionary
schema.

which is at the same time historical-interpretative and theological. History interprets, as well
as putting bits and pieces together. From the
historical-interpretative side, it looks like matter is coming together when subject and object
unite--if only for a moment--and we use the way
things are in a larger sense: they are one. This
is the view taken as far as it can go without
theological help. Theology could say that this is
the view one has when one sees the Cosmic Christ
being all in all; that all things are one and
moving into closer unity through him. But as far
as we can go, with the evidence thus adduced, is
to say that it looks like matter can think and
that there are times when it sees a unity. This
is as far as Nature Mysticism can go.

When man considers what to do about his
overall disunity--inner and outer--we have religion.
Religion begins, therefore, when either God comes
out of his heaven to begin the reunification
process, or man takes it-under grace-to do it for
himself, putting the God question on the back
burner.

CHAPTER IV

RELIGIOUS MYSTICISMS

(A) The Religious Use of Nature Mysticism

I have shown that the enthusiasms of Nature
Mysticism have a wild--untamed, and scmetimes dia-
bolic--side. I have demonstrated, further, that
Nature Mysticism is a type unto itself, different
from theism, at least, since there is no God present there, and, implicitly, different from religious mysticism since they have nothing of the
roistering expansions and contractions spanning
man's consciousness. But I have not demonstrated
this second point yet, but only menticned it
implicitly. It is my intention, now, to demonstrate that Nature Mysticism is different from
Indian mystical religions, first of all. I have
chosen two from India's "Mall of mysticisms":
Sāṁkhya, a dualism, and Advaita, a monism, or non-
dualism, to be more accurate. It is, by extension,
different from Buddhism, which is not essentially
different from mainline Indian mysticisms, and
Taoism/Zen, which bear an inner resemblance to
Indian religion, as I have shown. It is, lastly,
not the same as Muslim monism either.

Secondly, I intend to demonstrate that India
dealt with death and pain, either through the
religious use of Nature Mysticism, which is the
Ur level of the religion of the Upaniṣads, or by
using what I shall call Isolation Mysticism,
which deals with death and consciousness by cut-
ting out all but immortality in man.

Zaehner found that Nature Mysticism was man's
enjoyment of matter--albeit a diffused form of
matter--in its solidarity aspect. Conversely, what
he was to call Isolation Mysticism was the
enjoyment--blissful (nirvāṇa=Bliss)--of matter in
its solitary state, cut off from all and everything, within and without the Self. He said
that this is so because man is basically

145

isolationist; i.e., he wills to make it through
life, basically, alone.[1] This is not to say that
man is not gregarious, but that, in those things
which are most meaningful and important to him--
release from the alienation intrinsic to his
estate--he wills to find his own salve for the
wounds which fester in his consciousness.

Zaehner finds the religions of India delight-
fully empiricist, since they wish to deal with
what is salvageable in man. Man is in a sorry
state, so without turning to God, they set out
to do something about it. They found that they
could expect to experience something of that
which they buried deep within--namely, immortality--
by a process of manipulating consciousness, which
process they called Yoga. The Indians found that
there are two souls in man, the ego (Skt.=
ahaṁkāra) and the higher self, the ātman. The
ātman is in exile in the nether regions of con-
ciousness, what we would call the unconscious
today, and must be released (mukta=freed, liberated, the goal of Indian religions). What we
would call the transcendent is to be found, not
"out there" as in Semitic religions, but "in
there" in the religions of the East.[2]

(1) The First Step in Relgious Mysticism in
     India is Nature Mysticism

When Nature Mysticism brims over into its
expansive enthusiasms what appears is that the
subject and object become identical, up to a
point. What this means is that man's interiority
becomes one with the exteriority surrounding him;
or, to put it another way, that Nature Mysticism
is an intuition that microcosm is macrocosm. In
Christianity this appears, for Zaehner, with

---

[1]Zaehner, S/T, p. 174.

[2]Zaehner, Xt/O, p. 69.

146

Nicholas of Cusa, who said that man is not only the _imago dei_, but he is the _imago mundi_ as well. Further, it is possible for man to experience his identity with both, "for he is an analogy of both," according to Cusa, "For man is God, though not absolutely, for he is man. He is therefore God in a human way. Man is the world, too, not indeed all things compressed into a small compass, since he is a man. He is therefore man as microcosm."[3] Hinduism will place the emphasis of this on a non-theistic basis, but the logic runs the same for both Cusa and the early _Upanisads_. Therefore, Nature Mysticism and religion have something in common since they see a unity between man and things, and in the experience of this unity something, not only selfish, but something transcending man, can happen. This is the bridge Zaehner discerns between Nature Mysticism and religious mysticism. The breaking-off point between religious and non-religious (Nature) mysticism is involvement with the world. Nature Mysticism is totally involved with the world, with matter and the ego coalescing into something either happy or tormented-depending on whether the experience is expansion or contraction (in Medieval parlance, diabolic possession). Religion begins when man desires to do something about the situation in the world by just uniting with things as they are. Taoism is a unity with things just as they are. Max Weber realized this and delighted in it in the Chinese character. In his study of China Weber theorized that China (meaning, in this instance, Taoism) just leaves things alone and adjusts to them, but the religion of the West (which means Protestantism for Weber) sought to subdue the world through reason.[4] Taoism is a prime example

---

[3]Zaehner, S/P, p. 102, _apud_ Cusa's _De Docta Ignorantia_, 122, ii.3.

[4]Weber, Max, _The Religion of China, Confucianism and Taoism_, translated and edited by H. A. Gerth, The Free Press, N.Y., 1951, "Confucianism and Protestantism (Ch. 8), pp. 224-49.

of what Zaehner would consider religious Nature Mysticism, since it is religious and yet is a mysticism of matter. Non-religious Nature Mysticism would be an experience of the unity of man with the All, which did not happen by design, but by accident--as it happened with Zaehner, while reading his poetry at school. Religious Nature Mysticism, on the contrary, happens when one sets out to do something about one's situation in the world. For Zaehner, this is the bridge uniting the Sacred with the Profane. This is why he entitled his book Mysticism Sacred and Profane. When man decides to do something about his condition religion happens; whether he sets out by asking questions which are religious, which are to be found in the question of the sages in the Vedas and Upaniṣads, or by ritual, which Nature Religion is to be found in any manifestation in which man's interiority is found united with the environment. This is the sort of thing treated by B. Malinowski in his Magic, Science and Religion in seeing the religion of primitive peoples as being a vision wherein all things are one through interconnections. Malinowski, perhaps, throws light on Zaehner's thought when he links the ritual of primitives with magic whereby one's interior desires are brought to bear on events and physical things. This is sympathetic magic, and it is a conclusion of what can be called Natural Religion. It acts religiously on the vision of the sages, especially in India, who saw the link between mind and things. It endeavors ritually to effect what it desires since things are one anyway.[5] Nature Mysticism is really not a religionless mysticism, it is a godless one. Zaehner's thought seems defective in trying to make natural mysticism neutral in order to differentiate it from Isolation Mysticism and Theism and refute the

---

[5]Malinowski, op. cit., introduction by R. Redfield, Anchor Doubleday, Garden City, N.Y., 1954, chapter II, The Rational Mastery by Man of his Surroundings, pp. 25-35, passim.

philosophia perennis. Nor did he have to make
it neutral in order to show its ambivalence
morally. Nature Mysticism is less profane than it
is godless. It is a phenomenon which can be discerned when man is not addressing himself to his
conditions, and either has or seeks a euphoric
intuition of unity. It is religious most other
times since, as Lévy-Bruhl points out, primitive
man is in a mystical frame of mind most times, he
is not a frivolous man, but most sober[6] trying to
put the cosmos together by his own efforts which
are mystical/magical/ritual efforts.

All this is by way of introducing us to the
religious use of Nature Mysticism found in India,
and cultivated more in Islamic writings by Muslim mystics.

One more introductory note: Hinduism used
Nature Mysticism as a religious thing, but had
no systematics, at this early stage, whereby one
could distinguish between Being and the Good.
This easily led to the wildness we saw in Nature
Mysticism in the last chapter.[7] This lack opened
it up to the Dionysian side of religion, and the
introduction of a systematics of mysticisms and an
ontology depicting a domestication of the natural
mystical phenomenon by the introduction of a concept of a higher and lower soul in man. Whether
systematics was the cause or result of this domestication and peace in religion I cannot tell.
What I can say is that Zaehner discerned that the
lack of it is the root of such corruption as one
sees in the Soma cult, which used intoxicants to
induce mystical states.

So the religious use of Nature Religion
demanded some harnessing of the expansion

---

[6]_Ibid._, p. 25.

[7]Zaehner, S/P, pp. 116-8, _passim_.

phenomenon, which meant, for Islam and Hinduism, the domestication of the lower soul (ego) by the higher soul (Self). This domestication was taken care of by the second stage of religious texts, and religion, outlined by Zaehner: namely, what he calls Isolation Mysticism, which contracts man, not in the sense of the crushing depressions-- which looked so diabolical to our Christian fore- bears--but in the sense of stripping away all the material side of man. Since Nature Mysticism is an intuition of Nature in its material side, Iso- lation will be seen to be the exact opposite of Nature Mysticism; thus, the former is a stripping of man of all but immortality--which is the essence of the Self, and the latter is the expansion of the ego into infinity. The one goes towards infinity found outside man, and the other towards it found inside him.

What I intend to do here is to show that Iso- lation Mysticism is different from both Nature Mysticism and theism, but first I must show the relationship between natural mysticism and Isola- tion Mysticism since at times it leads to the confusion of mysticisms, making them look identi- cal, rather than inter-related. This confusion adds appeal to the philosophia perennis when it argues from assumptions which say that they are all alike anyway--which assumptions they decline to prove. Nature Mysticism relates with Isolation Mysticism and Theism, but is distinct from each as each is from the other. Mutuality and similarity do not make identity: this is the problem Zaehner had with the philosophia perennis. Indian religion, too, says that it has the same experience which those in the West have in theisms, and Zaehner's argument set the record straight on this by refut- ing it. But, to keep out the confusion, I do not intend to include in my systematics of Zaehner's argument his lesson in the evolution of religions, beginning with Nature Mysticism, and moving up through Isolation Mysticisms--both dualistic and monistic--and ending with Theism. This is interest- ing but not germane to our purpose, which is to refute

150

the philosophia perennis' argument and systematize Zaehner. My argument will be simple.

Firstly, the earliest form of what Zaehner calls Indian materialistic religion, by which he meant a religion using natural mysticism, is to be found in the Brāhmaṇas, which were the texts preserving the rituals of sympathetic magic which brought about the remaking of the cosmos. Early Indian sacrifice was practiced in order to reproduce the creation by the proper performance of some rites. These rites placed the individual egos of the tribe around the collective tribal ego at the time when creation began, a time of innocence when Primal Man (Skt.=puruṣa) walked the earth.

Hindu sacrifice, therefore, teaches three simple truths: i) through the performance, man knows and experiences that macrocosm is microcosm, or that the without of things is the within of them; ii) it teaches that man becomes the All, which is Nature Mysticism, expressed beautifully by Zaehner when he said that natural Mysticism is "an anamnesis on the part of the single fragment of the once unbroken whole;"[8] iii) and if one wishes to realize himself as the All, one must get rid of individual consciousness in order to become one with Universal consciousness. The Fall myth is used by Zaehner to explain the fact that man felt removed from an awareness of this Universal consciousness, which keeps on cropping up in his thoughts, and ritual repairs that rift.[9]

The next level of texts, the Upaniṣads, reveals to us another use of Nature Mysticism, and of a materialistic religion less "gross" than sympathetic magic, if less exciting in what it

---

[8]Zaehner, C/Sp, p. 85.

[9]Ibid., pp. 83-85.

holds out to us than its more primitive brother.
The Upaniṣads are, literally, sessions with a
teacher, sitting at his feet; nearby him, in other
words. Zaehner says that the salient feature of
the Upaniṣadic inner life was a Nature Mysticism
commencing in man's immortality; i.e., they start
with man, where he is, not with any god, as the
earlier Indian texts did. Its emphasis is on the
imago dei to the exclusion of the deus. This is
not a nonsense statement on Zaehner's part, but
merely means to tell us that what the texts say is
that man seems to be about re-doing something
which has been fragmented. We call it the imago
dei (the image of God), and later when theism came
back with the Indians, they began to deal with
something like the imago dei in preferring a
grace (Skt.=prasada=grace) religion[10] to straight
yoga or natural mysticism. The Upaniṣads began
with treatises on the substrate of all existence,
to the effect that the changeless ground of all is
the Brahman. Early on, the Brahman was accounted
as food, a living, material, substance which maintains everything in existence. At this level,
food and breath (Skt.=prāna) were the geminal symbols of the Absolute. But food was alive for
Zaehner. He found this in the Taittiriya Upaniṣad
(Tait. Up. 2.2), which said:

       From food indeed are creatures engendered,-
       Whatever (creatures) dwell on earth.
       Then again by food they live,
       And again pass into it at the end.
       But food is the chief of beings,
       Whence it is called the elixir of all things.
       Who reverences Brahman as food
       Gains all food.
       For food is the chief of beings,
       Whence it is called the elixir of all things.
       From food are (all) creatures engendered;

---

       [10]Cf. Gītā, 18:56, "...for by my grace he will
attain to an eternal changeless state."

152

When born, by food do they grow up.
It is eaten and eats all creatures.
Therefore is it called food.[11]

So, the without of food is the body, and the
within is the spirit of man. The within in food
is a self, therefore, since it has life. But
within that self is mind, and within the mind is
intellect, and within intellect is bliss (ānanda,
or nirvāna).[12] Hence, body is the without of the
self and mind; intellect and joy the within. One
can see how this concept, taken and refined, could
become yoga, which refined all things after split-
ting man apart body from soul; then it strips self
of mind, emotions and desires, thoughts, and then
even of the trances it induced along the way, to
leave only the intuition of Joy. This would come
later, when a dualism and monism would invest this
materialistic body of Indian religion, its materia
prima, with souls called Sāmkhya-Yoga and Advaita,
respectively.

So, on this level, matter was instinct with
what we call spirit. The two were "inextricably
entwined." The beauty of the Joy/Bliss was a constant temptation to which Indian religion, again
and again, succumbed mistaking its enjoyment for a
God. That Ātman is Brahman, which is not talking
about God but the Self as the Absolute, is a form
of this "succumbing" can be demonstrated since a
later scripture, the Gītā, would grant its
imprimatur to all preceding spiritualities, among
which was this monistic one stating the Self is a
god, and that this 'god' was the only Real; but
the Gītā went further in declaring that theism
and a religion of grace and devotion (bhakti)
were the highest of them all.

---

[11]Zaehner, C/Sp. p. 87.

[12]Ibid.

153

The materialism of this early state of Nature Mysticism is furthered, in Zaehner's view, when food pushes on towards becoming spirit, and thence on to become thought. So the outer dimension of food always tends inward, and the inner dimension always moves outward in food-become-man, which outward direction begins with an expansive joy, which itself becomes matter. This is Nature Mysticism pure and simple. Both matter and spirit meet in man in synthesis.[13]

Even better than the Taittirīya text is the Brhadāranyaka Up. (1.4.10), which says:

> In the beginning this (world) was Brahman.
> It took cognizance of itself, "I am
> Brahman." Therefore it became that All.
> Whosoever of the gods became aware of
> this, became that (Brahman). So too in
> the case of seers, and so too in the case
> of man...This is so now also. Who so
> knows, "I am Brahman," becomes this All.
> Not even the gods have the power to
> prevent him becoming thus, for such a
> one becomes their own self (or soul,
> ātman).[14]

Expansion into the All, to become the All, is Nature Mysticism. One expands into one's immortality. Thus death and pain have been faced, and these are the twin starting points (epitomized by the Sanskrit word dukha=wretchedness, sorrow, pain) of Indian religion in which man consciously faces down his fragmented existence. When immortality becomes expansive, therefore, it is Nature Mysticism. It is a materialistic form of religion, but a religion nonetheless since it is man dealing with the religious quest: "What are life and death about?" is really a question about

---

[13]Zaehner, C/Sp., p. 88.

[14]Zaehner, S/T, p. 53.

man, not God. Religion deals with man's doing
something about his status. Some have a god
irrupt to begin a process for him, and others, more
aggressive, begin it, seemingly, for themselves,
as we see in Indian religion and Taoism.

     In brief scope, the direction this material-
istic nature mysticism took is this: The All
of materialistic (early Upanisadic) Hinduism is
Brahman. So, to become the Brahman is to become
All. So Zaehner concludes that these early Upanisads retail a message of pan-en-henism in which
breath (Skt.=prāna) becomes consciousness; and
breath thus experienced is an experience of bliss
and immortality. This is to be found in the
Kausitakī Upanisad (3.4). So, the materialism of
the Upanisads proceeds to idealism; this, since
breath is more necessary than food. Hence, breath
is spirit, which is the immortal link sought by
our fathers in India.[15]

     Indian Nature Mysticism is a mysticism of
matter becoming aware of itself, in which man is
aware that he is alone, apart from the brood, and
in some way responsible for his loneliness. The
first experiences of Nature Mysticism were not
spontaneous, however. Zaehner says that they were
the result of yoga, a technique which aims at
putting one into direct contact with one's personal
immortality. Such an experience was subsumed by
religious men as Indian religion veered towards
seeing this immanent experience of the One as the
Transcendent as well.

     So Nature Mysticism, though it contains no god--
neither does Ur Buddhism--seems to be not irreligious
by essence, but neither is it a confessional religion. Other primitive examples could have been
shown by Zaehner, but were not, which could have
shown the magical use of this mystical outlook in
sympathetic magic. It is not placed in the

---

[15]Zaehner, S/T, pp. 64 f.

religious category by Zaehner since it is ambivalent. It can be non-religious, as in Huxley's
self-induced drug experience or Zaehner's experience with poetry, or, again with the anti-
religious Jefferies, but it can also be religious.
It can be anti-religious, too, as in its contraction stage which is crushing in its effects and
pulls man away from anything considered religious.
Further, Zaehner did not want to make it anything
but profane--thus the "Profane" of his title
Mysticism Sacred and Profane--since it would later
serve as the link between religious and non-
religious hopes, like Marxism, which see man coming together through matter. But this is theology.
At first blush, Zaehner's text-by-text study of
mysticisms, in order to refute the philosophia
perennis, caused him to see a type called Nature
Mysticism. It is not by essence religious, since
there is neither any god in it--though there can
be--nor any thought of addressing man's status on
this earth. It can address this status, though,
and then it is religious. It did this in India,
and it can be seen as the bridge leading from the
profane mysticism to the religious in what Zaehner
calls Isolation Mysticism. The sages of Hinduism,
whose experiences were written as the early
Upaniṣads, saw pan-en-henism as the goal of Nature
Mysticism and perfected yoga as a method for producing just that. The irrational use of the
natural experience came, in Zaehner's view, to
this form of early Hinduism because the sages had
divorced experience from revelation in using religion and a method of trance in conjunction. This,
in turn, leaves religion open to the types of
experiences people fancy. It is quite capricious;
too much so for Zaehner's taste. He said that the
modes used for producing the experience had to
put the rational faculty into neutral before the
contents of the unconscious side of man's personality could surface; which contents are irrational,
and can act contrary to one's well-being.[16]

---

[16]Zaehner, H/M, pp. 56 f.

Finally, the Upanisads contain so much philosophy since they were attempts to explain the experiences of these very sages. Hence revelation existed to explain the experiences of these yogins, which revelations we call the Upanisads.[17] The experiences they had were the end of a desire to make all one again. Man became the All in becoming the Brahman.

The next level of Indian experience desires to get away from all contact with matter and the temporal, both within and outside of man. It desired to isolate man in a small, circumscribed, place which was not temporal and material, and thus attain immortality without the expansion of Nature Mysticism. This form of mysticism is a contraction to the Self in order to enjoy it alone, without the All being involved at all.

---

[17]Zaehner, S/T, p. 44.

CHAPTER V

ISOLATION MYSTICISM

(A) Sāṁkhya

Zaehner sees three trends in early Indian religions which further our argument about mysticisms being different. The three are: i) the yogic, which isolates the immortal and puts one into a direct experience of it, ii) an experience of the self becoming all in the early Upaniṣads, which is a pan-en-henic experience, and iii) the philosophical speculation of the Upaniṣads, which makes the isolation experience a non-dualistic metaphysic (Skt.=advaita, meaning non-two-ism) in which the Self is the ground of all, including the self and even god.[1]

But more on the theory of yoga is necessary to see just how it fits into the scheme of Indian religions as Zaehner sees them. Yoga has been used in the West to induce states of manic enthusiasm. But this is not what it was intended for in India. Perhaps I should give an outline of the steps of spirituality which Zaehner has constructed so that one can see how and where yoga fits.

Zaehner sees three stages in spirituality among religions in general. I am talking, as did Zaehner, about Indian religions here, but he seems to mean that this applies equally well to religions in genere. So yoga stands in for asceticism generically. This is plausible since, for instance, Zaehner later quotes Ruysbroeck to the effect that one can induce states of peace (by which the Fleming meant what yogins mean by nirvāna without the agency of God if one only knows the technique). And, further, that it is a good emptying process (Mahāyāna Buddhists call

---

[1]Zaehner, S/T, p. 66.

their goal, śunyatā, which is Skt. for Emptiness)
on the way to God, but not including him. It is
a foyer on the way, and a good one. So, asceticism in general can be seen as inducing states
of what Zaehner called pan-en-henism; i.e., the
ego unites with matter within itself and with its
environment. So yoga was designed, not for such
lunacy as we find here in the West, where people
"indulge themselves by its use," but to isolate
one from anything to do with time and matter.

   So the first stage Zaehner outlines is a
yoga stage which frees the contents of man's
inner life, which causes an expansion of the ego
which we call Nature Mysticism. This can become
manic, but it was not designed for such in India.
It unites the ego with the world. This is of
paramount importance in understanding Zaehner's
system. Yoga is quintessential Indian religion
and it unites one with the world. One does not
leave the world, but becomes united with it, in
the first stage of movement towards the goal set
by the sages.

   The manic potential in this stage can be
handled by bringing the higher soul (purusa in
India and rūh in Islam) into play with its lower,
empirical, and mortal counterpart which Indians
call prakrti and Muslims nafs. More explanation
is needed here. Yoga is based on a two-soul
hypothesis, such as we saw in Proust's experience
of the ego and the "other" self. The system in
India which constructed the theory of the two
souls is called Sāmkhya. Yoga is not based on
monism, but on dualism and moderate realism; i.e.,
things really exist and are composites, cosmo-
logically. In Sāmkhya the human being, the soul,
is called person (purusa), which is the male
principle of everyone, male or female. Purusa
is eternal, and can be termed the Self of each
person. But purusa has become entangled with
Nature (Skt.=prakrti), which means matter, and
which is female. Nature (prakrti) is, in turn,
composed of three perpetually active elements:

160

sattva (which means light and truth), rajas (which means energy, activity and desire), and tamas (which means darkness, heaviness and sloth). Purusa (soul) has been trapped in matter (prakrti)--which latter is not a pernicious thing, but merely somewhat good but bothersome. So matter is a bond keeping the soul from its eternity, its home. The separation of isolation is the aetiology of each soul. Further, each soul is a monad and never has, nor will it have, any connection with any other soul. Union with either another soul or with God is ludicrous in such a system since it is an "every purusa for himself" affair. Zaehner mentioned that man is basically isolationist, a loner, in matters of doing something about his alienation and fragmentation, and here we have proof. God (Iśvara) is not only not the goal of purusa in a theistic type union, but he is merely a helper in the achievement of isolation by revealing Nature to him as a lovely dancer, who, having once revealed herself, is never more to be seen. Nature helps man to achieve his goal, even though it is never seen anymore. This "being seen" is the expansion experience of pan-en-henism which is produced as the first stage of yoga. When the soul has seen the beauty of Nature it moves on to achieve its original state and its final destiny, which is isolation to contemplate its own beauty. For the beauty of the soul is far greater than the beauty of Nature (prakrti, matter).[2] Up to now Zaehner saw nothing religious about this mysticism, but when purusa goes further than pan-en-henism, a union with the world, to become isolated from it, that, for Zaehner, is the beginning of religion. In Zaehner's estimation, religious mysticism, therefore, is a loss of ego in the Self. So Nature Mysticism is the aggrandisement of the ego--in its happy phase--in its unification with matter.

---

[2] Zaehner, S/P, p. 99.

Sāṁkhya's matter is always in flux. To Zaehner, it looks much like Aristotle's matter-with its three attributes of sattva, rajas and tamas informing it in the Aristotelian sense of that term. Matter for the Sāṁkhya is, according to Zaehner, that atomized/diffused, and potent, stuff in man's psyche which we saw with Huxley, who called it Mind at Large and other nature mystics who found something welling up out of them becoming autonomous and uniting with the environment. It is that stuff which seems to be common to others, what psychology calls collective unconscious, which is matter in the Sāṁkhya system. Zaehner calls this "matter" consciousness:

> ...the sum total of the phenomenal universe and life-force that keeps it in being. It is the world of perpetual flux in which no form is permanent, and yet where nothing irrevocably passes away. It is the stuff of which both body and psyche are made, always changing and never at rest,-not staying for one moment the same, but in its quantitive totality remaining, presumably, always the same though perpetually passing through different forms. It is Aristotle's matter.[3]

For Zaehner, matter is something so spiritual that even soul is made of it, in a way; at least the empirical soul, or ego.

The Indians were not the only ones to discover two souls in man. Like Avicenna, most Muslim psychologists distinguish the upper from the lower soul. For the Muslims the higher, rational, soul (rūh) strives upward for the knowledge of God. The lower soul (nafs) is composed of imagination, lust and anger (aggression). Lust and anger are a pair of opposites which

_____

[3]Zaehner, S/P, p. 99.

Avicenna says must be integrated, not suppressed.
The lower soul is ambivalent for Muslims. It is
both animal and bestial. The animal soul is
domesticated, the bestial one is a carnivore
ready to devour one if he is not careful.

Zaehner says that this parallels what he
found in the Sāmkhya. The components of _prakrti_
(matter) are not only components of things cosmo-
logically, they are the moral and psychological
components as well. Goodness in all things, and
a fortiori in the soul, is the quality possessed
by _sattva_. Energy and passion is the characteristic of a person or thing under the influence
of _rajas_. And darkness, heaviness or sloth of
soul, is the characteristic of one in whom _tamas_
is ascendant.[4]

What Zaehner seems to be driving at in all
this is that after the enthusiasms of yoga's
pan-en-henic phase pass, there is another facet
of the Nature Mysticism stage. This is the
domestication of the lower soul by the higher, or,
put better, the domination of the ego--with all its
drives and levels of conscious and unconscious--
by reason. The Self is not intellect but will
do nothing against reason. So intellect is the
highest agent of Self. Integration of higher and
lower soul means, basically, that matter and
spirit become one. This happened with Proust. It
is a healing form of Nature Mysticism, and has
nothing _per se_ to do with religious mysticism.
It has everything to do with it in the healing
arts in the West, especially with Jung, who
wished his healing method to be used in conjunction with religion. But in itself the wedding of
matter and spirit (_prakrti_ and _purusa_, _rūh_ and
nafs) in a peace brought by the healing facet of
pan-en-henism is not religious. This is the first
stage of mysticism, in Zaehner's estimation. It

---

[4]_Ibid._, p. 107.

can be done through yoga, which can yoke men together within. The very word yoga (the root is from the Sanskrit root yuj, which means to yoke) denotes an integration; it is its first formal effect, in Aristotelian jargon.

Zaehner thinks that integration contains and controls the ecstasies of the expansion phase of yoga in Indian and some Ṣūfi techniques of trance. He seems to further his argument here, even though he is using a psychological term in doing so. What he did was describe the phenomenon, and the best word he could find was a Jungian one: Integration. He went on to give long disquisitions linking Jung with mysticism, but it does not seem to further the argument very much. So ecstasy is the first step on the way to the goal: Isolation. The Ṣūfi master Abū Yazid of Bistam had such ecstasies and cried out, while they were in full spate, "I am He," which is a complete and utter blasphemy for a Muslim. But his commentator, Junayd, says that these were only the outpourings of a drunken neophyte and not, really, to be taken theologically.[5] Junayd and Zaehner seem to think that beginners fall easy prey to such enthusiasms of identity with the deity, an identity which the subjects seem to see as complete. The Sufi writer Junayd called these "drunken" ecstasies as opposed to "sober" ones. The temptation of this and all pan-en-henism is the philosophia perennis, according to Zaehner.[6] When these enthusiasms entered religion, as they did with the theist Abū Yazid, they split his loyalties between the transcendent Allah and absolute monism, a monism which Zaehner goes to great lengths to prove came from a Hindu

---

[5]Zaehner, S/P, p. 114, apud Abu Nasr, al Sarrāj's Kitāb al Luma', edited by R. A. Nicholson, Leyden, Brill, 1914, p. 381 of Arabic text.

[6]Zaehner, H/M, p. 3.

monist mentor.[7] Trance techniques, whether yogic
or Ṣūfi, tend towards pan-en-henism, and the tendency of pan-en-henism is to go further than a
simple "I am All" to say that there is really
nothing but the All and that "I am that One." The
flow of logic is from pan-en-henism to pantheism
(in which one sees god everywhere, and in which
one is still united with the deity) to the conclusion that there is only God, that one's higher
soul is that Absolute, whether one calls it God
or Brahman. Muslims see this danger as quite
prevalent in beginners, but it is strong all along
the line, if the monist explosion in Islam and
Indian religion, with Śankara, are to be taken
seriously at all.

The Hindu side of trance places man in a
deep, dreamless sleep (Skt.=suṣupti=ɡood sleep)
in which the soul imagines itself to be a god
or king; in fact, it sees itself as the whole
world, this all: "I am this (world), I am (the)
whole." The Brhadāranyaka Upaniṣad says of
this:

> As a man when in the embrace of a well-
> loved woman knows nothing, neither out-
> side nor inside, so does this man
> (puruṣa) when in the embrace of the
> intelligent self know nothing within or
> without. This is his form in which his
> desire is fulfilled, in which the Self
> is his desire, in which he has no desire
> and has passed beyond sorrow.[8]

The cumulative effect of this identity of the
ego with the all is that opposites are reconciled. The soul is "idam sarvo" (=this whole

---

[7]Zaehner wrote much of his Hindu and Muslim
Mysticism to prove Islam's debt to India for its
monistic Ṣūfism.

[8]Brhd. Up., 4.3.4, apud Zaehner's S/P,
p. 116.

world in Skt.), and so everything, being identical, is everything else. Rimbaud, while in his enthusiasms recognized this, and Zaehner quotes him as saying he was beyond good and evil (dispensé de toute morale).[9] In this land opposites are meaningless. The Brhadāranyaka says "In this land a father becomes no-father (Skt.= a-pita), mother no-mother, the worlds no-world, the gods no-gods, the Vedas no-Vedas. There a thief becomes no-thief, the murderer of an embryo no murderer of an embryo,...a mendicant no-mendicant, an ascetic no-ascetic..."[10] Zaehner notes that here we are not dealing with the madness of Custance and Rimbaud, but with holy writ. He interprets this reconciliation of opposites as an integration of man's parts, given its healing aspects. It puts spirit back with matter, part with part.[11] It is also an intregation with a moral aspect. It can tend to a complete amorality. The Gītā speaks of those on this level of pan-en-henism,who deal a death blow to an enemy, as not having killed at all, for no one kills or gives life; all opposites are reconciled (Gītā 2:19). This is so since, at bottom, no one is an agent. The Absolute is the agent of all. Gītā 3:30 says that God is the agent of all, so all should be cast on Him.[12] This early part of the Gītā is not theistic yet, but retails the classical Indian religion of yoga in which opposites are reconciled, and really do not matter. Only the Absolute matters, and neither the ego nor God matters, so morality, while important, does not matter, ultimately, since all things come together anyway on this proximate level; and on the absolute level there will be no

---

[9]Zaehner, S/P, p. 116, apud Rimbaud's Oeuvres Completes, op. cit., p. 243.

[10]Ibid., p. 117, Brhd. 4.3.22.

[11]Ibid.

[12]Zaehner's S/G, p. 99.

good or evil.

These Upanisads are, for Zaehner, the philosophical efforts of primitive men to enquire into
the nature of things. They delve into the ground,
or nature, of the universe, and discourse on yogic
meditation. The caveat of S. Dasgupta, the distinguished Indian scholar, is well taken by
Zaehner to the effect that there is, indeed, confusion in the Upanisads. There, diverse currents
are fused without benefit of systematics, and
opposites are reconciled in the highest principle
of being.[13] This confusion leaves Westerners
confused and does not even seem to bother Indians.
The root of the problem is indicated by Zaehner's
remark that, at this stage of their development,
the sages had not yet distinguished Being from
the Good. So Zaehner swipes at those who use
this reconciliation of opposites in Indian
thought and ally it with statements by Meister
Eckhart, which look just as amoral, in order to
prove the unity of all religions on the meta-
physical-transcendental level. The Indians are
dealing with a problem in pan-en-theism, and
Eckhart's message is from a theistic base. Theism obviously distinguishes not only between good
and evil but between God and his creatures. Pan-
en-henism runs good and evil together. The two
mysticisms are beginning from different places
and talking of something entirely different when
they depict things which look alike.[14]

So, on the level of purusa and prakrti, which
is pan-en-henism, matter is on the move, even in
flux. The direction matter is taking is an upward thrust evolving towards spirit (purusa). For

---

[13]Zaehner, S/P, p. 117, apud Dasgupta's
A History of Indian Philosophy, Cambridge, 1922,
vol. i, p. 42.

[14]Ibid., p. 118.

Zaehner, the highest evolute of Matter (Nature=
prakrti) is Mind (buddhi). It is like Huxley's
Mind at Large and the Universal consciousness we
have noticed coming forth during the enthusiasms
of nature mystics.[15] Matter slowly makes its way
back to its goal, which is Mind or the experience
of it through yogic techniques. This is as far
as this first stage of Mysticism can take us.
Matter evolves toward its goal: Mind.

The next stage of mysticism is Isolation
Mysticism as such. Sāṃkhya moves further, past
the expansion phase of yoga, to strip the immortal Self of all forms of matter, whether the
grosser forms of rajas, tamas or even the higher
ones of sattva (passion, sloth and virtue, respectively). The introduction of a god here
would not make any difference at all, or any
sense, since the goal is not god, but isolation
of the purusa (Eternal Self) from all things,
mind, body, or ego in toto.[16] So when Sāṃkhya
introduces Īsvara into the process, it is still
an atheistic system. Isvara (Skt.=Lord) is
merely a helper towards the pan-en-henic experience, not by giving grace--there is none here--but
by serving as an object of meditation. The yogin
uses the Lord as a tool for doing something in
his nature. You should remember my comments on
the philosophia perennis here: namely, Isherwood
and Schuon said that man, at bottom, is supernatural; which is to say, the removal of obstacles
through asceticism--read yogic meditation--allows
him to see his true nature and become such. Man
does it himself in Sāṃkhya. It is not so much
atheistic as it is a-theistic. So the yogins of

---

[15]Zaehner, S/P, p. 108.

[16]Ibid., p. 109. Ruysbroeck attacks the
Beghards for doing just that, i.e., introducing
God into a natural act and calling it super-
natural.

the Sāṃkhya are not interested in God, but in the quest for the Self (puruṣa).

This Self (puruṣa) may very well be the second self of Proust. The goal of yoga is the release of the Self (puruṣa) from the ego (ahaṃkāra), which is a composition of the three cosmological components of Nature (prakṛti), sattva, rajas and tamas. Beatitude for Sāṃkhya consists in a final, eternal release. In classical yoga, God was invented to explain how puruṣa got involved in prakṛti in the first place. The deity never served any other, more ultimate, purpose than that for Sāṃkhya. Zaehner says that this is the strangest concept of God in all religion.[17]

So the goal of yoga is release (mokṣa=release or liberation). It is the release from the trammels of matter, or Nature (prakṛti). As such the goal is an eternal death and eternal bliss; this is nirvāṇa. Isolation consists of stripping from the immortal all psycho-physical adjuncts. This is what the Islamicist Louis Gardet calls entasy, which is "...the soul contemplating itself in its essence."[18] In all this, the soul has returned, reverted would be more precise, to its newborn state. It is a return to innocence. So this return to the personality of the child, which Oscar Wilde called a personality cleared of all sin, is a sinless state. It is Limbo. Zaehner has it that both Rimbaud and the Sāṃkhya desire this return to the bliss and isolation of Limbo.[19] Hence isolation contracts the soul into

---

[17]Zaehner, S/P, p. 127.

[18]Ibid., p. 128, apud Gardet's Les Mardis de Dar el-Salam, Cairo, 1951.

[19]Ibid., p. 129

its essence: immortality, which is always a blissful experience. Integration, as we saw in Proust's pan-en-henic experience, on the contrary, puts the element shunned by isolation mysticism-namely, matter or temporality--together with the spiritual. The one contracts to immortality; the other contracts to a unity of matter/mind in its integration. Neither is the expansion of Qushayrī.

So, summing up, isolation for Zaehner is like Rimbaud's return to Limbo. As such it is a blissful experience divested of any trace of theism. In such a state a personality cannot develop. In fact, it is more an undifferentiated state than a developed one. It is a return to the way we were, not a thrust forward to what we will be in the developmental model which eschatological religions in the West use. It is something like a return to the womb, to a state of undifferentiated consciousness. Zaehner says that no category of depth psychology fits the isolation of Sāmkhya. Isolation is not only not a state of psychological integration, it is its very opposite. It is the isolation, not of the collective unconscious, but it is isolation from the collective unconscious.[20] In fact, Zaehner likens the process of the purusa entering prakrti to the Christian concept of a new soul entering a body. It cannot see God without the direct intervention of God's grace. If it does not receive such graces as are necessary to see God, through the agency of Baptism, then its only goal is a form of natural bliss. Sāmkhya seeks this, not after death, but during life. Zaehner sees this as the goal, not only of the Sāmkhya, but of all India's mainstream religions: Hinduism, Buddhism and Jainism. This is not a process of salvation, which is a making whole again of something which was fractured; but it is a separation of the

---

[20]Zaehner, S/P, p. 129.

170

temporal from the eternal. Therefore, it is not an integration of this precious eternal with anything.[21] Integration makes great sense in the West where one is dealing with the Judeo-Zoroastrian-Christian tradition; but it makes no sense in the Indian tradition at all.

So, for Zaehner, this second stage of mysticism is one in which the Self asserts itself. In the first stage, that of pan-en-henism, we saw the ego emphasizing itself to swell itself to grand proportions in an experience of unity beyond all expectations. In this second state we have the Self stripping the ego of all things transitory, even to stripping off the ego itself. This recovers the bliss of Eden. It is a passive state of being before the self in contemplating the Self. A Christian would say, here, that it is the Self before God contemplating either him or itself. Either way, Christian or Hindu, the Self can go no further. This is the limit of Isolation Mysticism. No God need be here necessarily, whether in a Christian or Indian context. In an Indian context, of a certainty, there is no God.[22]

Nature Mysticism is the polar opposite from Isolation Mysticism, for Zaehner. In Nature Mysticism one embraces the All, but this All is not God. Nor is this expansion experience anything like the isolation experience which breaks man down to his simples so as to enjoy immortality in such a stripped-down state. Isolation (Skt.=kaivalyam) of the Sāmkhya variety is outlined completely in the Bhagavad-Gītā, 2:55-72. Here is the essence of yoga, which is quintessential Indian religion, for Zaehner:

---

[21]Ibid., p. 130.

[22]Ibid., p. 151.

When a man abandons all desires which affect the mind, and by himself is contented in himself, then is he known as one whose mind is tranquil. The man whose mind is untroubled in the midst of sorrow, free from desire in the midst of pleasures, from whom passion, fear, and anger have departed, whose thoughts are steady, he is known as a sage.

He who is everywhere devoid of affection, taking the pleasant and the unpleasant as they come, neither welcoming the one nor detesting the other, he is firmly set in wisdom. When he withdraws his senses from their objects as a tortoise withdraws its legs on all sides, then is he firmly set in wisdom. Objects of sense disappear for the embodied soul who ceases to feed on them, yet their savour remains behind: this too disappears for one who has seen the highest. Though a man strive (for perfection) and be never so discerning, yet his senses harass him and carry off his mind by violence. With all his senses controlled, deep in meditation, a man should sit down contemplating Me as his final end. The man whose senses are under control, is firmly set in wisdom.

When a man dwells on the objects of sense, he will develop attachment to them. Attachment breeds desire, desire anger. Anger breeds mental confusion, mental confusion plays tricks with the memory. A memory so disturbed brings on insanity...Insanity destroys. When a mind is thus purified, his understanding will soon be recovered. An undisciplined man has no understanding, nor has he the power to concentrate. One who has no power to concentrate knows no peace. How should there be happiness without peace?

172

A mind that obeys the roving senses,
robs a man of wisdom, even as the wind
carries away a ship at sea. So he who
everywhere withdraws his senses from
their objects, is firmly set in wisdom.

In what is night for all (other)
creatures the disciplined soul keeps
vigil; but the time when (other) creatures are awake, is night for the sage
who sees. Even as the waters flow into
the sea which is ever being filled
yet remains motionless and still, so
do all desires flow into such a man.
He attains peace, not the man who
desires desire. The man who abandons
all desires and lives without craving
or thought of "I" or "mine" attains
to peace. This is the state of
Brahman: no one who has attained to it
is (again) confused. He who is fixed
in this state at the end of his days
attains the peace (nirvāna) of Brahman.[23]

The Gītā introduces us to the technique of
Indian spirituality in outlining isolation
(kaivalyam) for us. But the Gītā is not a
systematics of spiritualities but a compendium of
them. It keeps the door open for the other two
classic spiritualities in India as well: namely,
monism and theism. The Gītā is a compendium
which mixes spirituality with spirituality.
India rests easily with crosscurrents in
its religion; even when the crosscurrents seem
a hopeless confusion. India is not only a Europe
of countries but offers a home to its twenty-
three major language groups, with many tendrils
and offshoots of these coursing to and fro about
the country. Its cultures range from light-
skinned Aryan northerners to tiny black people
in the South.

---

[23]Zaehner, S/P, pp. 145 f.

Its scriptures reflect not only its multi-culturalism but its polychromed religiousness as well. This is offputting to Westerners used to things being more circumscribed in their religions--even the world religions. To have, within one country, a world religion having the appearance of being several religions, which Indian religion really is, leaves us limp with frustration in trying to fathom what is going on in Indian religion. The Gītā accurately reflects the three strands of Indian religion--pan-en-henic, yogic and bhaktic (devotional) theism--to be found in India. Since there is no pope, no doctrine, as such, and no magisterium, why should things be systematic? As a matter of fact, they are not very systematic, but they have been gathered into one "omnium gatherum" which is cohesive and depicts an evolutionary movement in religion. That "gatherer" is the Gītā. And it is to Zaehner's credit that he not only saw this, but fought with those, like Radhakrishnan, who would flatten out India's religious peaks into the banal plateaus of the philosophia perennis. The three mysticisms in Indian religion are different. There are three different religiosities there, therefore; which religious variants would be religions in themselves in other cultures. But these religious variants gather, somewhat, under the umbrella of the Gītā and devotional (bhakti, if you will) religion. This does not make one religion in India, but merely is to state that the Gītā portrays the three strands as very good, but chooses (Skt.=Iṣṭa=chosen, one has the option not only of religions but of gods in India) one, and that one is the religion of Viṣṇu and devotion (bhakti) to him as one's iṣṭadevata (chosen deity).

In sum, in India the three religious mani-festations--pan-en-henic, yogic and theistic--are interrelated, or can be.

Isolation is not only explained by a dualism, philosophically, but contains the seeds of monism

174

in it. Monism leads to isolation (kaivalyam)
of the Self from God, if one begins theistically
and floats into a monistic position to explain
one's religious experience, as happened in Islam
with Ṣūfism. Zaehner has been chided for having
a "thing" against monism,[24] but he did so precisely because he saw that it would deprive the
theist of the presence of God, if followed sedulously. The religious experience which takes
pleasure in the contemplation of the Self by the
self is a bliss taken in one's own immortality.
Isolation mysticism begins with the assumption
that one is already the Absolute, and that any
god is only an aspect of this.[25] But a religion
which is theist can end there as well. Hence,
the rather strange, to Zaehner, use of God in
the Sāṁkhya, which uses him as an object of
meditation, if at all. Sāṁkhya-yoga begins and
ends in the self. So, Zaehner, using his method
of comparison-interpretation, decided that monism
could lead one no further than the Sāṁkhya position. Pure Sāṁkhya feels that an absolute is
irrelevant; but that, if one insists, then,
immortality is that absolute; and the soul is
that immortality. Hence, cultivate one's soul
alone, and the devil take the rest. If one
begins from a monist position, such as advaitan
Vedānta (non-twoism), then one must get rid of
the contingent and get at the absolute, the
unqualified (nirguṇa=Skt., means that without
guṇa, the gunas being the three qualifiers of
Nature, sattva, rajas and tamas). The unqualified is the self (ātman), and self is Brahman
(the immortal, unqualified Absolute). Hence, one
should use a technique to get one to the self,

---

[24]T. Gelblum's review art. of Z's H/M,
in "Bull. of Sch. of Orient. and Afr. Stud.,"
no. 25,1962, says that Zaehner has a monotheistic
bias when it comes to Hindu monist texts
(p. 173).

[25]Zaehner, S/P, p. 146.

shortcircuiting all which is not this immortal
self. This technique is yoga. So in its effects,
Sāṃkhya isolation mysticism is the same as
advaitan "monistic" mysticism, even though the
metaphysics are diametrically opposed: Sāṃkhya
is dualistic, and Advaita says that the Brahman
is the only reality, and the Self (ātman) is
that. Hence we are presented with two philosophies, but one religious experience for both:
namely, yogic isolation.

In essence, then, Isolation suppresses the
contents of the lower soul, even to eliminating
it for good, in order to obtain peace. The type
of peace one obtains is another question. It
seems to be the peace of Nirvāna, but that is
to Zaehner what Roman Catholicism speaks of in
wishing for its dead a requies aeterna, the
coldness and stillness of complete rest, which
is precisely the way Hindus describe Nirvāna.
In other words, for Zaehner, a death is the
result.[26]

I conclude, therefore, that Zaehner has not
been able to fit theism into Isolation Mysticism
thus far, nor is it the same in essence as
Nature Mysticism. So we have Nature Mysticism
and Isolation Mysticism thus far, and the one is
not the other, and neither has happily admitted
the God of theistic mysticism to its experiences,
which mysticism is always a mysticism of love.
There has been no mention by Zaehner of love or
the inter-personal intimacy which attends it in
theism; there has been none because there is
none in the texts. The mysticisms are beginning
from different points and saying different things.
Hence Zaehner's initial contention has
held up so far.

Now I move on to another type of mysticism

---

[26]Ibid., p. 148.

which exercised Zaehner in that it saw all other
religious experiences as no different from its
own; theism was no different from its own, natural
mysticism was the same and so was pantheism. This
is religious monism. If it sounds peculiarly like
the philosophia perennis it is because it is the
very same thing as what Huxley and Schuon,
Radahkrishnan and Isherwood have been advocating.
It is, as such, quite absorbent and resilient,
popping up everywhere. It is more than resilient,
though, it absorbs all by negating the main
tenets of the other's religious self-consciousness. When St. Teresa of Avila says she experienced the living God and his love for her, which
is a dualistic relationship, philosophically
speaking, religious monism would say that this
merely means what Hindus mean when they experience the love of a god who is only relatively
divine and who created only for play (Skt.=
lila), and who will himself be destroyed at the
end of the age, since all is illusion anyway,
save Brahman--which exists above the gods--and the
ātman, which is Brahman. So monism relativizes
and neutralizes all religions by accepting them.
It says "Lord Jesus" but does not mean by that
what the ordinary Christian means: the All High
God, than whom there is no greater, the creator
and redeemer of all. It is this absorbency
quality in monism, which absorbs in order to
negate others, which so bothered Zaehner, and
seemed to bother Hans Küng.[27]

(B) Religious Monism

The Vedas are the Scriptures of all the
Hindus. They are the oldest of all their holy
books. The Rig Veda is older than any of the
books of the Old Testament. But it is the
Upaniṣad which forms the way in which Hindu

---

[27]Cf. Hans Küng's remark concerning the
exclusivism of such monisms, cit. supra.

spiritually comes to life. These writings are the summary of the Vedas as well as their summit and end (hence, Vedānta, which is Sanskrit for "end of the Veda"). If Sāmkhya sees each person as a monad, and allows for an infinite number of such monads, Vedānta is just the opposite. There is only one reality for Vedānta: viz., Brahman. Brahman is the Real, and nothing else is real. Sāmkhya's prakrti (Nature) is mere illusion (Skt.=māyā) to the Vedāntin. The ontologies of the two are vastly different. But, Zaehner cut through all the impenetrable undergrowth of Hindu philosophy and came up with the simple statement that, though their metaphysics are quite different, they are the same, as we have said, in praxis. Their contemplative techniques are identical. The aim of both is isolation from the world. Even in Sāmkhya the world ceases to exist, to be perceived, once it has been really seen. The askesis of both Sāmkhya and Vedānta withdraws one from phenomena until only the self exists.[28] In both systems one empties the self of all content. It is just about the same as the Emptiness sought by Mahāyāna Buddhism. Zaehner sees the spiritual reality of Indian religion as being pretty much the same, even though the philosophies explaining it are different. Hence the experience talked of by those in the Sāmkhya is the same as that in Vedānta.[29]

Generally the Upanisads teach that God is immanent and all-pervasive. God is all, the very stuff of man's soul. Zaehner runs down the list of the Upanisads' teachings very briefly: i) God creates from his own substance and enters creation himself; ii) God pervades all; iii) God and the universe are identical, which is pantheism, and iv) God and the soul are identical,

---

[28]Zaehner, S/P, pp. 134 f.

[29]Ibid., p. 135.

which is monism. Zaehner says that numbers
three and four tend to merge; i.e., pantheism
tends towards monism; which[30] is to say, a
diffused idea of God tends towards finding one's
bliss in the Self alone.

Where the sacred writings called the
Brāhmaṇas tended to control the microcosm and
macrocosm by ritual and formula, the Upaniṣads
have foresworn such complete control and treat,
rather, of the nature of the universe, of the
cosmos. Originally the key phrase "Brahman is
Atman" meant that man's vital organs--the
microcosm--correspond to those of the cosmos--the
macrocosm. The pantheism and monism Zaehner
sees in the philosopher Sankara's works developed
from just this simple microcosm/macrocosm relation. Zaehner sees more than Nature Mysticism
in the Upaniṣads. He sees in them a definition
of the Godhead in its relation with the individual. In one of the oldest of the Upaniṣads,
the Chāndogya, Zaehner chooses a passage which
he intends to bear out his contention:

> All this (world) is Brahman. Let one
> worship it in all quietness as tajjalan
> ("that from which one is born, into
> which one breathes and acts"). He who
> consists of mind, whose body is breath
> (spirit or life), whose form is light,
> whose idea is the real, whose self
> (ātman) is space, through whom are all
> works, all desires, all scents, all
> tastes, who encompasses all this (i.e.,
> the whole universe), who does not
> speak and has no care, He is my self
> within the heart, smaller than a
> grain of rice or barley-corn, or a
> mustard-seed, or a grain of millet, or
> the kernel of a grain of millet; this

---

[30]Ibid., p. 136.

is my self within my heart, greater than
the sky, greater than these worlds.
All works, all desires, all scents, all
tastes belong to it: it encompasses all
this (world), does not speak and has no
cares. This my self within the heart is
that Brahman. When I depart from hence
I shall merge into it. He who believes
this will never doubt.[31]

For Zaehner this is very similar to the
theory of St. Thomas Aquinas that God is present
in everything as its cause. Further, he lines up
St. John of the Cross to say that God is the
center of the soul.[32] Hence, for Zaehner, both
Christian mysticism and the Upaniṣads say that
God is infinite, an unextended point at the
center of man. Zaehner maintains that this
immanent God is different from the integrated
self of Proust since the saint is different from
the normally healthy man; which is what happened
to Proust: he became healthy, not holy. In this
Upaniṣad the teaching about Brahman, which had
previously been a rather primitive materialism,
begins to soar. Brahman, in the Chāndogya,
transcends spirit and maybe time. Zaehner says
that this is a primitive man's way of defining
something immaterial; i.e., by saying it is
small, infinitesimal like a seed.[33]

By this time the Hindu had begun to perceive
an eternal, changeless Being behind things. It
was the "real of the real," i.e., it was the
only reality, and it was identical with the
soul.[34] Hence the human soul is identical with

---

[31]Zaehner, S/P, pp. 136f. Chāndogya Up. 3.14.

[32]Ibid., p. 137.

[33]Ibid, p. 138.

[34]Ibid.

the ground of all being. This is the essence of Hinduism and of the Chāndogya (6.9 and 6.10), in Zaehner's estimation. The Upaniṣad said it this way:

> 6.9 As bees make honey by collecting pollen from trees in different places and reduce the pollen (collected) to a unity; and as the different pollens can no longer tell the difference (or say), "I am the pollen of this tree, or I am the pollen of that tree" so too when all these creatures reach reality, they do not know that they have reached it. Whatever they are, whether tiger, lion, wolf, boar...they all become that (the ultimate reality). That which is the subtlest of the subtle, the whole world has as its self. That is reality. That is the Self, and that art thou (Skt.= tat tvam asi).
>
> 6.10 These rivers flow, the eastern towards the West and the western towards the East; from ocean to ocean they flow. They actually become the ocean. And as they do not know which one they are, so all these creatures here, though they have come forth from Being, do not know that they have come forth from Being. Whatever they are, whether tiger, lion... they all become that (the ultimate reality). That which is the subtlest of the subtle, the whole world has as itself. That is reality. That is the self, and that thou art.[35]

Here Zaehner saw, not so much monism, as a merging of individual souls into a higher unity. This he terms the bridge between theistic mysticism and nature mysticism. If Christian mystics

---

[35]Zaehner, S/P, p. 139.

see God in their heart, the Hindus go the other
way and see nothing other than the self in the
self. Huxley called this downward transcendence,
and Zaehner rather liked this way of putting it.
This leads to solipsism which forecloses the very
possibility of any spiritual development. This
is somewhat important for Zaehner. Isolation
spiritually, or downward transcendence, is not a
mode of love, of the perfection of the individual, by putting him back together, but a mode of
self-preservation which achieves its goal by
breaking man down further, into his simples; and
saving that which will not perish: his immortality. It does not seem to Zaehner that this
view can be reconciled with the Christian, which
said that man's condition after the Fall can be
overcome. Hindu isolation spirituality does the
best it can for man on his own; which best is a
taste of immortality, which does not admit of
either grace or God or love.[36]

Zaehner does not see this period of Hindu
spirituality as being the endpoint of Hinduism.
He notes movement. He terms the Upanisads a
bridge between isolation mysticism and theism.
The first view he offers of the bridge is of
Brahman, which (not who), though almost invariably referred to as an impersonal principle,
is not irremediably so. He sees a personality
breaking through the vaulted impersonalism of
Brahman. This is a departure from the way in
which Hinduism is normally treated. Zaehner
seems to discern a pattern of growth towards
theism in Hinduism. It is certain that theism
does come to Hinduism with the Bhagavad Gītā,
with its rich Vaiṣnavite theism, which is dedicated to the God Viṣṇu; and in the South of
India, with its ardent Śaiva Siddhānta, dedicated
to Śiva, and startlingly close to Christian

---

[36]Ibid., p. 140.

piety and mysticism. In all this Zaehner discerns, overall, a move towards theism. It is a gradual evolution from matter, in the crude materialism of the early Upaniṣads[37] where matter is first brought to life, then moves ineluctably towards thought, and thence to divinity in a Upaniṣad like the Śvetāśvatara.[38]

In all his dealings with monism Zaehner is propounding a thesis to the effect that the monist locks himself into his system, which is a solipsist one, and cannot experience what the Christian experiences; but the Christian, on the contrary, can and does experience monism in its isolationist form.

What Zaehner means by this is that, in the comparison of monism with theism and vice versa, one moves beyond isolation to something else: namely, monism in its mystical form. Monism is a naughty word in Western philosophy, but in religion it takes on a different coloration. It is something which has attracted men for centuries untold. It is not that monism, in itself, is alluring, but that religion which means to take its bliss in the self-isolated, when given a philosophical explanation, becomes a monism quite easily; it has, in a word, moved one notch further than pure isolation mysticism. Where isolation admits of a duality, in monism that in which one takes one's pleasure, the self, is not only the only part that matters, it is the only thing which exists, full stop! Monism makes the self the All; and Zaehner says this is to make the self a god.

---

[37]Zaehner, S/P, p. 63, apud Taittirīya Up. 3.10.6.

[38]Zaehner, C/D, pp. 110 f. Śvetāśvatara Up. 5:1; 1:2, 8; 6:5, 11; 1:6, 9.

Hindu mysticism exhibits three basic types: i) the pan-en-henic, which says "I am this All," ii) isolation, or the realization of one's undifferentiated unities--this may be an experience interpreted by the dualistic Sāṁkhya system or the monist/pantheist Vedānta-advaita system--and iii) a loving union with God.[39] Indian religion begins with an experience of immortality and later moves on to philosophy and thence to God. One of the fallacies which most rankled Zaehner is the monist tendency to interpret everything in other men's religions in terms of monism; i.e., to turn everything into a monist experience. He says, "It is fatally easy to confuse all types of mysticism under one head."[40] For example, the Ṣūfi Abū Yazīd identified his experience of loving communion with the Vedantin (Indian) experience of identity with the Absolute. Zaehner says, "From identity of will he jumps forward to the idea, wholly revolutionary in Islam, of identity of essence."[41]

Zaehner said that the system of the great Hindu advaitan philosopher (non-dualist, or monist, for want of a better word) Sankara would fit into the Christian mystical umbrella under the rubric of a via purgativa. That is to say, that all ascetism, all the meditation, leads to the emptying out of sense impressions to free one to intuit his immortal essence, his ātman (self). Thus, it is an isolation mysticism, and so there is nothing of God in it as such. It is much the same, in Zaehner's view of things, in Christian mysticism. The soul has much to do in its own

---

[39]Zaehner, H/M, p. 19.

[40]Ibid, p. 111.

[41]Ibid., p. 112.

184

purification, by way of prayer and ascetical
practice. But God does not enter the picture
until after all the spadework has been done; not
that he has been absent when the purification
has been taking place, but Zaehner means to
interpret Christian spirituality over against
Hinduism, so he seems to downplay the operation
grace has in the first phase of the Christian process of deification in order to make sense of
the Hindu side, and, by way of "spinoff" to
garner some fresh insights into Roman Catholicism
as well. It is not only a trap for the monist to
see that his isolation is God. It is just as
much a trap for the Christian who has achieved
isolation--the Limbo experience--to think he has
gotten to God, finally. Further, it is a rather
modern fallacy, which occurs among those who use
yoga and Zen in Christian contexts, to think that
theirs is a Zen or yogic way of life, by essence.
It may be so per accidens, but the substance is
quite something else: they live by God, not by
self-effort.

So Zaehner says that the emptying out process in Christian mysticism can be an isolation
like the monist experiences, while the former is
on the way to God. But the monist is not on the
way to God, if we take what he says seriously at
all. What he says in his Upaniṣadic texts is
quite something else: he is on the way to the
Self, not God. Hence, the monist enjoys a monist
experience, but not a theistic experience of God.
The theist enjoys an isolation experience, too,
but only as a way-station on the move to God.

The heart of Śankara's Advaita system is a
psychological experience, from which he constructed a monistic interpretation of that trance
experience. Further, the experience is the same
as that had in the dualistic Sāmkhya system-yoga
is basically a dualistic system based, as it is,
on an upper and lower soul hypothesis. By impli-
cation, if one were to dig enough one could find
dualism in a-dvaita (non-dualism) as well. It

185

would be well to dwell on the heart of Sankara's
experience for a few pages in order to understand isolation mysticism from its monist side
and to see that it is neither Nature Mysticism nor
Theism.

Śankara bases his system on the passages in
the Upaniṣads which state that the soul (ātman) is
the Absolute (Brahman). Zaehner says that Brahman
is also the World Soul, or God, in Śankara's
thought. This normally leads the Western reader
to incalculable frustration and a desire to begin
skimming rather than pondering the text, since
such elasticity of terms is not ours here in the
West. Zaehner says that Śankara's teaching is
most easily found in his commentary (Skt.=kārikā)
on the Māndukya Upaniṣad, which is the shortest of
all the Upaniṣads. Śankara says, "This Upaniṣad,
with the Kārikā (of Gaudapāda) embodies in itself
the Quintessence of the substance of the entire
philosophy of the Vedānta."[42] The text speaks of
the four levels of consciousness which the ascetic
experiences. These may have seemed like science
fiction topics or arcane rubbish to the casual,
and to many serious, readers until a short time
ago. But the recent interest in Eastern religions, and in yoga, in particular, have put these
reservations to rest. Scholars accept these
states as they do those of the Western mystics
today. It is the explanation which differs: is
it of God or man? This is asked by theologians
of the experiences of both monistic and theistic
mystics. The four states are:

> All this is Brahman. This self (atman)
> is Brahman. This self has four parts.
> The waking state, taking cognizance of

---

[42]Zaehner, S/P, p. 153, apud Swami
Nikhilananda's ed. of Śankara, Mysore, Sri
Ramakrishna Ashram, 1949.

what is outside...experiences what is
gross: this,...common to all men is the
first part.

The state of sleep, taking cognizance
of what is inside oneself...experiences
what is subtle; this is...composed of
brilliance; it is the second part.

When the sleeper desires nothing
and sees no dream, that is deep sleep.
The state of deep sleep is a unified state,
a mass of wisdom..., composed of bliss:
it experiences bliss; its mouth (or head)
is thought; it is wise; this is the third
part. This is the Lord of all, the knower
of all, this is the inner controller,
the womb of all, the origin and end of
creatures.

The fourth state has cognizance of
neither what is inside nor what is outside, nor of both together: it is not a
mass of wisdom, it is not wise nor yet
unwise. It is unseen; there can be no
commerce with it; it is impalpable, has
no characteristics, unthinkable; it cannot be designated. Its essence is its
firm conviction of the oneness of itself;
it causes the phenomenal world to cease;
it is tranquil and mild, devoid of
duality. Such do they consider this fourth
to be. He is the Self; he it is who should
be known.[43]

So the four states are: i) our waking state;
ii) sleeping; iii) dreamless sleep (which is God);
and iv) a state beyond dreamless sleep (which
state is the Godhead). These are the four levels
of consciousness. The ultimate level, the

---

[43]Zaehner, S/P, p. 154, apud Māndūk. Upan.
nos. 2-7.

fourth, is even beyond God. It is the level of
the ātman and the Brahman, the Self and the Absolute. This Brahman cannot change or make anything
in this world, simply because it is not the cause
of anything in it. In fact, creation is God's
deception of himself.[44]   In Gaudapada's commentary on this Upaniṣad we find full-blown monism.
He says that there is only one reality. Also,
Brahman is identical with each soul. Brahman-
soul (ātman) did not create the world as we see
it. He imagined it, and this without any purpose
at all. Existence is purposeful, but the world
is not included in existence. It is an illusion.
The problem is that the Brahman-soul imagined the
world and then the world turned back and fooled
the Brahman into thinking that it is real. This
is the state of normal human consciousness. It
is categorically wrong. Consciousness is a
state of ignorance which binds us to a phenomenal existence. Release from this bondage comes
through the destruction of this illusion. The
illusion is imposed by the Self on the Self
against its will. Release comes in the state of
dreamless sleep. This is a state without qualities, much like the eighth stage of release in
Buddhism.[45]

In this state there is no perception of
feeling, and perception itself stops along with
discursive reasoning. One has not detached himself from them, as one does in Sāmkhya-yoga, but
one realizes that they just do not exist. The
only existent is the Self. This comes through
experience. Hinduism does not believe. It does
not have to. Thirty centuries of experience
have taught it that one can experience the immortal now. Therefore, experience tells the Self
that everything has no existence; not religion,
not gods, not people, not emotions, not thoughts,

---

[44]Zaehner, S/P, p. 154.

[45]Ibid., p. 155.

not feelings, not body,...etc. It is the most
uncompromising of experiences. It is not a system at root. It is an experience first, from
which experience one fashions an explanation.
Life antecedes its explanations. So the philosophy of monism came after the experience of
solipsism. This phenomenon is accepted as
valid today by students of religion and psychology. It is a stunning experience, therefore, and
must be dealt with. In this system there can be
no thought of union. What would one unite with?
Theists unite with god. Monists unite with
nothing and no one.[46] This is the basis of
Zaehner's continued assertion that there is no
teaching of love in Buddhism, which is another
isolation mysticism, despite its kindness and
compassion. Love demands a mutuality of personal
relationships, and isolation mysticism dis-
courages these at their roots.[47] Hence, Zaehner
sees no philosophical possibility of love in
early Buddhism (Theravada and Mahāyāna, the
types of the latter which see nothing but emptiness as real--i.e., that of Nagarjuna, to name
only one) nor in any isolation system. The
psychological possibility of love is another
matter. Buddhist mothers love their children as
much as do Christian mothers. The religion lived
is not the religion as taught.

So, Hindu mysticism begins with the Upanisads, which draw no clear distinction between the
soul, which is the eternal, and God. Hence,
Vedānta sees self-realization as a process of
becoming Absolute.[48] Of the same experience, the

---

[46]Zaehner, S/P, p. 156.

[47]Cf. Zaehner's C/D, pp. 207,220 and 303
for this important concept.

[48]Zaehner, H/M, p. 187.

Sāmkhya says that the soul enjoys its own immortality, its own eternity. So, Zaehner says that both Śankara and Gauḍapāda do pretty much the same thing in their monistic systems: both construct a metaphysical system out of a psychological experience. Both conclude to the non-being of everything but the self, after having an experience of supernal Oneness.[49] It is difficult, indeed, for phenomena to stand much of a chance before the euphoria and power of such an experience. The metaphysics may be procrustean, but it does not seem to bother monists very much. The metaphysics seem to soothe them and do not jibe at their experience of ultimate liberation.

So the fourth level is the level of the isolationist. It is beyond God, on the level of the Godhead. The level of God, the third, is merely a way-station on the way to the Real. God is merely an illusion, even in the interior life, for the isolationist. The Real is the Self, and all else is, ultimately, illusion.

In his review article of Zaehner's The Convergent Spirit[50] Bede Griffiths says that he agrees that in isolation mysticism one experiences "the soul in itself." But he would not agree with Zaehner that this experience is a dead end, or something closed. He contends that the isolation experience opens one up to all beings since in experiencing the ground of one's being one is "open to all beings" precisely in experiencing one's ground. It is a "living point, which opens on the infinite. In other words, it is at this point above all that man is open to God."[51]

---

[49]Ibid., p. 172.

[50]Ibid.

[51]In "Blackfriars," art. cit., p. 479.

It would appear that a compromise would put
Zaehner and Griffiths in agreement. If the
isolation experience is experienced as a last
end, an end in itself, from which one refused to
venture forth to God and one's fellows, then it
is a dead end, and Zaehner is right. If it is
experienced as the end of a process of self-
emptying in which one finds oneself blissfully,
and for the first time, as a part of a larger
process in which one means to go out to God and
one's fellows, then Griffiths is correct.
Zaehner's point in all this is that the experience is so powerful that it is a temptation, a
trap; one is so ravished by the direct and blissful experience of the self that one refuses to
go further. Later on Zaehner loosened up his
seemingly harsh judgment and dealt more benignly
with the other religions in his efforts to see
convergence, but in his argument against the
philosophia perennis he was interested in the
divergence of religious experiences to disprove
the contention of Huxley et al. that there was,
beneath it all, only one mysticism, and it is
both universal and perennial.

Zaehner has been thus far saying that
Huxley's experience was not either the Sat,
Chit, Ananda experience of the Hindus nor the
Beatific Vision of Christians because it is pan-
en-henic, which is to say it is Nature Mysticism.
It is real mysticism, but not the Sankhya nor
Advaita of Hinduism nor the theism of Christianity. Secondly, he has said that Nature Mysticism
(the pan-en-henic experience) is, or can be, the
first step in a religious experience, though not
religious at all in itself. It is the first
level of trance, in yoga, which produces a sleeping awareness that one is the All.

The second level of that experience is one
of isolation in which the Self rears its head and
throws off the assertiveness of the ego, which
latter had taken control in the pan-en-henic
experience to say "I am the All." But the second

191

level is one in which the Self demands that all,
everything, of body and mind and soul be stripped
from one so that only the upper soul be left in
an enjoyment of what we would call Self-contemplation, and what yogins would call Ānanda (bliss) or
Nirvāna (bliss), depending on whether they were
Hindus or Buddhists. The experience, however, is
the same. It is one produced by yoga which is an
ecstasy technique based on a bicameral psychology:
the upper soul is the eternal, the lower is
ephemeral and somewhat gross, though not necessarily evil, and even--in the case of Sāmkhya--
somewhat good, though bumbling. The heart of
Indian spirituality is here, and it is the heart
of the philosophia perennis, in my estimation.
Though Zaehner never says this, it is the next
step in his logic. Yoga, therefore, is based on
a dualism in which there is body and soul
(prakrti and purusa), whether it is the dualist
Sāmkhya system, or the advaitan system of Sankara.
Sankara has been called nondualist, but this is
an emphasis on his part, a philosophical emphasis, or an ontology. The psychology and
spiritual technique he and his yogins use is one
and the same as the Sāmkhya yogins use: namely,
a dualistic, bicameral, one. This should reduce
the confusion in the reader a bit. There are
two philosophical constructs: the Sāmkhya is
dualistic (body and spirit), and the advaitan is
monistic (there is only the One). There is one
spirituality: a bicameral one based on the
upper/lower soul psychology which is axiomatic
to all Indian thought.

Next, Indian spirituality is based on a
first yogic experience which says, "I am the
All." This is neither sāmkhyan nor advaitan but
it is yogic. The next level takes two directions: Sāmkhya says that there are other things
besides the Self (purusa), but when complete isolation is achieved it is as if there were
nothing else; Advaita, on the other hand, when
in the throes of isolation, explains it so that
the "All" and the Self are one and the same

thing, the only existent. Monism has flipped the
pan-en-henic experience and the Sāṃkhya experience
about to say "All is I, only I," or from the Absolute side, "the All is the Only Reality, and the
Self is that All." Monism is the temptation of
mysticism, in Zaehner's view. It seems so because
monism is a unitive experience, as is each mystical experience, and unity is either a combination
of two or more parts or it gives way to the next
step of the logic of a unitive experience, which
is identity. There is an essential difference
between unity and identity. Identity is what we
have here with monism, and unity is what one sees
in Christian, or theistic mysticism. There is,
therefore, an essential difference between Hindu
monism and Christian theism. So Isolation Mysticism, whether Sāṃkhya or advaitan, is not Christian Mysticism, though Christian Mysticism can
partake of isolation states and pan-en-henic
states on the way to the union of man with God.

It seems that the force of a trance technique can turn around either a polytheism, a non-
theism or a theism until it becomes a monism. In
Hinduism, with its profusion of gods, and its pantheism as well, one of the temptations of the use
of the trance technique outlined by Śankara is
that one go beyond the third level, that of God
or the gods, to a Godhead level, which is monistic in which everything is the same, in which all
are One, and there is no other. This is the
philosophia perennis, and it is universal when a
religion goes against itself. When Islam was
introduced to the trance technique of India,
through Abū Yazīd of Bistam's guru, this religion
of vaulted transcendentalism became monistic.
Zaehner's commentary on the Gītā argues that
Śankara's interpretation of the Gītā and the
Upaniṣads imposed a monistic interpretation on
them. There is no such thing as bad doctrine in
Hinduism, nor is there a magisterial body to
judge what is proper or improper, nor is there
any inclination to do so; that is either
Christianity or Islam or, in a much reduced

sense, Judaism. But the fact that Rāmānuja fought Śankara's interpretation so fiercely, and that his interpretation is the workaday one now in India, somewhat proves Zaehner's point that monism is both a temptation to religions and not the only interpretation of the trance experience one has had. Zaehner did not go this far, but I shall add, following out his line of reasoning, that monism is a sign of the breakdown of religions when enthusiasm makes the Real, and all others, to be a function of the Self. The interpretation of reality which does not assign some value to both spirit and matter, as did Sāmkhya and Aristotle, tends to make reality depend on one's interiority thus destroying any possibility, psychologically and ontologically, of there being any exteriority at all. This is the reductio ad absurdum, not only of religions, but of all normal life.

So I shall look, next, to a theism in which monistic trance-states are to be found: namely, Islam. The philosophia perennis states that what it holds is both universal and the only mystical experience. Zaehner's argument is that it derives from India, even in Islam, and is different from both theism and pan-en-henism.

Monism is not only to be found in Hinduism. It is strongly represented in Ṣūfic Islam. It is one of Zaehner's more creative interpretations that there is no such thing as an indigenous monism in Islam. He holds this in the face of a catalogue of Ṣūfi masters who were outrageously monist, and some good modern scholars who contend it is not so that Islam could not grow monism on its own soil. Zaehner maintains that Hinduism and Islam are moving in opposite directions as they live, grow and develop. The Hindu mystical tradition goes from monism in the beginning to theism in its latest manifestations. Islamic mysticism begins with an overarching theistic

194

religion and moves towards monism in which one realizes himself as God.[52] For Zaehner, only Indian religion makes mysticism the very basis of its system. This seems to be the reason why Zaehner made mysticism the basis of inter-religious dialogue: the commonality between East and West is mysticism. The slippage in the mystical tradition in the West forced him to include only Roman Catholicism in his dialogue with the East. Vedānta and Sāmkhya are philosophical attempts to explain mystical experience. Its dogmatism did not allow Islam the freedom of movement which all Hindus enjoy in a dogma-free religion such as Hinduism is.[53] Hinduism begins with a spirituality of identity and moves on to one of separation of matter from spirit. Islam begins with a religion of sharp separation in which God is "out there," and no one and nothing either can or does associate with him. Associating anything or anyone with God is a capital sin in Islam. But Islamic development ended with the identity of God and man in the writings of Al-Ghazāli and Al-Ḥallāj, both Ṣūfi masters. Mysticism grows very sparsely in religions of such transcendence, such as Judaism and Islam. The Kabala was a late comer to Judaism. Early on, Judaism had a strong tradition of ecstatic Prophets, but it did its best to discourage this as time wore on.

Neither transcendental religion, Judaism nor Islam, could give much leeway to mysticism, since their dogmatism held them to very tight boundaries. But the mystic is generous in spirit, and tends to see truth in all religions. This is why Zaehner says that the temptation of the mystic is the philosophia perennis. Without saying so outright, he says that the mystic tends to see

---

[52]Zaehner, H/M, p. 11.

[53]Ibid., p. 20.

all religions as an outer manifestation of a
single inner truth.[54] Hence, he concludes that
mysticism does not bloom in a monotheism which is
healthy and not under the heel of persecution.
Zaehner assumes that the primary Indian assertion,
that man's soul is at least potentially extra-
temporal, is as axiomatic as the basic monotheistic
assertion that God exists. In fact, he jibes, one
can prove the Indian assertion, but one cannot
prove the monotheist's assumption.[55] For example,
the Brhadāranyaka Upanisad (2.5.15) sees the Self
(upper self, ātman) as God. It does not see how
one can distinguish between the ātman and God
empirically. The Upanisad concludes that the
infinite within man is the infinite without as
well. The Sāmkhya does not go so far, but both
it and the great Hindu theist philosopher
Rāmānuja say that each soul is its own cosmos with
an infinite within it; it is not "the" cosmos,
but a cosmos separate from the others.[56] Śankara
says that there is only one thing worthwhile doing
in life: the realization of one's unity.
Rāmānuja counters by saying that this is just the
contemplation of the self, and that it has to
cease, and that one has to move into God's presence through love.[57] So Hinduism came to the
conclusion, against the Brhadāranyaka's assertion,
that one can distinguish between God and the Self.
This is the basic difficulty Zaehner discerns in
monism: that one mistakes the Self for the Real.
When the Gitā moved on, in its later chapters
(after chapter VI) to assign a value to love and
devotion, and value it more than yoga and self-
realization, Hinduism moved into another era
religiously. It moved away from monism to dualism

---

[54]Ibid., p. 3.

[55]Ibid., p. 87.

[56]Ibid., p. 88.

[57]Ibid., p. 89.

and love mysticism. This will be the third
stage of mysticism, the other two being the pan-
en-henic and the isolation states in which the
ego asserts itself to become the All and the
Self asserts itself to throw off all but the contemplation and enjoyment of its immortality.
This third stage began, Zaehner affirms, not with
either isolation or pan-en-henism, but with the
polar opposition of isolation: integration.
After one had integrated the self with the two
aspects of man's lower person, body and ego, then
love mysticism can begin. Zaehner sees this as
very much like Christian and Muslim love mysticism.

But, for Zaehner, just as there is no concept of love in the early part of the Gitā, which
outlines yoga, so there could be no question of
loving God in early Islam.[58] He was too far
removed, and it was sinful to even think of associating with him, even in so tender a thing as
love. But, as things wore on, Ṣūfism came into
Islam as a movement of the heart. It maintained
that those who wait with a loving heart for his
call can experience God. This leads to union
with him, which leaves some individuality to
them. Dhu'l-Nun and Muḥasibi are exponents of
this mysticism of love.[59] But how did such a
radical break come in a religion which held that
religion was a crystalline emptiness below the
fullness of god and his transcendence? A mysticism of love filled the crystal cup with the
heady wine of ecstatic religion. What, then, is
the origin of this love mysticism in Islam?

Love in the Qur'ān meant obedience. The
Traditions (Arab.=Hadith), which are the fonts
of doctrine second only to the Qur'ān, would

---

[58]Zaehner, H/M, p. 89.

[59]Ibid., p. 91.

have no love in Islam since love was only for equals. But love and the experience of it, a passionate longing for a God who chooses his lover, is to be found in both Dhu'l-Nun and in Rāmānuja. Zaehner made no more of this, maintaining that Muslim mysticism is a continuation of Christian mysticism anyway. He calls it "entirely derivative."[60] First, it came from Christian love mysticism. Later, mysticism came from the Vedānta through Abū Yazīd; i.e., in the ninth century of the Christian era. Zaehner makes no further move to elaborate the love element in Islam, since it is obvious to him that it derives from Christian, not Indian, devotion mysticism. But he goes to great lengths to prove that Abū Yazīd's mysticism derives from India. He does so since, if this be ture, then it cannot be said that Muslim monism proves that such monism is universal, as do those who teach the philosophia perennis. He uses Abū Yazīd to disprove the contention that there is a universal mysticism, always and everywhere the same. If Yazīd's came from elsewhere, so goes Zaehner's reasoning, it is not a manifestation of a universal tendency in man, but an import which took hold in another religion; a religion which had borrowed its love mysticism from elsewhere as well; i.e., from Hindu monks.

For Zaehner, Abū Yazīd's monism is like Islam's love mysticism: it is derivative.[61] Further, the experience of oneness which Abū Yazīd had caused him to fall into the monist's trap; this is to say, that he had an experience of his own oneness, and called it the Absolute, which is God in Islam. But, unlike Vedānta, which is by no means a monotheism, he had neither the polytheist background nor the philosophical background--the tools--to express his

---

[60]Ibid., p. 160.

[61]Ibid., p. 175.

experience. He concluded, therefore, that the experience of his own oneness was the experience of God. This is the trap of monism. The Ṣūfis had no distinction between a God who is beyond time and an experience of the Self within it. For the Ṣūfis, only God was beyond time. When they experienced ecstasy that which they experienced was the self beyond time; but, since they had no concept for eternity other than God's eternity, they concluded that an experience of inner eternity meant that they were God. So Al-Hallāj exulted, "I am God," and paid for it with his life.[62]

The first, and the prototypical, example of Muslim monism for Zaehner, therefore, was Abū Yazīd of Bisṭam. Bisṭam is a town in the province of Sind, in India. He took a guru to instruct him in Hindu prayer and trance techniques. In return he instructed his guru, whose name was Abū 'Ali, in the ritual of Islam. Abū 'Ali had converted to Islam from Hinduism. So, when Abū Yazid said things like "Takūnu anta dhāka" (Arab.=thou art that), it had no meaning whatsoever in Arabic, and certainly none in Islam. Sarrāj wrote about Yazid's mysticism. In one passage he said:

> Abū Yazid is reported to have said (Sarrāj tells us): "Once (God) raised me up and placed me before him, and said to me: "O Abū Yazid, verily my creation longs to see thee." And I said: "Adorn me with thy unity and clothe me in thine I-ness and raise me up unto thy oneness, so that when thy creatures see me, they may say: "We have seen thee (i.e. God) and thou art that." Yet I (Abū Yazid) will not be there at all.[63]

---

[62]Zaehner, H/M, p. 105.

[63]Ibid., p. 94, apud Sarrāj, p. 177. I can not find Zaehner's source beyond this page reference in his H/M.

It will be remembered that this phrase, "Thou art that," is one of the great phrases of Indian monism. In Arabic, the phrase is nonsense. It just does not make any sense to Zaehner at all, and he seems to be right in saying so. But translate it directly into Sanskrit and it becomes Tat tvam asi (thou art that), which is one of the mahāvākyāni (Skt.=great phrases) of Hindu monism. Zaehner says rightly that this is straight out of the Chāndogya Upaniṣad (6.9.10).[64] The great Arabist R. A. Nicholson does not try to go over to Hinduism to make sense of the phrase and, in Zaehner's estimation, makes a non-translation of it rather than commit himself. Nicholson's translation runs thusly: "and that only Thou mayst be there, not I."[65] Zaehner did not meet this phrase in Buddhism, Neo-Platonism or Taoism. It must, therefore, be Hindu, since it fits perfectly there, and does not fit anywhere else; certainly not in Islam.[66]

Zaehner's next offer of proof that Yazīd's utterances are Vedāntin in provenance is this: Śankara gives phenomena no quarter. They just do not exist on the real level. They are an illusion (Skt.=māyā). Sarraj says that Yazīd mentions the "tree of oneness," the very symbol of monism in Vedānta. Sarrāj says:

As soon as I reached (God's) unity...I became a bird whose body was of oneness and whose wings were of everlastingness, and I went on flying in the atmosphere a hundred million times as large; and I went on flying until I reached the expanse of eternity and in it saw the tree of oneness.

---

[64]Ibid., p. 95.

[65]Ibid., p. 94.

[66]Ibid., p. 95.

Then (says Sarrāj), he described the
soil (in which it grew) its root and
branch, its shoots and fruits, and then
he said: Then I looked, and I knew that
all this was deceit.[67]

The tree of life, for Zaehner, is the famous text
from the Katha Upaniṣad (6.1) and the Bhagavad-
Gītā (15.1-2). These texts are truisms in Hinduism. The Gītā says: "With roots above and
branches below the imperishable fig-tree has been
declared. Its leaves are the Vedic hymns. Who
knows it knows the Veda. Below and above extend
its branches nourished by the qualities (sattva,
rajas, tamas), and the objects of sense are their
sprouts. Below are extended the roots from which
arise actions in the world of men." This tree
appears in both the Mundaka Upan. (3.1.1-3) and
the Śvetāśvatara Upan. (4.6-10); the latter con-
nects it with māyā (illusion). God uses deceit
(māyā in Skt. and khud'a in Arab.) to fool men in
both Hinduism and in Islam. In both religions,
God uses deceit to bring about designs he has
made for the world. But the Arabs in no other
texts use khud'a to indicate God's deceit. This
is conclusive for Zaehner, since khud'a is an
exact translation for māyā. So both the word and
the sense fit perfectly into an Indian Vedantin
religious scheme.[68]

The clincher, theologically, is that the
Lord is the great deceiver in both religions
(Mahā Māyin=the great magician or deceiver in
Hinduism); but only in Hinduism is the world a
deceit. Yazīd uses khud'a for this very purpose;
and this has no meaning at all to Orthodox Islam
where the world was purposeful, proceeding on a
linear career towards the Eschaton, and had

---

[67]Ibid.

[68]Zaehner, H/M, p. 95, and S/P, p. 162.

201

intrinsic meaning. If Yazīd used it in the
sense that the world was deceitful it was,
therefore, meaningless to mainstream Islam but
very meaningful to mainstream Vedānta. Zaehner
did not think to add this theological explica-
tion, since his readers would already know it,
being mostly Indologists and Arabists; but I add
it to highlight the force of his argument, which
was not inconsiderable, and still stands without
refutation which is any more than partial.

Next, when Yazīd cried out "Glory be to me.
How great is my glory" (Arab.=subhāni, mā a'zama
sha'nī), it shocked his listeners' religious
sensitivities. Glory is to be rendered to God
alone in Islam. All piety is directed to God.
But the Sannyāsa Upaniṣad says "mahyam evo namo
namah," which means, "glory, glory be to me" in
Sanskrit.69

Lastly, Yazīd says "I sloughed off my skin
as a snake...I was He."70 Zaehner says that this
is a direct parallel to the Bṛhadāraṇyaka Upan.
(4.4.7), which reads, "As the sloughed off skin
of a snake lies on an ant-hill, dead, cast off,
so does this body lie. But this incorporeal,
immortal spirit is Brahman indeed, is light
indeed...If a man should know himself (his ātman)
and say: "I am He-, what could he possibly wish
for or desire that would make him cling to the
body?"71 Zaehner says that the two texts
resemble one another too closely to be mere
chance, something "fortuitous." The account
seems to be translated from a language which
makes no distinction between nafsi (my lower soul,

69Zaehner, S/P, p. 163, apud Otto Schrader,
The Minor Upaniṣads, Madras, 1912, vol. i,
p. 257.

70Zaehner, H/M, p. 99.

71Ibid., pp. 98 f.

in Arabic) and dhātī (my essence, in Arabic).
Sanskrit uses only one word for both: ātman.[72]
It looks as if Zaehner's argument is allowing him
to close in for the kill.

Hence, in all these instances, Yazīd's
phrases are either nonsense or blasphenous in an
Arab-Muslim setting, but fit quite well in a
Hindu Vedānta one. They fit here alone. Zaehner
concludes, "Thus not only are Abū Yazīd's ideas
pure Vedānta, the very words and phrases he uses
only make sense when seen in a Sanskrit context."[73] Therefore Hinduism came to Islam through
Abū Yazīd of Bisṭam. He was an uneducated man and
probably heard Vedānta from his guru, a former
Indian Vedāntin. He absorbed it unreflectively,
probably without knowing the roots of doctrine
contained in what he set out to teach. Zaehner
says that the sayings of Jesus and St. Paul came
into Islam in the very same way. Where else would
Yazīd have gotten the secrets of the Upaniṣads,
for secrets they were, not given freely to anyone
except the pauci electi, and then only taught
secretly in the woods, if Rāmānuja's way of learning them is any example? The latter learned them
this traditional way and then broadcast them--
illegally--from the pinnacle of the temple. Only
Birūni, a Muslim who had earlier published a book
on the teachings of the Hindus, could have
retailed such knowledge, but he did not; and
besides, even if he had, Yazīd was unlearned. So,
it seems that he learned these secrets fresh from
his Vedāntin guru, and that, since there is no
other source extant from which they could have
come, and since the translations of Zaehner seem
well within the realm of probability--that there
be so many coincidences in one man's life so as
to be able to reproduce the very words of a

---

[72]Ibid.

[73]Ibid., p. 99.

religious teaching he had never heard--Zaehner's argument seems probable. In putting forth the very heart of vedāntic teaching Yazīd shows a Hindu influence and a link with Indian monism.[74]

Yazīd's experience placed him beyond space and time; even beyond love. They left him in a state of complete, undifferentiated unity. His experience was an "I am this All" experience. The "All" was not Brahman for this Muslim; it was God Himself. He did not have the tools intellectually with which to express his experience. He could not, therefore, do with his experience what the Hindus did: viz., distinguish between God and God's mode of being (mad-bhāva, in the Gitā). He sees love and longing after God as a hindrance, as a consequence of his experience. Devotion, law and rites were useless as well. Zaehner says that this is very much like Yazīd's contemporary, Śankara's thought.[75]

Zaehner notes a radical change in this Muslim's thought, therefore. This change he thinks too radical without outside help; which help came from India or from an Indian. Śankara had just revived advaita. The liberated man, in Śankara's and Yazīd's thought, abandoned all, even God, but never the Self (ātman and ruh, the upper soul in Skt. and Arab. respectively).[76]

Later, the Ṣūfi master Junayd, who liked Yazīd and wanted to protect him from his enemies and to preserve his teaching within the confines of orthodoxy, said what we have been hearing all along from Zaehner about those with such strong experiences: what Yazīd experienced was a trap,

---

[74]Ibid., p. 100.

[75]Ibid., pp. 105-7, passim.

[76]Ibid., p. 109.

though set by God--in Nature Mysticism one sets
the trap for the self--to catch out the proud.[77]
If he wants, God shatters the first experience of
unity--an isolation experience--and enters into an
I/Thou relation with the soul in which he overwhelms the soul and appropriates it to himself.
The soul submits in suffering (Arab.=fanā=annihi-
lation) and joy.[78] Once the destruction of the
ego happens in Ṣūfism, nothing is left save God.
So one appears to be God. Even Ghazali holds
this, and he is the paragon of orthodoxy in
Islam, whom so many call the father of orthodox
Ṣūfism, since he cleansed it of its heresies and
offered the orthodox something they could
accept. For him, one appears to be God. This
looks just like Sankara to Zaehner, and Zaehner
appears to be correct.[79]

But, trap or not, Abū Yazīd's teachings
seeped into Islam and became common currency.
This made it possible for Ṣūfis to experience
the advaitan experience in a theistic context.
If advaita allowed the yogin to experience the
self as Absolute, then the same experience in a
theistic context made the illation that "I am
God" not only possible, but necessary. It was
necessary since the Ṣūfis had not sufficient
philosophical frameworks to handle the difficult
construction work necessary in making a distinction between isolation mysticism and theistic
mysticism. This is the trap of monism.
Reversed, it makes the monist think that everyone in the same and other religions experiences
the very same thing in the various ways which
are the religions themselves. This was, again,
Zaehner's purpose in writing Mysticism Sacred
and Profane and its companion volume Hindu and

---

[77]Ibid., p. 188.

[78]Ibid., pp. 188 f.

[79]Zaehner, H/M, p. 14.

Muslim Mysticism: to disprove the monist's fallacy. Hence Yazīd brought Vedānta to Islam. He was not condemned for heresy because he had such strong advocates, like Junayd, who talked the orthodox out of their hostile intentions against him.

Yazīd said that he had been annihilated in God. His annihilation (Arab.=fanā) meant that every sense of self, feeling, space and time, even the sense of the very loss of self is lost. There is just an awareness of undifferentiated oneness in which all creation, including the empirical self, vanishes. Yazīd attributes the experience to the Self, but Junayd "baptized" it by attributing it to God.[80] Yazīd was never condemned by Islam. Hallāj was, literally, crucified for saying the same things. Junayd knew Hallāj, and Hallāj's disciple Shiblī. He refused to have any truck with Hallāj, but kept up his friendship with Shiblī. However, he wrote a defense of Yazīd to allow the latter his life and afford Islam the opportunity to taste his doctrines. Yazīd never suffered physically for his teachings, though he was exiled from Bistam seven times for promulgating them.[81]

Yazīd was probably helped by the common appraisal of him that he was a madman. He once held his silence for thirteen years, just staring ahead with his chin resting on his knees. Muslims think that he underwent bast (expansion) and also severe periods of qabd (contraction).

What did Yazīd experience, precisely? His isolation (Arab.=tafrid) from all things, including himself, is the separation which we saw in Sāmkhya. Yazīd interpreted it as an intuition

---

[80]Ibid., p. 124.

[81]Ibid., p. 116.

of his own Godhood. Junayd amends it to say that it was an experience of the isolated soul contemplating the isolation of God. Zaehner says that this is exactly the same way that the theistic Sāmkhya-yoga interprets it: for it, God is a useful object for contemplation. This is what transpired with Yazīd.[82] Secondly, when Yazīd experienced all things in himself, he thought it was so because he was God. Zaehner thinks that this is an experience of Nature Mysticism where the self expands enough to include everything. This we saw in the Upaniṣadic experience. It looks as though he fell into the trap laid for one engrossed in the expansion experience.[83]

Thirdly, Zaehner's linguistic analysis of Yazīd's terminology evokes Hindu terms for the same experiences.[84]

Fourthly, Yazīd thought that he had gone to the very pinnacle of the mystical life while in the throes of his experience, but the Persian writer Aṭṭār said that the infinite is only the beginning of the mystical life.[85]

Hence, Yazīd said openly what his contemporaries had felt secretly, and had experienced, but never admitted to the public: namely, that the soul is God when it reaches Journey's end. The Ṣūfis did not have such a useful set of categories to work with as did the Hindus, with

---

[82]Ibid., p. 124.

[83]Zaehner, H/M, pp. 127 f.

[84]Ibid., e.g. Yazīd's "I-ness" (Skt.= ahaṁkāra), his "selfhood of self" (Skt.=ātman).

[85]Ibid., Zaehner says that Aṭṭar's version of the experience is found in Badawi's trans. of Aṭṭār, pp. 138-41, also in Zaehner's H/M, appendix B 1, pp. 198-218.

their ātman, etc. nomenclatures, in expressing
their experience in a way which would allow it its
unquestioned power and reality. The Hindu theist
Rāmānuja used ātman, an ancient term, as a point
of distinction between the self and God. Thus,
he saved the yogic experience, which was a real
experience, and the grace of God which was just
as real to him. So in not having such a term as
ātman, Yazīd had little alternative in his dilemma: either he was true to his experience or he
was true to God and orthodoxy. So he combined
the two and his experience became God. Again,
this is the monist's fallacy. Zaehner sees the
category ātman as being beyond space and time,
and, therefore, divine on that account, but which
is not the ground of being (God) itself.[86]

I offer both the criticisms Zaehner's colleagues offered his interpretations of Abū
Yazīd's teachings and my criticism of Zaehner in
his stand as well in the first appendix to this
book. In the second appendix I will show the
monism of both Al-Jynayd and Al-Ghazālī in outline
form. Suffice it to say for now that Zaehner's
typology stands up, and, a fortiori, so does his
argumentation in all this against the philosophia
perennis, which states that each type of mysticism is different, and that there is no universal
"type" of mysticism overarching all. Zaehner's
argumentation that there is no indigenous mysticism in Islam is not thoroughly convincing
since, derivative though it may have been, the
end-product is the important matter in religion,
not from whence the materials derive. Islam had
and has a mysticism, so Zaehner seems too zealous
to prove that the philosophia perennis is not
universal. Further, it is not a numerical universality which the philosophia perennis
preaches, but a qualitative one; which is to say
that they think that behind differing forms

---

[86]Zaehner, H/M, p. 134.

mysticisms and religions are the same. Ṣūfism is hardly even a different form, but is Isolation Mysticism and monism, with the same consequences we saw and discussed in Hinduism. But, nevertheless, Zaehner's argumentation is not destroyed by the criticism of scholars, nor are my criticisms of a nature as to do any more than domesticate his zeal a bit.

What Zaehner has done is to demonstrate the difference between Nature Mysticism and the two forms of Isolation Mysticism (Sāmkhya and Advaita) from one another, and from the Mysticism of Love in theisms.

(C) Summary of Hindu and Muslim Isolation and Monism

Sankara's system gives the yogin four states of consciousness: waking, sleep, dreamless sleep, and beyond dreamless sleep. This is the heart of Indian spirituality, its Ur experience, and the technique for obtaining it is yoga. The Godhead is the fourth state of consciousness; it is actually a state of trance called samādhi. God is the third level of trance. Thus one becomes God and then moves beyond him on the way to a dualistic or monistic isolation. God is not necessary on the whole, and not even present in the fourth, or end, stage. The fourth state means that there is no Becoming whatsoever; there is only Being. God, on the lower level, creates to deceive himself.[87] So God s creation is an illusion, and freedom (Skt.=mokṣa) comes through destruction of this self-delusion.[88]

In Zaehner's system a unio mystica is meaningless in Hindu monism because union demands two realities, and here there is only one.

---

[87]Zaehner, S/P, pp. 153 f.

[88]Ibid., p. 155.

Zaehner sees great similarities between the ontologies of the Māndukya Upaniṣad, on which both
Śankara and Gauḍapāda base their monistic metaphysics, and Ghazālī's thought. The latter says
that nothing exists save God. This is taken from
God's point of view; i.e., qua being things are
pure not-being (a-sat in Skt., and in monist
philosophy). Things do not exist in themselves,
they exist only in the divine being. For the
Hindu monist, man is God. For the Muslim monist,
man exists only insofar as he has been given
reality by God.[89] The latter is just normal Muslim doctrine. In the Māndukya Upaniṣad there is
a unity, but there can be no union, nor can there
be communion either since there is only one
reality involved, not two. In Islam Abū Sa'id
spoke of his union with God as a "they," adding
the Arabic honorific phi to the pronoun to indicate that the "they" means God.[90] When Ghazālī
is writing under the influence of ecstasy (what
Muslims call drunkenness) he can be monist. When
sober, he is orthodox and defends Junayd's sober
school of Ṣūfism. Zaehner says that Ghazālī is
inconsistent, therefore. When he is sober he
says that only God exists ontologically. Man is
nothing apart from God, and it is shirk (Arab.=
unbelief deriving from associating anything with
God) to say anything about a union with God.
Hence, nothing exists apart from God.[91] This is
the early orthodox, Ghazālī. The monist Ghazālī
is another matter.

Zaehner argues that mysticism in Islam is
entirely derived, either from Christianity or from
Hinduism. Any religion which is so wary of shirk
is not fertile soil for mysticism, which is based

---

[89]Zaehner, S/P, pp. 157 f.

[90]Ibid., p. 159.

[91]Ibid., p. 160.

on the immanentism of God, at least in potentia.
So monism derives from Abū Yazīd of Bisṭam, in the
Indian province of Sind. He learned it from his
guru, who was a former Hindu monist.[92] The instances in Yazid's writings, which are to be found
in Sarrāj's works, in which monism is openly
stated, are nonsense or blasphemy in a normal Muslim context, and make perfect sense only in a Hindu
setting where even the Sanskrit fits amazingly
well. Zaehner's detractors have not left me convinced that they have destroyed his position.[93]
So, it seems Ṣūfi monism derives from Sanskrit
linguistically, from Hindu monism and very likely
from Christian monasticism religiously, but from
within Islam most of all--this latter flies in the
face of Zaehner's strong assertion to the contrary. He made a serious error in this matter.

Zaehner criticizes both the Māṇḍukya Upanisad and Śankara, who used it as his chief source,
for going beyond the evidence. Elsewhere in
Hinduism, e.g., the Śāṇḍilya Vidyā text, both God
and world are accorded independent reality, and
God does exist in man's center: namely, the
heart. So it identifies man's center with God,
but both really exist.[94] Śankara, however, says
that nothing external to God exists. Zaehner
says that this is the position of the Sāṃkhya as
well. Therefore, absolute monism carries the
ascetic or mystic to isolation, not to God.
Zaehner concludes that isolation is only a way-
station in the process of deification, only a
via purgativa. He seems to see things moving in
an evolutionary pattern. The monist Hindus do
stop at monism and seem quite happy, but Hinduism

---

[92]Ibid., p. 162.

[93]Cf. Appendix no. 1 for a full treatment of the linguistic argument.

[94]Zaehner, S/P, p. 164.

211

itself did not stop there. There is a pattern of
movement in the Gītā in which things evolve
towards theism; Rāmānuja's thought, too, caps
this Indian religious evolution as does the rich
theism of South India, Śaiva Siddhānta. In a word,
Indian religion was moving towards bhakti which is
a theistic religion, or a religion of devotion.[95]

In its practice monism meant the isolation of
the self from others. This is true in both
Hinduism and Islam. Junayd formulated the Ṣūfi
doctrine of the soul thus: it existed in God
before one's birth. In this, Junayd resembles the
Sāmkhya and Vedānta's advaita, both isolation
mysticisms, in its annihilation of one's temporal
self, and in the idea of the self which exists
eternally in God. This it borrowed from Christianity, in Zaehner's estimation: one returns to his
first state, or "as he was before he was." Therefore, the idea of the soul as a pre-existent in
God is common to Hinduism, Islam and Christianity.[96]

In sum, there are three distinct types of
mysticism which Zaehner delineates: i) the pan-
en-henic; ii) Isolation Mysticism; and iii) the
return of the self to God. Christians would see
the first kind as a reversion to pre-lapsarian
innocence, in which man returns to an undifferentiated psychological state of being one with
everything. The second kind of mysticism isolates the soul from the psyche and from all
psycho-physical operations. The third finds the
spirit returning to its infinite ground, where it
is immortal; i.e., it returns to God. Zaehner
says that Christians would see one state beyond
all this: namely, the Beatific Vision, when
"matter in the shape of the body will share in

---

[95]Ibid., p. 165.

[96]Zaehner, S/P, p. 167.

212

the general deification, when "corruptible will put on incorruptible" and the whole man will be transformed in God, and God will be "all in all."[97]

Zaehner can fit pure monism into none of these categories. This is a very important conclusion for our argument. If the monist follows a pure yogic technique he should end up classed with Sāmkhya-yoga Isolation Mysticism. For, Zaehner adds:

> ...he is intent on realizing his immortal spirit in detachment from his mortal frame. This is his bliss...but so long as he sticks to his monistic view of life and feels that his philosophy is confirmed by his experience, then I do not think that his bliss can be identical with that experienced and described by the Christian and Muslim mystics, insofar as these remain theist, whose bliss consists rather in the total surrender of the whole personality to a God who is at the same time Love.[98]

In other words, monism does not fit into Zaehner's pattern thus far; it is a separate mystical category. It is a difficult phenomenon since it always seems to interpret its monist experience in terms of what the other fellow is experiencing in his religion. When the other religion happens to be theistic, the monist says that his and the theistic experience are precisely the same once the proximate religious notions (the wrappings) are removed from the nub of the experience. The kernel of the experience is the same as the monistic one. It sounds very much

---

[97]Ibid., p. 168.

[98]Zaehner, S/P, p. 168 f.

like the reductionism of some demythologizers in the West.

The logical sequel of monism is the renunciation of everything but Self; i.e., the sannyāsin (ascetic, renouncer in Skt.) in Śankara's system is to give up all religious ceremonies, any idea of divine grace, good or evil works as a repayment to one's enemies, and seek his goal through yoga.[99] Zaehner's argumentation for the distinction of theism from both natural mysticism and Isolation Mysticism draws on, not only Christian concepts of theism, but, also and especially, Hindu ones. Hinduism itself draws sharp distinctions between theism and what Zaehner calls Isolation Mysticism and Nature Mysticism.

---

[99]Ibid., p. xvi, apud Māndūkya Upan. Kārika (commentary on the Upan.), 2.35.

CHAPTER VI

THEISTIC MYSTICISM

In carving out his argument Zaehner does not leave us with an exhaustive definition of theism or theisms, but goes about the major work of his thesis: namely, refuting the <u>philosophia</u> <u>perennis</u> by showing that there are three main mystical types, which types are radically different from one another; and that theism, especially, is different from the other types. Theism was special to Zaehner because it was the base from which he worked. He knew from his personal faith that what Hindu monists experience, and claim, is not the same as the Christian experience--either mystically or just in the ordinary sense of the Christian experience of God--it is utter nonsense to say so; but it is nonsense which is quite well packaged and seductive to not a few Christians, theologians as well as non-theologians, who manifest an inclination to follow its line. As an example, I offer Hans Küng. He begins his remarks on world religions with the question, "Don't all the higher religions begin with 'the same perennial questions...? No one who has the slightest knowledge of world religions can dispute these facts.'"[1] I do, and so did Zaehner. This essay has amply demonstrated that religions are dealing with radically different problems, seeking the answers to radically different questions. When Küng says that all religions see God's goodness he is speaking from a western perspective. Buddhists do not give a fig for God's goodness. At least Theravada Buddhists do not. They "had it up to here" with the gods and their "friends," the Brahmins. So they set out to seek peace without Scripture, liturgy, law, and especially without gods--good or otherwise. Certainly Küng's statement betrays an alarming

---

[1] Küng, <u>op.cit.</u>, p. 92.

ignorance in uttering such a statement. It was
Zaehner's life's work to prove that the religions
begin from different places and say different
things. This book has dealt with what they said
so as to show that their religious experiences
are different, thus refuting the philosophia
perennis. The rest of Zaehner's corpus contented
itself with setting out an hypothesis on just
where the religions started from: Buddhism from
a desire to get away from pain through the dissolution of the concept of desire and person;
Chinese religions from twin starting places,
which I detailed above (in the overview of
Zaehner's theses)...

So when a learned and well-intentioned man
like Küng, who saw through the vaunted eirenicism
of Hindus who say they accept all religions-and
really are only preaching a Hindu monist exclusivism[2]--and really do not accept them, says what
I have quoted, I must say that I do not have to
dispute what he takes for "facts," the facts
themselves dispute him. He adds what he thinks a
clincher to his argument in saying that he thinks
all religions are seeking the same thing.[3]
Zaehner, and this book, have demonstrated that
all religions are not seeking the same thing. Isolation Hinduism, Muslim monists and Buddhists are
seeking a peace in the immortality of the Self,
while Christianity is seeking the peace of God.
The two "peaces" could not be more different. So
I will set up Zaehner's argument to manifest just
how he answers the type of questions Küng posed,
which questions were asked by both Christian and
Hindu monists, both of whom thought they had experienced God when all they had experienced was
the peace of the Self, not the peace of God.

---

[2]Kung, op.cit., p. 103.

[3]Ibid., p. 93.

First off, Zaehner outlines two instincts in all mysticisms: i) the first is the instinct to self-preservation; this one tends to <u>isolation</u>, a mysticism of pride in being an individual; ii) the second instinct tends to <u>union</u>, the loss of individuality or the merger of the self in a larger whole, which is a desire to become one with one's surroundings in terms of some intimacy.[4] On the whole, Zaehner thinks that Nature Mysticism leads to a selfish type of union with the All, while Theistic Mysticism, being from God himself, leads beyond the self to God as "other." Further, the instinct to self-preservation leads one beyond Nature Mysticism to Isolation Mysticism, in which one seeks to enjoy one's own immortality, not God's.

Nature Mysticism is a mysticism of the lower soul, the <u>prakrti</u> of Sāṁkhya and the <u>nafs</u> of Ṣūfism. Neither will see God, and neither intends to see him. In Christian terms the lower soul is the soul of the first Adam, whose soul was, in Paul's terms, "flesh and blood."[5] The Adam of the spirit is the Christian analogue for the upper soul in both Hinduism and Islam. Zaehner says that both the Adam of the Spirit and <u>purusa</u> and <u>nafs</u> will see eternity. Further, in <u>Vedānta māyā</u> (Skt. for "illusion," the illusion of phenomena) will not see eternity either, but the <u>ātman-Brahman</u> (the eternal principle, <u>Brahman, is</u> the soul, the <u>ātman</u> or Self) shall see it. In Islam, only man's angelic nature, which is eternal, will see God. His animal and bestial souls will not

---

[4]Zaehner, S/P, pp. 141f.

[5]<u>Ibid.</u>, p. 144.

see him.[6] So in the four traditions (Sāṁkhya and Vedānta in India, and the Christian and Muslim traditions) Zaehner discerns a dualism; this, even in the a-dvaita (non-dualist, or monist) tradition of Vedānta. In a-dvaita, māyā (illusion) includes all contingent being; this is one principle. The other is Brahman-ātman, which is self-existent. Zaehner states that the greatest of the advaitans, Śankara, taught a doctrine of māyā which distorted the Upaniṣads, and it is dangerous for those in search of beatitude to follow it.[7] It is dangerous because even Hinduism has gone beyond it to theism, as we shall see with the Gītā and Rāmānuja's thoughts on it.

The Gītā, as does Zaehner himself, details three stages of spirituality or deification. Zaehner will go on to say that Christian spirituality, if one looks hard enough, sees these three stages as well. The three states are: 1) personal integration, which puts the ego and Self together, and which can either be the product of yogic method, can happen spontaneously or come about in the West through psychotherapy. It is a psychological phenomenon. ii) Then comes the religious phase, that of isolation, which is to be achieved by the complete withdrawal of mind and sense into the self. This is the end of the line for the monist. He can go no further. iii) It is at this point that God begins his direct action. He leads the soul out of its isolation and begins to change it into his own substance. Muslims speak, at this stage, of

---

[6]Śankara, like most Hindu commentators on the Upaniṣads, infuses these writings with his own pre-conceived notions. This is a rather commonly held view among students of Hinduism. So the non-dualist comes to the scriptures and finds them non-dualist...etc.

[7]Zaehner, S/P, p. 144.

annihilation (Arab.=fanā) and abiding (Arab.=baqā),
and the annihilation of annihilation, which
Zaehner sees as analogous to the Hegelian "negation of negation;" i.e., the soul remains itself,
though it has been transformed into the divine
essence, like a container is to the wine itself.

So the first stage is a return to an undifferentiated unity in its more primitive manifestations; in its integration phase the more
personal side of man, his ego, fuses with the
collective side, the unconscious, and what emerges is a whole personality, as we saw with Proust.
So the self emerges and the ego is subjected to
it.[8] Isolation finds bliss in jettisoning all
things transitory; and Zaehner says that Christians would term this blissful state of both
Sāṁkhya and Advaita the bliss of Limbo. It is a
return to the Garden of Eden, with its innocence
regained. But here the soul must stay unless God
steps in. In theism the soul is passive from
here on in. It must play the bride to God's
groom. Eckhart said, "if man remained always a
virgin, no fruit would proceed from him. If he
is to become fruitful, he must necessarily be a
woman. 'Woman' is the most noble word one can
apply to the soul, more noble than virgin."[9]
Both the Christian Suso and the Muslim Ghāzalī
corroborate what Eckhart said. The soul falls
violently in love at this stage and wishes
nothing so much as to be ravished, annihilated by
its lover. Its ravishment accomplishes its
deification in God.[10] We saw the first stages of
spirituality, that of yoga, in the Gītā (2:55-72),
in both its dualistic and monist manifestations:

---

[8]Zaehner, S/P, p. 150.

[9]Ibid., p. 151, apud Eckhart's Serm. 8,
Pfeiffer, p. 34.

[10]Ibid., pp. 150f.

isloation can take both forms at this level of the
Gītā. But it is Zaehner's thesis, not destroyed
by scholarly antitheses, that the overriding preoccupation of the Gītā is theism. The Incarnation of the god Viṣṇu, Krishna, outlines classic
Indian spirituality to the warrior Arjuna, in the
Gītā. It is Viṣṇu who is the centerpiece of the
Gītā, not previous spiritualities. Hence, the
Gītā is a shameless eirenicon, mixing spirituality
with spirituality. India rests easily with crosscurrents in its religion; even when the crosscurrents seem a hopeless confusion. Hinduism is
not an "ism" at all. The name was imposed, as I
said earlier, by Westerners to circumscribe the
religion of the people around the Indus (whence,
"Hindu," because the Persians have a different
form of the word) River. There never was "a"
religion of India. There were religions. The
"great religions" tradition of the West imposed
the name Hinduism on Indian religion because it
fit our categories quite well. It did the same
to the religiousness calling itself today
Buddhism. Both names have had disastrous consequences in the West, since it expects to find
analogues abounding in the East. Where we have a
Saviour, a pope, a doctrine, ... we expect to find
one there--and tend to impose one if not found. So
the unsystematized spiritualities found in the
Gītā rather throw all but the most persistent and
astute reader and student for a loss.

However, the Gītā reveals the clamor of
religions in India, but does so in an hierarchical
way, and this is Zaehner's thesis. The Gītā
accepts the old religions and their yogic technique. But the way to liberation (mokṣa) was by
grace through a loving God, from a loving God.
This is a startling new revelation, and the Gītā
takes its time in revealing it as it moves along.
However, it does so from its very beginning,
though implicitly, since the very setting of the
scripture is theistic.

Hence, the Gītā goes beyond monism to theism, while retaining Sāṁkhya-yoga as its asceticism for those on the way to a higher religion: namely, theism.[11] Zaehner notes, in both Islam and Christianity, a tendency in theology towards transcendentalism which makes God so over-arching as to place him out of reach. In reaction to this, both Christian and Muslim mystics have a tendency towards monism in order to offer a counterweight of immanency to their respective religions. In India the one to react was Rāmānuja. But it was not against transcendentalism that he reacted, but against the dreadnaught of monism represented by Sankara. He saw too much immanence in Indian religion, and Sankara was its paramount spokesman. So the two are forever sparring within the various schools which they founded. Rāmānuja focused on a trend in religion which would emphasize transcendence. Hence, God was to be worshipped. This is nothing very startling for Christians, Muslims or Jews. But for those who see God as a way-station towards liberation, and as something relative and built on māyā (illusion), this was a revelation. Devotion was and is no novelty to Western religion, but it is a distinct break with the anti-nomian and anti-devotional strand represented by Śankara's monism. Monism in general tends away from gods, rite and laws. Not that it is anti-religious or immoral. It is not. But it sees them as useful for the initiate--however, not necessary—and, perhaps, as hindrances to complete isolation in the One. So Zaehner's plea was that we should beware of monism since it leads away from God to a bliss which is isolation, not a loving union. It leads away, therefore, from God and his religions of theism to ones of monism, in one way or another. Frequently one will retain the name Christian or Muslim, but the reality is monist, and the religion is Hindu. The appendices on Al Junayd and Ghazālī will

---

[11]Zaehner, S/P, p. 146.

show this in detail. But Zaehner sets forth an
example for us in Christian history which is both
interesting and germane to his and my argument.
It is the phenomenon of Quietism which confronted
the Flemish mystic Ruysbroeck.

> (A) Ruysbroeck's argument against Beghard
>   Quietism and Zaehner's use of it for
>   his argument

What Zaehner found empirically, working text
by text in carving out his mystical types,
Ruysbroeck found pastorally. It came to his
notice that the Beghards were moving past Church,
past rite and law and even God, into something a
Hindu monist would call Nirvāna. In terms
startling in both their similarity of style and
content to that of Hinduism, Ruysbroeck outlines
his argument against Christian monists by saying,
in a word, that monism in Christian mysticism is
unhealthy.

Zaehner makes yeoman use of Ruysbroeck's
mystical theology, set out in the latter's The
Spiritual Espousals,[12] forging it into a divining
rod to discern healthy from unhealthy theistic
mysticisms--or theisms become unhealthy by becoming monism.

Both Ruysbroeck and Suso blasted the
Beghards for their Quietism. Zaehner finds that
the Beghards' views, mutatis mutandis, are akin
to Śankara's. Both hold that all works are to
cease. Śankara held such since, at bottom, man
is what Christians would call God, and what he
called Ātman-Brahman (the Real Self). The reader
should recall that the philosophia perennis says
that man is supernatural. The Beghards saw
themselves as perfect, which is the same as saying

---

[12]Translated by Eric College, London, Faber
and Faber, 1952.

ātman (i.e., that the Real Self had been attained in their own Self). Hence the Beghards renounced all religious works as superfluous, since they were incapable of sin. In his Spiritual Espousals Ruysbroeck said that they were seeking tranquility in themselves:

> Now observe, that whenever man is empty and undistracted in his senses by images, and free and unoccupied in his highest powers, he attains rest by purely natural means. And all men can find and possess this rest in themselves by their mere nature, without the grace of God, if they are able to empty themselves of sensual images and of all action.[13]

Zaehner is startled by the accuracy of Ruysbroeck's statement. Though he did not know Hindu mysticism, he wrote about it as accurately as if he had experienced it. In Hindu terms the empty man has attained the highest Brahman, which is the essence of advaita for Zaehner.[14] But Ruysbroeck saw this emptying-out process as only the beginning, not the end of things, and that those who know and have experienced God's grace are aware of this as fact.[15] The Hindu theist, Rāmānuja, too, says about the same thing: once isolation has been achieved, the process is only beginning.[16] God is beyond the isolation process. Both the Christian mystics and the later Muslim

---

[13]Zaehner, S/P, p.170, apud Ruysbroeck, op. cit. pp. 166-67.

[14]Ibid.

[15]Ibid.

[16]Zaehner, H/M, p. 188.

mystics of Persia say that God is love, so the
self and its experience are lower forms of mysticism. The Bhagavad-Gītā, which outlines isolation mysticism (yoga) in its first six chapters,
ever faithful to classical Sāṁkhya, begins to open
up to an integration model in its psychological
aspect. This same Gītā, in chapters ten and thirteen, affirms a higher mystical doctrine: loving
devotion to God, called bhakti.[17] This is the
most secret doctrine of the Gītā, and its revelation as well. Sankara has only disdain for those
who continue to worship "illusory gods." He advocates that this come to a stop. Ruysbroeck
places himself over against all this in his refutation of the Beghards; and Zaehner pits him
against Sankara for the same reasons the Christian
mystic posits against Quietism. Ruysbroeck says
that there are two types of peace: i) one is a
rest in the Self, and ii) the other is a rest in
God through love. The first type means that the
Self is contemplating the Self by itself without
sin. This is original innocence, though it is
separated from God due to the Fall.[18] It is significant that Ruysbroeck, without knowing anything of yoga and the techniques of the East
employed to bring about this state of bliss
(peace) in isolation by the self, yet knew that it
could be done by one's own powers--i.e., without
grace, if one but knew the technique. It would
seem to be in man's nature to do so. The peace
of Ruysbroeck's first type places one beyond rite
and law, as it does for Sankara. In it one is
isolated from man, Nature and God, and cannot
advance in virtue since one is the Absolute.[19]
The consequences of this are all too obvious:

---

[17]Zaehner, S/P, p. 170.

[18]Zaehner, S/P, p. 170.

[19]Ibid., p. 171.

license follows close on its heels, usually sexual.[20] The state of being Absolute makes good and evil convertible. Morality makes sense only on the relative level. If one is the Absolute, living beyond the relative, then the terms good and evil have meanings which are irrelevant and devoid of content.[21] In Hinduism relativities (phenomena) are the spokes of a wheel. When one realizes his essence--which is that he is the Hub (ātman-Brahman)--then the spokes, which are relativities like good and evil, disappear. This frightens Zaehner when applied to theistic mysticism. And it is this which exercised Ruysbroeck about the Beghards and their Quietism, which was a monism in which all things are convertible: evil to good and vice versa, since they were perfect and above all morality and sin.

So Ruysbroeck has no truck with Christians who wish to remain at rest in the self, since it is not union with God, but a rest in which man contemplates himself in his own eternity. It is done in innocence, true enough, but an innocence cut off from God.[22] So Ruysbroeck agrees with Zaehner's conclusions that this stage is one of Limbo, happiness without God, and innocence without grace. But Ruysbroeck says that the rub comes here. Such men, living in peace, think they are holy-"the holiest men alive"-yet he says they are living lives counter to God, the saints and all good men.[23] This belief that they cannot

---

[20]Zaehner details this in his S/G, when dealing with Charles Manson's murder cult.

[21]Cf. Zaehner's S/G, the chapter entitled "The Ghost of Heraclitus" for a fuller treatment of this.

[22]Zaehner, S/P, pp. 170f.

[23]Ibid., pp. 170f. apud Ruysbroeck, op.cit., p. 173.

go further in perfection is the greatest barrier to grace: "they maintain that they cannot advance, for they have achieved a life of unity and emptiness beyond which one cannot advance and in which there is no exercise."[24] But where is love in all this? If a mysticism does not end in prayer and love, it is not Christian. Rimbaud himself used this as a rule of thumb with which to discern that his own experience was a lie, as far as being a Christian experience was concerned. It was a true experience, but not a Christian one. That was what he wanted. What he had was not so. Hence it was a lie.

Further, since Islam inherited more than it knows from Christianity, any experience which does not end in love is not Muslim either; the two mysticisms--Christian and Muslim--are that alike in their healthy forms.[25] This religion of love finally breaks forth in Hinduism in the Gītā (chap. 10:8-10,"...for I loved them first"), where God, in the form of Viṣṇu, demands love--certainly a revelation in Hinduism--and says that it is because he had loved man first. So there is a religion of love (Skt.=bhakti, devotion) and there are religious experiences of non-love: e.g., in Sāṁkhya's and advaita's isolation.[26] There are religions which manifest no love. Zaehner says

---

[24]Ibid., Zaehner, ibid., Ruysbroeck.

[25]Ibid., P. 174.

[26]Cf. the article by W. L. Newell in Geist u. Leben, Okt. 1975, 48 Jahrgang, Heft 5, entitled "Buddhistische u. Christliche Liebe" for a fuller treatment of what is meant by this. Briefly, isolation means just that. There can be no real relationship between persons in this system since at bottom it tends to solipsism. Hence there can be no love.

that, "self-satisfied monism" is always lurking
behind the love portrayed in the Gītā; and it is
a real Hindu religious experience, this monism.
Zaehner seems to judge this complaisance as something evil in se; but this would be wrong. Monism
is a real religious experience. If it comes into
Christianity and any other theism, by Zaehner's
own canons, then it is wrong since it is self-
satisfied and self-righteous. Monistic isolation
is all right and healthy in Hinduism and Buddhism,
and Taoism and Zen too, but it is quite unhealthy
in any theism; this includes Christianity, Islam,
and theistic Hinduism. Why else is there such a
battle between the Śankara followers, with their
monism, and Rāmānuja's advocates of theism? The
two are always at loggerheads at best. Monism
and theism do not mix within the same religion.
So when the philosophia perennis makes its bland
assertions to the contrary its protagonists have
to explain what they mean, and explain their
vast--unproved--assumptions that we are all the same
and that their isolation experiences are the same
as those of theistic love mysticisms. There
simply is no love in Isolation Mysticism and
theism is always a love mysticism. All the
theisms of world religions--Hindu, Judaic, Muslim
and Christian--are love mysticisms. That is a
salient which the philosophia perennis refuses
to climb in its bland assumptions. It goes
around the salient, but never climbs it, nor does
it attempt to, and Zaehner appears to have nailed
down this illogic in them. Nor have the protagonists of the philosophia perennis changed.
Huston Smith's new book referred to above simply
makes the assertion that there is a primordial
tradition and goes on about his business explaining it, but not proving it one bit-unfortunately,
for he is a great scholar and student of religions.

Monism is not a religious manifestation in
which love is possible. In it God seems to serve
as a function of the self, as he did with Sāṁkhya.
So when Zaehner goes on to say that there can be

227

no love in monism, it is very important for any understanding of Isolation Mysticism in general to know what he means; this includes not only the Sāṃkhya and Advaita in Hinduism, but also Theravada Buddhism, Mādhyamika Buddhism, Zen, Taoism and any form of monistic religious technique or monistic understanding of religion. Zaehner catches much flack for this position, but it seems defensible from the argument thus far laid down.[27]

---

[27]In W. C. Smith's review of Zaehner's C/D, art. cit., Smith finds it incredible that Zaehner makes a Buddhistic virtue of dukkha (wretchedness, sadness in Pali; Zaehner's translation=despair). Dukkha is the Pali for the Sanskrit dukha, which word is the key in the phrase "all life is wretched" which is, perhaps, the beginning point of all Indian religion. How both Buddhism and Hinduism deal with this phrase makes them what they are. The Buddha, and his Mahāyāna followers, especially Nagarjuna and the whole of his camp called the Middle Path (Pali=Mādhyamika), make Nirvāna consist of an experience of emptiness (Pali=Śūnyatā), which is not a nihilism, as so many would like to see it in the West, but a positive intuition of wisdom (jñāna=Pali) into the reality of the life situation that Nirvāna is Sāmsara (the infinitely played out barbed wire of life-after-life-after-life...etc.). The experience that wretchedness is Bliss (Nirvāna) makes wretchedness (Zaehner's despair) a virtue, the cardinal hope of Buddhism. Zaehner's chapter (XIX) in C/D is dealing with the reconciliation of opposites. Smith's biting comment betrays an alarming lack of insight into the Middle Path, whose logic is a reconciliation of opposites making wretchedness (dukkha, or despair) into a virtue. Smith's comment on Zaehner's conception of dukkha (in C/D, p. 207) runs thusly: "One is left haunted by a wondering whether he is perhaps basically misunderstanding what the mystics' assertions are all about (and especially the Buddha's,

The nub of the argument here is that in the findings of what Proust calls the "second self"- bringing it out into the open-the "aspirant" thinks that he has arrived at the goal, that the second self (ātman in Hinduism) is God. If such a state of "emptiness" and "unity" is arrived at,

---

whom he incredibly interprets as a man of despair)." (Art.cit. p. 380.) It seems that Zaehner did not so much interpret Buddha incorrectly as did Smith Zaehner. Zaehner's statements make the Buddha a man of over-arching hope in the midst of a rotting wretchedness; this is the essence of Buddhism: look within! there is hope, not without! For further reference please cf. Eliade's Yoga: Immortality and Freedom (p. 165) where truth is to be experienced and known; truth is experimental. The monk creates a new body in meditating on dukkha. All three of Suzuki's vols. of essays are good in showing that Nirvāna is Samsara. Lastly Arya Deva, Nagarjuna's student and co-founder of the Mādhyamika wanted men to free themselves from phenomena and thought forms; once done one sees (experimentally) that the śūnyatā (emptiness) of one is the śūnyatā of all" (apud ChatuhSatakam of Arya Deva, restored into Skt. by Professor Bhattachara, Vishvabharati, Shantiniketan, 1931, pp. 139-40). So, if anyone is lacking in the knowledge of what the Buddha is talking about it does not seem to be Zaehner, at least in this matter. He loves to shock. He does in saying that sadness is hope. But that is precisely what the Buddha was trying to do as well. I have tried out these ideas on Professor Nagatomi, the distinguished Japanese Buddhist scholar of Harvard, and they were found not only acceptable, but that they seem to have captured the Mādhyamika from the inside; i.e., to have an Einfühlen, the goal of historians of religion. Zaehner seems to have had the same here.

according to Ruysbroeck, the trap is laid.
Zaehner battens on these two words used by
Ruysbroeck since they are of capital importance
to his argument. The first word Ruysbroeck uses
(emptiness) is the very essence of the Mādhyamika
experience in Mahāyāna Buddhism, where one arrives
at one's interiority, one's immortality, which is
called "emptiness" (Skt. and Pail=śūnyatā). The
second word, "unity," Zaehner sees as the essence
of the Vedānta experience. Neither is a Christian
experience as such, since there is no love in
either. Both can be stages in the Christian
experience, but neither is its goal. Zaehner
says, "Emptiness is the prelude to Holiness,"
but that remaining there is dangerous[28]since it
is the Gospel's clean-swept house which is open
to seven more devils. Ruysbroeck's claims for
man's unity with God were so exorbitant that he
was suspected of heresy, yet he himself felt the
greatest threat to religion was monistic Quietism.
Zaehner sees an abyss yawning between theism and
monism.

What Zaehner sees in Ruysbroeck's attack on
monistic quietists is this: monistic Quietism
(read isolation for Quietism) seems to place one
beyond good and evil.[29] So moral laws are beneath
quietists; a state beyond which they do not wish
to go has been achieved, and this with no reference to God. This is the state of the question.
What Zaehner makes of it is this: monistic
Hindus, and monists in general, tend to think
that their experience is the same as that experienced in theisms, as I have said. But Zaehner
demonstrated before that their experience is not
of God, when dealing with Isolation Mysticism, and
now he does it from an example of monism in
Christianity. So how can their experience be a

---

[28]Zaehner, S/P, pp. 173f.

[29]Ibid., p. 175

theistic one, or the same as a theistic one, once
God has been stripped of his "local" relativity?
This relativity is the monist's way of saying
that each religion is just a localization of a
transcendent metaphysical Truth. Theisms like
Islam and Christianity should be the arbiter of
their own experience. When asked, "Is this a
theistic experience?" theists in Christianity--
like Ruysbroeck--and Islam, when faced with
Ḥallāj's enthusiasisms, react with shock and anger.
It most certainly is not the experience one has
in a theism, it is not an experience of God at
all. So how can it be theistic? What Zaehner has
done here is to say that Huxley has been disen-
franchised. He has lost his vote in Christianity.
He cannot say what a Christian has, nor can the
Ṣūfi Schuon, nor can Radharkrishnan, nor Isherwood,
nor Coomeraswami, because they are based in
another experience. They can say what they experience, and they do. What they say is monistic. When they judge it over against Christianity and Islam, they say it is theistic; and that
is pure nonsense. This is why Zaehner bristled
at the very name Schuon. The latter claims to
be mainline Muslim, but he is a type of Ṣūfi who
does not fit into a theism at all. Ṣūfi he is,
mainline Muslim he is not. Zaehner does not
leave it up to himself to judge this. Muslim
theology itself says that Schuon's thought expressed, not theology, but blasphemy since it is
guilty of Shirk (associating something with God).
Zaehner does not have to judge for Islam. It
does so for itself. And he reserves the same
right for Christianity. But it is supernally
galling to him to have the protagonists of the
philosophia perennis explain not only their
experience, but everyone else's as well-and in
particular his own. So theists see such assertions as meaningless in theology and blasphemy in
religion. God, in theology, is he beyond whom
one may not go. Neither Jew, nor Muslim, nor
Christian will have any truck with any such
monist reasoning; and this is not because of any
rampant dogmatism, but because they are the judges

231

of what they experience. None of them have accepted monism into their religion. When it came to Islam it had to be changed sufficiently to keep the law, God and man in their assigned places. Further, Ghazālī's monism was held secretly, and published only when he was an old man. It is still not held by mainline Islam. It is suspect to this day. Monists, and these are mainly Hindus of the East or West, make the illation that their legitimate religious experience is the only experience in any religion. Hence their eirenicism in accepting any religion at all. But I have stated that theirs is less an eirenicism than an exclusivism. In saying theirs is the same as a theist experience they make all their own, and leave no room for anyone else. How exclusivist can one get? So everything is relative: Jesus, Qur'ān, Yahweh, ... Hence such Hindus can easily accept Jesus as an incarnation of Viṣṇu since even that gentle deity will be dissolved at the end of each time cycle (Yuga cycle in Hinduism). So no other God threatens, since none has ultimacy. None came in time except the God of the West, Jesus. Hindu incarnations come in mythical time; there is no date and no place for them, ever.

Further, from the Sāṁkhya point of view, Qur'ān will go at the end of the cycle, and so will Allah, and with him, Yahweh. God is useful only as an object of meditation. In monistic advaita God serves the same function, but, really, there is no God at all. So Hindus must mean that theists experience ātman. And Zaehner pounces on this to say that ātman is not God. It is the self, or Self--it makes no difference to Zaehner how it is spelled--which counts here.[30] Zaehner says that one may experience monist emptiness as a good and wholesome experience on the way to God, but that it is in no way an experience of God. It is the experience of the Self emptied

<hr />

[30] Ibid., p. 171.

232

of ego; which Self is on the way to God. Later, Hinduism was to agree with Zaehner, with the advent of Rāmānuja's doctrine which said that God was beyond the monist's experience of Self; that the experience of the ātman was not the experience of Viṣṇu. Hence Zaehner argues from Semitic sources and from Hindu sources that the monists' argument, to the effect that their experience is the same as the theistic union with God, is just plain wrong. Buber's warning rings out to the same effect;[31] so does Ruysbroeck's. To say that one has experienced God when all one has experienced is the Self is, to Zaehner, to repeat the Fall.[32] Suffice it to say, in theism, such an act is consummate hubris, which is the very essence of the Fall.

In Christianity one loves the ens Realissimum, but not in advaita. In Christianity one can love Absolute Reality because it is also Absolute Good; again, this is not so in Vedānta. The Absolute is not good in advaita, not only not "the" Good, but not even good. Zaehner points this out, and it is a significant statement. Goodness is one of the qualities of God's essence in theistic systems. But Brahman, the Hindu ultimate, is beyond moral qualities; this means that its essence is nirguna (=Skt. for "qualityless, without the components of phenomena such as sattva, rajas and tamas). So Brahman is not good; it is without moral qualities, least of all love, which Zaehner says, demands duality.[33]

What is so confusing in all this discussion about monism versus theism is that it is so full of inconsistencies when fleshed out in life. For

---

[31]Ibid., Buber, op.cit., pp. 24-5.

[32]Zaehner S/T, p. 90.

[33]Zaehner, S/P, p. 188.

233

instance, some of the most beautiful hymns in
Hinduism were written by Śankara:

Day and night, evening and morning,
winter and spring ever return;

Time, sports and life passes away;
yet the breath of hope brings no release.
Worship Govinda, worship Govinda, worship Govinda, deluded man. When Time is
finished and rolled up, rules of grammar
cannot avail you.

With fire in front of him and the sun
on his back, knees tucked up to his chin
at night, beggar's bread in the palm of
his hand, his dwelling beneath a tree,
even (to such a religious mendicant) the
toils of hope bring no release. Worship
Govinda.... Yet if a man study the
Bhagavad-Gītā a little or drink only a
drop or two of the Ganges waters or worship Krishna only once, how should death
pay attention to him? Worship Govinda,
... O Krishna, in this phenomenal world
so hard to traverse and so much to be
pitied, ward off from us rebirth and re-
death, ward off yet another sojourn in a
mother's womb,... Worship Govinda,...
etc.[34]

This is the religion of devotion (bhakti),
written with soaring lyricism. Yet the monist
only tolerates bhakti since it produces states
of natural mysticism which, though diametrically
opposed to the isolation of the monist--since it
unites with all--is still akin to it because it is

---

[34]Ibid., pp. 177-78, apud Swami Nikhilananda,
Self Knowledge, Madras, Sri Ramakrishna Math, 1947,
pp. 287-89.

an experience of unity.[35] So Śankara advocates
the use of hymns to produce a state of self-
induced hypnosis. Zaehner says that God has no
value *in se* for the monist.[36]

But,worship is a much inferior technique to
yoga in Śankara's eyes; and worship is of not
much value in itself, but mostly for its strength
as an induction device for altered states of
consciousness. Repetition tends to free the mind
from its moorings.[37]

So Zaehner mined Ruysbroeck's argumentation
against the monist Beghards to provide a foil for
the monism of the Hindus and their Western allies,
the protagonists of the *philosophia perennis*.
Ruysbroeck says that such monism is healthy only
as a way-station for a person on the move to God,
and that there was no going past God; he is the
end of the line. But monism in a theism is
unhealthy mysticism. It is a peace in the Self
counterfeiting the peace of God; both good in
themselves and in their proper places. Theism
must, however, go beyond the first peace to the
second in order to be theism. If there is no
love there, Zaehner reminds us, it is neither
Christian nor Muslim mysticism. True theistic
mysticism leads to love and prayer. Further,
monism means that one thinks himself beyond good
and evil. So Zaehner says that the *philosophia
perennis* has mistaken the peace of the Self for
the peace of God; and has mistaken the ātman for
God. This is a capital mistake, persistently
and blandly made and assumed, but never proved.
Zaehner leaves this part of the argument with the
assertion that monists do not love the Real, and

---

[35]*Ibid.*, p. 179.

[36]*Ibid.*

[37]*Ibid.*, p. 180.

235

love is the essence of theistic mysticism, and it is so because God is good, but the Brahman is beyond all that. So the philosophia perennis speaks on many levels at once, and seems to want it both ways: monist and theist. And Zaehner says one has it one way at a time since the two are mutually antagonistic and exclusive.

> (B) Zaehner's thesis: Vedānta's goal (emptiness) is Theism's beginning. Hence they are different.

Zaehner launches out, once again, on his own, leaving Ruysbroeck behind, to do battle with text after text in order to refute the philosophia perennis once and for all, and this time on its own ground: Hindu Vedānta, or what he considers the source of the philosophia perennis. He attacks Hindu monism obliquely, from its Ṣūfi offshoot, to begin with. He enlists Ṣūfism as an ally, however. The Ṣūfi who is theistic seeks to be annihilated in his Beloved, while the monist yogin (Skt.=Sannyāsin, an aspirant for perfection (Skt.=muni), literally it means a "renouncer") seeks bliss in an emptiness devoid of all qualities (Skt.=nirguna) of mind and heart, body and ego. The Ṣūfis see themselves as rays of light returning to their source. The yogin monists are drops of water who imagine themselves to be the ocean. Zaehner says that such is so with monism since, "it has no experience of the ocean nor can it adequately conceive what the word means."[38] This is the essence of Zaehner's argument against monism and the philosophia perennis. The monists argue to the universal knowledge of religious experience from an experience of a particular nature, an experience which Zaehner seems to think is very limited. Hence when they argue to universal knowledge and that they have a universal

---

[38]Zaehner, S/P, p. 179.

experience, Zaehner can only say, in plain language, that they do not know what they are talking about. What they have is valid, but not universal; and it certainly does not apply to the theistic experience.

Further, Śankara's arguments are drawn from Upanisads which could only prove monist arguments; so rigidly monist are they. There are others which can prove otherwise, like the Śvetāśvatara and the Chāndogya, which open the way for theism, not monism. But, Zaehner says, Śankara cultivates the attention only of those who argue for his preconceived notions, whose notions are monist. He scores Śankara for overlooking many texts which say that God is the cause of all, that he creates out of his own substance--i.e., that God is the material cause-- and instead ends up with man being a monad and God a metaphysical impossibility.[39] A merely surface resemblance to Eckhart's mystical utterance is admitted by Zaehner: the monists make capital of these similarities, liking to use them as proofs of the universality of the one mysticism. But Zaehner is quick to add that the German's distinction between God and the Godhead--a distinction well beloved of advaita-- is only a homiletic device, not a metaphysical conclusion. Eckhart was out to shock his listeners, not philosophize for them. Śankara distinguishes between the supreme Brahman (Skt.= para-Brahman) and the lower Brahman (apara-Brahman). The latter creates the world through its own ignorance (avidyā) or self-deception (māyā). So there may be a verbal basis for comparison between Śankara and Eckhart, but the realities betray nothing in common. Eckhart never said that reality was only the Godhead, and that all else was nothing, as did Śankara when he said that ātman-Brahman was the Absolute,

---

[39]Zaehner, S/P, p. 179.

and "Thou art That."[40]

Further, Śankara's and Eckhart's experiences are fundamentally different. Śankara's is a liberation (Skt.=mokṣa) experience in which one is liberated absolutely from all things interior and exterior to it. One cannot go beyond this experience in Śankara's monism. Eckhart, however, does not experience the highest stage of liberation, but a never-ending deification. Liberation is a lower stage; it is the emptying-out process which begins deification, belonging to a very primitive, but necessary, time in God's coming to man, but it is a time of "clearing-out" before God actually gets there. Identification is a "beyond which one cannot go" process. Deification, on the contrary, never ends. There is the difference. When one knows that one is Brahman at bottom, then one has arrived. The theistic process of deification is not an identity; deification just goes on and on forever, from union to deeper union. Śankara's reality is "One without a second," and a "Thou art That" reality. The attainment of this state means peace (Skt.=śāntih). Śāntih is to be seen as linked with death since it is a state of Nirvāna, which is the purest bliss in a death-like trance. Nirvāna is a coldness like unto death, a situation in which all flame is gone, nothing burns to cause life and, therefore, pain. Hence monist peace is death-like. Zaehner links this with Ghazālī's reflections on ignorance, which belongs to darkness; but darkness is of rest, and rest is akin to non-existence. Ghazālī sees deep, dreamless sleep as spiritual death; it is not something devoutly to be hoped for or sought in Islamic mysticism. But the Brhadāranyaka Upaniṣad (4.4.1-2) regards

---

[40]Ibid., p. 182.

[41]Zaehner, S/P, p. 182.

238

dreamless sleep as a death, a state in which the
person becomes one.[42] Zaehner thinks this "...
is ... the unity brought about by the cessation
of all activity and therefore of all multiplicity, the unity in other words, of complete unconsciousness. Such an opinion, however, is
belied by the text itself and the sequel shows
that this is not the Upanisad's interpretation
of what happens at death."[43] For him, the text
is capable of monistic interpretation, but it
has not gone that far as yet. It is still either
a pantheistic text, or better, a pan-en-henic
one. The passage itself says:

> When this self becomes feeble and, as it
> were confused, then do these breaths
> gather round him. He collects these
> particles of brilliance together and
> goes down into the heart. When the
> person in the eye departs back (to the
> sun which is its source), then does he
> cease to see forms. "He is becoming
> one," they say, "he does not see."
> "He is becoming one," they say, "he
> does not taste." "He is becoming one,"
> they say, "he does not speak." "He is
> becoming one they say" ... hear ...
> think ... feel ... know." The tip of
> his heart begins to shine. Lighted by
> this brilliance the self departs, either
> by the eye, or by the head, or by other
> parts of the body. As he goes out the
> spirit follows him. As the spirit goes
> out all the breaths follow it. He be-
> comes conscious. What has consciousness
> follows after him.[44]

---

[42]Ibid., p. 183f.

[43]Ibid., p. 184.

[44]Ibid., pp. 183f., Bṛhad. Up. 4.4.1-2.

239

This could be interpreted monistically,
Zaehner admits, but the sequel (Brhad.Up. 4.4.13)
says differently. It is pantheistic: thus, "He
who has found and become aware of his self and
entered into this impenetrable abode, he is the
maker of all, the maker of the whole world, he is
the whole world."[45] This text could fit into two
of Zaehner's types of mysticisms: namely, pantheism, since the soul is the universe; also,
it could be fitted into theistic mysticism where
the soul feels one with God through identity.
But Zaehner objects that no theistic mysticism
can lay such exhorbitant claims, such power to
create, etc., which are proper to God alone.
Neither in Islam nor in Christianity do mystics
lay claim to preternatural powers.[46] It does
not fit at all into the category of Isolation
Mysticism, where the flesh is to be completely
separated from the spirit, the eternal from the
temporal in an ecstasy of non-unity. But
Zaehner says that this latter passage of the
Upanisad fits well with Nature Mysticism,
especially with fits of mania like John Custance's.
In fact this passage of the Brhadaranyaka Upanisad sums up with what he has had to say about
Nature Mysticism: viz., that mania and the
pan-en-henic experience are analogues.[47]

The monist experience says that the world
is inside oneself because one has dreamt it so.
So man is the creator of the world. Thus far,

---

[45]Ibid., p. 184.

[46]Zaehner appears to be ignorant of the
exorbitant claims made for Muslim desert mystics.
Cf. Guillaume's remarks on them in Prophecy and
Divination Among the Hebrews and Other Semites,
London, 1925, p. 151.

[47]Zaehner, S/P, p. 185.

monism and the pan-en-henic experience are alike.
But the world is the many, and the many do not
exist, ultimately, for the monists. Nature mystics admit of a "many" and of a unity of the many.
Monism can admit of no such thing. The many is a
chimera for them. Ultimately, one is everything.
Nothing else exists for the monist. So, the first
stage of unity with all, which is the pan-en-
henic experience, can agree with monism when
trance removes the many in dream and the ego is
"oned" with the All. But, if the ego dreamed
the many, then phenomena are unreal. The next
stage of the monist experience is trance, a
dreamless sleep, in which the without of the world
is removed along with the within save the essence
of the Self. This essence is seen as <u>Brahman</u>.
But if the Self created it in the pan-en-henic
experience, and if Brahman is the ground of all,
then I am Brahman. So the Self (ātman) is the
Brahman. All that remains is yoga which aids in
detaching oneself from the illusion which one has
conjured. The Self is not one among many Selves,
like the <u>puruṣa</u> of the Sāmkhya, but it is the
only reality.[48]

Where Hindu monism resembles Christian and
Muslim speculation is in the thinking of the
advanced mystics which say that one becomes the
All, the Absolute. Zaehner says that where this
resemblance is deceptive is in the fact that God
is not Good in Hinduism; but Being is the Good,
and Love itself, in Christianity. Zaehner counts
this as the main difference between theism and
monistic mysticism.[49] In fact, <u>Kauṣitaki Upani-
sad</u> reveals that there is wickedness in God, as
well as an indifferent attitude towards evil as
his Part:

---

[48]<u>Ibid</u>., p. 186.

[49]Zaehner, S/P, pp. 186 f.

Understand me as I am. This indeed I deem
to be what is most useful to men--to understand me. I slew the three-headed son of
Tvastr; I delivered the Avāṅmukhas,
ascetics, to the hyenas. Transgressing
many compacts I transfixed the people of
Prahlāda in the sky, the Paulomas in the
atmosphere, the Kālakakṣyās on earth. Yet
not one single hair of mine was injured.
So with one who knows me, his world is
injured by no deed whatsoever, not by the
murder of his father, not by the murder of
his mother, not by theft, not by the
slaughter of an embryo. Whatever evil
he does, he does not blanch.[50]

Ghazāli, Junayd and Ruysbroeck railed
against just such an amoral tendency in monism
as the Upaniṣad manifests here. In his Our
Savage God Zaehner plays on this theme again
very noticeably with his rehearsal of the Charles
Manson story and both Marxism's and Teilhard's
putative easy conscience before mass murders in
the World Wars. Therefore, the Brahman is beyond
good and evil, and so the Brahman is not good.
It has no moral qualities at all (Skt.=guṇas,
i.e., Brahman is not "gunated" to use the Indian
term, which means it is not qualified by anything,
good or evil), least of all love.[51] It takes two
to love; in monism there is only One. So Zaehner
holds it as axiomatic that: a monist can have
only a monist experience since God is a fiction
for him; but a theist can have the monist (pan-
en-henic and isolation) experiences of emptiness
on the way to God.[52] Zaehner combines the pan-
en-henic experience of the self as the All with

---

[50]Ibid., p. 187.

[51]Ibid., p. 188.

[52]Ibid., p. 189.

242

the monist experience of the self as the One and
says it is very nearly John Custance's experience. But how would this fit in with theistic
mysticism? Zaehner says that if this is theism,
then God is merely Nature, the subtle stuff which
energizes the cosmos; and he will have none of
this.[53]

Theists see man's end differently, however.
He does not participate in God in Gaudapāda's
monistic fashion; i.e., as an "insensible object,"
or as an animal, but as a rational person, as the
image of God himself. Zaehner says that this is
the modality which is shared only by man himself.
It is a personal way of participating in God. As
a person, man is a rational substance which is
individuated--this is Boethius' classical Scholas-
tic definition; and it is the basis of Zaehner's
model for theistic mysticism.[54] God deifies
according to the eternal idea of that which is
in his mind. Both Christianity and Sūfism are
clear on this point. Zaehner exemplifies his concept by using St. Thomas' teaching of God as the
first exemplar of all things.[55] In Sūfism Junayd
said that the mystic is looking for himself as
his own final cause, and comes to realize himself
as an idea of God's essence. Suso says something
rather stunning which Zaehner quotes in extenso:
"Note, however, that all creatures exist eternally
as God in God, and are not distinguished in him
essentially, except in the sense already mentioned. They are the same life, essence and
power, so far as they are in God, and are the

---

[53]Zaehner, S/P, p. 189.

[54]Ibid., p. 189.

[55]Ibid., apud Thomas' Summa Theol., art. 3,
trans. by Pegis.

same One and nothing less...etc."[56] Suso was a disciple of Eckhart, but went further than his illustrious master, or than Junayd, to say that man as he exists in the world has more worth as creature than he possessed as an idea in God's mind. So man on his own account has more dignity than he had as an idea in God. Man as creature possesses his own essence, he is an individual substance. In acknowledging himself as a creature and God as creator he attains such dignity. In God, man could not love God as Creator; in the world he can do so.[57]

Zaehner made a distinction between the monistic way of going to peace and the Christian way in saying it depends not only on grace, but on the way one understands Original Sin. Man, as created and in grace, is valuable since he is free of God; i.e., he is distinct from him in his freedom. This freedom allows man to return to him in love of his Creator which it could not have done in God as God.[58] As free, man's soul can rest "in its own derived existence unaware that this existence is from God. This is what Adam did, and this is original sin."[59] Thus, since Original Sin is inherited, man's condition is not wholly a rejection of God. What Zaehner calls Adam's "absurd egotism" causes man to be born unaware of God's very existence. What he says next is the capsule form of his idea of the difference between monism and theistic mysticism:

---

[56]Ibid., apud Suso's Little Book of Truth, chap. iii, trans. by J. M. Clark, London, 1953, p. 180.

[57]Zaehner, S/P, p. 191.

[58]Ibid.

[59]Ibid.

In the dreamless sleep of the embryo, as the psychologists have told us, there is a blissful unconsciousness, a physical union with the mother, a native innocence to which the individual in his "manic," "mystical," "inspired," or merely lunatic moments aspires to return: for we are all one in Adam, and this oneness we, at rare moments or under the influence of drugs, can and do feel. Yet every human being repeats the sin of Adam in that he separates himself from his fellows as Adam separated himself from God. The instinct that makes a child say "I" at a certain stage of his development is the inherited self-assertion of the First Man who made the supreme mistake of seeking eternal happiness in himself in his ātman, rather than in God. So it is that in every discipline that calls itself mystical, the first step must be the taming, or rather the destruction, of the sense of individuality: only then can one say, "I am Brahman," "I am this all," thereby identifying oneself with the undifferentiated Man or farther back still with undifferentiated Nature. And "in this emptiness rest is sufficient and great, and it is in itself no sin, for it is in all men by nature, if they know how to make themselves empty."[60]

Here Zaehner, in brief compass, defines both Isolation Mysticism, Nature Mysticism, and their relationship to Theistic Mysticism. The first stage of mysticism is: i) a trance state (dreamless sleep, which is the God of isolationistic mysticism), ii) which is a return to innocence, described mythically/psychologically by Zaehner to make it a return to one's mother in union, and this return comes about through a

---

[60]Zaehner, S/P, p. 191.

condition of morbidity (mania), or one of mysticism; and iii) this reunion reconstructs our original oneness with Adam. This is both Nature Mysticism (one with the All) or Isolation Mysticism; the one when it is a union with the All, the other when it is a separation of the Self from the All in order to seek--through this death to the ego--a bliss in the Self (ātman, or Brahman). This is sinful for man in general; it is a preternatural egotism in which one is mystically (preternaturally) allied with one's Self for the first time in joy. It is a sin, then. But does Zaehner mean to say that this is what Indian religion, and all religions like it, are? Not in the least. It is merely to say that, for the First Man (whatever that means) it constituted a sin, but for us it constitutes a desire which is noble and religious: the religious desire being, for Zaehner, the quest for the oneness of innocence, which oneness was the experience of the First Man; and the experience of the first man was the unconscious experience of immortality. Zaehner is, implicitly, saying that the unconsciousness of Indian religion (trance) reconstitutes the unconscious state of man's innocence/immortality. It is a contrivance, but religion is a contrivance when it is not a grace religion, but it still remains religion and holy for Zaehner.

Adam, for Zaehner, represented the fusion of the orders of nature and grace. At death, Adam went to Limbo where yogins go when they die. Neither Adam nor the yogins can go elsewhere since both were out of contact with the source, which is God, and could not find it. The yogins found the only thing they could be in contact with: the eternal bliss of the soul. To do this they had to separate the soul from all that was transitory and "ungodlike;" this, even though they did not know God. The soul's bliss consisted in contemplating itself as it came from God, as the imago dei. Zaehner says, therefore, that the yogins and others who know this bliss before

246

death often mistake it for heaven.[61] It is not
Zaehner's intention, here, to read Hindu holy
men out of heaven, leaving it a preserve for
theists only. It is his intention, and mine,
to show that the philosophia perennis is wrong
in saying that the monist experience is the same
as the theist. The bliss of heaven is an enjoyment of God in his "entirety," his essence, and
his "eternity." Zaehner offers as proof that
this bliss of the monist is different from the
Beatific Vision of Christianity and the bliss of
Islam, and of theism in general--including Indian--
is to be found in the difference of approach
which separates monist from theist. The monist
achieves bliss by his own efforts since there is
no God there to offer him help or with whom he
can unite. The theist mystic, on the contrary,
is sought by God first; and it is God who makes
him fit for union.[62]

This does not read non-theists out of
heaven, I reiterate. What it does is to eluci-
date what they say of their own experience, not
what derivative thinkers such as those of the
philosophia perennis say about them. The yogins
themselves, the writers of the sacred Upaniṣads,
said that they are separate from grace, gods,
body/mind and heart...and from all but Self.
This is to take them at their word--which is the
essence of Zaehner's methodology: to take the
orthodox at their word, not what others say of
them, but what they say of themselves. Theistic
Hindus intend to go to God through God's actions,
coupled with yogic asceticism, but the action of
God is first and foremost in the theism of the
Gita and Rāmānuja and Śaiva Siddhānta. This
makes it a different religion from Hindu monism.
This is all Zaehner intended to say. The religions are different. As proof he offered the

---

[61]Zaehner, S/P, p. 191.

[62]Ibid., pp. 192 f.

247

radical differences which persist among the varieties of mystical experiences which he broke down into three categories. So in a religion of monism one does it oneself. In a theism God divinizes one and unites with the soul. Monism unites with no one since there is no one but the Self, and the Self is All, the Ultimate Being. Does this preclude the possibility of grace helping the yogin to empty the Self of ego? Naturally not, but this is another question, one Zaehner took up in the other three theses discussed earlier. In a word, however, grace is lacking to no one. But we must proceed as if it were in order to take the other religion at its word, and in order to make the proper distinctions as if the grace of God were not there. For the rest of his life, and the rest of his corpus, Zaehner will use and drop the "as if" device depending on whether he will speak of divergence or convergence in religions. Divergence is helped by not speaking of grace. Convergence is helped along by including it in the discussion.

Hence Vedānta cleans the mirror of the Self so that bliss in immortality can be attained in beholding the imago, the state of man's nature, even though flawed. Man has forgotten that he is from God, so the view of one's nature must be blissful, if the yogins are to be believed, and if one is to believe the expressions of theologians these many centuries reflecting Christian consciousness to the effect that man's nature is good. Any intuition of the good in man is blissful. This is as far as Vedānta does and can go. Theism begins its work here, when God begins to empty the Self of Self in the annihilation which precedes full union with him in the ultimate state of Christian mysticism short of the Beatific Vision: namely, a fullness of union with God and consciousness of that here and now, if only for a while. What Zaehner has indicated is that at the bottom of man's nature is a bliss in the very way he is made; this, yogins and anyone can attain on one's own. But beneath that is a bottomed-out man, emptied by God to be filled with God's own life; and that is a bliss as well. It is the difference between a human bliss and a divine one. And that is what Zaehner has pointed out: the difference between the orders of nature and grace, and the close proximity in which they live. But the distinction must be made between them or else suffer the fate of Prometheus: hubris, the essence of the Fall was that God hated man at his best, not that man at his best could not, and did not steal God's fire. Yoga can and does steal the fire of God which we call the imago dei by isolating and enjoying it. But it is hateful to God when man says that is as far as one can go. God can and does, in theism, come into man's heart with another bliss, infinitely greater than the first bliss. To say that man can go no farther than first bliss is what we Christians would call a sin against the Holy Spirit. It is to say that God can do no more for us than we can do for ourselves. This is the thing which piques Zaehner when he reads the writings of the philosophia perennis: in saying it is all the same, what they are saying is that all one can do is get to first bliss, a monist bliss. Zaehner had to make things distinct again in order to begin the discussion among religious men, not end it. The philosophia perennis closes down the discussion before it can begin, since, if we are all the same, then what is all the fuss about? This is not only the reductio ad absurdum of mysticism, but the end of religions as well. Yoga is not hubris if there are other religions. But it is if it is all man can do. If so, we are back with Adam and Prometheus, but after the crime, not when they were at their best.

Zaehner's work began as a refutation of the philosophia perennis. His writings followed hard on the heels of Huxley's The Doors of Perception in order to refute that author's assertion that drugs were a religious surrogate. Just one week before he died,

...at a time when he /Huxley/ had reached a stage in which he thought that under the influence of LSD he could remain indefinitely in a state of timeless bliss which the Tibetan Buddhists call the 'Clear Light of the Void,' he realized that this was probably a gross misrepresentation of what was actually happening...his wife made a tape-recording of their conversation...(he said), "This whole thing has been very strange because in a way it was very good--but in a way it was absolutely terrifying, showing that when one thinks one's got beyond oneself, one hasn't... I began with this marvellous sense of this cosmic gift, and then ended up with a rueful sense that one can be deceived... It was an insight, but at the same time the most dangerous of errors...inasmuch as one was worshipping oneself."[63]

Zaehner had the last word. He would die only two years after this himself. Huxley admitted what Zaehner had proved: Huxley's experience was of the self, not God. And Huxley admitted it on his deathbed.

---

[63]Zaehner, Drugs..., op. cit., pp. 108 f, apud Laura Archera Huxley's This Timeless Moment (Chatto and Windus, London and Farrar, Strauss and Giroux, N.Y., 1968, pp. 268-9, Mrs. Huxley's emphases, not Zaehner's.

CHAPTER VII

SUMMARY AND CONCLUSIONS

(A) Summary

(1) Nature Mysticism

Mysticism is, generically speaking, being
one with something or with someone. This unity
bespeaks an integration, a unity or it may even
mean a disintegration--which is an oddity for us
in the West, though it is not in the East with
Hinduism and Buddhism. It becomes a 'mysticism
of matter' when one is united with matter in its
undifferentiated, spiritualized state. When one
views matter on the cosmic plane this form of
matter can be termed 'mind,' 'ego,' or even
'Super-Mind.' Teilhard de Chardin said matter
was "an ambiguous unquiet, the combined essence
of all good and evil."[1] This means that matter
is alive. It moves not just mechanically, but
it has 'impulse,' a vital life-spirit, a tension
causing interiority (life). This is what J.
Boehme meant by his 'throes of matter,' which
Marx and Engels picked up from the former.[2] This
idea of matter sees one as merging with the All,
with that impulse that gives all life and movement, which is the essence of matter for Marx.
Marxism, therefore, has not only an economic-
social justice-attraction; it also has a quasi-
religious one. It is, then, a mysticism of
matter.

The Mystical and Prophetic religions come
together through matter; and so do Christianity

---

[1]*Hymn to the Universe*, Harper and Row, N.Y.,
1965, pp. 59 f.

[2]Cf. K. Marx and F. Engels, *The Holy Family*
(E. tr. Moscow, 1956), p. 172.

and Marxism, typologically. All come together
dialectically clashing and renewing each other,
à la Hegel, to keep the flow of history, i.e.,
matter, going. For a teacher solidarity subsumes
the solidary religions (Hinduism and Buddhism)
and all men and women into one community: namely,
Christianity. God clashes with matter in creation
and the Incarnation and matter clashes with God
in Marxism and resolves in history and religion:
i.e., in Christ's history prolonged in our history in the Church. Therefore, Word became
Flesh so that Flesh might become Word; so that
unredeemed flesh, unredeemed, thinking matter
might become divinized; and history, our history,
might not only be touched by God, but become God's
life in time.

But, as always, there is a <u>caveat</u> here. The
convergence theme so beloved by theologians and
historians can take the place of goodness and evil
in time. Convergence can become a trap because it
seems to force one beyond one's own religion into
something theological, but not religious; into a
theology without God, which is meaningless and
aimless.

If this mysticism of matter is a basis for
religion and economics, it is also the basis for
psychotherapy, a healing for man seen as a frac-
tionated, material/spiritual being. Freud pic-
tures healing as a coming to oneness of the transcendent self beyond the ego; i.e., it is having
an experience of one's intimacy with matter to
experience the 'collective unconscious' immedi-
ately--i.e., in an unmediated way. Herein lies
the trap: Chardin's experience of his oneness
with matter is, really, the end-product of healing on the psychological level.[3] But Chardin
saw matter as a warm trap: warm because we are
matter, and it is endearing at its best: a trap

---

[3]Chardin, <u>loc. cit.</u>

because it is so necessary, so powerful, so
beautiful and healing that we can come to worship it, which is to say we come to worship ourselves, and this is to break the commandment we
think least about: "I am the Lord, thy God.
Thou shalt have no strange gods before me." Prometheus was man at his best. He successfully
stole the fire of the gods. But the gods hated
man at his best. This myth seems to say that, in
some way, we intuit that we have limits; that we
have a proper place in the scheme of things; and
that to be so successful that we transgress those
limits is to commit the sin of Prometheus:
hubris. I see mysticism of matter as a good thing
in itself, but it is instinct with pitfalls--some
warm and rewarding, others so frightening that
they lead us to self-hatred and border on insanity. And Greek religion, in its mythology,
'remembers' that some success is a danger to our
well-being. I think that this 'remembering' is a
centerpiece in the religions of both East and
West as 'anamnesis,' which is to recall us to our
reality, which we have forgotten (amnesia) by
Fall or some other device or cataclysm which
alienated us from such 'recall.' This is the
alienation which both Marx and psychotherapists
have vaunted so; and this is merely the theme
about which religions move either as center-poles
or as ends in themselves. In the East, when one
has attained to such knowledge (jñāna), then
one has remembered the Self (ātman), and the end
of the road has been reached. In the West, this
is a way-station on the road to God, but it is
central nonetheless.

Rimbaud's enthusiasms were those of the matter mystic. He attained his goal through his
poetics, aided by turning every moral law and
human relationship upside down and inside out.
This induced madness temporarily, a state in
which one becomes one with the All. On this
level one is beyond good and evil. This is the
materialist's mind, not Christianity's God.
Union came through dissolving the conscious mind

thus fleeing to the unconscious. Rimbaud thought that he had become nature. He thought that he had become a deity, too. Theisms flee this doctrine because it is a diabolic mysticism and produces only bad fruit. The <u>Cloud of Unknowing</u> says that desiring to 'un-be' is the devil's work, not God's; that both God and the devil have their contemplatives. The author knows this from the fruit of both of these genuine mysticisms.

Seeking the Self can be good in Hinduism and Buddhism because this is the way their religious coordinates work; grace and transcendence vector them differently from us--i.e., speaking as a Christian theologian, not an historian of religion or as a phenomenologist, I see grace operating in all religions, but in radically different ways. This is what I mean by Hinduism and Buddhism having different coordinates. The coordinates in different religious systems may touch, but they are not the same, nor do they lead to the same goals. To confuse this is to end up with the <u>philosophia perennis</u>. Having said this, it is necessary to say that, for a Christian, Jew or Muslim to set out wanting only the Self would be improper and mischievous; but it is the very goal of Buddhist and Hindu Isolation Mysticism. Rimbaud sought union with God whether God wanted it or not. His shortcut to God was through perversion. He achieved ecstasy, but not God's peace; there is a distinct difference. This state is one without God and is to be found on man's unconscious level. Rimbaud had a conversion in which he felt that all his sins were forgiven. It was in one of his enthusiasms that this happened. But psychotic enthusiasm has the same result: namely, one feels that one's sins have been forgiven. And Rimbaud's psychosis was quite temporary. When he came out of it, he knew that his sins were not forgiven. He said later that it was a false conversion because there was no desire to pray and no peace of heart involved, both of which are the hallmarks of Christian mysticism. I add that there was no desire to

254

change his life by doing penance either; and this
is usually the tipoff whether one's experience is
genuine or not. Prayer, or the desire to pray,
and to change one's life for the love of God, are
the signs of a genuine conversion. His enthusiasm
showed another mark determining it as a non-
Christian mysticism: self-hatred. God does not
call us to hate the self.

Nature Mysticism has two phases: expansion
and contraction. Expansion is the phase of the
experience in which the ego balloons to include
all, to become one with the All, to become the
All. In Muslim mysticism this is called bast and
is connected with the virtue hope. This movement
takes delight in the body and is not horrified by
its needs; but it is a delight which can turn into
horror after the enthusiasm wears off. It is very
near the manic side of the manic-depressive psychosis. It is the hopeful feeling novices feel
at the start of the spiritual journey. It follows
the spiritual life as a 'good news' thing. This
is not to say that novices cannot have genuine
consolation, but that, in retrospect, those who
crash quite heavily reveal that their 'ups' have
been more Nature Mysticism by dint of the very
way they came down. All come down, but there is
a coming down in the Lord and a coming down in
the self. More on this in a moment. Now I am
considering the 'up' side of things in which one
wants to take care of everyone, sell all one's
goods and give everyone a good time with them,
help all men and women...etc. It is expansion
in excelsis and lasts only a short time.

Some rules for handling expansion are in
order. The Muslim spiritual master Qushayri says
that when in a mood like this one can keep one's
equilibrium merely by following the canons of
good breeding: namely, behave like a gentleman
or gentlewoman even though one feels like being
wildly enthusiastic. This state is one of
mania, says Qushayri, and is to be considered a
trap because beginners mistake it for progress,

and it is not. It is joy, but not God. There is
a difference. It is not bad joy, but it is not
God either. The trap is in mistaking one for the
other. A good time is a good time and God is God.
When God gives one a good time the results are
different. One desires only to be with him, to
please him, to change one's life, to pray. There
is a great self acceptance in feeling oneself
repose in God, yet there is a great pain in feeling sinful, yet one's repose is greater than one's
pain, even though it does not lessen the pain. It
just does not matter because one is loved, which,
in turn, exacerbates the pain. Repose and pain
are in a healthy tension. The ego is not ever
crushed in self hate. Instead it is loved and
revealed and led (challenged) beyond itself.

Contraction (qabd in Arabic, pronounced
"qabz") is connected not with the hope (raja) of
expansion (bast), but with fear (khawf). So the
binary pairs run thusly: expansion/hope........
contraction/fear. See it that way and you can
see the usefulness of expansion as well as its
trap side. Contraction has no useful side. It
is utter abandonment to oneself in oneself. It
is depression, not the dark night of the soul
enjoying the consolation of God in great pain,
but just a dark self-hatred from which there is
no exit. In this state one is overwhelmed by a
sense of sin--whereas in Christian mysticism one
may be flattened by a sense of sin, but it is a
flattening which leads one to pick oneself up
and try again. Here one is flat, period. The
soul is utterly alone; one's only companion is
sin. One feels only disgust for the body and
for the self, whereas in expansion one felt only
joy and tremendous self-acceptance in both.
There is terrible fear here like only those who
begin the spiritual life for the first time can
feel. It is a fear which freezes into inaction.
In this state one is obsessed by damnation.
Luther seems to have felt this and not the dark
night of the soul. The dark night sends a shaft
of love into one, the pain of which is almost

overwhelming, but which leads to love and adoration; and it induces a tremendous pain in one's sinfulness, but there is not _any_ sense of being overwhelmed by one's sins. How can one be overwhelmed by one's sins when one is overwhelmed by love? One is in great pain because of sin, but only because one is so loved. The Christian knowledge of sin is a gift which attends one's experience of being loved. God never sends the revelation unless it is both sides of the revelation: that one is a loved sinner, not a sinner period, but a loved sinner. The feeling of being loved is always greater than the sins because Christ has conquered sin. Anything else is not Christian, but neurotic; not healthy guilt, but sick guilt; not God, but the ego or the evil one mauling one horribly, for this is a terrible state. This is the diabolic side of Nature Mysticism, and anyone who plays with it lightly-by using drugs or other techniques-is courting such an experience.

Some rules for handling contraction: Don't struggle against this state because it increases one's morbidity. So do nothing to overcome it. Submission to the state allows it to pass; like the jet pilot who must push down on the stick of a plane in a crash dive after breaking the sound barrier in order to pull it out: press down, not pull against it, but go with it. The ego in God is strong enough to pull out of it, but it seems that any struggle sends one deeper into the depths. This is a depressed state, and as such is different from desolation; or, as we said, it can be, or can have, its diabolic side, and then desolation enters with its frozen blackness. St. Teresa of Avila said that the knowledge of her sins _always_ led her to pray because it called her to God's mercy and an awareness of it. Her sins not only did not depress her, but made her aware of God's love and her own salvation in progress.

A bad expansion experience leads one beyond

the laws of religion. The tipoff of what kind of experience it has been is in what kind of life one leads after. Huxley called this type of expansion 'downward transcendence.' Expansion, therefore, always leads one to a state beyond the law, which is not per se a sinful place to be, but can be and has been so often in the history of religions.

Therefore, expansion is Nature Mysticism in its 'up' phase. Contraction is Nature Mysticism in its diabolical or depressed phase. But some expansions can become diabolic if they lead one to do dionysiac things. Yogins use Raja-yoga to expand the ego with the same results: some lead holy lives, and some do not.

I will define Nature Mysticism again, to wrap up this section on the mysticism of matter, but I will not expand on it as I did in the text. I will dwell on a few matters which need more amplification, however. Nature Mysticism is a preternatural experience, placing one beyond the norms of subject/object, space/time continua, in which the ego is expanded to identify with all things and thus unite with its objects, carrying it beyond good and evil; and in which personal immortality is assured; in which no god is necessarily involved; in which one is aware of his intimacy with his environment, which is to say, with one's material side.

Nature Mysticism is an experience on a primitive, but powerful, level. Its name is merely a descriptive term, not a philosophical definition. The rest, or peace, one achieves in expansion or integration, especially in the latter, for expansion is rather more a joyous excursion than something quiescent, can be on the way to God, but is not so per se. It ends with the ego, and the ego is not even the Self, let alone God. Drugs or a low-level yoga can produce Nature Mysticism. Here the ego expands, not the Self.

The unity of Nature Mysticism is a material one, so it is not a unity with the Self, which includes materiality, but transcends it as well. There's the rub, isn't it? We still have not found a philosophical system to rid us of the bicameral psychology (upper and lower soul). Possibly we cannot find one because sin has alienated us from the Self, so no merely human interpretative framework can put us back together, even in a tentative way as would be done philosophically. Further, the matter experienced in Nature Mysticism is in an undifferentiated state. This means that it is not in its human, self-conscious, state, but in a previous state of perfection. That is what we mean by a participation mystique: when men and women were much younger as a race they reacted like animals. There was a group mentality, something like animals. The herd instinct kept us together and impelled us to live together. The individual was not known at all, but only the group, the herd. So human consciousness, matter in a humanly conscious form, was less defined, less differentiated, in those days. To experience this participation mystique is a return to an earlier form of consciousness. This may be why Nature Mysticism is so charming: it is a form of religious nostalgia in which we return to 'the way we were.' It is a return to a more primitive state by a gymnastic leap to a form of group think. As such, religious nostalgia is no better than any other nostalgia, and is even worse since it uses incense to trivialize the past. Nostalgia trivializes the perfections of the past, which perfections were high achievements in their day, but to which we cannot return since we have grown, changed. It may be a necessity psychologically to return to the past in order to be healed. But to buy a home there and set up shop is not only delving in trivia but trafficking in it. It is not paying homage to the ancients to wish to go back with them. Rather, it is a lack of courage and hope in the only life we have religiously and psychologically to live at one or

259

several removes from our present level of achievement. Such would not be religious at all, but a form of infantilization. In this sense, Nature Mysticism can only be a condiment in either psychological healing or religion, otherwise it becomes toxic if one wishes to make a meal of it. And this is precisely what Huxley did. He made a meal of this piquant condiment and in doing so made a botch of it. On his death bed his wife recorded his words to the effect that Nature Mysticism did not put him in touch with God, but with the ego, and this not in a healthy way.

Beyond space/time means beyond good/evil because one need not consider the consequences of one's acts. God means something only within the bounds of the here and now. God is always contextual. That is why he is always called the God of Abraham, Isaac and Jacob. He is the God of history, of contexts in which men and women live. And space/time is the human context. Anything else is to say that God has not taken possession of us and our world, which is to go against reality. Morality means, therefore, a here-and-now God. There need be no morality in eternity because all is holy there. Morality is for those on the way to the Holy. Nature Mysticism is one of the ways to short-circuit the nettling consequences of being in a fallen/risen state. It puts one into eternity bypassing the necessity of love, of people, of doing good, of being decent. This is why the Charles Manson phenomenon in California is so important here. The drug culture of Manson and his 'family' made good become evil and vice versa. This is because they altered their consciousness so much that they flipped it out of its human context. This is Nature Mysticism precisely. In this way there is a great similarity between Manson and Rimbaud, both of whom used perversion to achieve a state beyond the ego in order to throw off the burdens of normal human life. But the rub is that the Incarnation is frightfully normal. God is to be found in the normal, in the material, in the psychological, etc. Being beyond space and time means that one does not have to take himself or his world seriously. Again, trivialization! Again, infantilization! I hate to homilize, but it is necessary to point out that this form of mysticism is fraught with pitfalls. One must take himself and his world seriously. Space and time allow us to take ourselves seriously, they give us frameworks of reference. This allows us to have meaning in our lives. Without space and time there is no meaning, and without meaning there cannot be love and joy. Nature Mysticism is a 'cheap thrill' when used to take us out of the possibility of the present. It is hard enough to have a present without undercutting it completely. And without the present there cannot be a future. This is the point. It is the reason why so many misuse alcohol and drugs: to get out of the present for a while. But this is despair. Hope means that God is a God of the context, of the present, and that he will perdure in the presents of which our future is compounded.

In Taoism there is the reconciliation of evil with good, male with female, light with dark-all this is the reconciliation of opposites I spoke of above--and this seems like a likely root of the diabolic possibilities of Nature Mysticism. It is not that Taoism is diabolic. Certainly not. What I am driving at is that over and over we see this reconciliation flipping one out beyond the context of one's religion or normal life into an area of wildness and joy, often fraught with danger and sadness personally. This is so because expansion is often followed by contraction, which medievals in the Church called diabolic possession. The experience of joy in the expansion phase is often followed by a blunted moral sense, or at worst a distorted one. Death seems impossible because one is beyond space and time. Being without space gives one the feeling of omnipotence one has in the expansion phase; being without time gives one the feeling of immortality. Both of these feelings are transitory, but quite powerful.

261

This is not a theistic experience at all.
This is so because, quite simply, there is no
relationship with any person; and personal
relationship is the basis of the Christian experience: God is love and he who abides in love
abides in God. But in Nature Mysticism the ego
is the starting point and the terminus of the
experience. This feeling of unity with all things
is not a unity of equals since the ego feels
superior to all of them. If the person with the
experience calls this a god experience, it may be
pantheistic since pantheism is not a relation, but
an identity put into words: it is man/woman
united with his/her environment, which he/she
calls a god. This is next to religion, but not
there yet.

Therefore, Nature Mysticism is not religious
because it doesn't do anything religious. Religion begins when one attends to one's fallen
state, to one's alienation, to one's pain. In
Semitic religion God makes the first move towards
us. This is the theistic process. In Indian
religion (Hinduism and Buddhism, for our purposes) man begins the process of doing something
about his sad estate by stripping away the ego
and its relations, which are the roots of sadness, to enjoy immediate bliss in the Self.
Religion begins when God or man begins to empty
the ego in order to get at the Self. The ego
is either full of self or expanded to include all
nature. Therefore, Nature Mysticism is the best
man and woman can hope for without religion. It
is a Limbo experience of a sort: a happiness in a
locked-in ego, that is a happiness without God;
even though the ego is expanded, it is locked in
on creatures and on the shallowest, most ephemeral level of human nature. There is no death
because there is no time involved. There is no
responsibility because there is no place involved
to contextualize human loves and hates. It's
just a happy union with the ego, at best. It
tends, though, to self-worship because one feels
omnipotent and immortal, both of which are

elements of the divine nature. Diabolical Nature
Mysticism is not religious because no religion
preaches the destruction of the self and self-
hatred as is felt in contraction. Nature Mysticism recognizes no values and religion begins
with the sorting out of values.

Matter has been experienced as something
alive in Nature Mysticism. When matter comes
together, the inner and outer dimensions are seen
to be one in man and things. It appears that
matter can think in its non-human forms. It is
obvious that it can think in its human form; and
it is in this human form that matter sees its
own unity. Religion begins, though, when man
and woman in a non-euphoric state want to do
something about the obvious disunity of things
and people.

(2) Religious Nature Mysticism

Nature Mysticism is not religious per se
because it does not address the human condition
in order to do something about it, but is merely
a voyage into the expanded or contracted ego.
But if one wished to face up to reality, this
would be an ideal place to start, if one only
knew the proper techniques for altering one's
consciousness. The Indians knew these techniques
superbly: yoga. Religious Nature Mysticism
shows up the first time in the Hindu ritual
texts called the Brahmanas. Here the Hindus
found that through sacrifice man experiences
(knows) that the 'without' of things is one with
his 'within'; i.e., that macrocosm is microcosm.
Also they found that ritual causes one to
remember (the anamnesis theme) that before a Fall
one was part of an unbroken whole. If one
wanted, therefore, to restore this wholeness he
had to remove individual consciousness, which
was the effect of the Fall. Before the Fall
consciousness was a communitarian thing; all
were one with a unitary, non-indivualistic consciousness. So rite repairs the rift the Fall

263

caused in consciousness restoring Universal Consciousness. So, there were two awarenesses: a
lower one residing in the ego, and a higher one
called Universal Consciousness. This resided in
the Self.

The second level of Nature Mysticism is to be
found in the Upaniṣads. These start with man and
where he is, not with a god; they deal with his
immortality. It is the human situation again.

Quite simply, these Upaniṣads saw food and
breath (prāna) symboling the Absolute, which is
called Brahman. The latter is an impersonal
Absolute, and as such is the substrate of all
beings. So the Brahman is food, which, being
alive, maintains life thereby. The 'without,' or
exterior, of food is the body, and the 'within'
is man's spirit, which is a self. Within the
self is a mind; within the mind is an intellect;
within the intellect is bliss (Nirvāna). Therefore, the body is the self's and mind's exterior,
and the interior is intellect and joy. Yoga then
enters to split the self, body from soul and
refines both further. Then the self is stripped
of mind, emotions and desires, thoughts and even
of trances (ecstasies). All that is left is a
quiescent joy. The Taittirīya Upaniṣad is
especially good on this 'food' theme. It is
quite an early Upaniṣad.

On the first level of religion, which was
religious Nature Mysticism, Hinduism constantly
mistook its enjoyment--its religious joy--for the
Absolute, or what we would call God in our context. So when a Christian, for example, has such
an experience, his/her context is theistic and
so he/she tends to make the mistake that the
experience is of God when it is only matter (the
ego in a spiritualized state) which has been
experienced. The context leads one powerfully
to conclude that one's experience is in terms of
one's own religion. This is not always the case.
Christians have Nature Mysticism experiences as

well as experiences of Isolation Mysticism and so on. But they tend to conclude that such is God. It is not; not at all! Our history is a highway along whose shoulders bleach the bones of those who have made this mistake and persisted in it by making it the bread and butter of their lives, and calling this bread God. God names himself. We don't do the naming in theism.

So food pushed on to become spiritualized (prāna=breath, or life force), and thence it moved on to become more spiritualized by becoming thought (buddhi). The outer dimension of food always tended to move inward; and the inward tended outward to become a man or woman. The outward direction began with an expansive joy which becomes matter. Nature Mysticism is matter and spirit meeting in synthesis in man and woman.

So one expands to one's immortality. The pain and death have been faced. Religion has begun. Man has consciously faced his fragmented existence. When immortality became expansive, it became Nature Mysticism. This is materialist religion--look at Marxism this way and you see it in a different way! This materialism in religion is true religion--not ours, but true. (And we must remember that the Incarnation is God becoming self-conscious matter. At least that.) Questions of life and death are really questions about man, not God. To face them opens one to the possibility of God.

The expansion to become the All led Hinduism, ultimately, to move further to become the Brahman, which is the substrate of the All. Materialism showed matter's thrust: a lively movement towards what we call spirit. Leave matter alone and it seems instinct to move back towards spirit. It shows what we would call the leftovers of the Fall: alienation of matter from spirit, of ego (matter), from Self (spirit). It also shows that there is an elan vital in matter, a force pushing it; and Jacob Boehme's 'throes of matter,' picked

265

up by Engels and Marx, show what Karl Rahner means
when he says that matter is moving instinctively
back to spirit, that matter's nature is to develop
back towards spirit;[4]that the cosmic-corporeality
is present to itself in each of us...as one cosmos but present in many ways in men.[5] When the
Hindus talk of materiality it is not a gross matter, but a spiritualized stuff that they treat.
When Rahner and the young Marx talk of matter this
is what they mean. So, at its best this materialism is not gross. At its worst it is wild and
Dionysiac....gross and ugly as religious and
political history show with materialisms, including Catholicism, which is quite materialistic.

Breath (prāna) becomes consciousness after
it is refined by the process of digestion. So
the process runs: from food to breath (prāna)
and breath to consciousness, the direct experience
of which is bliss (immortality). So matter moves
to thought and then to bliss because real thought
is happy/good. Again an optimism. At man's base
is goodness and the way to get there is first
through matter. But here is where the comparison
begins to weaken since Hinduism is going to get
where it wants to go by getting away from matter
as quickly as possible. When Hinduism began, its
materialism looked like ours. The comparison ends
there since Hinduism then split men and women
from their bodily base. We cannot abide that.
That would be the heresy of the Manichee all over
again in the Church. Therefore materialism proceeds to idealism in the Upanisads because
breath is more necessary than food. Breath is
spirit. This is the link between phenomena and
the all.

---

[4]K. Rahner, Foundations of Christian Faith,
Seabury, N.Y., 1978, p. 186.

[5]Ibid., p. 190.

Indian Nature Mysticism is matter become
aware of itself because man has faced the fact
that he is alone, apart from the brood and responsible for this alienation in some way.
Therefore, to put oneself in touch with prāna
in its expanded state--which means that it has
become the All--means that matter and the ego
have been united. To do this they used yoga
for the first time. Or put another way, using
yoga they discovered that they were in touch
with matter. Now what did they want to do with
that experience? They have now had an experience of their personal immortality in an
intuitive (contemplative) way.

So Nature Mysticism is not irreligious,
though it can be, but religious. It can be non-
religious in a modern sense when attained to by
drugs. Hinduism's sages (seers) saw becoming
the All as the goal and perfected yoga to effect
this desire. The irrational use of the experience came when the sages divorced experience
from revelation in using religion and trance in
conjunction. Yoga put the rational in man in
neutral, opening the gates for the irrational
contents of the unconscious to emerge.

The Upanisads are the sages' religious
attempts to interpret their experience. Hence
they are philosophical. These experiences were
the results of attempts to make all one again.
This is close to our idea of salvation in its
desire, but far from it in its mode of accom-
plishment.

Conclusion: In this first state of mysticism (Nature Mysticism) matter evolves toward
its goal: Mind; ego units with matter as well.
In the second stage (Isolation Mysticism) the
Self will assert itself. Up to now the Self has
kept quiescent. But from here on it will aggre-
sively pull away from the ego and its ecstasies
for a much deeper joy. It wishes to recover
Eden's bliss, not Limbo's. The second form of

mysticism will be a matter of the Self contemplating the Self. This will be as far as humankind can go. Without God we can do no more. But it should be remembered that if one knows the correct technique one can enjoy immortality on two levels. Religion begins when one seeks to do something about one's situation. The third stage of mysticism, the third radically different kind of religious experience, is that of love mysticism. This is theistic mysticism. It can be given only by God, no matter how shrewdly one applies this or that technique. In the first, or Nature Mysticism stage, yoga frees the contents of one's inner life to become one with the inner world. The ego becomes one with the world, it doesn't leave it.

(3) Mysticism of Spirit: Isolation Mysticism

Yoga, and asceticism in general, can induce states of peace which are the expansion phase of Nature Mysticism in which the ego unites with matter within and without to become one with the All. Here, man's inner life disburses all its contents in a joyous expansion. Therefore, yoga unites one with the world; one never leaves the world in this form of asceticism.

Isolation Mysticism as such begins with the stripping of sattva, rajas and tamas from the Self. This means that the ego is sloughed off; the ego, remember, is composed of Prakrti, nice but a trap. So matter is considered, not an evil, but a diversion from one's aim: Self-realization. The goal is Nirvāna, which is an eternal, deathlike bliss. The Self comes home, at last, to the Self. Isolation contracts the soul to its essence: immortality, the enjoyment of which is a bliss (Ānanda) called Nirvāna.

This bliss in the Self is totally devoid of theism and is, therefore, radically different from Nature Mysticism's expansion or integration.

268

Here the personality cannot develop because it has become undifferentiated, not developed. It's a return to where we were, to the womb, not a thrust forward, as it is with Semitic religions: a thrust into the God of history and the history of God. On the contrary, it is the undifferentiated consciousness of the womb. This is enstasy, not ecstasy.

No category of depth psychology can fit Isolation Mysticism because it is the opposite of integration and therapy; it is isolation from the collective unconscious, or any kind of unconscious.

Therefore this type of mysticism is not salvation, which makes us whole--because we were fragmented by sin--but it is a separation of the eternal from the mortal. It is a liberation in separation. Comparison of the categories of salvation and liberation which forget this fact are in trouble. Further, the categories follow from the experiences which they interpret, which are radically different.

The Self asserts itself in Isolation Mysticism, the ego in Nature Mysticism. Isolation is an active stripping of the ego, which becomes a passive contemplation of the Self in the Self.

Isolation Mysticism begins with the assumption that one is the Absolute. God is, therefore, a function of the Self in this system, if he is anything at all. In our system God is not a function of anyone or anything. He is free, absolutely. In fact, an absolute seems somewhat irrelevant here, though, because immortality is the only reality worth cultivating.

Therefore, Sāṁkhya supresses the contents of the lower soul (ego) to achieve a peace which is deathlike (Nirvāna).

So, if being one with matter is one direction of mysticism, the other is being one with

269

one's spirit, with the Self. The French thinker
Peguy said that the temptation of the truly great
people in spirituality is precisely this unity
with the spirit to the exclusion of the body. So
the two heretical tendencies--and remember, heresy
is a teaching compelling us to be somebody whom
we are not--in Christianity are: i) to be one with
matter to the exclusion of the spirit, and ii) to
be one with spirit to the exclusion of the body.

The Buddhists, too, wish to forget matter's
unquiet, its dis-ease, its pain and the ill of
matter or life (dukha in Indian spirituality is
the wretchedness connected with what we call
matter and its entails: love, enjoyment,
family...) All leads to pain (dukha), and religion is at base, what man (in Hinduism and
Buddhism) or God and Man (in the Semitic religions of the Book: Judaism, Christianity and
Islam) do about this painful condition.

The three characteristics of matter--in its
solid as well as its atomised (more spiritual)
state--in Buddhism are: impermanence, unsubstan-
tiality and unease. Marx and Engels couldn't
agree with Buddhism more in this case,[6]because
they both see matter as unsubstantial, changing,
in flux, devoid of self, the same and not the
same.

Indian thought goes back before time to a
period of bliss without matter, without time.
Indian spirituality wants to stop the pain by
voiding its causes: matter and time. Hence
theirs (Hinduism and Ur Buddhism) is a salvation
from matter, not in matter. It is not the Word
(Logos) taking on the undignified stuff of matter (sarx) for them, but it is becoming what they
are in reality: not-selves (an-atta, in Buddhism).
This produces the surcease of pain and induces
the bliss they call Nirvāna.

---

[6]Cf. Anti Duhrung, p. 27, and Zaehner,
Dialectical Christianity and Christian Marxism,
p. 34.

The young, humanistic, Marx wanted, not the
present state capitalism of Russia and its satel-
lites, but a new materialism, a new humanism
which, in its philosophical aspects, limned out
by Engels, is a mysticism of matter. Again, it
is a way of dealing with the pain, and therefore
very enticing. But it is also a trap, pushed too
far, as I said above.[7]

Evolution for both Engels and Teilhard was
this: The emergence of life from dead matter;
secondly, it was the emergence of consciousness
from this life; and thirdly, it was the emergence of self-consciousness from animal awareness.
But Indian spirituality, which is a spirituality
of the spirit, says that one is to find <u>Nirvāna</u>
in the midst of the endlessness of matter's pain,
which endlessness is called <u>Samsara</u>, indicates
that as we are, as things are (<u>Tathatā</u> in Sanskrit) they are supernally good. So get to the way
we are by divesting the self of matter and all its
entails: time and body, family and intimacy,
love and anything which brings attachment. For
the root of pain (<u>dukha</u>) is in attachment, and
the root of attachment is desire. So, we
Christians disagree with Indian spirituality
because it strips us of something we need: matter
and time. Christ's spirituality is an inclusivism:
it includes the total man, not just a part.
Indian spirituality works, though. That is its
attraction. But Christ takes life as it is in a
more radically real sense: he takes on life, and
matter and pain and sin and ecstasy and sadness...putting in order what is disordered and
forgiving what needs forgiving. Christ takes on
man and woman as they are: body and soul. We
are redeemed in matter, not from it. And our
redemption does not move us to worship matter,
but God. The tension is this: God took on matter, became it; matter not only supports God in

---

[7] Cf. Marx's <u>Theses on Feuerbach</u> for substan-
tiation of my claims of mysticism in Marxism.

the Incarnation, it symbolizes him since human matter is the marriage partner--indissolubly, in some way--of the spirit. Thus Christ's matter, and that of the Sacraments, draws us beyond ourselves; beyond our egos, that is, to the real lasting Self. And where the Self is, there is God. The Self of humanity is inextricably involved with matter and time. Hence our spirituality must deal with both head on. Matter Mysticism is, therefore, partial; and so is Spirit Mysticism. Christian spirituality is paradigmed by Christ. The Incarnation is our model. Person is both/and: both spirit and matter; or, what is more evident: both matter and spirit.

The Incarnation is Christ's forgetting (amnesia of himself into matter. It is his emptying (kenosis) of himself, in Pauline terms, which is a "forgetting." As he grew, he became aware that he had to "forget" (i.e., empty himself of) even his ego, now grown to full maturity.

But this growth (which growth is a "remembering," or anamnesis, which is what we do at the Eucharist in remembering precisely who we are in reality, in God) is Jesus' remembering that he is man. And this human growth, this remembering, this anamnesis, begets a remembering that he is also God; i.e., his vision of his deepest reality (that he is Trinitarian) came to maturity as he came to full manhood according to the human laws of growth. This is his emptying, his forgetting: viz., that he left "being God" with all its prerogatives, and came to follow, to be, what it is to be human. He follows our laws without doing violence to either humanity or divinity.

Thus, there are two amnesias: forgetting that he is God in becoming man, and the forgetting of his ego in his total loving, obedience to the Father. And secondly, there are two

272

anamneses: growth into full manhood and then
giving up that perfection in the fuller perfection of the creature's obedience to the reality
of creaturehood, which is death. Thus, two
kenoses: two pleromas (fullnesses).

So Christianity is a radical, hard-headed
acceptance, a transcendent positivism rooted in
matter, yet its transcendence is not from matter
but in matter; hence our sensuousness manifested
in our liturgies and our "stickyness" in not
wishing to give up our visibility as Church for
a more "spiritual" ecclesiology. Our way is
never without matter and its laws. And Christ
took our ways in order to open up His Way to
us.

"This is my body" and "This is my blood" are
scandalously material ways of opening up the
"Way." The reality of the Church is to be found
in matter and time, in the body and in both
history and historicity. This is the dynamic
reality of the myth we call our religion, that
truth which compels our belief must be bound
inextricably to matter and time. These are the
lineaments of our faith, the continua in which we
work. The myth means that he takes us just as we
are and transsubstantiates us in (of) our sins
into someone justified. It is a case of "This
is myself, and I forgive you." He has remembered
the way in and of us. To forge a new "Way" would
be not only fraudulent, but unreal. Our
anthropology is founded on the truths of the way
things are; the greatest "way things are" is the
Incarnation. Christ's coming changed all, for
always. His coming is so powerful that it over-
flows all the way back to Adam. In order to be
retroactive, it had to have been really active in
time and body/spirit. And it was.

The goal in yoga is trance induction, to
slough off the ego and enjoy the Self in bliss.
This trance, Samādhi, is the thing sought in
Isolation Mysticism in India.

273

In this stage one has realized one's ātman.
The trance (enstasy) is a happy experience which
perdures (immortality) but without benefit of any
ego (impersonal, transpersonal) needing to be the
subject of this eternal bliss. Thus the bliss is
one of subjectivity without ego, which is beyond
person. So when I say "Self" I do so in a different way (sense) than I would if I were speaking in a Christian context. I use "Self,"
though, so as to make it easier to understand
and to transfer this technique to Christian use,
as long as one is aware of the differences. So,
one has attained to the direct experience of the
ātman and this trance is called samadhi. Sam=
perfection, fulfillment. Dhā=to place; and a=
towards. So one has been placed within one's
reality, finally. This is enstasy, not ecstasy.
And it is obtained by one's own aggressive act,
not by grace. Grace comes in Indian thought
much later, and is found in conjunction with the
yogic technique in the Bhagavad Gitā. But that
is another story.

So one has achieved the reconciliation of
opposites on this level in a much more wholesome
way than one did in Nature Mysticism. But it
can be just as much of a trap here as there,
especially for a Christian using the technique.
Refer back to the pages on the Philosophia
Perennis and you will see what the impact of this
thought is on one in a Christian context. One
feels beyond good and evil, beyond religion and
the divinity itself. This is why I have difficulty when Westerners like the great R. Otto
compare the German mystic Meister Eckhart with the
advaitan (quasi monist) Šankara.[8] Both, Otto said,
speak of being beyond God. But Otto erred badly
in not seeing that the contexts were radically
different. When Eckhart said beyond God he was

---

[8]Cf. Otto's Mysticism East and West.

speaking as a pious Christian (a theist) and he meant it within a religious context in which religion and its rules were to be kept. When Sankara spoke it meant that one is holy but beyond the gods, rules and observances of religion. One must be painfully aware of the difference in contexts. Huxley and his cohorts in the philosophia perennis were unaware of the need for context. Present-day Marxism is aware of this need, especially the Frankfurt School of Sociologists like Habermas. So what is holy in one context--Hinduism--would be wicked in another like Christianity if, for instance, one were to say that one is beyond good and evil and beyond one's history, one's time and place, beyond one's materiality itself. This would be to deny the Incarnation.

Isolation Mysticism and Nature Mysticism can be--and are--done by the unaided self. Theistic Mysticism's emphasis is on God, not to the exclusion of a vibrant response on man's part, however. But Love Mysticism is the effect of God, who is free. He willingly relishes our lives from the inside: his delight is to play with the sons and daughters of men (Prov. 8:30).

The seductive thing about Nature Mysticism is that its expansive phase must be thrown over for a less scintillating phase of integration. But this integration seems the price faith asks when God moves one to a deeper intimacy with him. It seems that we must fall apart again to be made over by him. Intellect and interiority go awry. Only the will is at peace, but it is a darksome peace, since the light has gone out with intellect's meander through the halls of our interiority. God has taken us in his great gourd-heart and gentled us with such brilliance that it seems dark. Aristotle says that the most obvious and brilliant truths seem darkest to us. God is the hidden self-evident of our lives buried in the striations of our muscularity. When God comes "alive" in contemplation, joy gives way to the cottoning of our souls. We feel

275

emptied but filled with a dry lightness like
cotton puffs. It leaves one helpless but loved.

So Nature Mysticism's integration can be just
as much a trap as the expansion phase, more so
even, since it seems to be all the more "spiritual"
and close to the way things are meant to be. But
we move from perfection to perfection. Expansion
is a perfection, and so is integration. Isolation is a soaring perfection. We move from
integration to love in the West. Indians move
from isolation to love in their theism. It
depends on one's context. Isolation is one form
of transcendence in which one empties the cup of
ego to fill it with the emptiness of subjectivity
(Self). This seems like limp poetry, but the
interpretative metaphor the Buddhists use to
symbol their experience is "Emptiness" (Śūnyatā):
Saṁsāra=Nirvāna=Tathatā=Śūnyatā. This means that
within the pain of everyday life and lives
(Saṁsāra) there is a Bliss (Nirvāna), which
bliss is to be found at the bottom of the way
things are, exactly (Tathatā): and all this is a
feeling of Emptiness (Śūnyatā). This is the way
the Buddhists express their experience, and we
take them for honest religious people. Take the
others seriously! is the axiom of history of
religions. And Buddhism is just an Indian
spirituality, so it applies just as well to Hindu
spirituality. Buddhism is not "just" that, it is
much more, but to see it as anything other than
in the mainline of the Indian tradition is to miss
the boat.

Now in theism, God moves into one's life and
shatters the emptiness with a fullness which
plunges us into darkness. The moment of fullness
is so new it looks and feels dark. One has been
used to a peace in emptiness (kenosis in Christian
terms). Now God moves in with a fullness (pleroma)
and its novelty sends us into a vertiginous period
because we haven't eaten in so long, nor exercised
with him in the Garden of an evening since Eden.
We have "forgotten" the old feeling of closeness

and the new is the better of its father-so much
so that it all but overwhelms one. The ecstasies
of the saints are so powerful because our poor
stuff cannot stand so much closeness. The best
we had was to see his back, but to see the face
of God is a pain like suddenly coming out of the
cinema on a Saturday afternoon with the other
kids and being blinded by the happy Saturday
sunlight. So God shatters the first experience
of unity (integration) in the emptiness of
Isolation Mysticism--if one is a Christian ascetic/
yogin--and enters the soul in an I-Thou relationship which appropriates us to himself. We lose
our center. Hereafter we are centered in God.
Therefore vertigo! until we get used to our new
estate. The soul submits in suffering and joy.
The Sufis say the annihilation (fana) is a joy
as well.

When a system has no philosophical base with
which to interpret one's religious experience it
is easy to conclude that one is God, the union
is so complete. This is obvious in the Isolation
experience, which cannot be ungraced in the good
men and women who experience it. So, in Hinduism,
both the quasi monists (advaitans) and dualists
(samkhyans) experience the same yogic delights
psychologically but conclude philosophically to
being the Ultimate. The advaitans do it in a
monistic way and the samkhyans in a dualistic.
But atman and purusa are both seen (concluded to)
as the Ultimate. There is not a union with the
Ultimate in either system. One is the Ultimate.
This is the difference between this and the
Christian mystical experience: the Hindu experienced identity, the Christian experiences what
he/she calls union. There is an essential difference here. The experience of unity is so
powerful that even in Islam, whose vaulting
transcendentalism sees it to be mortally sinful
to have anything to do with God, the mystics concluded that they were identical with him. So,
both Hindu and Muslim monists concluded that: "I
am the One," or "There is only the One, and I am

277

that," or "I am God."

Conclusion: In a religion of the Book, when there is an experience which either goes against the grain of the revelation or which goes with it but in so potent a way that it is quite easy to conclude to heterodoxy by saying "I am God," then the tendency is to absorb each experience and put it someplace safe within that religion, if it is at all possible. This is easy when one's revelation is not one Book but many, as in Hinduism. But in a religion where one must obey the Book, as in Judaism, Christianity and Islam, it is a case of conform one's experience to the experience of the Book or get out. The supreme experience is obedience to the Book of God and the God of the Book. Any other experience is secondary. So in Islam some--like Hallāj--were executed because they said ,"Glory be to me," or "I am He," in concluding from their isolation experience that the Self is God. It is interesting that the Muslims were taught Hindu techniques and shortly after began to experience isolation and write about it in a monistic way. This happened when Abu Yazīd catechized a former Hindu and was taught the latter's ascetical techniques in return. Other Muslims were tucked within the folds of the ample skirts of Islam because they either accommodated their teaching to the religion or had it done for them by friends who convinced people that this new teaching could be accepted by the orthodox.

Therefore, God and the Book and the People keep us and our experiences in line. But where there is not a philosophical tool to use, it is easy to conclude that one is the Absolute, whether this be God or the Brahman or Allah. Hinduism is more generous because it absorbs all and then converts it into its own modalities; but Semitic religion is not so generous since its experience is its truth; and part of that experience is the revelation of God; another part is the God of the Revelation; and a third part is both of these in the mix called a religion, or People of the Book.

278

(4) Christian Mysticism

In his Spiritual Espousals the Flemish mystic
Ruysbroeck had to deal with the false mysticism
called Quietism; i.e., it was a true mystical experience, but it was false to say it was "the" Christian experience. Many experiences can be Christian
experiences, but to aver that they are "the"
experience of Christ leaves the proof to the one
asserting so. Ruysbroeck said that the peace
which the Beghards (Quietists) had was not the
peace of God but another peace which anyone could
have if he knew the proper technique of ridding
himself of distractions, images, and leaving the
higher powers free. The rest one attained to was
a true rest, but is a rest without the grace of
God. Such rest is the consequence of ridding
oneself of images and all actions, not God's
action at all. So many men and women seek peace
at any price, and what they achieve may well be
peace; but it is entirely another thing to say it
is God and his love they are experiencing. There
are two types of peace then: i) peace in the Self
without God's grace, and ii) peace in God through
his love and grace. How different these forms of
peace are. In a Christian context the consequences of the other type of peace are license,
usually sexual. This is not to say that the
achievement of, for instance, Isolation Mysticism
by Hindus or Buddhists leads to this. Their
religious context is different. They try to do
different things: namely, to aim for a peace in
the Self regardless of anything else. It is a
way of dealing with the results of the Fall. In
the Christian context one does not start out looking for religious experience as a way to deal with
the pain; rather one has a love relationship with
God and religious experience may or may not come
in one way or another. It is a question of emphasis. We have religious experiences, but we do not
seek them; to do so would be an evil for us since
no one can manipulate God. Experiences come and
go, and may even be a danger to one if one battens
on them by placing more importance on them than

279

on loving God. Our eyes focus on the God of
experience, not on the experience of God. Experience is always in the picture, but not in the
foreground. God is. So what is quite religious
in one religious context, namely seeking the religious experience called isolation, would be not
only fatuous but would be downright evil in a
Christian context. So it seems that God is contextual and so is religious experience. If God
works in the other religions, and he does, then
he does in a radically different way. The other
religions are different "vocations," or karmas, as
the Hindus would say. We know they are different
from us because what they are conscious of is so
radically different from our own religious
experience and tradition; and this is not just a
cultural difference; when one flattens out those
differences they are still worlds apart. They
are as radically different as men are different
from one another.

So, let's get down to brass tacks. Since I
have spent all this time in telling you that,
i) the other experiences are true, but not Christian, ii) and in outlining in depth just what
kind of mysticism it is, then what is Christian
Mysticism? There are many mysticisms in Christianity, but generically it is a process of
divinization in which man/woman is changed
interiorly into something divine. How does this
happen?

The Process: to see the bits and pieces is
the first step in the process. What do we see?

We see pain. The other religions began with
pain too. How do we see it-this is our context?
We see it as a mix of sin and goodness; sin since
in some way pain is connected with sin; goodness
since we perceive our hunger for happiness and a
cessation of pain as our bottommost level. So we
see pain and sin as coming from outside, as less
internal than goodness. Our deepest longing, then,
is for happiness. The very fact that I feel my

280

contingency so keenly is an expression of the deeper need for happiness--which need expresses the anthropological fact that we are good, and that our first impulses are for the good, i.e., that our will has an inbuilt inclination to seize on the good, not that it wills it, but that it knows/loves it. At bottom, then, we are good and love the good. The awareness of this need is also more interior than my feeling of difference from others and from myself.

But this feeling of contingency is, as Spinoza says, a sadness, "a passion by which the soul moves to a lesser perfection" (Spinoza, Ethics). This is the sadness of being finite with an infinite appetite. This suffering successively walls man in on himself more and more, isolating his consciousness from his deepest level thus denying one's very innermost self.

The feeling of not coinciding with others and with the Self is a basic "No" built into our being from the outside. All evil, moral and physical, comes from the outside; i.e., good is at our bottommost level, not evil. The sadness of being finite, limited, fragile goes deeper and progresses geometrically as it travels inward. Can it overcome one? Can the powerful feeling of sadness stemming from one's state of being fragmented (not coinciding with the Self) overpower one? I'll answer this in a moment.

But first, man, philosophically speaking, is a limitation. He is an Infinity mediated by the finite. So his feelings are in deep conflict. He feels good about himself and badly at the same time. Feeling reveals the human predicament, always. It reveals man as a "primordial conflict."[9] But what clashes with what?

---

[9]P. Ricoeur, Fallible Man, p. 216.

Underneath the negative phase of the conflict is the more primordial level of what K. Rahner calls the "Yes" (Foundations of Christian...) and Ricoeur calls the "original affirmation,"[10] and what II Corinthians 1:17-21 calls the "yes" which Christ is, buried deep within us--i.e., God in Christ accepting and affirming us because we are good. So, theologically and philosophically man is good. The guilt of our state making us alien to the Self (called original sin, which term is confusing) and the personal guilt we have earned from our failures of love do not wipe out our most primordial structure: we are created good and God has made us good (better, in fact) through Christ after the inner rift in our nature set up this conflict of feeling, which is emblematic of our whole state: viz., fragmented. But our deepest level anthropologically and theologically shows that the inner "Yes" is a joy buried in us so deeply that evil and the geometrically expanding sadness can never overcome us. The sadness, which grows as it is allowed deeper in us, will never get on our deepest level to destroy it. This is so because we would die first. Our deepest level, the "Yes," is intact through creation and salvation (second creation). So our most primordial level is the yes of being (of the creature, since being is better than non-being) and of redemption.

What has revealed this conflict? Feeling has revealed it. What has the conflict revealed? Evil and good. So how does one get to the good? Through the evil. One knows, philosophically, that one is good because one knows that one is evil and should not be. The tension reveals one's deeper nature: goodness and the appetite for happiness, which is the possession of the good. What the "Yes" is is a joy. So man is happy on his most primordial level.

_____

[10]Ibid., p. 208f.

So this joy (the "yes") is found together with a profound sadness in being finite, limited, fragile. So man is a "fragile mediation for himself," in the words of Ricoeur.[11] What this means is that he projects the rift into his work, into his world. This rift is his very being, and that is the terrible rub. So: we summarize just in what condition we find man in this way:

i)   At bottom, man/woman is an original joy.

ii)   The fact that man/woman finds him/herself not coinciding with the Self means that not only is the external world an "other," but the very Self is to be construed as an other philosophically and theologically because that is precisely how it is "felt," or found in human experience.

iii)   Human fragility allows us to know the other two levels and mediates them. But fragility is not only a way to know, it is the ability to do evil. Evil has been done and we find its possibility in ourselves in our tender capacity to go out of focus, not to coincide with the Self.[12]

Our fallibility can be the occasion of evil, the window through which evil can enter one's life and the life of the world. The very fact that we have a science of ethics means that man has tried to synthesize humanity and has failed. Police exist because fragility has become evil.

Philosophy is fallibility (fragility) questioning oneself, one's place in the world and one's lack of happiness. And evil is the shadow our fragility throws on our goodness. We

---

[11]Ibid., p. 215.

[12]cf. Ricoeur, p. 215.

283

know we are good because we have been bad. We
know we are a joy because we are sad. So, the
primordial can only shine through the fallen
because that is precisely what/where we are. But
evil need never overcome our original affirmation, or primordial joy because anguish is not
on this level; good and joy are there and are
irremovable; if we want them to be conquered that
is our business, but the ruination is of a joy
and good which are still there. That is why hell
is to horrible: we suffer because we see that we
are good and have chosen "No" instead of what we
are: a "Yes." The cards are stacked in our
favor. The worse primordial anguish can do to
us is to evoke a deeper response, or a response
from a deeper level of our being: namely, the
will to live, which is the revelation of the very
original affirmation, our primordial joy in
action.[13]

Summary: What have I done so far? I have
determined philosophically (and philosophy is
our joy turned into a question: Why?) that we
are fragile; that it is our fragility, not evil
in itself, which reveals our ambivalent nature.
There are two valences: i) fragility turned evil,
into what we call sin, and we know sin since we
know how it feels: guilty. And ii) fragility
revealing a deeper level, which is the bottommost
level, which is a joy, a "Yes," an original
affirmation. What the Creator made was good and
the creature enjoys that good. We go to the
knowledge that we are good by going through our
evil, and the deeper we go the more sad we
become because we know our nearness to death the
more. But the deeper we go, the more good we can
know about ourselves, and the more we do know.
We can never have a knowledge of sin which will
kill us since our good outweighs our evil. We

---

[13] Ricoeur, History and Truth, p. 291.

may die, but it won't prove fatal. Joy and happiness are in existence, not in non-existence.

So our way of moving runs right at the fullness of our being: good and evil. This is a radically different way of dealing with the human situation from the way the Hindus and Buddhists proceeded. They stripped away time and matter, space and fragility by going into the joy. They saw the pain but would not deal with its cause: sin. We do. If we care to deal with sin it is not because we are more moral than the Buddhists and Hindus; certainly not! Our history is a concatenation of saints amid the sinners, holy gentlefolk amid mostrous boors. No, we can face up to more of our reality because we have help. Alone it seems the Hindus and Buddhists made the best deal man could hope for. Forget the evil and go for the joy they knew was buried within! We have a different experience. In time we were met by God who allowed us to live in time and face its consequences. India could not face time since the consequences, without God, were too terrible. Time demands an accounting and space a reason for one's impotence. So they bent time back on itself and said we all come back over and over. In stripping away matter (the ego) they had to strip away time and space. But God is a contextual God. He forces one to look at the fullness of the self in time and space. This is only bearable because of our experience of Jesus and the Spirit in our lives in time. Without time we deal in a coinage of myth. And our pain and desire for joy are pressingly real.

Now, does man shape the experience or the experience the man? Hindus wished to experience the joy at the bottom of the barrel and did so, and still do. But we Christians know that we are at the altar of the transcendent mystery, and that we do not shape the mystery but that it shapes us. The Indian experience is something

285

the Indians control aggressively up to the point
of experiencing Nirvāna. It seems that they do
not control the experience, though, even though
they come in and out of it. They control the
means to go into it, and to come out of it, but
they do not seem to be in control of the experience. They are in possession of the Self,
but the Self experiences a sense of self-
transcendence with no term. The mystery is un-
named, and in this sense I agree with K. Rahner's
anonymous Christian. They witness the transcendent in a nameless, unthematic way. But their
own Self is quite fully thematized. They experience the joy that we are. And this is an important human discovery. But Christians neither
shape nor control their transcendent. They are
in the presence of mystery and cannot control it.

So the bits and pieces fit into a pattern of
good and evil as the human poles. They relate
with one another as we have outlined above. The
second step of the process was to put the bits
and pieces into patterns which fit the realities.

The Third Step of the Methodology: Let us
step back and see what all this means now that we
have given the literal interpretation of the
phenomena. This step means that we show how the
Christian life works, in brief scope.

Firstly, divinization is the process of
becoming, in some way, divine. It means that
one is radically changed into Christ. It is to
become an alter Christus (another Christ). Where
are we to find Christ? Just where we found our
human situation, which is that we are a battle-
ground of good and evil feelings: namely, we
hunt for God in our feelings.

Secondly, divinization will follow the laws
of human self-discovery because God does not like
to create twice what can be done once--otiosa
restringenda sunt. The law of normal

self-disclosure says that one follows the line of
one's pain to arrive at one's joy; this means
that, negatively, to experience pain, to know it
and to have more pain because of the pain is a
way of saying that the pain should not be there,
that there is something positive and joyful--at
bottom--forming man's and woman's constitution.
So evil is the prism through which we know that
there is a good which we love all the time, even
though we don't follow it. We don't coincide
with ourselves. The will naturally is complaisant
in what it loves naturally, and it loves the good
naturally, even though it does not follow it all
the time. So evil reveals our good, and good
reveals itself as good. So all reveals the good
either negatively or positively. Now, when God
comes to us he will follow his own laws, respect-
ing our condition--our use of the constitution he
handed us in creation. God will take us as we
are. So man is the joy of the "Yes" in the
sadness of the finite. But if we look only to the
Self then we bog down in a morass of sadness because we don't find ourselves privy to our present
status: saved or not? So, what to do?

God's movement into our lives pulls our gaze
inward past the Self, through the Self and past
it is more accurate, to him. He pulls our gaze
to his Son in trust and love. This makes us begin to coincide with ourselves at the same time
that we begin to coincide with him.

Thirdly, the laws of human action are through
consolation and desolation, through joy and sadness. These are the twin laws of humanity unredeemed, and these are the laws of humanity redeemed. Christ took on the rhythms of humanity
as he found it. So if we wish to find God in
our lives, look within our psychological rhythms.

Fourthly, it is impossible to present all
Christian mysticisms, or even all Catholic ones,
in such a small book. Hence I would like to
content myself with a modestly reasonable and

287

short presentation of Ignatian Mysticism.

The Spiritual Exercises of St. Ignatius of
Loyola have the effect of using images (the active
imagination) to confront all that is within us,
both consolation and desolation. They take
feelings quite seriously. If nothing is going on
in any particular prayer then one is either not
praying, or there is a block of fear or anger.
Something always happens when one confronts the
Self.

The Spiritual Exercises (hereafter Sp. Ex.)
both take one out of the Self (ecstasy) and into
the Self (enstasy) in a new way. There is a
Christocentric movement away from (beyond) the
Self, and an anthropocentric movement in which
the Self is found, healed and liked for the
first time--possibly--in one's life. This goes
beyond Nature Mysticism since the ego and the
Self are healed and enriched in God, not just
the ego alone, as in integrative Nature Mysticism.
The consolations are, moreover, personal joys in
the other which enrich (make one love) the Self
too. Unlike Huxley's ecstasies which were joys
of an expansive type but completely impersonal,
these are joys in interpersonal love. There is
a Presence within one calling one deeper in the
Self, so deep that one goes beyond the Self to
the Other as one's Self. Thus the alienation
within the Self and between one and the other
is ended. One is reconciled with the Self, one
coincides with the Self--the ego with the Self,
in a happy integration and subordination--and with
the divine other. In this instance Christ is the
human other and the divine Other. In one fell
swoop one's alienation in the interior and exterior spheres is ended. In God the Self is
enriched and challenged to go beyond in love.
Man is the mediator of all things, but the Sp.
Ex. show him/her that he/she is not the measure
of all things. God is. The Sp. Ex. draw one to
one's deepest mystery, to that which is so clear
and obvious in se that it has been obscured and

288

hidden by the detritus of one's personal trage-
dies and those of the race. Aristotle, John
of the Cross and K. Rahner all say that the most
luminous truth is the most obsured one; the more
obvious a thing is the more easily overlooked
or suppressed. This is true about God; this
is true about the Self.[14] The things which are
most obvious to your friends, and especially
your enemies, are hidden to you. Your hidden
sins aren't hidden from them, but from you.
The Sp. Ex. open one up in love to examine and
accept them in a context of loving change
(metanoia means a change of the heart, this is
penance a reconciliation with the self as no
longer other, with the other as self and with
God as self).

The reason why the Self is so elusive is
that it is a subject, not an object. As a
subject it is impatient of direct examination.
You can't put soup in a pants pocket! One is
never quite sure who one is because one is subject and one cannot approach the Self directly.
Rahner says that one approaches the Self of God
asymptotically-i.e., that one gets close and it
moves away just before one has it because it is
a curve coming close to the figure viewed, then
it curves away into infinity. One approaches
the human self indirectly too. One cannot symbol
the self directly. Ricoeur is good on this in
his Symbolism of Evil (the first and last chapters). He says that the symbol of one's evil
is never out in the open directly. I would go
further. The symbol of one's good is never
out in the open either. One is subject. So
one's examination of conscience is always
approximate, never right on the mark. The

---

[14] cf. Jn. of the Cross' Bk. II, Drk. N. of
the Sp., ch. v., 3 on this. Cf. K. Rahner's
work cit. supr. on this.

Council of Trent said that one cannot know with
absolute certainty that one is in the state of
grace--this in response to Lutheran claims. But
the thing about the Exercises is that they keep
one's gaze where it should be: on Jesus. If
one is so loved that one's sins just keep oozing
out to bring one great pain within such love then
one will not get locked in on false guilt. The
latter is a solitary confinement with one's
sins...without God and his love. Contemplation
(mysticism) is a loving awareness of God and
the Self as loved/sinner. It is a balanced knowledge of who one's deepest Self is: one's new
self is God and one's own Self raised to a new
power; but this does not discount the heavy
reality that one is in process; time is important here for without it one would have no
theater in which to act out (get rid of) one's
evil. One knows one's sins in the encounter
with Christ. But they seem less important since
one is so loved. But such love is so awesome, so
wraps us out of ourselves that our sins are
unbearably apparent and painful. Love is a
sweet knowledge of our goodness and our badness.
Neurotic knowledge is without God, without love,
without any option...And God is the God of options
in any and all contexts. There is always a way
out. In neurosis there is no way out.

But if there is no way out with neurosis,
there is no way back with expansive Nature
Mysticism. We are subjects and the subject/
object polarity is gone in Nature Mysticism. So
how is one to deal with the fact that one is
subject and that subject can only be subject if
there is an object? Hence Nature Mysticism is a
short-run thing. It takes one there and leaves
one there...to crash in greater sadness when the
experience is over. Nature Mysticism is not a
Way at all, but a blind alley--happy, but blind.
And Jesus is a Way. Huxley was looking for a
Way out of the boredom of the ego, which boredom is one of the anguishes tormenting us back
into our joy. Why is one so sad when one knows

that one should be happy? Huxley's Nature
Mysticism is a sprint to a truncated freedom
which leaves one all the more enslaved when the
experience vanishes. Jesus' Way is to go within
the reality, to face the sadness, not to escape
it. Look at the Cross! That is not an escape,
it is a redemption! Jesus is fully realistic,
scotching out nothing from the contents of our
lives, from his human life. He faced the full
rhythms of human living: the sadness and the
joys, God and man. He sidestepped nothing of
reality in his life, and his religion would
have us sidestep nothing either--when it is
healthily lived. Buddhism does not deal with
the God question but sedulously avoids it
saying, "The house is on fire, don't ask who
made it. Get out of the house!" Isolation
Mysticism in general slips the question of God
as an absolute. If it treats him at all it is
as a less than absolute object of meditation--as
it does in Sāṁkhya. God is never an object,
he is the subject par excellence. The
experience of emptiness, holy and joyful as
it is, is a muted experience, because it is
purposefully an end. Christians pray, "World
without end" because history is linear. It
perdures. God is forever and we perdure with
him. How can emptiness be anything but a start?
God is a fullness. To stop at emptiness would
be an insult for a Christian. God is contextual,
so are religions. What is holy for one would be
unholy in another if done in the same way with
the same intention. We can use the techniques
of the Hindus and Buddhists but only to produce
the emptiness which God wishes to fill so
lovingly. This is the radical difference between
experiences and religions. Mysticism is therefore the center of religions, not just religion
but religions. When St. Teresa and St. John of
the Cross spoke of mysticism it was called mystical theology, not mysticism in this compartment
and theology in another; but it was together.
The experience is the theology. Recently a religious told me that she did not want to do

theology, but spirituality. On the other hand to do theology and not realize that it is one's experience and that of the whole Church that one is putting into an interpretative framework is to forget the way the Fathers and Mothers of the Church saw it so early on and continued to see it for centuries. Mysticism is not a luxury but the center of our religion. The fact that it has produced so many loonies in the Church should not allow us to forget that it has produced saints and doctors like Ignatius Loyola, John of the Cross, Teresa of Avila, Francis de Sales... Mysticism is Christianity, or better, Christianity is a mysticism. It is hard to handle, as I have tried to show in this essay. It slides one into happy, and sometimes horrible, pockets and leaves one there. Or it is the very loving presence of God himself. Bad mysticism tends to drive out good mysticism. It is Gresham's law of economics applied to religion. But that does not deter us from the fact that we are a mysticism first and a religion second. K. Barth's theology hated the fact that we had made religion a third party: there was Christ, there is ourselves and there is religion, that strangest of all distillates. Religion is the relation between Christ and ourselves. Barth, however, scanted mysticism. Like so many in the Reformation tradition he saw how foolishly we Catholics had followed our mystic trail. Pity he did not know that the very relation with Christ was a mysticism. What is primary in Christianity is mysticism, not the epiphenomena of mysticism like visions and ecstasies and the like, but the stuff of mysticism, which is a loving relationship with Christ. Mysticism in my sense, in the Catholic sense--and I see myself in the Ignatian tradition of the Catholic tradition--is the experience of God in which one is loved, knows/feels one is loved and wishes only to love in return. As such it is a loving and knowing experience of God, and the Self in God, which leads to loving exchanges between the lovers (prayer and confidences) and a change of heart on both sides.

God changes by revealing more of himself and the human person changes by dint of the power to change one's heart (penance) which this experience is.

Mysticism, then, means to change one's heart and mind giving the beloved the heart and mind of Jesus. The intellect understands through God's wisdom and the will loves through the Holy Spirit's purity. One's inner faculties have a foretaste of glory and the affections are renewed with God's delight.[15] Ignatian mysticism agrees with this. One's inner life takes on Christ's. He took on our binary rhythms (consolation/desolation) and we take on his.

Therefore the Sp. Ex. are ways of going to the Self and God through the felt/known (*sentir* of Ignatius). They use the active imagination to free the whole content of the body/soul in a context of love. God comes in our context, which is a joy hidden by the sadness and aggressions of philosophy, on the highest level, and by the primal screams of history on lower levels, and he takes us into a context of love, which is his context. Thus history is God's context with men and women. Other traditions tried a coronary bypass around the clogged arteries of history to the joy they knew existed primordially in man. But to do this they had to bypass God and sin. Thus Indian mysticism seen on the way to Christ is good for them and for us. Seen as an end it would be good only for Hindus and Buddhists. For Christians to take it in the Indian context would be to deny Christ and history, to deny the full panoply of human emotions, with their loves and fears, viciousnesses and soaring nobilities. The context of Christ is the context of the

---

[15]cf. John of the Cross, *op.cit.*, II, iv., 2.

293

Sp. Ex.: man and woman, sinful and loved, to be turned by divine logic into man and woman loved and sinful in a context of history in which love increases and sin decreases--(He must increase and I decrease).

History is the way of Christ and of Ignatius. Take men just as they are. Since we are subjects we cannot get at the realities frontally, so we use indirect methods like the images of the Gospel. So myth in the sense of image, not in the sense of not being historical, is the lever which pries God out of us along with our darker side. The tool is the image. The effect is a change in love. The goal is divinization. Our felt/knowns, our knowledges will become loves, our loves wisdoms in God. Our very inner life will be revealed in its beauty and ugliness, but the latter only in a context of such great love that one wants it revealed and changed because it pains one so to be so loved and so sinful.

Discernment means, then, to get to the will in its pristine element. The will always falls in love with the good, not that it always does it. Go to your heart without fear and pray to do what it wants, for it wants only the good. And God is good!

APPENDICES

APPENDIX I: An Appraisal of Zaehner on Abū Yazīd

  When his Hindu and Muslim Mysticism appeared
in 1960, Zaehner had already published his
critically acclaimed masterwork, Zurvan: a Zoroastrian Dilemma (1955), his Mysticism Sacred and
Profane (1957), and his At Sundry Times (published
as The Comparison of Religions in the U.S. in
1962, but in 1958 in the U.K.).   Hence his
theories about mysticism were well known, as was
his reputation for scholarship.   Hindu and Muslim
Mysticism, as I have said, is a tandem to
Sacred and Profane; the earlier volume gave the
groundwork and the latter merely filled it in a
bit.   In his review of the book, Frits Staal
called it an important work because it is one of
the few studies on comparative mysticism done by
one linguistically equipped to do it.[1]   He says
that the translations are generally accurate, but
that the interpretations are not.   He finds
Zaehner more one-sided in his treatment of Hinduism than in his treatment of Islam; this is
because Zaehner does not like Hindu ritual, and
battens on the later form of the religion known
as bhakti (devotion) and its companion and adver-
sary advaita (monism, or non-dualism).[2]   But
Stall's criticisms on Zaehner's interpretation of
Abū Yazīd are most to the point here.   He thinks
the most interesting chapter in the book is
chap. V, "Vedānta in Muslim Dress," in which
Zaehner treats Abū Yazīd and the influence of
Vedānta on Islamic mysticism, if any.   He is
convinced that Zaehner's interpretation is

---

[1]Staal, Frits, review of Zaehner's H/M in
Journ. of Am. Orient. Soc., 82 (1962), p. 96.

  [2]Ibid.

probably correct, especially the interpretations
on tat tvam asi and māyā (Zaehner, pp. 94-97) in
which the mystic utters things which make the Self
a god, and the world an illusion, respectively.[3]
Zaehner's religious allegiance piques Staal. He
finds it too much in the foreground; as such, it
obscures the differing points of view. Further,
though readable, he finds Zaehner too emotional.[4]
By 1975, some thirteen years later, Staal's book
on mysticism,[5] does a volte face on this, stating
that Zaehner is found out to be wrong on Abū
Yazīd, too. He bases his judgment, which was done
on his own power before, on the notions of Profs.
A. J. Arberry and T. Gelblum. It repays treating
both here.

Gelblum published his review in 1962 in the
prestigious Bulletin of the School of Oriental and
African Studies (25, pp. 173-76). He finds
nothing very new in the book as far as information
is concerned, but Zaehner's interpretation is
quite new. After some preliminary criticism, he
gets to Zaehner's main thesis. He finds Zaehner's
interpretation "... highly questionable as regards
both method and fact."[6] He finds Zaehner's words
on the Chāndogya Upan. text (6.8ff) "tat tvam asi"
to be convincing, at first blush, and impressive
(cf. Zaehner, p. 94). But Gelblum says that
Zaehner's hypothesis amounts to "an improbable
solution of a nonexistent difficulty."[7] He
maintains that Zaehner's translation of the

---

[3]Staal, art. cit., p. 97.

[4]Ibid., p. 98.

[5]Exploring Mysticism, Penguin ed., Middlesex,
Eng., 1975, p. 68.

[6]Gelblum, art. cit., p. 173.

[7]Ibid., p. 174, Zaehner's H/M, p. 94.

Arabic pronoun dhaka (that, which is the parallel,
according to Zaehner, of the Skt. tat=that) does
not refer directly to God at all; its context
could refer to God, but only the context. Hence,
he says that the Arberry translation (appearing
in his Revelation and Reason in Islam, London,
1956, p. 95) and that of Nicholson, which Zaehner
tore apart, are both impeccable. Neither scholar
translated the text as did Zaehner. Nicholson
said the text went thus: "... so that when Thy
creatures behold me, they may say they behold
Thee, and that they behold Thee, and that only
Thou mayst be there, not I." We shall deal with
Arberry at length in a moment. He thinks Zaehner
disregarded those elements in the Arabic texts
in question which would not help his argument.[8]
He concluded that Zaehner created textual diffi-
culties in the Hill and Edgerton translation of
the Gitā which were not there. Hence, he does
not accept Zaehner's main conclusions in the
book, though it was a book "marked by profound
erudition."[9] In mentioning Nicholson's work,
one wonders why Gelblum did not think to say
that Nicholson maintained that there "is certainly, I think..." an Indian origin in Ṣūfism;
that the doctrine of fanā (annihilation in Arab.),
in which the empirical self is destroyed in God,
seems to have come from Yazid's guru Abū 'Ali
al-Sindi.[10] In re-reading Nicholson one gains
new respect for Zaehner who, more modestly than
Nicholson, said that Nicholson theorized that
the Ṣūfi doctrine of fanā "might have derived"
from Indian sources.[11] One wonders why Gelblum
who enlists Nicholson's aid against Zaehner's

---

[8]Gelblum, art. cit., p. 174.

[9]Ibid., p. 175.

[10]R. Nicholson, The Mystics of Islam
(London: 1963), p. 17.

[11]Zaehner, H/M, p. 93.

hypothesis, overlooked something in Nicholson which corroborated Zaehner's central thesis: that Vedānta came to Islam through Abū Yazīd's guru. What Gelblum charges Zaehner with might well be laid against him: he overlooks evidence which disproves his counter-claims against Zaehner.

Why does such a good and fair scholar over-look the obvious--whether Zaehner is correct or not is not the question for a moment? What the question is is this: what made Gelblum overlook Nicholson's outright assertion, which backs up Zaehner? Perhaps he answers it for us himself. In his earlier review, on Zaehner's At Sundry Times (cit. supra) Gelblum accepted Zaehner's main thesis on Mysticism: that there were types, and that these types were radically different; and that this was proved by Zaehner. He rejoices that Zaehner has blasted the indifferentists. But here, as in the article under consideration, he bemoans Zaehner's "enormous assumption" that revelation is progressive: from lower to higher (theistic) revelations.[12] He criticizes Zaehner for uprooting concepts from their native con-texts in order to make a point: e.g., that the Trinity is like the Hindu sac-cid-ānanda.[13] He says that Zaehner makes the same methodological error which the indifferentists make; and he seems correct in this. But the same line of argumentation may be turned back on Mr. Gelblum in our present instance: Zaehner is trying to find the proper context for Ṣūfi ideas; hence the attempt is both worthwhile and yet to be disproved. We have Zaehner's word against Gelblum and the vacillating Staal. What seems to bother Gelblum is Zaehner's "monotheistic bias" which slants his translations: e.g., "soul" is

---

[12]Gelblum, S/T review, p. 610.

[13]Ibid., p. 611.

298

the Sanskrit ātman.[14] He chides Zaehner for his
implied value judgment in seeing Hindu religion
moving from monism to theism and Islam in the
opposite direction.[15] But he does not say this is
incorrect; he says it needs many substantial
qualifications. Zaehner did not say that At
Sundry Times was anything but painting with the
broadest of strokes. As long as one accepts his
outline, and that is all he is giving--an outline
of theological histories--At Sundry Times, Convergent Spirit, Concordant Discord and Dialectical
Christianity and Christian Marxism, then Zaehner
would say that his purpose was complete. Gelblum
seems to have accepted the outline of Zaehner's
systematics--with qualification--in his At Sundry
Times review. In his later review he rejects
Zaehner's main thesis because it is based on
imaginary problems. But he overlooks Zaehner's
corroborative evidence which Nicholson supplies
for him. The linguistic evidence is one thing,
but the corroborative evidence is quite another.
Again, Zaehner's assertions stand. It is his
assumptions--evolution in religious revelations--
which seem to bother Gelblum. He has disproved
neither, and in doing so his work has revealed
his own unproved assumptions.

More pointed still is the critique of
Zaehner given by Prof. A. J. Arberry. In his
book, Zaehner says that Arberry had rejected,
but had not proved, Nicholson's view favoring
Vedānta influence on Sūfism.[16] The book Zaehner
refers to is Arberry's Revelation and Reason in
Islam (London, 1957, p. 90). In his review of
Hindu and Muslim Mysticism Arberry sets out to
put the record straight. In the Bulletin of the
School of Oriental and African Studies,

---

[14]Gelblum, H/M review, p. 173.

[15]Ibid., Zaehner, p. 11.

[16]Zaehner, H/M, p. 93.

299

U. of London (25, pp. 28-37), Arberry delivers
himself of a major review of Zaehner's assertions.
He moves point by point through the translations
offered by Zaehner and comes to the conclusion
that Zaehner's

> ...presumption that Abū 'Ali came to
> Abū Yazīd as a convert from another
> religion is no more than a presumption.
> My own presumption, which is no more
> than a presumption, is that Abū Yazid
> took Abū 'Ali, a village Muslim of
> little or no formal education, through
> the religious and legalistic meaning
> of the ritual and common duties of
> Islam, and to his surprise discovered
> in his pupil a mastery of the 'real'
> and mystic apprehension of God. If
> this guess is right, then Abū 'Ali
> would belong to a type of simple saint,
> intuitively privy to the divine
> secrets, which is by no means un-
> common in Ṣūfi hagiography.[17]

More on this in a moment; suffice it to say that
whatever Arberry says will not destroy Zaehner's
contention completely, since neither seems able
to prove it linguistically. It is the conten-
tions which vie, ultimately, not the reasons
lodged in their favor.

When Zaehner says that khud'a was māyā (the
Arabic meant exactly the same in both instances,
for Zaehner, p. 97), that is, that both mean
"deceit," Arberry admitted that it was a non-
Qur'anic term, but offered what he considered
sufficient evidence to say that it is an

---

[17]Arberry, art. cit., pp. 36 f.

extension of the Qur'anic picture of God.[18]
Arberry's second criticism is of Zaehner's handling of the subhani (glory be to me) text
uttered by Yazid. He feels that the rest of the
text ("how great is my glory") is a gloss, and
was never uttered by Yazid. He does this on the
basis of textual variants, and eschewing the
Sanskrit in which he possessed no competence, he
still feels that the Sanskrit "homage" is rather
remote from the Arabic subhan (which he thinks
means "admire," connected with the Arabic 'ajab[an],
which means "an admired human being").[19] Further,
Zaehner overlooked Massignon--a scholar of monumental importance in modern Islamic studies--in
his deliberations. Arberry does not deem it
necessary to repeat Massignon's evidence, since
it is so well-known in the field. Hence he says,
"The attempt to find a Hindu source for this
celebrated shath seems so unlikely as not to call
for further discussion."[20]

---

[18]Ibid., p. 31. God is the master beguiler
in the Qur'an: Suras IV, 141; VII, 182; LXVIII,
45. He wishes to test one's faith and worship
by guile.

[19]Arberry, art. cit., pp. 31 f.

[20]Ibid., p. 32. Cf. Massignon's Essai,
pp. 249-51. Perhaps it is well to include here
Massignon's views on outside influence on Islamic
mysticism, given in this classic work whose full
title Arberry did not give since it is so well
known: Essai sur les origines du Lexique
Technique de la Mystique Musulmane (Paris, 1954).
Massignon's thought, in capsule form, is this:
W. Jones (in Asiatic Recherches, 1803, III,
353f, 376) said that there is a possibility of
Hindu influence on Ṣūfism, but did not back it
up with serious demonstrations. (81) He means
(footnote continued)

20 continued

Vedānta influence on Sūfi monism. Tholuck,
Kremer, Rosen, and Goldziher hold the same in
different degrees (81). Massignon admits to contact between Islam and India in science; calculus,
trigonometry and astronomy were gotten from India
by Fazari in 771 A.D., as were medical arts,
which came, perhaps, via Pahlavi translations
made by Muslims. But this contact was brief, and
ended very quickly (82f). Contact ceased after
the third century A.D. The first Indian-Muslim
hybrid doesn't appear until after the Muslim
missionaries came to India (11th century A.D.),
which was long after Yazid (fl. 9th cent. A.D.).

    Massignon's true colors come out when he says
that in every milieu where there are reflective
men one finds mystics (63f). Mysticism is to be
found everywhere, since it is a human phenomenon
(64). Hence, Massignon rejects out of hand the
theory of the Aryan provenance of all mysticism,
which Gobineau pushed along with anti-Semites like
F. Delitzsch (Die grosse Tauschung) (64). These
held that the Semites were absolutely without any
aptitude in arts and sciences and that, therefore,
mysticism in Semitic religion derives from the
Aryan peoples (64). Renan, P. de Legarde,
Reitzenstein, Blochet and E. G. Browne (whom
Zaehner cites) held this racist theory (64).
Applied to the theory that there was Iranian influence on Sufism, this means that the Aryan
Iranians gave Islam Ṣūfism. Massignon says that
this is indemonstrable. It is further said that
the Muslim sect Shi'ism, which is fobbed off by
many as an exclusively Persian "heresy," was
brought by colonists who were "de pure race
arabe." The local Kurdish tribes and the Afghans
were against Shi'ism, says Massignon (64f). So
Massignon is against any theory which smacks of
cultural colonialism and which says that mysticism cannot spring up by itself anywhere. This
is not the philosophia perennis, but something
                         (footnote continued)

302

Arberry's thoughts about Zaehner's equation
of the Arabic anta dhaka (thou art that) with the
Sanskrit tat tvam asi, though himself recognizing
the oddness of the pronoun construction, run to
these: "It would appear . . . that Abū Yazid was
intending to say no more than that "that" which
the creatures were seeing (in a "middle place
between the near and the distant") was God, and
that Abū Yazid had ceased to exist as a contingent
entity apart from God. If this interpretation is
correct, then there is no need to drag the
Sanskrit tat tvam asi into the arena."[21]

Arberry's criticisms are, as he said, his
presumption against Zaehner's. His linguistic
critique seems based on a presumption that monism
was home-grown; therefore, to have been based on
Massignon's argumentation. Both men, Arberry and
Zaehner, offer linguistic evidence, but only
Zaehner offers such in conjunction with a much
larger theory of comparative mysticisms, and a
systematics of mysticisms. It will be remembered
that Zaehner scored Arberry for presuming too
much about mysticisms being the same everywhere.
The linguistics appear secondary to the sparring
convictions about mysticisms in general. Perhaps
it would be well to give the reader the state of
the question concerning possible Indian influence
on Islamic mysticism. I have begun this already;

---

20 continued

quite different, which we will have to put to
Zaehner's theories, especially about Jewish mysticism, and here concerning Sūfism. Massignon did
not say all were the same; but he did say that
mysticism happens everywhere. In part he agrees
with Zaehner. But he disagrees with Zaehner's
theories that monism, like mysticism in Islam,
is "entirely derivative" (Zaehner, H/M, p. 167).

[21]Arberry, art. cit., p. 34.

I merely take up the threads begun by Nicholson and Massignon. Nicholson says that modern research has rejected such sweeping assertions as that which sees Ṣūfism as an Aryan reaction to the Semitic religious/political conquerers.[22] This would make Ṣūfism a Persian thing. But Nicholson would have none of this. The link has not been established between the assertion and historical evidence. The early Ṣūfis were natives of Syria, Egypt and Arabia by race. Further, Indian influence belongs to a later epoch. Ṣūfism is too complex for such easy assertions as Vedāntin, Buddhist or Aryan hypotheses.[23] So Nicholson slowly plods through the evidence and says that the early Ṣūfis learned ascetical techniques and love-mysticism from the Christian monks.[24] Neo-Platonism had its role, too; e.g., the Pseudo-Dionysius, who "may have been a Syrian monk."[25] Gnosticism helped in giving the goal of the Ṣūfi: to escape the prison of the body.[26] Ṣūfis learned the use of repetitive prayer, e.g., rosaries, certainly from Buddhist monks. Further, Nicholson affirms that Ṣūfi ethics, meditation practices, and abstract thought patterns "owes a good deal to Buddhism."[27]

But it is his assertion about the Ṣūfi doctrine of fanā (annihilation) which interests us most in this search for the worth of Zaehner's

---

[22]Nicholson, op. cit., p. 8.

[23]Ibid., p. 9.

[24]Ibid., p. 11.

[25]Ibid., p. 12.

[26]Ibid., p. 16.

[27]Ibid., p. 17.

argument. Nicholson has stated that fanā is certainly Indian in origin. Yazīd (Bayāzīd in
Nicholson's orthography) was the first exponent
of fanā. He may have received it from his Sindi
guru.[28] He goes on to say that Yazid's stuff is
not Buddhism, per se, but Vedānta pantheism
(Zaehner's monism). Fanā is made to appear very
close to the Vedānta concept of Nirvāṇa--vanishing
into the "Universal Being." But it looks, on
balance, to be Buddhist influenced--with its
ethical bent demanding the extinction of passion,
as well as by "Perso-Indian pantheism."[29] He
makes a statement which seems amazing in the light
of Massignon's views to the contrary, that

> ...the receptivity of Islam to foreign
> ideas has been recognised by every
> unbiassed inquirer, and the history
> of Sufism is only a single instance of
> the general rule. . . Even if Islam had
> been miraculously shut off from contact
> with foreign religions and philosophies,
> some form of mysticism would have arisen
> within it, for the seeds were already
> there. . . (such as) an ascetic revolt
> against luxury. . . (a) counter movement
> towards intuitive knowledge and emotional
> faith (against rationalism). . .[30]

J. Spencer Trimingham echoes these latter senti-
ments of Nicholson's in seeing Ṣūfism as a
personal expression of religion over against a
prevailing communalism. It is a bubbling to the
surface of something natural; namely, man's
right to a contemplative life. So Ṣūfism
developed naturally from within Islam, and owed

---

[28]Nicholson, op. cit., p. 17.

[29]Ibid., p. 19.

[30]Ibid.

little to non-Muslim sources.[31]

Where does this put Zaehner and his argument?
Zaehner sets out to draw Ṣūfi monism, primarily.
He finds that it simplifies his argument if Ṣūfism
is Indian in its _leitmotif_ and not home-grown. It
is a brilliant connection, if he can make it hold.
It appears not to ruin what he says about his
typology of mysticisms if Ṣūfi monism is not
Indian Vedānta, but it enhances the brilliance of
his presentation if it is so. Further, Massignon's
work seems to be cogent in that Semites can be
mystics in their own right: "Since they are, they
can be." Ṣūfism proves Semites are mystics.
Zaehner violates a prime rule in the history of
religions in his presuppositions: which are that
Vedānta influence is inordinately powerful in
Ṣūfism, so much so that Hinduism looks more opera-
tive there than Islam. In the history of religions what matters is not where ideas come from,
but what happens to them after they get there.
Jesus, Joseph and Mary appear in Islam, but
vastly changed. They are Islam's Jesus, Joseph
and Mary, and to quibble that such is not so, is
to deny Islam its existence as a World Religion.
Themes and persons take on new souls, new identities in other religions. Zaehner's linking of
Ṣūfism with Vedānta is very illuminating-and
Arberry has not sufficiently destroyed Zaehner's
arguments or his presuppositions, so they still
stand--but not as important as what Zaehner will
say about monism as an ideal type of mysticism.
This section on his linkage and the criticism it
has received meant to throw the insides of
Zaehner's thought open--with its presuppositions
and its methods--together with those of his
critics. They attack his linguistics when they
have a chance, but they have not destroyed them.
Further, as Arberry says, their presuppositions
remain intact. The one is as good as its arguments. And it is Zaehner's arguments about types

---

[31]J. S. Trimingham, The Ṣūfi Orders in
Islam (Oxford, 1971), p. 2.

of mysticisms which is primary here, since he
builds his theology of religions and the rest of
his theological thought on it. His typology is
attacked less and less, and still remains both
useful and vigorous. _In the ninth century of the
Christian era Abū Yazid began to voice a movement
within Islam: monist mysticism. The appendices
on Al-Junayd and Al-Ghazālī will treat these more
incisively than we could in the book proper.

APPENDIX II: Al-Junayd

Junayd's mystical doctrine begins with God's relation to the higher soul (Arab.=rūh). It is an eternal and unique relationship in each case. God reveals this relation to the soul in a flash, which shows the individual that it is outside time and related uniquely and forever with God. So the object of the revelation is the relationship between God and the soul.[1] The vision passes and the soul begins to pine and sorrow due to its loss. It longs for God in its emptiness. It decides to achieve God again; this time on its own. It achieves nothing but enstasis, the total isolation of the self in the self. It is a happy, powerful experience, an experience of Nature Mysticism. The soul loses its awe of God and becomes bold towards him. Junayd says that this is a trap set by God for the unwary and proud. The state of enstasis so easily becomes one of spiritual pride. God comes again and humiliates the soul, which now knows God as its only goal and joy. Its suffering becomes a joy. The soul loses nothing in all this, but gains joy in loving and being loved by God.[2]

Junayd defined union as ". . . to isolate eternity from origination."[3] Zaehner says that this is very much like Sāmkhya-yoga, the theistic brand. Further, he says that the yoga of the Gītā (cf. 6:25-27) is almost the same as Jung's integration. It integrates, it does not isolate.[4] But Junayd's doctrine of tawhid (Arab.= uniting, or affirming unity) means isolation or

---

[1]Zaehner, H/M, p. 152.

[2]Ibid., p. 152-3.

[3]Ibid., p. 135.

[4]Ibid.

separation, while yoga comes from the Sanskrit
for "uniting," but means its very opposite in
Sāmkhya. This means that yoga says unite, but
means separate. Junayd says unite, but means
God's separation from his creatures. This is so
since he is eternal.[5] Yazīd said that the mystic
was separate from all things, but Junayd twisted
this to suit his need to prove Yazīd's orthodoxy.
Zaehner says that Junayd formulated Ṣūfism in a
way that the orthodox could accept. He is, therefore, regarded as the father of all Ṣūfi brotherhoods.[6]

Junayd is an uncompromising transcendental-
ist, according to Zaehner, who rejects Massignon's
appraisal of Junayd's doctrine as monism. Zaehner
feels that it is a dualism as frank as Sāmkhya's.[7]
But how to bridge the gap between God and man
without compromising God's unity and transcendence? Junayd felt that the sure way to God was
through love. God is a hidden God. He reveals
himself as a giver of love and enkindles a yearning for him in his creatures' hearts. The chief
aim of the mystic was to "be as he was before he
was," i.e., he returns to a state of being an
idea in the divine mind. For Junayd, this is
deification. God merely says the word "Be" and
the idea in his mind becomes a person. The soul
reverses the process, in Junayd's view of the
mystical odyssey: it utters the word "union"
(Arab.=tawhīd) and it becomes one with God again
as idea, God's idea. God can now say to the
soul, "O Thou I;" and it can say in return, "Oh
I," which is to recognize its divine origin.[8]

---

[5]Zaehner, H/M, p. 136.

[6]Ibid., p. 137.

[7]Ibid., p. 138.

[8]Zaehner, H/M, p. 140.

The soul participates in the divine because the flesh has died through a process of annihilation (Arab.=fanā), or destruction. Again, the mystic Junayd says union (tawhīd) and means separation or Sāmkhya isolation of the soul (Self) from all that is not itself--this, especially means matter.

First, God chooses the soul, then he voids it of self to isolate it in order that it be able to deal directly with him, or to have commerce with him at all. In God's bringing this about time ceases, and one enters eternity alive.[9] This is the first stage of Junayd's isolation. The soul is pre-ordained to a share in God's life. It is isolated in God from "what belongs to the soul, and in itself from what belongs to God."[10] So the soul is isolated in itself, by itself, from all creatures. This is exactly Rāmānuja's concept of isolation, where the soul is isolated in itself through God, according to Zaehner. So, in the first stage, the soul realizes itself as eternal and then that it shares God's nature. Both Rāmānuja and Junayd concur on this first stage. In the second state, according to Junayd, God isolates the soul and annihilates it. The isolation is in the eternal essence, not in the ego. This brings the soul into a relationship with God himself: "from God to God," Junayd's doctrine has it. So the soul receives an infused knowledge of God, but knows that God is forever isolated from it.[11]

Junayd liked Yazīd, but thought that his experiences labeled him a beginner as a mystic.

---

[9]Again, it is not belief, but experience which makes the Hindu a Hindu. In accepting this Junayd teaches something which does not look like Islam.

[10]Zaehner, H/M, p. 142.

[11]Zaehner, H/M, p. 143.

He eschewed any quietism or the dropping of works.[12] For Junayd, intimacy (Arab.=uns) is a cessation of shyness without loss of awe for God. Further, the higher soul (Arab.=rūh), Skt.= ātman) is aware of God's presence when it arrives at the second state, but neither the lower soul-- which is the whole human psyche (Arab.=nafs)--nor the senses have any awareness of God's presence.[13] Zaehner says that both Junayd and Rāmānuja hold that only God's intervention can cause the soul to realize its immortality in isolation.[14] Junayd says that the trance of isolation monism is a trap which God uses to catch the proud. As a result of its pride God removes the rapture which the soul enjoys and it begins to suffer the acute loss of God and to thirst for him. This is God's method of asserting his authority over the soul.[15]

Zaehner has exposed Yazīd's thought. Now he sees if there is a pattern into which it fits. He says that Śankara's and Gauḍapāda's doctrine of "undifferentiated oneness" experienced nothing but the self--so far they are both just like Sāṁkhya, the a-theistic yoga. But both went further and said that the freed soul was the ground from which all things in space and time grew. This is the message which their experience had for them. But their ordinary perception told both of them that this obviously was not true. They were, in Christian and Muslim terms, God. So, they concluded that everything was an illusion except their experience. Phenomena and interiority were baseless, except the deepest

---

[12]Ibid., p. 145.

[13]Ibid., p. 149.

[14]Ibid., p. 151.

[15]Ibid.

level of man, beyond the human psyche; which is to say, the Self in the Self (which is ātman).

Yazīd imported these ideas into Islam and made the mistake of equating Allah with Brahman. Zaehner says that it is plain that the God of Abū Yazīd's mystical experience was not Allah, the God of the Qur'ān. Junayd accepted Yazīd's doctrine and openly faced the heresy inherent in it. He did so by seeing the experiences as genuine. They were experiences of an Absolute, which both Zaehner and Buber called the "pre-biographical unity of the soul."[16] Rimbaud and Zaehner say that this is an experience of Limbo, of innocence-returned. Junayd saw this as a part of the way up to God: each soul in its pre-biographical unity. So Yazīd, who felt that he had gone beyond God, was deflated by Junayd. The latter found a place for Yazīd. It was in this way that Junayd preserved a new and very exciting set of experiences in Islam while, at the same time, preserving God's "majesty and uniqueness."[17]

---

[16]Zaehner, H/M, p. 157. This is Louis Gardet's idea. Zaehner does not cite his source for this statement beyond giving the name of its author.

[17]Ibid. This section was received rather well. In a review in Blackfriars (42, 1961, by Norman Daniel, pp. 180-82) the reviewer says that "what Margaret Smith did for al-Muhasibi, or Massignon for al-Hallāj, he will one day ("he" being Zaehner) do for Junayd; he prints an excellent translation of a part of the Kitab al-Fanā. . . Prof. Zaehner's is a wise and stimulating approach to often intractable sources." (p. 181).

APPENDIX III: Al-Ghazālī

Many say that Junayd was the father of the
Ṣūfi brotherhoods. But the man who is considered
the father of Ṣūfism in general--i.e., as a phenomenon accepted by orthodoxy--is Al Ghazālī. He was a
respected philosopher whose own orthodoxy was
above reproach. He dropped out of things for
quite a while and became adroit at Ṣūfi techniques. He then turned his hand to writing again
in an effort at making Ṣūfism acceptable. His
writings are accepted as a model of balance and
orthodoxy. So it is with surprise that one sees
Zaehner's statement to the effect that, secretly,
Ghazālī taught two heresies: i) the soul is God,
when denuded of all its qualities; ii) God is in
man--which was taught by Hallāj and is found in
religion as the imago dei tradition. Further,
Zaehner says that in Mt. 25:36-40, one is to be
judged as worthy of God's eternal presence or not
according to whether one has seen God in his most
wretched neighbor or not.[1] It is not the
wretchedness of the neighbor, but the Presence,
which is important.

Zaehner says that Ghazālī borrowed his ideas
from Yazīd, Hallāj and Khayr. The works where
these "heresies" show up most are the Kimiyā and
the Mishkāt.[2] These he published late in life,
when he had already established himself as a
redoubt of orthodoxy. His most secret doctrine
is Vedāntin, according to Zaehner. It is the
doctrine of unity (Arab.=tawhīd). It holds that
nothing existed except the One. Zaehner says
that this is as advaitan as Śankara's Vedānta
doctrine: that the soul is "God," and that God
is the soul is pure monism, the same as Ātman is

---

[1] Zaehner, H/M, p. 163.

[2] Ibid., p. 165.

315

<u>Brahman</u> and vice versa.[3]

Another of Ghazālī's linchpin doctrines is
the one of the <u>Dhikr</u> (Arab.=remember). It is a
technique of meditation in which one repeats the
same thing over and over in order to alter one's
consciousness, more or less considerably. <u>Dhikr</u>
is seen as annihilation (Arab.=<u>fanā</u>) in its last
stage; i.e., everything vanishes save the object
of meditation, which, in this instance, is God.
So all becomes non-existent, too, because man
has even forgotten himself. When the world and
the self do not exist only God exists. Since
only God exists for the individual, he himself is
God. Simply put, you are what you are conscious
of. In meditating on God, one becomes God. God
is what one's meditation makes of him.[4] This is
not so much a Vedāntin doctrine as it is Sāmkhya-
yoga, since Sāmkhya places one in touch with one's
immortality (read, infinity) by the use of meditation. So meditation's object is the Self. But
if the Self is infinite, immortal, then one
becomes the object of the meditation. The object
is infinite. So one is infinite. Meditation
makes the man in Sāmkhya. God serves only as an
object for meditation there.

Zaehner concludes that the Ṣūfi doctrine of
meditation, which Ghazālī formulated, is the same
as that found in the Bhagavad-Gītā (chap. VI),
except that in the Gītā the Self is the object of
meditation. Hence Ghazālī says that in meditation the meditator is: i) one with God; ii) then
he projects this on to all creatures becoming one
with them. This particular union with God is an
identity. So Zaehner says that this is monism.
The unity with all creatures is pantheism as
expressed in Ghazālī. But Zaehner says that

---

[3]Zaehner, H/M, p. 166.

[4]Ibid., pp. 167 f.

this is monism. The unity with all creatures is pantheism as expressed in Ghazāli. But Zaehner says that Ghazāli combined them into a cohesive doctrine.[5]

Another indication of Ghazāli's late-life monism is to be found in his doctrine of friendship, which has him actually become the "other," and vice versa. Zaehner says that this is exactly the same as the teaching of the Kausitaki Upaniṣad where one is the All. He concludes that Ghazāli advocates in the Kīmiyā-yi Sa'adt two heresies: i) identity with God, and ii) that God and the universe are co-terminous.[6]

Ghazāli's early fame and seriousness gained for him an easy acceptance among his peers, both intellectual and political. So, what Zaehner calls his later frivolities in doctrine, which would have earned a lesser man censure at the very least, were accepted benignly or even with enthusiasm. So, Zaehner concludes, Ghazāli opened the way for Ṣūfism's later excesses.[7] Ghazāli also imported Neo-Platonism into Islamic thought, with its doctrine of Universal Soul and Universal Intelligence. Zaehner says that this import gave a philosophy to the new monism in Islam. Hence God became a "timeless being experienced in ecstasy."[8] This timeless Being had no part in becoming. In Ghazāli's doctrine of mysticism, the personality of the mystic is disintegrated into the One. It is not an integration (Skt.=yukta) as in the Gitā, or a

---

[5]Zaehner, H/M, p. 168.

[6]Ibid., pp. 170 f.

[7]Ibid., p. 169. Zaehner says that the Ṣūfis soon placed themselves above all morality and religious observance. In no time pederasty was used as a meditative aid. Cf. Zaehner's Drugs, Mysticism, p. 100.

[8]Ibid., p. 171.

317

Jungian integration either--in which Jung would
have it that the thinking ego is overwhelmed by
the formless collective unconscious. But Zaehner
sees Ghazālī moving in the same direction here as
did Śankara and Gauḍapāda in Hinduism. In the
latter religion God had to become a relative
Being, with no ultimacy at all. In fact, God was
created and destroyed with the end of each cycle
of time. Hence, God was relative, and, ultimately, an illusion like the rest of phenomena--
both exterior and interior. The only absolute
was the Self. Hence, with these two Hindus, the
Self was God, was all, was everything. If pushed,
the Self was not everything, since everything was
just accidental being. Hence, at base, the Self
is the only being. Ghazālī, in taking up this
direction, was bound to have to get rid of Allah.
He could not do this, so he introduced the
"Obeyed One" as a substitute for God. This Neo-
Platonic intermediary he took from Hallāj's
Tasin al-Siraj. God could remain, and a relative
figure like the "Obeyed One" could come and go
like a Neo-Platonic Demiurge. Thus, Ghazālī
preserved orthodoxy and his mystical experience,
and those of his peers, intact. He had done
what Śankara and Gauḍapāda before him had done:
namely, constructed a philosophical system out
of a psychological experience. He had experienced a oneness. Hence, nothing but the One
existed;[9] but now, enter a philosophical distinction to preserve God for the faithful.
Śankara and Gauḍapāda preserved God and religious
rites for the masses, but the pauci electi should
have nothing to do with it unless necessary.[10]

---

[9]Zaehner, H/M, p. 172.

[10]Śankara advocated one thing, but was practical enough to do what was necessary. He had
said not to do normal religious functions, but he
still went to his mother's obsequies, and he wrote
most beautiful hymns--at least a tradition says
that he wrote them.

It had become, for Ghazālī, what Max Weber called a religion of the esoteric and exoteric. Zaehner says that it looks like either Muhammad or the Archangel Gabriel had become the "Obeyed One" for Ghazālī.[11] Ibn Arabi, one of Ghazālī's successors, liked the Neo-Platonism and made of it a system much like Śankara's Vedānta. Ghazālī had moved Ṣūfism away from an experience-oriented movement to something now vectored back towards theory.[12]

Thus, both Buber and Zaehner again affirm that it is a mistake to confuse the Sufi and advaitan experiences of seeing one's "pre-biographical unity" in a flash of intuition as having experienced God himself. Further, the conditioning process which made it possible, both in Ṣūfism and advaita, to do so, also made it somewhat necessary for Zaehner that it be done. But Zaehner scores both advaita and Ṣūfism for going in this direction. The explanation is that since God was so great in both religions, and their experiences were so overwhelming, then their experience pushed them to conclude along the lines of their conditioning: namely, that they were God. So Muslim mysticism, which began to develop early on along Christian lines which demanded that one approach God with reverence and love, changed radically with Ṣūfism moving towards monism. Zaehner says that then outside, Indian, influences changed their experiences around, with the introduction of yoga and ecstatic techniques, then dance and music led to the introduction of boys as tools for meditation. Ṣūfism had become more interested in ecstasy than in God.[13]

---

[11]Zaehner, H/M, p. 173.

[12]Ibid., p. 175.

[13]Ibid., p. 176.

BIBLIOGRAPHY

Primary Sources

Books:

Zaehner, Robert Charles. Mysticism Sacred and
Profane, An Inquiry Into Some Varieties of
Preternatural Experience. Oxfcrd University
Press, 1957.

--------. At Sundry Times, An Essay in the Comparison of Religions. London: Faber and
Faber, 1958. Published in the United States
as The Comparison of Religions, Religion
East and West. Boston, 1962.

--------. Hinduism. Oxford University Press,
1962.

--------. The Teachings of the Magi, A Compendium of Zoroastrian Beliefs. London:
Sheldon Press, 1956.

--------. Zurvan, A Zoroastrian Dilemma. Oxford
University Press, 1955.

--------. The Dawn and Twilight of Zoroastrianism. London: Wiedenfeld and Nicholson,
1961.

--------. The Convergent Spirit, Towards a
Dialectics of Religion. London: Routledge
and Kegan Paul, 1963.

--------. ed. The Concise Encyclopedia of Living Faiths. Boston: Beacon Press, 1959.

--------. Hindu and Muslim Mysticism. New York:
Schocken Books, 1960.

--------. Christianity and Other Religions. New York, 1964. Published in England as The Catholic Church and World Religions, a Faith and Fact Book. London, 1964.

--------. Hindu Scriptures. Selected, translated and introduced by R.C.Z. London: Dent, Everyman's Library, 1966.

--------. The Bhagavad-Gita, With a Commentary Based on the Original Sources. Oxford: Clarendon Press, 1969.

--------. Dialectical Christianity and Christian Materialism. Oxford University Press, 1971.

--------. Concordant Discord, The Interdependence of Faiths, being the Gifford Lectures on Natural Religion, Delivered at St. Andrews in 1967-1969. Oxford: Clarendon Press, 1970.

--------. Evolution in Religion, A Study in Sri Aurobindo and Teilhard de Chardin. Oxford: Clarendon Press, 1971.

--------. Drugs, Mysticism and Make-Believe. London: Collins, 1972.

--------. Our Savage God. London: Collins, 1974.

--------. The City Within the Heart. London/ Boston, Unwin, 1980.

Articles:

Zaehner, Robert Charles. "Can Mysticism be Christian," New Blackfriars, 46, October, 1964, pp. 21-31.

--------. "Hinduism," The Listener, 72, 3 December, 1964, pp. 869-71.

--------. "Theology, Drugs and Zen. 1. The Irrelevance of Theology," The Listener, 84, 5 November, 1970, pp. 623-4.

--------. "Theology, Drugs and Zen. 2. The Other God," The Listener, 84, 12 November, 1970, pp. 654-6 il.

--------. "Theology, Drugs and Zen. 3. Salvation," The Listener, 84, 19 November, 1970, pp. 695-6 il.

--------. "The Climate of Our Unbelief," The Times, 6 March, 1971, p. 14.

--------. "Roman Catholic Attitudes," The Times, 27 March, 1971, p. 14.

--------. "The Other God: Theology, Drugs and Zen," Theology, 74, August 1971, pp. 350-5.

--------. "Salvation Through Death: Theology, Drugs and Zen," Theology, 74, September 1971, pp. 391-6.

--------. "Theology, Drugs and Zen," Theology, 74, September 1971, p. 14.

--------. "Learning From Other Faiths: Hinduism," The Expository Times, 83, March 1972, pp. 164-8.

--------. "Mysticism Without Love," Religious Studies, 10, September 1974, pp. 257-64.

--------. "The Wickedness of Evil, On Manson, Murder and Mysticism," Encounter, 42, April 1974, pp. 50-8.

--------. "Why Not Islam?" Religious Studies, 11 July, 1975, pp. 167-79.

Secondary Sources

Books:

Arberry, A.J. Sufism, an Account of the Mystics of Islam. New York: Harper Torchbook, 1970.

Aurobindo, Sri. Essays on the Gita. Pondicherry: Sri Aurobindo Ashram, 1970.

Baeck, Leo. The Essence of Judaism. New York: Schockey Books, 1961.

Bakan, David. Sigmund Freud and the Jewish Mystical Tradition. Boston: Beacon Press, 1973.

Basham, A.L. The Wonder That Was India. New York: Grove Press, 1959.

Bharati, Agehananda. The Tantric Tradition. New York: Doubleday Anchor Book, 1970.

Brown, John B. The Darvishes, or Oriental Spiritualism. London: Frank Cass and Co., 1968.

Buber, Martin. Between Man and Man. Translated and introduced by R.G. Smith, Collins, Fontana Library, 1974.

Bucke, Richard Maurice, M.D. Cosmic Consciousness. New York: Dutton Paperback, 1969.

Butler, Dom Cuthbert. Western Mysticism, The Teaching of Augustine, Gregory and Bernard on Contemplation and the Contemplative Life. London: Constable, 1922. Some things on nature ecstasy appear in an appendix.

324

Campbell, Joseph. The Flight of the Wild Gander. Chicago: H. Regnery, 1972.

Cassirer, Ernst. An Essay on Man, An Introduction to the Philosophy of Human Culture. New Haven: Yale University Press, 1944.

--------. The Philosophy of Symbolic Forms. 3 vols. New Haven: Yale University Press, 1955.

Chang, Garma C.C. The Practice of Zen. New York: Harper and Row, 1970.

Clark, James. Meister Eckhart, An Introduction to the Study of His Works with an Anthology of His Sermons. Edinburgh: Thomas Nelson and Son, 1957.

Confucius. The Analects of. Translated and annotated by Arthur Waley. New York: Vintage Books, 1938.

Conze, Edward. Buddhist Scriptures. A translation. Middlesex, England: Penguin Classics, 1959.

--------. Thirty Years of Buddhist Studies. Selected Essays, B. Cassirer. London, 1967.

--------. The Perfection of Wisdom in Eight Thousand Lines and Its Verse Summary. Wheel Series 1. Bolinas: Four Seasons Foundation, 1973.

--------. Buddhist Meditation. New York: Harper Torchbooks, Harper and Row, 1959.

--------. Buddhism: Its Essence and Development. New York: Harper Torchbooks, Harper and Row, 1959.

--------. Buddhist Thought in India. Ann Arbor Paperbacks, University of Michigan Press, 1967.

--------. The Large Sutra on Perfect Wisdom with the Divisions of the Abhisamayalankara, Part I. London: Luzac and Co. 1961. Parts II and III printed but not published by the College Printing and Typing Company, Madison, Wisconsin, 1964.

--------. The Prajnaparamita Literature. The Hague: Mouton and Co., 1960.

--------. Vajracchedika Prajnaparamita, Serie Orientale. Vol. xiii. Rome, 1957.

Coomeraswami, A.K., and M.E. Noble. Myths of the Hindus and Buddhists. New York: Dover Publ., 1967.

--------. Buddha and the Gospel of Buddhism. New York: Harper Torchbook, 1964.

Curtiss, Samuel Ives. Primitive and Semitic Religion Today, a Record of the Researches, Discoveries and Studies in Syria, Palestine and the Sinaitic Peninsula. Chicago, 1902.

Danielou, Alain. Hindu Polytheism. New York: Pantheon Books, 1964.

Dasgupta, S.N. Hindu Mysticism. New York: Ungar, 1971.

DeBary, William, ed. Sources of Chinese Tradition. Vols. 1 and 2. New York: Columbia University, 1964.

--------. ed. Sources of Indian Tradition. Vol. 1. New York: Columbia University Press, 1969.

DeVries, Jan. The Study of Religion, A Historical Approach. Translated by K.W. Colle. New York: Harcourt Brace, 1967.

326

Deussen, Paul. The Philosophy of the Upanisads. Translated by A.S. Geden. New York: Dover Publ., 1966.

Dulles, Avery, S.J. Theological Resources. A History of Apologetics. New York: Corpus Books, 1971.

Dumoulin, Heinrich, S.J. A History of Zen Buddhism. Translated from German by P. Peachey. Boston: Beacon Press, 1959.

Earhart, H. Byron. Japanese Religion: Unity and Diversity. Belmont, California: Dickenson Publ., 1969.

Edgerton, Franklin. The Bhagavad Gita. Translated and interpreted. New York: Harper, 1965.

Eliade, Mircea. Yoga, Immortality and Freedom. New Jersey: Princeton University Press, 1958.

--------. Shamanism, Archaic Techniques of Ecstasy. New Jersey: Princeton University Press, 1974.

--------. Cosmos and History, The Myth of the Eternal Return. Translated by W.R. Trask from the French. New York: Harper, 1959.

--------. The Sacred and the Profane, The Nature of Religion. Translated from the French by W.R. Trask. New York: Harper, 1957.

--------. Patterns in Comparative Religion. Translated by R. Sheed. Translated by R. Sheed. Cleveland: World Publishing Co., April, 1963.

--------. From Primitives to Zen, A Thematic Sourcebook on the History of Religions. New York: Harper and Row, 1967.

Enomiya-Lassalle, Hugo, S.J. Zen Meditation, Eine Einfürung. Zurich: Benziger Verlag, 1975.

--------. Zazen u die Exerzitien des heilgen Ignatius, einbung in das wahre dasein. Koln: Bachem, 1975.

--------. Zen Way to Enlightenment. London: Sheed and Ward, 1966.

Fackenheim, Emil L. Encounters Between Judaism and Modern Philosophy; A Preface to Future Jewish Thought. New York: Basic Books, 1973.

--------. The Religious Dimension in Hegel's Thought. Boston: Beacon Press, 1967.

--------. God's Presence in History, Jewish Affirmations and Philosophical Reflections. New York: Harper Torchbook, 1970.

Ferre, Frederick. Language, Logic and God. London: Collins, Fontana Book, 1962.

Fu Feng, Gia and Jane English. Tao te Ching of Lao Tsu. A new translation. New York: Random House, 1972.

Gadamer, Hans-Georg. Truth and Method. New York: Seabury, 1975.

Goldziher, Ignace. A Short History of Classical Arabic Literature. Translated, revised and enlarged by J. Desmogyi, Hilsesheim. G. Olms, 1966.

Gonda, J. Vishnuism and Shivaism. A Comparison. London: University of London, 1970.

Guillaume, Alfred. Prophecy and Divination Among the Hebrews and Other Semites. London: Hodder and Stoughton, 1938.

Hegel, G.W.F. <u>The Phenomenology of Mind.</u> Harper
     Torchbook, ed., and translated by J.B.
     Baillie, introduction by G. Lichtheim, New
     York, 1967.

Hicks, John. <u>Evil and the God of Love.</u> London:
     Collins, 1975.

Hitti, Philip K. <u>A History of the Arabs from the
     Earliest Time to the Present.</u> New York:
     McMillan, 6th ed., London, 1958.

Hopkins, Thomas J. <u>The Hindu Religious Tradition.</u>
     Encino: Dickenson Publ., 1971.

Huxley, Aldous. <u>The Doors of Perception and
     Heaven and Hell.</u> Penguin, 1974.

--------. <u>The Perennial Philosophy.</u> New York:
     Harper Colophon, 1970.

Ibn-Khaldun. <u>Prolegomena.</u> Translated from the
     Arabic by de Slane, 3 vols., 1863.

Inada, Kenneth. <u>Nagarjuna, A Translation of his
     Mulamadhyamakarika, With an Introductory
     Essay.</u> Hokuseido Press, 1970.

Isherwood, Christopher. <u>Vedanta for the Western
     World.</u> Isherwood ed., New York: Viking
     Press, 1969.

James, William. <u>The Varieties of Religious
     Experience.</u> New York: Mentor Book, 1958.

Jastrow, Morris, Jr. <u>The Religion of Babylon
     and Assyria.</u> Boston, 1898.

Jesuit Scholars. <u>Religious Hinduism. A Pre-
     sentation and Appraisal.</u> Allahabad: St.
     Paul Publications, 1968.

Johnston, William. <u>The Still Point, Reflections
     on Zen and Christian Mysticism.</u> New York:
     Fordham Press, 1970.

--------. Silent Music, the Science of Meditation. New York: Harper and Row, 1976.

Kitagawa, Joseph M. Religions of the East. Enlarged edition. Philadelphia: Westminster Press, 1960.

Knowles, David. The English Mystical Tradition. London: Burnes and Oates, 1964.

Kristensen, W. Brede. The Meaning of Religion, Lectures in the Phenomenology of Religion. The Hague: M. Nijhoff, 1960.

Küng, Hans. On Being a Christian. London: Collins, 1977.

Lamotte, E. Le Traite de la Grande Vertu de Sagesse de Nagarjuna. 3 vols. Louvain, 1944, 1949, 1970.

Langer, Susan K. Philosophy in a New Key, A Study in the Symbolism of Reason, Rite and Art. New York: Mentor Paperback, 1951.

Levi-Strauss, Claude. Structural Anthropology. Translated from French by C. Jacobson and B.G. Schoepf. New York: Harper Torchbook, 1963

Löwith, Karl. From Hegel to Nietzsche. New York: Harper Anchorbooks, 1967.

MacDonald, Duncan Black. The Religious Attitude and Life in Islam. Chicago: University of Chicago, 1906.

MacNicol, Nicol. Indian Theim, from the Vedic to the Muhammedan Period. Delhi: Oriental Publishers, 1968.

Maimum, Moses ibn (Maimonides). The Guide for the Perplexed (Moreh Mebhukhim). Translated by Friedlander. London, 1925.

330

Malinowski, B. Magic, Science and Religion.
Introduction by P. Redfield. New York:
Anchor Doubleday, 1954.

Mannheim, Karl. Ideology and Utopia, An Intro-
duction to the Sociology of Knowledge.
Translated from the German by L. Wirth and
E. Shils. New York: Harcourt Brace, 1936.

Marechal, Joseph, S.J., Studies in the Psychology
of the Mystics. Albany: Magi Books, 1964.

Massignon, Louis. Essai sur les origines du
Lexique Technique de la Mystique. Paris:
Muselmarie, 1954.

Marx, Karl. Karl Marx Selected Writings in
Sociology and Social Philosophy. Translated
by T.B. Bottomore. Edited by Bottomore and
Rubel. Middlesex, England: Pelican Book,
1961.

--------. Karl Marx Early Writings. Edited by
T.B. Bottomore. New York: McGraw-Hill
Paperback, 1963.

--------. Marx and Engels on Religion. New
York: Shocken Books, 1964.

McLelland, David C. The Roots of Consciousness.
Princeton, New Jersey: van Nostrand Insight
Book, 1964.

Monod, Jacques. Chance and Necessity, An Essay on
the Natural Philosophy of Modern Biology.

Murti, T.R.V. The Central Philosophy of Buddhism,
A Study of the Madhamika System. London:
George Allen and Unwin, 1955.

Naranjo, Claudio and Robert E. Ornstein. On the
Psychology of Meditation. New York: Viking
Press, 1971.

331

Needleman, Jacob (ed.) The Sword of Gnosis, Meta-
    physics, Cosmology, Tradition and Symbolism.
    Essays by F. Schuon, R. Guenon and others.
    Penguin, 1974.

Nicholson, R.A. Studies in Islamic Mysticism.
    Reprint. Cambridge; 1967.

--------. Rumi, Poet and Mystic. London: George
    Allen and Unwin, 1950.

Nietzsche, Friedrich. Beyond Good and Evil.
    Translated by W. Kaufman. Vintage Book,
    1966.

--------. Thus Spoke Zarathustra. Translated by
    R.J. Hollingdale. Middlesex, England:
    Penguin Classics, 1969.

--------. The Twilight of the Idols and the Anti-
    Christ. Translated by R.J. Hollingdale.
    Middlesex, England: Penguin Classics, 1968.

Nikhilananda, Swami. The Upanisads, abridged
    edition. New York: Harper Torchback, 1964.

Nisbet, Robert. The Sociological Tradition. New
    York: Basic Books Inc., 1966.

Otto, Rudolf. Mysticism East and West, a discus-
    sion of the nature of mysticism, focusing on
    the similarities and differences of its
    two principal types. Translated by B.L.
    Bracey and R.C. Payne. New York: MacMillan,
    1960.

Panikkar, Raymond. The Unknown Christ of Hindu-
    ism. London: Darton Longman and Todd, 1968.

--------. L'homme Qui Devient Dieu. Aubier,
    1969.

--------. Die Vielen Gotter u. Der Eine Herr.
    Otto Wilhelm Barth-Verlag, 1963.

Parrinder, Geoffrey. Mysticism in the World's
    Religions. New York: Oxford University,
    1976.

Progoff, Ira. Jung's Psychology and Its Social
    Meaning. New York: Anchor Book, 1973.

--------. Jung, Synchronicity, and Human Destiny,
    non-causal dimensions of human experience.
    New York: Julian Press, 1973.

--------. Depth Psychology and Modern Man. New
    York: McGraw-Hill Paperback, 1973.

Radhakrishnan, S. The Bhagavadgita, with an
    introductory essay, Sanskrit Text, English
    Translation, and notes. London: George
    Allen and Unwin, 1956.

--------. Eastern Religions and Western Thought.
    Oxford University, 1969.

--------. The Principal Upanisads. Edited with
    introduction, text and translation. London:
    George Allen and Unwin, 1969.

Raju, P.T. The Philosophical Traditions of India.
    London: George Allen and Unwin, 1971.

--------. Introduction to Comparative Philosophy.
    London: Feffer and Simons, 1970.

Rahner, Karl. Theological Investigations.
    Vol. IV. London: Helicon, 1974.

--------. Foundations of Christian Faith, Seabury,
    N.Y., 1978.

Raines, John C. and Thomas Dean. Marxism and
    Radical Religion. Philadelphia: Temple
    University Press, 1970.

Ramanuja. On the Bhagavadgita. A condensed
    rendering of his Gitabhasya with copious
    notes and an introduction by J.A.B. van
    Buitenen. Delhi: Motilal Banarsidass, 1968.

Reuther, Rosemary. The Radical Kingdom, The
Western Experience of Messianic Hope. New
York: Harper and Row, 1970.

Richardson, H.W. and D.R. Cutler. Transcendence.
Boston: Beacon Press, 1969.

Ricoeur, Paul. Fallible Man. Trans. fr. the
French by Charles Kelbley, H. Regnery Co.,
Chicago, 1965.

Ringgren, Helmet and Akev Strom. Religions of
Mankind Today and Yesterday. Edited by
J.C.G. Greig and translated by Nieils L.
Jensen. Philadelphia: Fortress Press, 1967.

Robinson, Richard H. The Buddhist Religion, A
Historical Introduction. Belmont, California: Dickenson Publ., 1970.

Rowland, Benjamin. The Pelican History of Art,
the Art and Architecture of India, Buddhist,
Hindu, Jain. Baltimore: Penguin Books, 1953.

Scherbatski, T. The Conception of Buddhist
Nirvana. Leningrad, 1927.

Schuon, Frithjof. In the Tracks of Buddhism.
London: George Allen and Unwin, 1968.

--------. Gnosis, Divine Wisdom. Translated from
the French by G.E.H. Palmer. London: John
Murray, 1957.

Shah, Idries. The Sufis, introduction by Robert
Graves. New York: Anchor Book, Doubleday,
1971.

Shankaracarya. Eight Upanisads, the commentary
of Shankara. Translated by Swami Bambhir-
ananda, 2nd ed., 2 vols. Calcutta: Advaita
Ashrama, 1966.

334

--------. The Brhadaranyaka Upanisad, with
    Sankara's Commentary. Translated by Swami
    Madhavananda, introduced by Professor S.
    Kuppuswami Shastri. Calcutta: Advaita
    Ashrama, 1965.

Smart, Ninian S. The Religious Experience of
    Mankind. New York: Scribner's 1969.

Smith, Huston. The Religions of Man. New York:
    Harper Colophon, 1964.

--------. The Forgotten Truth, The Primordial
    Tradition. New York: Harper and Row, 1976.

Smith, Margaret. An Introduction to the History
    of Mysticism. London, 1930.

--------. Readings from the Mystics of Islam.
    London: Luzac & Co., 1972.

--------. The Way of the Mystics: The Early
    Christian Mystics and the Rise of the Sufis.
    London: Sheldon Press, 1976.

Smith, Wilfred Cantwell. The Meaning and End of
    Religion, A New Approach to the Religious
    Traditions of Mankind. New York: Mentor
    Book, 1962, 1963.

--------. Religious Diversity, Essays by W.C.
    Smith. Edited by W.G. Oxtoby. New York:
    Harper and Row, 1976.

Smith, W. Robertson. The Religion of the
    Semites. London, 1889.

Söderblom, Nathan. The Living God, Basic Forms
    of Personal Religion. Gifford Lectures,
    1931. Boston: Beacon Press, 1962.

Staal, Frits. Exploring Mysticism. Penguin,
    1975.

335

Stace, W.T. Mysticism and Philosophy. Philadelphia: Lippincott, 1960.

Streng, Frederick J. Understanding Religious Man. Belmont, California: Dickenson Publishing Co., 1969.

--------. Emptiness, A Study in Religious Meaning. Nashville: Abingdon Press, 1967.

Suzuki, D.T. On Indian Mahayana Buddhism, edited with an introduction by E. Conze. New York: Harper Torchbooks, 1968.

--------. Mysticism: Christian and Buddhist. London: George Allen and Unwin, 1957.

--------. Outlines of Mahayana Buddhism, Prefatory Essay by Allan Watts. New York: Schocken Books, 1963.

--------. Studies in Zen. Edited with a foreword by Christmas Humphreys. New York: Delta Book, 1955.

--------. Essays in Zen Budhism, First Series. Evergreen Original, 1961.

--------. Essays in Zen Buddhism, Second Series. London: Rider & Co., 1970.

--------. Essays in Zen Buddhism, Third Series. New York: Sam. Weiser Co., 1976.

--------. Studies in the Lankavatava Sutra. London: George Routledge and Sons, 1930.

--------. Self-Realization of Noble Wisdom, A Buddhist Scripture, based on Professor Suzuki's translation of the Lankavatara Sutra. Published by Dwight Goddard, 1932.

Tart, Charles T., ed. Altered States of Consciousness. Garden City, New York: Anchor Book, 1969.

Thompson, Laurence G. Chinese Religion, An Introduction. Belmont, California: Dickenson Publishing Co., 1969.

Thurston, Herbert, S.J. The Physical Phenomena of Mysticism. Chicago: Regnery, 1952.

--------. Surprising Mystics, edited by H.H. Crehan. Chicago: Regnery, 1955.

--------. The Church and Spiritualism. Milwaukee, 1933.

Tilmann, Klemens. Die Führung zur Meditation. Zurich: Benziger Verlag, 1974.

Trimingham, J. Spencer. The Sufi Orders in Islam. Oxford, 1971.

Underhill, Evelyn. Translation of Jan van Ruysbroeck's The Adornment of the Spiritual Marriage. London: J.M. Dent, 1916.

--------. The Essentials of Mysticism and Other Essays. London: J.M. Dent, 1920.

--------. The Mystic Way: A Psychological Study in Christian Origins. New York: E.P. Dutton, 1913.

--------. The Mystics of the Church. New York: Schocken, 1964.

--------. Practical Mysticism. New York: Dutton, 1960.

--------. Mysticism. New York: Dutton, 1961.

337

Van der Leeuw, G. Religion in Essence and Mani-
    festation. Translated by J.E. Turner, with
    appendices to the Torchbook edition by Hans
    H. Penner. 2 vols. Gloucester, Mass.:
    Peter Smith, 1967.

Varenne, Jean. Yoga and the Hindu Tradition.
    Translated from French by D. Coltman.
    Chicago and London: The University of
    Chicago Press, 1973.

Wach, Joachim. The Comparative Study of Reli-
    gions. Edited with an introduction by J.M.
    Kitagawa. New York: Columbia University
    Press, 1958.

Waley, Arthur. The Way and Its Power, A Study
    of the Tao te Ching and its place in
    Chinese thought. New York: Evergreen,
    1958.

--------. Three Ways of Thought in Ancient China.
    New York: Doubleday, 1939.

Walleser, Max. The Life of Nagarjuna from
    Tibetan and Chinese Sources. Hirth Anniver-
    sary Volume, pp. 424-255. London, 1923.

Watkin, E.I. The Philosophy of Mysticism.
    London: G. Richards, 1920.

--------. Poets and Mystics. Freeport, New
    York: Books for Libraries Press, 1968.

--------. The Bow in the Clouds. New York:
    Macmillan, 1932.

Watts, Alan W. The Way of Zen. Pelican Book,
    1971.

Weber, Max. The Religion of India. New York:
    Macmillan, 1958.

--------. Ancient Judaism. New York: Macmillan, 1952.

--------. The Religion of China. New York: Macmillan, 1951.

Welbon, Guy. The Buddhist Nirvana and Its Western Interpreters. Chicago: University of Chicago Press, 1968.

White, John, ed. The Highest State of Consciousness. Garden City, New York: Anchor Book, 1972.

Winternitz, Maurice. A History of Indian Literature. Vol. 2. Calcutta: University of Calcutta, 1933.

Wright, Arthur F. Buddhism in Chinese History. New York: Athenaeum, 1969.

Articles:

Anonymous: A review of Zaehner's Our Savage God, Expository Times, 86, pp. 193-4, April, 1975.

Balmforth, H. Review of Zaehner's Dawn and Twilight of Zoroastrianism, Journal of Theological Studies, ns9, pp. 210-2, April, 1958.

Barclay, R.A. Review of Zaehner's At Sundry Times, Scottish Journal of Theology 12, pp. 420-3, December, 1959.

Barclay, W. Review of Zaehner's Drugs, Mysticism and Make-Believe, Expository Times, 85, p. 64, November, 1973.

Bloesch, D. Review of Zaehner's Our Savage God, Christianity Today, 20, p. 35, December, 1975.

Carman, J.B. Review of Zaehner's Hinduism,
    Journal of Biblical Religion, 32, pp. 90-1,
    January, 1964.

Clavier, H. Review of Zaehner's Concordant Dis-
    cord, Review History of the Philosophy of
    Religion, 52, no. 2, pp. 196-99, 1972.

Day, T.R. Review of Zaehner's Concordant Dis-
    cord, Frontier, 14, pp. 188-9, August, 1971.

--------. Review of Zaehner's Evolution in
    Religion, Frontier, 15, pp. 189-90,
    August, 1972.

Deotis, J. Review of Zaehner's Concordant Dis-
    cord, Journal of Religious Thought, 31,
    pp. 82-3. Fall-Winter, 1974.

Donnelly, D.K. Review of Zaehner's Evolution in
    Religion, Theological Studies, 32, p. 744,
    December, 1971.

Durwood, A. Review of Zaehner's Our Savage God,
    Religious Life, 45, pp. 124-5, Spring, 1976.

Fleming, J.R. Review of Zaehner's At Sundry
    Times, Southeast Asia Journal of Theology,
    2, pp. 63-4, July, 1960.

Gill, R.M. Review of Zaehner's Drugs, Mysticism
    and Make-Believe, Scottish Journal of The-
    ology, 26, pp. 506-7, November, 1973.

Griffiths, B. Review of Zaehner's Concordant
    Discord, Journal of Ecumenical Studies,
    9, pp. 644-6, Summer, 1972.

Gundry, D.W. Review of Zaehner's At Sundry
    Times, Church Quarterly Review, 161,
    pp. 241-2, April-June, 1960.

--------. Review of Zaehner's Dawn and Twilight
    of Zoroastrianism, Church Quarterly Review,
    163, pp. 379-80, July-September, 1962.

Hayward, V.E.W. Review of Zaehner's Dawn and
Twilight of Zoroastrianism, Review of the
History of Philosophy of Religion, 40, no. 1,
p. 85, 1960.

Hinnells, J.R. Review of Zaehner's Concordant
Discord, Church Quarterly, 4, pp. 94-5,
July, 1971.

Hughes, Robert D. III. "Zen, Zurvan and Zaehner:
A memorial tribute to the late Spalding Pro-
fessor of Eastern Religions and Ethics, Oxford
Studies in Religion/Sciences Religieuses.
Vol. 6, No. 2, 1976-77, pp. 139-48.

Johnston, W. Review of Zaehner's Concordant Discord, Theological Studies, 33, pp. 349-53,
June, 1972.

Klausner, S.Z. Review of Zaehner's Dawn and Twi-
light of Zoroastrianism, Journal of the
Scientific Study of Religion, 1, pp. 228-29,
April, 1962.

Leech, Kenneth. Review of Zaehner's Our Savage
God, Theology, 79, pp. 52-3, January, 1976.

Long, J.B. Review of Zaehner's Evolution in
Religion, Anglican Theological Review, 55,
pp. 254-6, April, 1973.

Lonergan, Bernard. "The Ongoing Genesis of
Methods," apud Studies in Religion, 6, 4,
1976-77, pp. 341-55.

--------. "Doctrinal Pluralism," 1971 Pere
Marquette Lecture, Milwaukee: Marquette
University Press, 1971.

MacQuarrie, J. Review of Zaehner's Christianity
and Other Religions, Journal of Ecumenical
Studies, 2, pp. 489-90, Fall, 1965.

Mascall, E.L. Review of Zaehner's Dawn and Twilight of Zoroastrianism, Church Quarterly
Review, 158, pp. 524-5, October-December,
1957.

341

Meynell, H. Review of Zaehner's Concordant Discord, Journal of Theological Studies, ns23, pp. 317-8, April, 1972.

Neill, S. Review of Zaehner's Concordant Discord, The Churchman, 85, pp. 302-3, Winter, 1971.

Newell, W.L. "Buddhistische u. christliche Liebe." Geist u. Leben, Okt. 1975. 48 Jahrgang, Heft 5.

Parrinder, G. Review of Zaehner's Gita, Religious Studies, 7, pp. 169-74, June, 1971.

Robert, J.D. Review of Zaehner's Hinduism, Journal of Religious Thought, 25, no. 1, p. 83, 1968-69.

Robertson, E.H. Review of Zaehner's Concordant Discord, Expository Times, 84, pp. 26-7, October, 1972.

Selby, P.S.M. Review of Zaehner's Dialectical Christianity..., Modern Churchman, ns15, pp. 267-8, July, 1972.

Smart, N. Review of Zaehner's At Sundry Times, Journal Theological Studies, ns11, pp. 239-42, September, 1960.

Smith, D.H. Review of Zaehner's At Sundry Times, Modern Churchman, ns2, pp. 171-3, March, 1959.

Smith, M. Review of Zaehner's Dawn and Twilight of Zoroastrianism, Anglican Theological Review, 44, pp. 231-4, April, 1962.

Smith, W.C. Review of Zaehner's Concordant Discord, Journal of Religion, 53, pp. 377-81, July, 1973.

Solomon, Jon. Review of Zaehner's Our Savage God, Frontier, 18, pp. 127-8, Summer, 1975.

342

Tinsley, E.J.   Review of Zaehner's Concordant
    Discord, Theology, 74, pp. 319-20, July,
    1971.

Tiwari, J.D.   Review of Zaehner's Evolution in
    Religion, Indian Journal of Theology, 22,
    pp. 81-5, April-June, 1973.

Watkin, E.I.   Review of Zaehner's Drugs, Mysti-
    cism and Make-Believe, Downside Review, 91,
    pp. 156-62, April, 1973.

--------.   Review of Zaehner's Concordant Discord,
    Downside Review, 89, pp. 236-43, July, 1971.

Younger, P.   Review of Zaehner's Hinduism,
    Theology Today, 23, pp. 435-9, October,
    1966.

--------.   Review of Zaehner's Matter and Spirit,
    Theology Today, 23, pp. 435-9, October,
    1966.

Zinger, D.   Review of Zaehner's Matter and
    Spirit, Lutheran Theological Quarterly,
    17, pp. 171-2, May, 1965.

Abandonment, 130, 256
Absolute, 8, 61, 66, 73-75, 77-78, 80, 99, 108,
   152-153, 165-166, 175, 186, 188-189, 198, 205,
   224-225, 237, 241, 264, 278, 291, 313
  quest for the, 11
Adam, 30-31, 83, 217, 244-246, 249, 273
Adoration, 257
A-dvaita (Skt.=non-two), 61, 204-205, 218-219,
   223, 226, 232-233, 274, 277, 295, 319
Advaitan Vedānta, 8, 39, 71, 74, 78-79, 108, 133,
   145, 153, 175-176, 184-185, 191-193, 205,
   209, 212, 228
Agapes, drunken, 105
Aham brahmasmi (Skt.=I am Brahman), 108n
Ahaṁkāra (Skt.=I-ness, ego), 146, 169, 207n
Aitareya Upaniṣad, 53, 108n
À La Recherche du temps perdu (Proust), 114
Alcohol, 101, 105, 261
'Ali al-Sindi, Abū, 199, 297, 300, 305
Alienation, 140, 146, 262, 265, 267, 288
All, 16, 19, 29, 39, 60, 80, 104, 106-110, 115,
   115, 125, 134, 136, 138, 154-155, 157, 171,
   183, 191, 204, 241-242, 246, 248, 253, 255,
   265-268, 317
  identity with the, 136-138, 165
  unity with the, 148
Allah, 139, 164, 232, 278, 313, 318
All Souls College, iii, vn
Ambivalence, moral, 99-100, 112
Amiel, Henri Frédéric, 96
Amnesia, 33, 253, 272
Anamnesis, 33, 151, 253, 263, 272-273
Ānanda (Skt.=bliss), 1, 84, 100, 140, 153, 191-
   192, 268
An-atta (Pali=not-selves), 270
Anglicanism, Evangelical, 81
Anguish, primordial, 284
Anima, 99
Animal soul, 163, 217
Annihilation, 205-206, 212, 219, 248, 277, 297,
   304, 311, 316-317

Anta dhaka (Arab.=thou art that), 303
Anthropocentric movement, 288
Anthropology, 12, 273
Anti-nomianism, 221
Apara-Brahman (Skt.=lower Brahman), 237
Apathy, 88
Apologetics, 26, 38
Apophatic tradition of Christian mysticism, 51
Arberry, A.J., 55-56, 296-297, 299-303, 306
Archetypal race experiences, 98
Aristotle, 3, 164, 194, 275, 289
Arjuna, 17, 220
Artificial Paradises, 90
Arya Deva, 229n
Asceticism, 21, 64, 72, 115, 118, 120, 159-160,
    168, 184-186, 214, 221, 247, 268, 278, 304-
    305
  penitential, 72-73
  religious, 77
Ātman, 61-62, 66, 71, 74, 78-80, 108n, 118-119,
    146, 153-154, 175-177, 179, 184, 186, 188,
    196, 202-204, 207-208, 217-218, 222-223,
    225, 229, 232-233, 235, 237, 241, 245-246,
    253, 274, 277, 299, 312-313, 315
At Sundry Times, an Essay in the Comparison of
    Religions (Zaehner), 4-5, 23, 46-47, 50,
    58, 100, 109, 120, 146, 154-155, 233, 295,
    298-299
Attachments, 12, 172, 271
'Attār, Farid ud-din, 207
Aufgehoben, 34n
Augustine (St.), 37, 135
Avicenna, 98, 162-163
Avidya (Skt.=ignorance), 61n, 237
Awe, 312
Ayam atma brahma (Skt.=Ātman is Brahman), 108n
Baeck, Leo, vii
Bakan, David, 136
Balzac, Honoré de, 37
Barth, Karl, 292
Bast (Arab.=expansion), 130, 134, 206, 255-256
Baum, Gregory, vii
Beatific Vision, 1, 84, 101, 110, 191, 212, 247-
    248

Beauty, 64, 87, 153, 294
  of Nature, 100
Becoming, 209, 317
Beghards, 127, 168n, 222-236, 279
Being, 70, 83-84, 110, 149, 167, 180-181, 209, 241
  contingent, 218
  great, 16
  principles of, 138, 167
  timeless, 317
  Ultimate, 248
  Universal, 305
Bestial soul, 163, 217
Bhagavad-Gītā, iii, 10, 16-17, 23, 28, 30, 44, 74,
    153, 173-174, 182, 193, 196-197, 212, 218,
    224, 227, 234, 247, 274
  2:19, 166, 204
  2:55-72, 171, 219-220
  3:30, 160
  chap. 6, 316-317
  6:25-27, 309
  10:8-10, 226
  15.1-2, 201
  18:56, 152n
  translations of, 297
Bhakti (devotion), 10, 16-17, 25, 44, 74, 153,
    174, 212, 224, 226, 234, 295
Bhakti cults of Krishna, 10
Bias, 46-47
Bicameral psychology, 192, 259
Birūni, 203
Bits and pieces, 49-51, 280, 286
Blasphemy, 14, 164, 211, 231
Bliss, 9, 13, 15, 19, 21, 28, 84, 86, 110, 122,
    140, 145-153, 155, 179, 183, 187, 191-192,
    219, 221, 224, 228n, 236, 238, 245-250, 264,
    266-267, 270, 273, 276
  Body of, 25
  death-like, 268-269
  eternal, 169-171, 246, 248-249, 268, 274
Blochet, 302
Bodhisattvas, 31
Body, 9, 14, 23, 29-30, 32, 90, 130, 153, 162,
    168, 170, 179, 189, 192, 212, 236, 247, 255,
    256, 264, 270-271, 273, 304

347

of Bliss, 25
construct, 25
transcendent, 30
Body of the Buddha, Dharma, 25, 84, 103
Boehme, Jacob, 251, 265
Boethius, 243
Brahman, 17, 61, 66, 78, 80, 108n, 119-120, 152-
   155, 157, 165, 173, 175, 177-180, 182, 186,
   188, 202, 204, 217-218, 223-225, 233, 236,
   238, 241-242, 245-246, 264-265, 278, 313, 316
 lower, 237
 supreme, 237
Brāhmanas, 12, 151, 179, 263
Breath, 96, 99, 113, 120, 152, 155, 179, 239,
   164-266
Brhadāranyaka Upanisad, 108n, 154, 165-166, 196,
   202, 238-240
Browne, E.G., 56-57, 302
Buber, Martin, 58-60, 112, 135, 139, 233, 313,
   319
Bucke, Richard Maurice, 98, 111
Buddha, 10, 12-13, 16, 18, 22-24, 27, 30-31, 228n,
   229n
 Cosmic, 25
 Dharma, 25
 Dharma Body of the, 25, 84, 103
 triune, 25
Buddhi (Skt.=mind), 168, 265
Buddhism, iv, vi, viii, 5-6, 8, 10, 12-13, 15, 20-
   22, 24-25, 30-31, 51, 61, 82, 92-93, 99, 104,
   120, 137, 140, 145, 155, 170, 192, 200, 220,
   227, 229n, 251-252, 254, 262, 270, 276, 279,
   285, 291, 293, 304-305
 love in, 189
 Mādhyamika, 228, 229n, 230
 Mahāyāna, see Mahayana Buddhism
 release in, 188
 Theravada, see Theravada Buddhism
 Tibetan, 250
Buddhistic scriptures, Pali canon of, 13
Catholic Church, 9, 31-32
Catholic Church and World Religion (Zaehner), 6
Catholic interiority, vii

Catholicism, Roman, viii, 27, 38, 82, 176, 185, 195, 266
Catholic mystics, 97
Center, man's, 9
Chāndogya Upaniṣad, 11, 108n, 179, 181, 200, 237, 296
Chatūh Satakam (Arya Deva), 229n
Ch'i (Chinese=matter), 21
Childhood, innocence of, 87
China, 7, 17-18, 21, 31, 140, 147
Chinese religion, 17, 32, 39-40, 56, 216
Chit (Skt.=thought-mind), 1, 84, 101, 191
Christ, 10, 24, 30-35, 37, 74, 105, 127, 257, 271-273, 287-288, 290, 292-294
  another, 286
  Cosmic, 143
  God in, 282
  heart of, 38
  mystical knowledge of, viii
  as risen, 25
Christian experience of union, 111, 230
Christianity, 6-7, 9, 20, 22-23, 26-28, 30-33, 35, 39-40, 61-62, 68-69, 74, 76-77, 79, 92, 102, 104-105, 108, 139, 146, 171, 193, 212, 215, 218-219, 221, 226-227, 231, 240, 243, 251-253, 273, 275, 278
  defense of, 5
Christianity and Other Religions (Zaehner), 6-11, 13, 16, 25-32, 146
"Christianity and the World Religions" (Zaehner), 11-16, 32
Christianity as mysticism, 5, 292
Christian love, 25, 108
Christian monism, 216, 222
Christian mystical experiences, 2, 79, 101-102, 112, 142
Christian mysticism, 17, 62, 102, 105, 117, 125, 133, 180-185, 193, 198, 235, 254-256, 249-294
  apophatic tradition of, 51
Christian mystics, vi, 58, 80, 122, 132, 213, 223-226
Christian pantheism, 35-36

Christian spirituality, 81, 185, 218, 271-272,
    291-292
Christocentric movement, 288
Christ's history, 252
Church, 222, 252, 273
  Catholic, 9, 31-32
  fathers of, 292
  mothers of, 292
Civilization, industrial, 90
Cloud of Unknowing (Ghazālī), 121-122, 254
Collective unconscious, 98-100, 111-112, 118, 162,
    170, 252, 269
Communion, 210
  with God, 14
Comparison, 45, 175
The Comparison of Religions, Religions East and
    West (Zaehner), 4, 295
Compassion, 19-20, 27, 31, 189
  long-suffering, 31
Competition, 4, 46
Concordant Discord (Zaehner), iii, 3, 18-22,
    24-29, 33n, 34n, 41-45, 47, 50, 54n, 58-59,
    100, 111, 183, 189, 228n, 299
Conduct, 8, 131
Conflict, primordial, 281-282
Confucianism, 7-8, 17, 19, 21-22
  Neo-, 8, 21-22, 25
Confucius, 19
Consciousness, 93-94, 108n, 145-146, 155, 163,
    259, 266, 271
  communitarian, 263
  cosmic, 35, 98-99, 111
  four levels of, 186-190, 209
  lower state of, 34
  matter, 162
  grace, 135
  reservoir of, 99
  undifferentiated, 170, 269
  universal, 151, 168, 264
Consolation, 97, 287-288, 293
Constricted soul, 130
Contemplation, 27, 72, 77, 88, 97, 269, 275, 290,
    305
  diabolic, 122, 127

divine, 127
of God, 28
self-, 28
Contextual God, 285, 290-293
Continuum, 70
  among religions, 4
Contraction, 130-132, 135, 145, 147, 150, 170,
  206, 255-258, 261, 263, 268
Convergence of religions, 7, 24-40, 252
The Convergent Spirit: Towards a Dialectics
  (Zaehner), iv, 7-8, 33n, 38, 45, 100, 151-
  154, 190-191, 299
Coomaraswami, Ananda, 57, 60-61, 70, 101n, 231
Cosmic consciousness, 35, 98-99, 111
Cosmic principles, negative, 71
Cosmos, 19, 151, 179, 243
Creation, 30, 33, 38, 80, 83, 151, 178, 188, 199,
  209, 252, 282, 287
  principle of, 71
  second, 282
Creator, 10, 80, 177, 244, 284
Creatures, 10, 80, 109, 167, 199, 262, 282, 284,
  310, 316
Cults
  bhakti, 10
  murders, 225n, 242
Custance, John, 125, 128-130, 134, 140, 166, 240,
  243
Daniel, Norman, 313n
Darkness, 71, 161, 163, 238, 276
Dark Night of the Soul, 29, 256
Dark Night of the Spirit (John of the Cross),
  289n, 293
Dasgupta, S., 167
Death, 13, 115, 129, 139, 141, 145, 154, 176,
  238-239, 246-247, 261, 265, 273, 284
  conquest of, 11
  eternal, 169
  spiritual, 238
Deathlessness, 13, 15, 19
Death-like bliss, 268-269
Death-like trance, 238
Debate, mysticism as grounds for, 5

Deceit, 201-202, 300
Deeper self, 7-8
Deification, 185, 211, 213, 218-219, 238
Deity, 174, 254
Delitzsch, F., 302
Delusional insanity, 97
Demiurge, 71, 318
Depression, 130-131, 135, 138, 150, 256-258
Depth psychology, 170, 269, see also Freud,
     Sigmund; Jung, Carl Gustav
Desire, 153, 157, 161, 165, 172-173, 179-180,
     254-256, 264, 271, 285
Desolation, 97, 257, 287-288, 293
Despair, 228n, 261
Destruction of the self, 263, 311
Development of religions, 15
Devil, 71, 97, 121-122, 132, 254
Devotion, 10, 25, 126, 153, 174, 196, 204, 226,
     295
  religion of, 16-17, 44, 212, 234
Devotion mysticism, 198, see also Love mysticism
Dhaka (Arab.=that), 297
Dharma Body of the Buddha, 25, 84, 103
Dhu'l-Nun, 197-198
Diabolic contemplation, 122, 127
Diabolic mysticism, 97-98, 111, 117, 125-126,
     131-132, 138, 141, 145, 150, 254, 258
Diabolic possession, 138, 147, 261
Dialectical Christianity and Christian Material-
     ism (Zaehner), 33n, 36-37, 142n, 299
Dialogue, mysticism as grounds for, 5
Dionysian side of religion, 149, 258, 266
Discernment, 294
Disciplina arcana, 48
Discursive reasoning, 85, 139, 188
Disgust, 130-256
Divergence in religions, 4-24, 33, 39
Divine contemplation, 127
Divine nature, 72, 263
Divinity, 62, 68-69, 77, 183, 272
Divinization, 286, 294
Doctrine, 174, 220
Dogma, 68, 77

The Doors of Perception and Heaven and Hell
    (Huxley), 53, 55, 80-82, 86n, 101, 104, 249-
    250
Dreamless sleep, 29, 62, 79, 165, 187-188, 209,
    238-239, 241, 245
Drug experiences, 100, 109, 156
Drug mysticism, v-vi
Drugs, iii, 1, 81, 88, 104-105, 123, 133, 137,
    245, 249, 257-258, 261, 267
Drugs, Mysticism and Make-Believe (Zaehner),
    35, 100, 249-250, 317n
Drunken agapes, 105
Drunken ecstacy, 164
Dualism, 39, 65, 74, 79, 145, 150, 153, 160, 174,
    176-177, 183-185, 196-197, 209, 218-220, 277
    non-, see Non-dualism
Du coté de chez Swann (Proust), 114
Dukha (Skt.=sadness, despair, pain, sorrow,
    wretchedness, Dukka (Pali)), iv, 154, 228n,
    229n, 270
Earth, 96, 113, 138
Eastern religion, 9, 22, 82-83
Eckhart, Johannes (Meister), 51, 53, 83-84, 167,
    219, 237-238, 244, 274
Ecstasy, 28, 94, 100-101, 105, 113, 117, 123,
    127-128, 164, 195, 197, 199, 210, 254, 264,
    269, 271, 288, 292
    drunken, 105, 164, 210
    of non-unity, 240, 274
Eden, 127, 171, 219, 267, 276
Edgerton, Franklin, 297
Ego, 9, 19, 80, 116n, 136, 139, 141, 146-147,
    150-151, 160-163, 166, 168-169, 171, 219,
    233, 236, 241, 246, 248, 251-252, 255-269,
    272, 274, 288, 290, see also Lower Soul
    diabolic flagellation of the, 141
    elimination of, 92, 94-95, 100, 105, 123, 129,
    285
    empirical, 127
    expansion of the, see Expansion of the ego
    inflation of, 29, 39
    see also Self; Soul
Einfühlung, 48-49, 229

353

Eirenicism, 43, 63, 70, 173, 216, 220, 232
Élan vital, 128, 265
Eliade, Mircea, 229n
Elite, spiritual, 66-69, 77
Emotion, 64, 97, 153, 188, 264
Empirical approach to religious experience, v, 11,
    42
Empirical methods of liberation, 12
Empirical religions, 12, 146
Empirical self, 7-8, 11, 13, 30, 62, 89, 206, 297
Empirical study of religious texts, 26
Emptiness, 18, 28, 51, 86n, 140, 160, 178, 223,
    226, 228n, 229-230, 232-233, 236-250, 276,
    309
Energy, 121, 127, 129, 161, 163
Engels, Friedrich, 32, 36-38, 251, 266, 270-271
Enlightenment, 92
    Buddha's, 23
    European, 21
Enstasy, 28, 169, 269, 274, 277, 309, 319
Enthusiasm, 131, 159-160, 168, 194, 231, 253-255
Environment, 134, 140, 142, 160, 162, 258, 262
Escape, 89-93, 100, 101n, 291
Eschaton, 12, 15, 201
Esoteric tradition, 67-69, 71-73, 319
Essai sur les origines du Lexique Technique de la
    Mystique Musulmane (Massignon), 301n
Essence, 10-11, 14, 203, 243, 247
Esthetics, 118
Eternal bliss, 169-171, 246, 248-249, 268, 274
Eternal self, 12, 168
Eternal substratum of man's being, 11
Eternity, 17, 25, 30, 36, 85, 161, 170-171, 190,
    199, 217, 247, 260, 309, 311
Eucharist, 68, 272
Euphoric experiences, 2, 19, 62, 113, 116, 127,
    134, 138, 190
Euphoric intuition of unity, 149
Evangelical Anglicanism, 81
Eve, 9, 31
Evil, 6, 8, 15, 18-19, 29, 36-37, 71, 78, 97-99,
    111-112, 120, 123, 129, 132-133, 138, 141,
    166-167, 225, 230, 235, 241, 251, 253, 258,
    260-261, 268, 275, 279-285, 287, 289

354

deliverance from, 15
in se, 227
Evolution, 35, 37-38, 142n, 271
  among mysticisms, vi, 30
  among religions, 28, 150, 174, 211-212
Evolutionary thrust of matter, 32, 167-168, 183
Exclusivism, 20, 43, 62-63, 69, 78, 177n, 232
Existentialism, 32
Exoteric tradition, 67-70, 73, 77, 319
Expansion, 130-132, 134, 138, 141, 145, 147, 149-
    150, 154, 157, 164, 170-171, 206-207, 253,
    255-258, 261, 268, 275-276, 290
  of the ego, 29-30, 89, 109, 113, 115, 133-134,
    137-138
Experience, 42
  archetypal race, 98
  drug, 100, 109, 156
  euphoric, see Euphoric experiences
  God of, 280
  of God, 280
  of immortality, 7, 9, 14, 82, 95-96, 100, 115,
    116n, 184, 188, 246, 267-268
  knowledge, 22
  of matter, 263
  mystical, see Mystical experiences
  preternatural, see Preternatural experiences
  religious, see Religious experiences
  of the Self, 30, 191, 224
  unitive, 137, 193, 235, 237, see also Inte-
    gration
  Zaehner's, 134, 148, 156
Fackenheim, Emil, 33-34, 74
Faith, 5, 20, 23, 41, 65, 82, 139, 273, 301n,
    305
The Fall, 7, 9-11, 18, 23, 39, 100, 140, 151,
    224, 233, 249, 262-263, 265, 279
Fallible Man (Ricoeur), 281n, 282
Fallibility, 283
False mysticism, vi, 279
Fanā (Arab.=annihilation), 205-206, 219, 277,
    297, 304-305, 311, 316
Fazari, 302
Fear, 130-131, 172, 256, 288

Feelings, 131, 188-189, 206
Flux, 162, 167, 270
Food, 120, 152-155, 264-266
"Foolishness to the Greeks" (Zaehner), 3, 26, 40-41
Forgetting, 253-272
Forms, 3, 162, 164, 229n
Fragility, human, 283-285
Francis de Sales, 292
Frankfurt School of Sociologists, 275
Freedom, 11-12, 125, 146, 209
Freud, Sigmund, 252
Gadamer, H.G., 47, 49
Gandhi, Mohandas Karamchand, 8
Gardet, Louis, 169, 313n
Gauḍapāda, 186, 188, 190, 210, 243, 312, 318
Gelblum, T., 26n, 175n, 296-299
Geometric designs, 68
German idealism, 74, 96
Gestalt, 48, 50
Ghazālī, Abu-Ḥāmid
  Muḥammad al-, 98, 121-122, 195, 205, 208, 210, 219, 221, 232, 238, 242, 307, 315-320
Gilson, Etienne, 1
Gītā, see Bhagavad-Gītā
Glory, 202, 293, 301
Gnosis, 72, 90
Gnosticism, 14, 20, 90, 304
Gobineau, 302
God, 9-10, 13-17, 23, 27, 29-39, 62, 64-65, 73, 79-80, 103, 107-109, 113, 116-123, 126-129, 132-135, 139-143, 145-146, 153-156, 159, 161, 165-171, 175, 177-190, 193, 195-196, 198-202, 204-213, 217-225, 231-233, 235, 237, 243, 246-247, 249-250, 252-254, 256-257, 260-262, 264-265, 268-269, 271-272, 274-249, 285, 287-291, 294, 303, 310, 312-313, 315-318
  attributes of, 128
  in Christ, 282
  communion with, 14
  contemplation of, 28
  contextual, 285, 290-293
  existence of, 66

356

experience of, 280
of experience, 280
above God, 70
grace of, 223
history of, 269
of history, 260, 269
identity with, 164
image of, see Imago dei
immanentism of, 211
Incarnate, 40
Kingdom of, 13
listening to, 13-14
living, 177
love of, 30, 35, 78, 121, 204, 257, 290, 292
of love, 73
loving, 220
man's attitude toward, 13-14
man's relation with, 15, 23
meetings with, 12
mercy of, 130, 257
of Nature, 122
obedience to, 6, 13-14, 78, 273
peace of, 216, 235
personal, 12, 17, 21, 69, 112
philosopher's, 22
Qur'anic picture of, 300-301
remembering of, 33
revolt against, 91-92
Self of, 25
of self, 25
Son of, 38, 62
union with, 8, 27, 79, 95, 98-99, 111, 123,
    184, 193, 210, 225, 247
unity with, 28, 51, 201
vision of, 101
wickedness in, 241-242
Godhead, 11, 84, 187, 193, 209, 237
intuition of the, 64, 79
Gods, 19-21, 24, 215
illusory, 224
Goldziher, Jo, 302
Good, 6, 8, 18-19, 36-37, 71, 78, 97-99, 111-112,
    120, 123, 129, 134, 138, 141, 149, 166-167,
    225, 230, 235, 241-242, 251, 253, 258, 260-
    261, 266, 271, 275, 281-288, 287, 294

Absolute, 233
for man, 15
Goodness, 18, 36, 163, 215, 233, 266, 280, 283
Gopis (cattle girls), 10
Gospel, 16, 294
Govinda, 234
Grace, 62, 72, 84, 105, 118, 133, 143, 152-153,
    170, 182, 208, 220, 225-226, 244, 246-248,
    254, 274, 279
divine, 214
of God, 223
order of, 249
religion of, 65n, 79
state of, 290
Gresham's law, 292
Griffiths, Bede, 190-191
Die Grosse Tauschung (Delitzsch), 302
Guenon, Rene, 57, 67, 70
Guile, 301
Guillaume, Alfred, 240n
Guilt, 257, 282, 290
Guṇa (Skt.=one of the three qualifiers of
    Nature), 175, 242
Gurus, 199, 203
Habermas, Jürgen, 275
Ḥadīth (Arab.=The Traditions), 197
Ḥallāj, al-, 195, 199, 206, 231, 278, 313n, 315,
    318
Happiness, 12, 141, 172, 225, 262, 266, 280-281,
    283, 285
Harmony, 9, 18-19, 32, 41
Haughey, Jack, ix
Healer, language of the, 111
Healing, 136, 163, 166, 252, 260
Healthy guilt, 257
Healthy-minded mysticism, vi, 90-91, 94-95
Heart, 38-39, 64, 182, 236, 247, 254
Heaven, 19, 96, 118, 129, 143, 247
Hegel, Georg Wilhelm Friedrich, 33-34, 36, 73-78
Hegelian systems, 33, 219, 252
Heraclitus, iii, 36
Heresy, 90, 205-206, 230, 270, 315-317
Heterodoxy, 3, 42, 278

Higher self, 9, 17
Higher soul, 9, 31, 149-150, 160-163, 165, 312
Hindu and Muslim Mysticism (Zaehner), 3, 23, 26,
    45, 51, 55, 59, 156, 164, 165n, 184, 189-190,
    195-208, 223, 295-297, 299-300, 303n, 309-
    313, 315-319
Hinduism (Zaehner), iv, 44n
Hinduism, vi, 1, 5-6, 8, 11, 13, 16-17, 19, 25,
    28-31, 44n, 54, 61-63, 66, 68, 71, 74-75,
    79-80, 82, 92-93, 99, 101, 104, 101, 119-120,
    128-129, 133, 137, 139-140, 147, 149-150,
    155-156, 170-171, 177, 182-185, 188, 191-196,
    199-201, 203-204, 207, 209, 216-218, 220,
    227-229, 232-234, 251-252, 254, 262, 264-266,
    275, 277-279, 285, 291, 293, 295, 301, 306,
    318
"Hinduism and Buddhism" (Coomeraswami), 60-61
Hindu isolation, 209-214
Hindu monism, 3, 74, 165, 193, 200, 204, 209-216,
    222, 236, 241, 247
Hindu mysticism, 17, 110, 112, 184, 189, 223, 226
Hindu pantheism, 16
Hindu ritual, 12, 263, 295
Hindu Self-ultimate, 62
Historicity, 273
History, iv, 12-13, 26, 33-34, 98, 143, 252, 273,
    275, 285, 291, 293-294
  Christ's, 252
  God of, 260, 269
  of God, 269
  God's dealings with man in, 11
  of religions, iii, v, viii, 5, 23, 26-27, 34,
    40, 42, 48-49, 82, 100, 111-112, 135, 142,
    229n, 254, 258, 276, 306
  religious, 34
  theology of, 38
  world, 34
Holmes, Liz, ix
Holy Spirit, 33, 38, 62, 96, 249, 285, 293
Homosexuality, 123, 254, 317n, 319
Hope, 5, 39-40, 125, 130-131, 156, 228n, 229n,
    256, 261
Hubris, 233, 249, 253
Hugh of St. Victor, iii, 28

Human condition, 6, 9
Human fragility, 283-285
Human nature, 10-11, 14, 19, 262
Human predicament, 281
Human situation, 40, 264
Husserl, Edmund, 50
Huxley, Aldous, iii, v-vi, 1-2, 22, 25, 39,
    41-43, 51, 53-55, 57, 60, 63-65, 70, 72,
    76-77, 139, 142, 162, 168, 177, 182, 231,
    249-250, 258, 260, 275
Huxley, Laura Archera, 250n, 260
Huxley's experience, 80-88, 133, 156, 191, 288,
    290-291
  meaning of, 88-112, 118, 132-133
Hysterical personalities, 79
I and Thou, 59, 139, 205, 277
Ibn Arabi, 319
Idealism, 74, 96, 155, 266
Identity, 46, 50, 65, 195, 240
  with the All, 136-138, 165
  with God, 164
  pantheism of, 35
Ignatian mysticism, 288-294
Ignatius of Loyola (St.), 288-294
Ignorance, 61n, 188, 237-238
Illusion, 96, 119, 177-178, 188, 190, 200-201,
    209, 217-218, 221, 296
Image of God, see Imago dei
Images, 223, 279, 294
Imagination, 162, 188, 288
Imago dei, 7, 29-30, 71, 108, 147, 152, 246,
    315
Imago mundi, 147
Immanence, 31, 221
Immortality, 11, 128, 133, 139, 145-146, 150-151,
    154-155, 157, 159, 170-171, 175, 182, 216-217,
    230, 248, 261-262, 264-269, 274, 312, 316,
    see also Mortality
  belief in, 7
  experience of, 7, 9, 14, 82, 95-96, 100, 115,
    116n, 184, 188, 246, 267-268
  personal, 134
  see also Mortality
Inaugural Lecture, see "Foolishness to the Greeks"

Incarnation, 3, 16, 30-31, 33, 37-38, 220, 232, 252, 260, 265, 271-273, 275
Inclusivism, 20, 62, 70, 271
India, 10-11, 13, 17-18, 145-146, 148, 156, 173, 193-194, 198, 285
Indian materialistic religion, 151, 153-155
Indian mysticism, 14, 29, 80, 122, 145, 293
Indian religions, iv, vi, 2, 5-8, 11-13, 15, 24, 28, 31-32, 39-40, 100, 140-141, 146, 150, 166, 170, 174, 184, 195, 246
  early, 10, 159-160
Indian spirituality, 17, 44, 122, 127, 192, 270-271, 276
Indian tendency, 58n
Infantilization, 260-261
Infinite, 43, 70, 74, 150, 190-191, 281, 316
Innocence, 151, 212, 219, 224-225, 245-246, 313
  of childhood, 87
Insanity, 97, 172, 253, see also Lunacy; Madness; Neurosis; Psychosis
Integration, 17, 25, 98, 115, 163-164, 166, 170-171, 197, 218-219, 224, 251, 258-269, 275-277, 288, 309, 317-318, see also Experience of unity
Intellect, 65-66, 153, 163, 264, 275, 293
Interiority, 41-42, 45, 47-49, 51, 146, 230, 251, 275, 312
Interpretative level, 26-27, 143, 175
Intimacy, 134, 217, 252, 271, 275, 312
  with matter, 35
Intuition, 53-54, 64, 79, 150, 206-207, 319
Iran, 6, 302
Iranian religion, 24, 39-40
Isaac, 123, 139, 260
Isherwood, Christopher, 60-63, 70-71, 168, 177, 231
Islam, vi, 6-9, 13, 15, 22, 28-31, 54, 69, 80, 100, 107, 116n, 121, 130, 134-135, 139, 149-150, 160-164, 175, 193-195, 197-203, 205-206, 208, 210-212, 216-219, 221, 231-232, 240, 254, 277-278, 295, 298-300, 305-307, 313, 317, see also Shi'ism
Islamic mysticism, 194

Ishness, 83-84
Isolation, 8, 116, 135, 142, 169, 223-224, 226-
    228, 230, 234, 242, 280, 309, 311-312
  Hindu, 209-214
  Muslim, 209-214
Isolationisms, 7, 216-220
Isolation mysticism, vi, 2, 8, 39, 60, 65, 77,
    116, 124, 129, 133, 136-137, 145, 150, 156,
    159-214, 240, 245-246, 254, 265, 207-279,
    291, see also Mysticism of Spirit
Israel, religions of, 6, see also Semitic reli-
    gions
Istadevatā (Skt.=chosen deity), 61n, 174
Iṣṭigheit, 83-84
Īśvara (Skt.=lord, god), 161, 168
Jacob, 123, 139, 260
Jainism, 5, 170
Jalāl-uddin Rūmī, 53
James, William, 90-91, 93-100, 130
Jaspers, Karl, 63
Jefferies, Richard, 112-113, 128, 156
Jesus, 25, 32-33, 40, 74, 203, 232, 272, 285,
    290-291, 306
  Lord, 177
Jewish mysticism, 303n
Jñāna (Pali=wisdom, knowledge), 17, 21, 72, 79,
    228n, 253
John XXIII, iii
John of the Cross (St.), 29, 180, 289, 291-283
Jones, W., 301n
Journal Intime (Amiel), 96
Joy, 123, 125, 134, 153-154, 205, 246, 256, 261,
    264, 267, 275, 277, 282-287, 290-291, 293
Judaism, 6-9, 13-16, 22, 31-32, 40, 69, 139, 194-
    195, 227, 278
Judeo-Christian religion, 78
Judeo-Zoroastrian-Christian tradition, 171
Junayd, Al, 164, 204, 206-208, 210, 212, 242-244,
    307, 309-313, 315
Jung, Carl Gustav, 35, 96, 98-99, 118, 163-164,
    309, 318
Jungian psychology, 98, 112, 164, 318
Kabala, 195
Kabir, 53

Kaivalyam (Skt.=isolation), 171-175
Kant, Immanuel, 73, 81
Karma, 280
Katha Upanisad, 6.1, 201
Kausitaki Upanisad, 107, 153, 241-242
Kenosis, 272-273, 276
Khawf (Arab.=fear), 130, 256
Khud'a (Arab.=deceit), 201, 300
Kimiya-yi Sa'adt (Ghazali), 315-316
Kitab al-fana, 313n
Knowledge, 17, 21, 65, 72, 236, 253, 305
Kraemer, Hendrik, 48-49
Krishna, 10, 17, 31, 220, 234
Kristensen, Brede, 48-49
Kundalini yoga, 128-129
Küng, Hans, 62-63, 177, 215-216
Lang, D.M., 104
Lau Tau, 53
Law, William, 53, 103
Law, 132, 204, 215, 221-222, 224, 232
   eternal, 65
   moral, 230-253
Laws, 49, 258, 273, 287
Legarde, P. de, 302
Lenin, Nikolai, 32
Levy-Bruhl, Lucien, 120-149
Liberation, 11-12, 15, 17. 27, 92, 146, 169, 204,
   220-221, 238, 269
License, sexual, 225-279
Lichtheim, G., 74n, 75n
Life, 77, 86n, 154, 179, 183, 201, 238, 251, 265,
   270-271, 283
   human, 291
   inner, 111, 160, 268
   spiritual, 256
   terror in, 10
Life-force, 113, 128, 162, 265
Lila (Skt.=play), 177
Limbo, 127, 141, 169-170, 185, 213, 225, 246,
   262, 267, 313
Limitation, 281
Logos, 22, 25, 33, 270
Lonergan, Bernard, 26-27, 49-50, 98

Lotus Sutra, 10, 24, 30-31
Love, 10-12, 17, 23, 28-31, 40, 95, 130, 139,
    182, 196, 204, 219, 224, 226-227, 233, 235-
    236, 241-242, 256-257, 261-262, 270-271, 276,
    279, 281, 287-288, 294
  in Buddhism, 189
  Christian, 25, 108
  divine, 126
  failures of, 282
  God of, 73
  121, 204, 257, 290, 292
  interpersonal, 288
  in Islam, 197-198
  mysticism of, see Love mysticism
  religion of, 8, 19-20, 226
  of the world, 121
Loved sinners, 257,290
Love mysticism, vi, 7-8, 30, 40, 60, 73, 77, 108,
    110, 124, 176, 197-198, 209, 227, 275, 304
Loving union with God, 184
Lower soul, 9, 149-150, 160, 162-163, 185, 192,
    202, 217, 259, 269, 312, see also Ego
LSD, 250
Lunacy, 86-87, 123-124, 126, 160, see also
    Insanity; Madness; Neurosis; Psychosis
McLelland, David C., 136
Macrocosm, 146, 179, 263
Mad-bhāva (Skt.=God's mode of being), 204
Mādhyamika Buddhism, 228, 229n, 230
Madness, 86-87, 118, 121-122, 138, 166, 253,
    see also Insanity; Lunacy, Psychosis
Magic, 103, 130, 148-149, 151, 155
Magician, great, 201, 301n
Mahā Māyin (Skt.=great magician, great deceiver),
    201, 301n
Mahāvākyāni (Skt.=great phrases), 200
Mahāyāna Buddhism, 6, 8, 18-19, 21-22, 31, 86,
    133, 140, 159-160, 178, 189, 228n, 230
Malinowski, Bronislaw Kasper, 148
Man, 11-12, 32, 38-39, 62, 64, 73, 77, 79-80,
139-141, 155, 195, 210, 232, 263, 281-282, 291
  First, 245-246
  material side of, 150
  Primal, 151

Resurrected, 40
Way of, 19
Mandūkya Upaniṣad, 58, 108n, 186-188, 210-211, 214n
Mani, 90
Mania, 159-160, 240, 246, 255
Manic-depressive psychosis, 106, 126, 128-131, 135, 255
Manichaeanism, 90, 266
Man's attitude toward God, 13-14
Man's being
  eternal substratum of, 11
Man's nature, 10-11, 14, 19, 262
Manson, Charles, 225n, 242, 260
Mantra, 68
Marga (Skt.=way), 61n
Marx, Karl, 32-33, 36-38, 251, 253, 266, 270-271
Marxism, iii-iv, vi, 21, 32-33, 35, 37-40, 156, 242, 251-252, 265, 271n, 275
Marxist-humanism, v
Mary (St.), 306
Mass, 68, 272
Massignon, Louis, 301-306, 310
Materialism, 155, 180, 183, 265-266, 271
Matter, 12, 14-15, 17-19, 27, 29, 31-39, 74, 96, 113, 120, 142, 145, 147, 153-157, 160-163, 166-170, 183, 194, 251-252, 256-273, 285, 311
  in motion, 21
Matter and Spirit: Their Convergence in Eastern Religions, Marx, and Teilhard de Chardin (Zaehner), iv
Matter consciousness, 162
Māyā (Skt.=illusion), 119, 178, 200-201, 217-218, 221, 237, 296, 300
Meaning, 50-51, 261
Mediation, fragile, 283
Meditation, 21, 172, 175, 184, 229n, 232, 291, 304, 316
Meeting of religions, mysticism as grounds for, 5
Mencius, 19
Merton, Thomas, 11
Mescalin, 53, 82-83, 87, 89, 93, 98, 100, 104-105, 125, 139

Messiah, 31, 40
Metanoia, 289, 292-293
Metaphysic, 65-66, 72, 110
Metaphysics, 16, 66, 178, 190, 210
Method, 74
  religion of, 64-65, 72, 80
  Zaehner's, see Zaehner's method
Methodology, vii, 26n
Meysenburg, Malwida von, 96
Microcosm, 146-147, 179, 263
Middle Path, 228n
Mind, 74, 110, 148, 153, 168, 170, 179, 235-236,
   247, 251, 264, 267
  conscious, 253
  at Large, 98, 118, 162, 168
  unification of, 115
  universal, 118, 120
Mishkāt (Ghazālī), 315
Moksa (Skt.=freedom, release, liberation), 11, 17,
   27, 169, 220, 238
Monads, 161, 178
Monism, 2, 38-39, 44, 61-63, 65, 69-72, 74, 77-78,
   99-100, 107-110, 136-137. 145, 150, 153, 160-
   161, 165, 173-175, 177-179, 218-221, 225, 227-
   228, 230-242, 244, 247-248, 274, 277. 295,
   299, 301, 303, 305-307, 312, 317, 319
  absolute, 164, 211
  Christian, 216, 222
  Hindu, see Hindu monism
  Muslim, 145, 165, 198, 209-214
  religious, 177-214
  Ṣūfi, 211
Monotheism, 196, 198
Monotheistic bias, 175n, 298
Moral ambivalence, 99-100, 112
Morality, 71, 78, 166, 225, 260
Moral qualities, 233, 242
Morbidity, 129-131, 246, 257
Mortality, 11, 15, 27, 114, see also Immortality
Motion, matter in, 21
Muhasibi, al-, 313n
Mukta (Skt.=freed, liberated), 146
Multiplicities, 53, 239

Mundaka Upaniṣad 3.1.1-3, 201
Muni (Skt.=perfection), 236
Murder cults, 225n, 242
Muslim desert mystics, 240n
Muslim isolation, 209-214
Muslim monism, 145, 165, 198, 209-214
Muslim mysticism, 198-199, 210, 223-224, 235,
    238, 255, 295, 319
Muslim mystics, 102, 104-105, 132, 149, 213, 226
Muslim psychology, 162
Muslim theology, 116n
Mystery, 285-286, 288
Mystical experiences, 45-46, 89, 114-115, 134-135
Mystical intuitions, 54
Mystical religions, 6-7, 12, 32, 251-253
Mystical theology, 98, 222, 291
Mystical union, 32, 41, 62
Mystical unity, 41
Mysticism, iii, vii, 14, 22, 27, 33, 82-83, 106,
    108, 148-149
  Aryan provenance of, 302-304
  Christian, see Christian mysticism
  Christianity as, 5, 292
  comparative, 295
  devotion, 198
  diabolic, see Diabolic mysticism
  drug, see Drug mysticism
  dualistic, see Dualistic mysticism
  emptiness, see Emptiness mysticism
  epiphenomena of, 292
  false, vi, 279
  healthy-minded, vi, 90-91, 94-95
  Hindu, see Hindu mysticism
  of matter, vi, 32, 37, 148, 155, 251, 258, 271
  paraphenomena of, 79
  religion as, 5
  of self, 8
  sick, 90-91, 94
  of spirit, 268-278, see also Isolation mysti-
    cism
  systematics of, see Systematics of mysticism,
    vi, 3, 124, 167
  theistic, see Theistic mysticism

unhealthy, vi, 235
Mysticism Sacred and Profane: An Enquiry into
    Some Varieties of Preternatural Experience
    (Zaehner), 1-2, 23, 26, 45, 51, 55, 56n, 57,
    59-60, 67, 79, 81-85, 87-97, 101, 103-106,
    108-110, 113-115, 118-132, 138, 147-148,
    156-157, 162-173, 175-183, 186-189, 201-202,
    205, 209-213, 217-219, 221, 223-226, 230,
    232-245, 247, 270, 295, 298
Mystics
  Catholic, 97
  Christian, vi, 58, 80, 122, 132, 213, 223-226
  Jewish, 14
  Muslim desert, 240n
  Protestant, 81-82
The Mystics of Islam (Nicholson), 297
Myth, 140, 253, 273, 285, 294
Nafs (Arab.=lower, empirical, or mortal soul),
    160, 162-163, 202, 217, 312
Nagarjuna, viii, 18, 189, 228n, 229n
Nagatomi, D., viii-ix, 229n
Natural mysticism, 18, 99, 111, 150-152, 177, 214,
    234
Natural pantheism, 35
Natural religions, 18, 20-22, 38, 76
Nature, 19, 28, 38-39, 62, 77, 88, 113, 117, 119,
    121, 129, 134, 136, 160-161, 168-169, 175,
    178, 224, 243, 246
  Beauty of, 100
  Buddha, 10, 24
  corrupt, 103
  divine, 72, 263
  God of, 122
  God's, 11
  half-angel, half-beast, 23
  human, 10-11, 14, 19, 262
  intuition of, 150
  order of, 249
  supernatural, 71-73
  union with, 80, 111
  unity with, 100, 135-136
Nature Mysticism, vi, 2, 10, 24, 28-30, 34-36,
    38-39, 42, 45, 60, 70, 72-73, 77, 79-143,
    145-157, 160-163, 168, 171, 176, 179, 181,

186, 191, 205, 207, 209, 214, 217, 240, 245, 246, 251-269, 275-276, 288, 290-291, 309, see also Pan-en-henism
Neo-Confucianism, 8, 21-22, 25
Neo-Platonism, 200, 304, 317-319
Neo-Scholastics, 1
Neurosis, 90-94, 101n, 114-115, 257, 290
Newell, William L., 226n
Nicholson, R.A., 200, 297-299, 304-305
Nicolas of Cusa, 36, 147
Nihilism, 228n
Nirguṇa (Skt.=qualityless, unqualified, without guṇa), 175, 233, 236
Nirvāna (Skt.=bliss), 13, 19-21, 24, 27, 86n, 122, 140, 145, 153, 169, 173, 176, 192, 222, 228n, 229n, 238, 264, 268, 270-271, 276, 286, 305
Nitrous oxide, 93, 97
Non-Christian heterodoxy, 3, 42
Non-dualism, 108, 145, 159, 184-185, 192, 218, 295
Non-existence, 238-285
Non-two, 61, 71, 108, 159, 175
Nostalgia, religious, 259
Not-self, 86-87, 103-105, 107, 110, 270
Obedience, 6, 13-14, 78, 197, 272-273, 278
Objects, 21, 29, 49, 133, 172, 201, see also Subject/object relation; Union of subject and object
"Objective scholars" of religions, 43-44, 46-47, 49
Ocean, 236
Old Testament (OT), 14, 27, 177
Omnipotence, 121, 139, 261-262
On Being a Christian (Küng), 62
The One, 19, 53, 63, 70, 107, 155, 246, 277, 317
Oneness, 8, 11, 53, 187, 190, 199-200, 312, 318
Opposites, 37, 97, 167, 228n, 261
Order, cosmic, 17
Original affirmation, 282, 284
Original joy, 282-284
Orthodoxy, Christian, 3, 42-43
Otto, Rudolf, 44, 274
Our Savage God (Zaehner), 46, 100, 112-113, 166, 225n, 242

"Overreach," 33-34
Oxford University, iii, vii
Pain, vii, 10, 18, 31, 130, 154, 145, 238, 256-
    257, 265, 270-271, 277, 280, 285, 287, 290,
    294
Pan-en-henism, 2, 70, 88, 106-109, 133, 136, 155-
    156, 159-161, 163-168, 170-171, 174, 184, 191,
    193-194, 197,212, 239-242, see also Nature
    Mysticism
Pantheism, 69-70, 107-109, 116, 129, 136, 140,
    165, 177, 179, 184, 239-240, 262, 305, 316
  Christian, 35-36
  Hindu, 16
  of identity, 35
  Natural, 35
  of unity, 35
Parable of Matter, 36
Para-Brahman (Skt.=supreme Brahman), 237
Paradises, artificial, 90
Paraphenomena of mysticism, 79
Parinirvāna (Pali=beyond nirvāna, beyond bliss),
    24
Parrinder, Geoffrey, iii, 44
Participation mystique, 120, 259
Passions, 12, 64, 163, 168, 172, 281, 305
Patterns, 49-52, 85-86
Peace, 21, 27-29, 126-127, 159, 172-173, 176,
    224, 238, 254, 268-269, 275, 279
  death-like, 269
  of God, 216, 235
  of heart, 254
  of self, 216, 235
Peak states, 39
Pederasty, 317n, 319, see also Homosexuality;
    Perversion
Peguy, Charles Pierre, 270
Penance, 117, 255, 293
Penitential asceticism, 72-73
People of the Book, 278
Perception, 45, 89, 188
The Perennial Philosophy (Huxley), 53, 64, 84,
    103-104
Perfection, 172, 226, 236, 259, 273-274, 276
Person, 160, 163, 272

Personal God, 12, 17, 21, 69, 112
Personality, 18, 135, 170, 182, 219, see also
    Integration
Personal survival, 14-15
Personal unconscious, 98-99
Perversions, 123, 254, 317n, 319
Peuch, H.C., 90n
Peyote, 54
Phenomena, 70, 200, 217, 225, 229r, 233, 266, 312
Phenomenal universe, 162, 187-188
Phenomenology, vii-viii, 50, 254
The Phenomenology of Mind (Hegel), 74
Phenomenology of religion, 62
Philo Judaeus (of Alexandria), 53
Philosophia perennis, 1, 4, 20-22, 39, 41-42,
    44-46, 48, 51, 53-78, 82, 88-89, 93, 97, 101,
    106, 126, 133, 139, 149-151, 156, 164, 168,
    174, 177, 191-195, 198, 208, 215-216, 222,
    227, 231, 235-236, 247, 249, 254, 274-275,
    302
Philosophy, 21, 25, 32, 34, 48, 53, 64-66, 69,
    157, 159, 184, 283-284, 293, 317
  Hindu, 178
  Platonic, 83
Pleroma, 273, 276
Plotinus, 53
Poetry, 88, 121, 125-126, 134, 148, 156
Polar feelings, 131
Polytheism, 122, 193, 198
Positivism, transcendent, 273
Positivist "objectivity," 43, 51
Possession, diabolic, 138, 147, 261
Praeparatio evangelica, 24, 39
Prajñānam brahma (Skt.=consciousness is Brahman),
    108n
Prakṛti (Skt.=nature, lower soul, matter, time),
    12, 21, 160-161, 163, 167-170, 178, 192, 217,
    268
Prāṇa (Skt.=breath, life force, vital force), 99,
    113, 152, 155, 264-267
Prasada (Skt.=grace), 152
Praxis, 178
Prayer, 117, 185, 199, 235, 254-257, 288, 292

    repetitive, 304
Prejudice, 47, 67
Presence, 6, 10, 68, 288, 315
Preternatural experiences, 81, 88-89, 95, 110,
    118, 133-134, 258
Primal Man, 151
Primordial anguish, 284
Primordial conflict, 281-282
Primordial joy, 282-284
Primordial tradition, 67, 77
Profane, 148, 156
Prometheus, 249, 253
Prophecy and Divination Among the Hebrews and
    Other Semites (Guillaume), 240n
Prophetic religions, 6-7, 13, 32, 251
Prophets, 12, 14, 195
Protestantism, iv, 8, 27, 81-82, 147
Proust, Marcel, 109, 114-117, 134, 136, 160, 163,
    169-170, 180, 219, 229
Pseudo-Dionysius, 51, 304
Psyche, 142, 162, 212, 312-313
Psychology
  bicameral, 192, 259
  depth, see Depth psychology
  Jungian, 98, 112, 164, 318
  modern, 131
  Muslim, 162
Psychosis, 118, 254
  manic-depressive, 106, 126, 128-131, 135, 255
Psychotherapy, 218, 252-253
Puruṣa (Skt.=eternal self, spirit, higher soul,
    person, man), 12-13, 21, 151, 160-161, 163,
    167, 169-170, 192, 217, 241, 277
Qabḍ (Arab.=contraction), 130, 135, 206, 256
Quietism, 56, 222-236, 279, 312
Qur'ān, 197, 232, 300-301, 313
Qushayrī, 130-132, 170, 255
Radhakrishnan, S., 44, 63, 70, 76, 174, 177,
    231
Rahner, Karl, vii, 266, 282, 286, 289
Rajā (Arab.=hope), 130, 256
Rajas (Skt.=energy, activity, passion, desire),
    161-163, 168-169, 175, 201, 233, 268
Rāja-yoga, 128-129, 258

Rāmānuja, 194, 196, 198, 203, 208, 212, 218, 221, 223, 227, 233, 247, 311-312
Rationalist approach, 47
Rational soul, 162
Real, 48, 53, 62, 153, 178, 180, 194, 196, 235
Reality, 1, 64, 178, 180-181, 194, 237, 260, 270
  Absolute, 233
  divine, 53
Real Self, 78, 222-223
Reason, 65, 73, 147, 163
Reconciling of opposites, 97, 167, 228n, 261
Redemption, 15, 271, 282, 291
Reductionism, 54, 214
Reitzenstein, Richard, 302
Release, 89-90, 105, 169, 188
Religion, vii, 15, 32, 34, 38, 41-42, 54, 75-77, 98, 142-143, 188-189, 252, 262
  beginning of, 161, 268
  Chinese, 17, 32, 39-40, 56, 216
  communal, 7
  confessional, 155
  of devotion, 16-17, 44, 212, 234
  Eastern, 9, 22, 82-83
  of grace, 65n, 79
  Greek, 24, 40, 253
  Hindu, 74, 299
  Indian materialistic, 151, 153-155
  Iranian, 24, 39-40
  Jewish, 6
  laws of, 258
  of love, 8, 19-20, 226
  materialist, 265
  of the Mean, 19
  of method, 64-65, 72, 80
  monistic, 2
  as mysticism, 5
  Muslim, see Islam
  Phenomenology of, 62
  Semitic-Christian, 6
  terror in, 10
  union of mean of, 67
  continuum among, 4
  convergence of, 7, 24-40, 252

development of, 15
divergence in, 4-24, 33, 39
empirical, 12, 146
28, 150, 174, 211-212
gaps between, 4
growth in, 4, 6, 272
history of, iii, v, viii, 5, 23, 26-27, 34, 40,
   42, 48-49, 82, 100, 111-112, 135, 142, 229n,
   254, 258, 276, 306
Indian, see Indian religions
of Israel, 6
missionary, 5, 46
modes of, 74
moral, 13
mystical, 6-7, 12, 32, 251-253
national, 6
natural, 18, 20-22, 38, 76
"objective scholars" of, 43-44, 46-47, 49
other-worldly, 8
prophetic, 6-7, 13, 32, 251
revealed, 55, 106
Semitic, see Semitic religions
solidarity, 7, 252
solidary, 7, 252
theistic, 2, 212
theologies of, iii, vi, 2, 307
this-worldly, 8
traditional, 67
typology of, 6-7, 110, 240, 252
unworldly, 11-12
world, 18, 174, 306
Religious experiences, v-vi, 47, 54, 134, 236,
   279
systematics of, v, 173
theology of, vi, viii
types of, 63-64
Religious monism, 177-214
Religious mysticism, 38, 80, 137, 145-157, 161
Religious nature mysticism, 263-268
Remembering, 253, 263, 272, 316
of God, 33
Renan, Joseph Ernest, 302
Renouncers, 214, 236

374

Revelation, 23-24, 35, 46, 85-86, 156-157, 221,
    267, 278, 298
  gradual, 11
Revelation and Reason in Islam (Arberry), 297,
    299-300
Revelations, competing, 5
Richard of St. Victor, 28
Ricoeur, Paul, 281n, 282-284, 289
Rig Veda, 177
Rimbaud, Arthur, 46, 56, 72-73, 117-121, 123-127,
    138, 140, 166, 169-170, 253-254, 260, 313
Rites, 42, 47, 68, 151, 204, 221, 222, 224, 318
  magical, 103
Ritual, 12, 148, 151, 179, 263, 295, 300
Roman Catholicism, iv, v, viii, 27, 32, 38, 82,
    176, 185, 195, 266
Rosen, 302
Rousseau, Jean Jacques, 18, 21, 119-120
Rūh (rational soul, higher soul), 160-163, 204,
    312
Ruysbroeck, Jan van, 53, 58, 127, 159, 168n,
    222-236, 242, 279
Sadness, 18, 140, 228n, 229n, 261, 271, 281-283,
    287, 291, 293
Sages, 148, 157, 160, 167, 172-173, 267, see also
  Seers
Sa'id, Abu, 210
Saints, 79, 100-101, 105, 180, 225, 277, 285
Saison en enfer (Rimbaud), 124
Saiva Siddhānta, 182, 212, 247
Salvation, 6, 98, 130, 257, 267, 269, 282
  individual, 31, 68
Samādhi (Skt.=trance sleep), 29, 62, 79, 209,
    273-274
Samkhya-Yoga, 2, 8, 12-15, 21, 24, 30, 39, 65,
    71, 74, 133, 145, 153, 159-178, 184-185,
    188-196, 206-207, 209, 211-213, 217-219,
    221, 224, 226-228, 232, 241, 269, 277, 291,
    309-312, 316
Samsāra (Skt.=peace, endlessness), 13, 21, 228n,
    229n, 271, 276
Sāndilya Vidyā text, 211
Sankara, 53, 165, 179, 184-186, 190, 192-194,
    196, 200, 204-205, 209-211, 214, 218,

221-222, 224, 227, 234-235, 237-238, 274-275,
    312, 315, 318-319
Sannyāsa Upaniṣad, 202
Sannyāsin (Skt.=ascetic, renouncer), 214, 236
Śāntih (Skt.=peace), 238
Sarrāj, 199-201, 210
Sat (Skt.=being), 1, 84, 101, 191
Satori, 27-28, 115, 140
Sattva (Skt.=light, virtue, truth), 161-163, 168-
    169, 175, 201, 233, 268
Saviours, 13, 19, 172, 220
Schizophrenia, 87, 130
Schleiermacher, Friedrich Ernst Daniel, 81
Schoun, Frithjof, 22, 52, 57-58, 64-78, 90, 109,
    126, 168, 177, 231
Sea, 96, 113, 142
Secularity, 34n
Secular spirituality, 81
Seers, 118, 154, 267, see also Sages
Self, 8, 10, 13, 19, 30, 61, 66, 71, 73-74, 78-80,
    99, 103, 117-119, 121, 123, 127, 135, 137-
    138, 141, 145, 150, 153-154, 157, 159-161,
    163, 169, 171, 175-176, 178-179, 181-184,
    186, 188, 194, 199, 204-206, 208, 217, 219,
    232-233, 239, 241-242, 246-248, 250, 252-
    253, 258, 262, 264-265, 267-274, 276, 281-
    282, 286, 288-289, 311, 313
  deeper, 7-8
  destruction of the, 263, 311
  empirical, see Empirical self
  eternal, 12, 168
  experience of the, 30, 191, 224
  forgetting of, 33
  god of, 25
  of God, 25
  higher, 9, 17
  immortal, 7, 11, 168
  mysticism of, 8
  natural, 18
  Not-, see Not-self
  peace of, 216, 235
  preoccupation with, 92
  real, 78, 222-223
  second, 229

temporal, 212
transcendent, 8-9, 11, 30, 62
transcendental, 7, 17, 136
upper, 196
whole, 17
Self-conscious matter, 265
Self-consciousness, 75, 177, 271
Self-contemplation, 28
Self-hatred, 253, 255-256, 263
Self-loathing, 135
Self-realization, 196, 268
Self-ultimate, Hindu, 62
Self-worship, 141, 262
Semitic religions, 7, 39, 140-141, 146, 233, 262,
    269, 278, 302-306
Senses, 172-173, 201
Separation, 80, 269, 310-311
Sexual license, 225, 279
Shibli, 260
Shi'ism, 302
Shirk (Arab.=unbelief), 210, 231
Sick guilt, 257
Sick mysticism, 90-91, 94
Sin, 6, 30, 36, 125, 130, 135, 138, 169, 223, 225,
    246, 249, 254, 256-257, 269, 271, 273, 280,
    284-285, 289-290
  original, 36, 99-100, 244, 282
Sinfulness, 256-257
Sinners, 79, 105, 257, 285, 290
Siva, 16, 139, 182
Skill in means, 18, 25
Sleep, dreamless, see Dreamless sleep
Sloth, 161, 163, 168
Smart, Ninian, 5, 46
Smith, Huston, 22, 77, 227, 228n
Smith, Margaret, 313n
Smith, Wilfred Cantwell, iii-iv, 47
Solidarity, 7, 23-33, 35, 252
Solidary religions, 7, 252
Solipsism, 182-183, 189, 226n
Soul, 9-10, 12, 14, 16, 23, 28-29, 32, 103,
    108-109, 123, 129, 153-154, 170, 178, 180,
    186, 188-190, 205, 207, 219, 240, 246-247,
    256, 264, 271, 309, 311-312, 315

animal, 163, 217
bestial, 163, 217
constricted, 130
Dark Night of the, 29, 256, 289n, 293
embodied, 173
empirical, 31, 162
higher, see Higher soul
inner, 31
lower, see Lower soul
personal, 117
rational, 162
Ṣūfī doctrine of the, 212
unification of, 115
unity of, 29, 60, 313, 319
Universal, 317
upper, see Upper soul
World, 186
Space/time continuum, 11, 96, 133, 138-139, 258, 260-261
Spinoza, Benedict, 281
Spirit, 17, 32, 37, 39, 60, 75, 99, 153-155, 163, 166-167, 179, 192, 194, 202, 217, 240, 265-266, 270-273
life, 251
mysticism of, 268-278, see also Isolation mysticism
Spiritual elite, 66-69, 77
The Spiritual Espousals (Ruysbroek), 222-223, 279
Spiritual Exercises of St. Ignatius of Loyala, 288-294
Spirituality, vii, 37, 39, 124, 159, 173, 192, 218-220
Christian, see Christian spirituality
Indian, see Indian spirituality
secular, 81
Staal, Frits, 46-47, 295-296, 298
Stace, W.T., 58-59
Starkie, Enid, 56
Struggle, 131
Subhanī (Arab.=glory be to me), 301
Subject, 21, 29, 49, see also Union of subject and object

Subjective methodology, 26n
Subjectivity, vii-viii, 43, 276
Subject/object relations, 2, 258, 290
Submission, 131, 257
Suffering, 13, 35-36, 121, 205, 277
Ṣūfi masters, 98, 164, 184, 194-195, 204, 231
Ṣūfis, vi, 97, 199, 207, 277
Ṣūfism, 3, 29-30, 69, 71, 76, 118, 130, 164-165,
    175, 197, 205, 209-212, 217, 236, 243, 297-
    302, 303n, 304-306, 310, 315-317, 319
Ṣun, 113, 128, 142
Sūnyatā (Pali, Skt.=emptiness), 18-19, 21, 51,
    86n, 140, 160, 228n, 230, 276
Supernatural nature, 71-73
Supra-Personal Divinity, 69
Suso, Henry (Blessed), 101-102, 219, 222, 243-
    244
Suṣupti (Skt.=good sleep), 165
Suzuki, D.T., 84
Svetāsvatara Upaniṣad, 17, 183, 237
Symbols, 26, 47-48, 50, 66-69, 96, 109-110, 152
Systematics of mysticism, v-vi, 3, 124, 167, 173
Tafrid (Arab.=isolation), 206
Tagore, Rabindranath, 8
Taittirīya Upaniṣad, 152, 154, 183, 264
Takūnu anta dhāka (Arab.=thou art that), 199
Tamas (Skt.=darkness, heaviness, sloth), 71, 161-
    163, 168-169, 175, 201, 233, 268
Tantra, 68
Tao, 10, 17, 19, 22, 40
Taoism, 5, 17-19, 21-22, 24-25, 28-29, 120, 133,
    137-138, 140, 145, 147-148, 155, 200, 227-
    228, 261
Tasin al-Siraj (Hallāj), 318
Tathatā (Skt.=suchness), 22, 271, 276
Tat tvam asi (Skt.=Thou art that), 80, 108n, 136,
    181, 200, 296, 303
Tawhid (Arab.=uniting, affirming unity), 309-311,
    315
Teilhard de Chardin, Pierre, vi, 32, 35-39, 242,
    251-252
Tennyson, Alfred, 95-96
Teresa of Avila (St.), 97, 130, 177, 257, 291-292

Text by text, 45, 65
Theism, 2-3, 20, 28-29, 39-40, 61, 70, 77, 99-100,
    107, 124, 139, 145, 148, 150, 152-153, 167,
    170, 173-177, 182-183, 186, 189, 191, 193-194,
    205, 209, 213-215, 219-221, 227, 230-231, 233,
    235-250, 254, 265, 268, 276, 299
Theistic mystical experiences, 2, 55
Theistic mysticism, 8, 29, 73, 80, 95, 102, 110,
    121-122, 176, 181, 185, 193, 215-250, 268,
    275
Theistic religions, 2, 212
Theological methodology, vii
Theologies of religions, iii, vi, 2, 307
Theology, 12, 16, 26-27, 37, 52, 69, 100, 135,
    142-143, 156, 231, 254
  Catholic, 116, 127
  Christian, 101
  of history, 38
  Muslim, 116n
  mystical, 98, 222, 291
  Natural, 5
  of religious experience, vi, viii
  spiritual, 38
Theravada Buddhism, 8, 12, 24, 31, 133, 189, 215-
    216, 228
Theses
  indicator, v
  Zaehner's, see Zaehner's theses
Theses on Feuerback (Marx), 271n
Thinking matter, 120, 252, 263
This-worldly religions, 8
Thomas Aquinas (St.), 37, 117, 180, 243
Thought, 37, 39, 96, 110, 153-154, 183, 188, 264-
    266
Throes of matter, 251, 265
Tibetan Buddhism, 250
Time, 11-12, 15-17, 19, 25, 27, 36, 75, 85-87,
    115, 117, 120, 129, 134, 138-139, 141, 160,
    208, 270-273, 275, 285, 290
  mythical, 232
Tonbridge School, 45, 54n, 81
Tradition, 25, 67-73, 77, 319
Traditions (Hadith), 197

Trance states, 29, 62, 79, 83, 95, 129, 153, 156,
    164-165, 185, 191, 193-194, 199, 209, 238,
    241, 245-246, 264, 267, 273-274
Transcendence, 31, 132, 182, 254, 258, 273, 276
Transcendentalism, 193, 221, 277, 310
Transcendental self, 7, 17, 136
Transcendent self, 8-9, 11, 30, 62
Traps, 252-256, 268, 276, 309, 312
Trimingham, J.S., 306n
Trinity, 25, 133, 272, 298
Truth, 61, 66-69, 73, 76, 106, 161, 231, 289
Two-self hypothesis, 11
Typology of religions, 6-7, 110, 240, 252
Ultimate, 61, 70, 277
Unconscious, 9, 11, 120, 146, 163, 219, 254, 269
  collective, see Collective unconscious
  personal, 98-99
Unconscious experiences of immortality, 246
Unhealthy mysticism, vi, 235
Unifying power of matter, 32-33
Union, 11, 14, 35, 41, 120, 209-210, 217, 310-311
  Christian experience of, 111, 230
  with God, 8, 27, 79, 95, 98-99, 111, 123, 184,
    193, 210, 225, 247
  of men of religion, 67
  mystical, 32, 41, 62
  with nature, 80, 111
  with a principle, 79
  of subject and object, 137, 143
Unitas mystica, 41
Unitive experiences, 137, 193
Unity, 9, 17, 29, 46, 50-51, 120, 193, 210, 219,
    226, 229-230, 239, 251, 259, 309-310, 315,
    317
  with the All, 148
  experience of, 137, 193, 235, 237, see also
    Integration
  euphoric intuition of, 149
  fictitious, 50
  with God, 28, 51, 201
  mystical, 41
  with Nature, 100, 135-136
  pantheism of, 35
  pre-biographical, 59

of soul, 29, 60, 313, 319
Universal consciousness, 151, 168, 264
Unworldly religions, 11-12
Upaniṣads, 11-12, 86n, 145, 148, 151-152, 157,
    167, 177-180, 182, 185-186, 189, 193, 203,
    206, 218, 237, 264, 266-267
  early, 109, 117, 134, 140, 147, 155-156, 159,
    183, 264
  see also Aitareye Upaniṣad; Bṛhadāraṇyaka
    Upaniṣad; Kaṭha Upaniṣad; Kauṣitaki
    Upaniṣad; Māṇḍūkya Upaniṣad; Muṇḍaka Upani-
    ṣad; Sannyāsa Upaniṣad; Śvetāśvatara Upani-
    ṣad; Taittirīya Upaniṣad
Upaya (Skt.=skill in means), 18, 25
Upper self, 196
Upper soul, 185, 192, 204, 217, 259
Vaiṣṇavite theism, 182
Vedānta, 16, 20, 57, 61-62, 71, 76, 86, 108, 110-
    111, 117, 119, 127, 134, 186, 189, 195, 198,
    200-203, 206, 217-218, 230, 233, 236-250,
    295, 298-301, 304-306, 315, 316, 319
  advaitan, see Advaitan Vedānta
  meaning of, 178
  monistic, 8
Vedas, 11, 148-149, 177-178, 201, see also Rig
    Veda
Via purgativa, 184, 211
Vijñānālaya (Pali=reservoir of consciousness), 99
Visions, 79, 86, 101, 292, 309
Viṣnu, 16-17, 31, 139, 174, 182, 220, 226, 232-
    233
Waking state, 186-187, 209
Way, 19, 31, 61n, 273, 290-291
Weber, Max, 81, 147, 319
Whole, 48, 50-52, 67, 77
Wickedness in God, 241-242
Wilde, Oscar, 169
Womb, return to the, 170, 269
Woodstock Center, ix
World, vii, 11-12, 21, 33, 38-39, 53, 69, 109,
    128, 147-148, 154, 161, 165, 180-181, 201-
    202, 211, 260, 268, 283
  love of the, 121
World religions, 18, 174, 306

Wretchedness, iv, 18, 154, 228n, 229n, 270, 315
Yang, 21, 138
Yantra, 68
Yazīd, Abū (of Bisṭam), 29, 164, 184, 193, 198-
    201, 203-208, 211, 278, 295-307, 310-312, 315
Yes, 282, 284, 287
Yin, 21, 138
Yoga, vi, 11, 17, 24-25, 29, 39, 62, 65, 72-74,
    78, 82, 119-120, 122, 124, 127. 137, 140, 146,
    152-153, 155, 157, 159-161, 163-169, 171, 174,
    176, 185-186, 191-192, 196-197, 205, 208-209,
    214, 218-220, 224, 236, 241, 246-247, 249,
    258, 264, 267-268, 273, 277, 310, 313, 319
  Kundalini, 128-129
  Rāja-, 128-129, 258
  Sāmkhya-, see Sāmkhya-Yoga
Younger, Paul, iv
Yukta (Skt.=integration), 317
Zaehner, Robert Charles, iii-ix
Zaehner's experiences, 134, 148, 156
Zaehner's method, 26, 40-52, 98, 175, 286, 295
Zaehner's theses, v, 1, 5, 39-40, 296, 298
  fifth of, 24, 32-40
  first of, 1-4, 39-40
  fourth of, 24-32, 39
  second of, 2-4. 39-40
  third of, 5-24, 39
Zen, 5, 7, 24-25, 27-29, 84-85, 115, 120, 133,
    137, 140, 145, 185, 227-228
Zoroaster, 14, 23, 32
Zoroastrianism, iii, 6-7, 9, 14-15, 24, 28, 32
Zurvan, A Zoroastrian Dilemma (Zaehner), iii,
    44n, 90n, 295